W9-ARS-340

Cover Art
The Accolade, 1901 (oil on canvas)
by
Leighton, Edmund Blair (1853-1922)
Private Collection

TO CRISPEN COURAGE
The Divine Annihilation

by
William L. Roth, Jr.
Foreword by Timothy Parsons-Heather

The Morning Star of Our Lord, Inc.
Springfield, Illinois
www.ImmaculateMary.org

Published by The Morning Star of Our Lord, Incorporated
Used with permission.
Copyright © 2005
William L. Roth, Jr. & Timothy Parsons-Heather
All rights reserved.

Publish date: July 4, 2005

ISBN: 0-9671587-6-1
Printed in the United States of America

Message Transcription Citations

1991	a	1998	h
1992	b	1999	i
1993	c	2000	j
1994	d	2001	k
1995	e	2002	l
1996	f	2003	m
1997	g	2004	n
		2005	o

001-366 day   x - (ff) line

Dedication
to
Archbishop Fulton J. Sheen

Born - May 8, 1895
Ordained - September 20, 1919
Consecrated Bishop - June 11, 1951
Into Eternal Rest - December 9, 1979

"If you believe the incredible, you will end up doing the impossible!"

"All we need do is to voice these two petitions: Dear Lord, illumine my intellect to see the Truth, and give me the strength to follow it."

Let us honor this great leader of faith who showed the world the most noble use of our communication media. This beloved pastor and obedient servant of God accomplished more for the purification and redemption of humankind in his first catechetical broadcast than the entire journalism profession has produced in recorded history. Let us pray for his intercession that the Light of Christ may flourish again through every venue at the disposal of our technologically advanced age.

To Crispen Courage
The Divine Annihilation

Table of Contents

To Crispen Courage

"Now comes your Holy Mother to speak to you again inside the wonder and splendor of the loveliness of God. I have blessed your lives since before the very hour you were born, and long since you have been raised into adulthood. Please understand that these are only timely things because your soul belongs to the Eternal. My purpose is to call you to holiness so that you will be fully prepared to be reunited in the perfection of Heaven. My children, you are also My teachers of your brothers and sisters on the Earth for Jesus—His Voice, Wisdom, Light, and Peace. He has made you these things in your acceptance and imitation of Him. This is the last Sunday of this month, meaning that time will go onward tomorrow, and you will be able to rise from your beds with the purpose of the conversion of the world in mind. Yes, you must go about your daily chores to sustain yourselves, but you must never forget that your prime mission in life is to follow the call of Jesus that you hear interiorly. For, what else would I do with My gratitude if I did not offer it to you? And, too, I realize that your mortal existence is a very difficult process. There are too many distractions, and you have far too many enemies of the Holy Cross with which to cope and battle. Never mind that they do not accept what you already know to be the Truth! Converting them does not imply that you will see its immediate effects. Your lessons and legacies are their conversion, for each of them must comprehend your emulation of Jesus through their own set of eyes. This takes time, and such time is always on your side. This is another reason why I have come to speak to you today about the tenacity that you must embrace if your goals are to succeed. When I speak of being tenacious, I am attesting to the fact that you are My soldiers of righteousness for Jesus on the Earth. He has sent you into battle against both evil and indifference, the latter being as great an enemy as the first. God is asking you to be His carpenters for His Kingdom, the potters of His works of clay that He has placed into your hands upon the spinning world. Above all this, My children, you must have courage. You must be strong and brave, determined, perseverant, prayerful, and always ready to make the most of every situation you are proffered to exalt the message of the Holy Gospel.

My Special son, please take your dictionary in hand. Search for the word 'crisp.' Brisk, sharp, decided. Invigorating, firm and fresh. Now, look at the definition of the word 'crispen.' What am I asking you to do with the courage of other men? To make it brisk, sharp, decided, invigorating, and fresh. Hence, I am asking all of My children, especially My messengers and seers, 'To Crispen Courage.' No one has ever thought that this would become the title of a magnanimous work about the conversion of the world to the Cross of Jesus Christ. I am giving it to you for such a purpose. It is very important that you know what this really means. Does it imply to you that you must make rank-and-file warriors of everyone you meet? No. (Because) this is a choice that must be made by the individual human will, as much as accepting human Salvation in the Blood of the Cross must be done by each and everyone. To become a warrior for Christianity implies that their courage has become crisp according to the way that only the brave-of-heart can truly understand. I am telling you these things because I wish to support and ratify the tenor of your present writing. It is the true warriors for Divine Love who will eventually defeat the forces of evil in their most physically prevalent form. Your writing is in the process of giving untold numbers of sinners the courage to rise above their own faults, enter the ranks of soldiers for the Kingdom of God, and stand tall in the Grace that I am dispensing to them. You see, therefore, that the mission of your present writing is 'To Crispen Courage.' Please do not be concerned that your writing will be offensive to those to whom it is directed. Indeed, I wish it to be! Time is now very short, I have told you this before. This is not the time to be shy about your transmission of the serious nature of the Judgment of God and the sorrowful condition of His Church on Earth. I support the work that the Holy Spirit is penning through your humble heart as it is transcribed by you onto the page.

I have come to speak to you only briefly today... You will continue to do the work that God has given you to do, 'To Crispen Courage' wherever you see that it may be weak, and to never surrender to the dailiness of mortal life. You are strong and still very young. You and your brother have a great deal of work yet to do for Me before your days are done... You are My children, you are worthy of the dignity that you are refused in certain circles, and I will not send you into places where your honor is under attack... I give you both now My humble blessing. + Thank you for offering Me your obedient hearts! I will speak to you again at the beginning of the new month of September! I Love you... Goodnight!"

Blessed Virgin Mary
Sunday, August 31, 2003 1:25 p.m.

Foreword
by
Timothy Parsons-Heather

This is the sixth book that William L. Roth, Jr. has asked me to introduce to everyday readers, philosophers, theologians, secular iconoclasts, and anyone else God leads to Bill's extraordinary work. When I was born in a rural village in southern Illinois more than a half-century ago, I had no way of knowing why I first came into being, from where I had come, in whose bosom I had been laid, what identity I would adopt, and how or why God would give me the breath of life that oftentimes seems so anonymous to the present generations of men. I have never been a staunchly religious person; and I suspect I would never have garnered a serious penchant for the universal Truth of Roman Catholicism if the Blessed Virgin Mary had not guided me there through Bill's family in the small hometown in which we were both reared. Indeed, it was no ordinary guidance that the Holy Mother offered me through the years, but one filled with lessons and teachings about human suffering, the unredressed plight of the socially impoverished, the incalculable enlightenment that comes from the tragedies and complexities of everyday life, and those few, rare individuals whose inherent relationship with God always seems greater than we might ever imagine our own spirituality to be.

I began having interior locutions and apparitions of the Mother of God in February of 1991 during a time when I was enjoying the highlights of my career as a professional public administrator. I had always considered myself to be somewhat of a philosophical pragmatist before then, having read, studied and written about the precepts of reasoning and rational thought as the kinetic particulars and principles of manual human existence. Of course, I attended church as a practicing Christian because it was a matter that seemed important to my parents and my smattering of close friends. To be sure, my relationship with God seemed much like that of anyone else. I knew He was there; and I knew that He knew I was here. But, any deeper relationship than this seemed rather insignificant to me. I don't hide the fact that He made me awfully apprehensive in times past by some of the poignant things He allowed to happen during my youth, back when I was in my most impressionable days, trying to grasp the greater meaning of the concept of "living." Who am I kidding?—I probably don't have a complete grasp on it now. Anyway, I have discovered since those earlier times that God grows our relationship with Him through a strange spiritual stratagem designed to place the core of our souls into the body of Jesus Christ, at least at some time during our mortal years. Why? Because we can never understand the idea of being raised from the dead unless we die unto ourselves. It is almost like seeing God as our real Father, but one whose presence is strangely missing from His place at the dinner table every evening. So, Jesus Christ has stepped forward in God's stead as our spiritual guardian, a more approachable conservator who has seen God because He is God, the Second Person of an inexplicable Trinity who has supped with God in His beatific presence. Now, that's something we can never boast to have done.

I viewed both God and Jesus Christ in that context until the Blessed Virgin Mary spoke to me in the predawn hours on that February night in 1991. And, to say that my world was turned upside-down would be putting it mildly. I literally heard the voice of the Mother of Jesus Christ, whom I have since learned to be also the Mother of God, with my own ears—at least the ones fashioned inside my head. For anyone who wants to know more about these unprecedented circumstances, I refer you to the Web site we have created for "The Morning Star of Our Lord, Incorporated" whose address is located at the front of this book. I doubted the prospect that the Virgin Mary would even know who I am, let alone bother to say something to me. However, my sense of anxiety was relieved when, soon after I heard Her voice, Our Lady began speaking to Bill Roth, too. Henceforth, we have recorded everything we could transfer from the Immaculate Heart of the Virgin Mary to the temporal world as best we knew how. Our earliest messages were extraordinarily difficult to comprehend because they were filled with euphemisms, parables, metaphors and mystical images. We secured the spiritual guidance of Roman Catholic priests who were close to us, and who knew what advice to give us during those difficult circumstances. I have always wished to be well liked by my friends, colleagues, peers and other people I meet for the very first time. However, I was not even feebly prepared for the rejection Bill and I would eventually receive from them all. I cannot accurately describe the feelings of ridicule, mockery and disdain we underwent during the early years of Our Lady's intercession. The priests who were counseling us told Bill and me to put the value of our reputations behind us, subdue our human will, and allow the Blessed Mother to accomplish precisely what She came to do. If not for the miracles we both saw during the first months of Her messages, I am unsure we could have believed even ourselves at times.

Even though I had studied speech forensics in undergraduate school, my chosen field of profession was in public management; and writing about spiritualism was the last thing on my mind. But, Our Lady was persistent while I prayed for stronger faith; and I eventually was able to open my heart to the Holy Spirit in a magnitude sufficient to allow for the continuance of our mission. I have learned from speaking to other people that it isn't so much how we communicate that matters the most, but *what* we communicate. This, too, is a lesson I garnered from the Queen of Heaven. And, the work you are about to read in this book is a product of Bill Roth's scripted obedience to this same Virgin Mary whom I have come to venerate and admire. Bill wrote his part of this manuscript of his own accord, under the Holy Mother's discretion; and the rest of the book is Bill's recording of the messages he has received from Her. I must admit that I have never seen or heard such profound messages in all my years of life. There is nothing I can say in this Foreword that could prepare you for the shocking revelations Our Lady is dispensing to humanity through Her messages to Bill. And, his ability to internalize and comprehend Our Lady's intentions for Her modern children bears an uncanny resemblance to the Apostles of the first century who received the power of the Holy Spirit in enlightened tongues of fire. We should rejoice that Our Lady has inspired William Roth to write *To Crispen Courage* as a means of teaching, leading, emboldening, admonishing and preparing humanity in advance of the Second Coming of Jesus Christ. Those whose hearts are given to the wide and varied possibilities that God gives His earthly people to understand His Will have already begun the journey of faith to the mountaintop of Divine Love; and they will enjoy reading this book with angelic jubilation. Some theologians will be apprehensive, and others even crass, in their response to the authoritative tone in which the Mother of God has spoken to Bill Roth in Her messages in this book. And, I suspect that some cavalier naysayers will categorically deny their authenticity altogether without ever reading a single page. It is for these poor souls that my heart aches the most, because God is touching us through His Mother in so many new ways during the present times; and we should open our lives as wide as grand canyons to receive Her Grace. I hope Bill's readers enjoy the revelatory dimensions to which Our Lady ascends humanity's spirit by Her messages in *To Crispen Courage*, and that everyone joins me in thanking William L. Roth, Jr. for his kindness and devotion in serving as an humble medium between God and humankind for the advancement of the Eternal Salvation of the world.

Section One
A Synopsis of Miraculous Legitimacy

"My forceful one, we have just begun. My Son is with you..."
February 22, 1991 - 2:45 a.m.

And, with these words in the pre-dawn hours of a winter morning at the close of the second Pentecostal millennium, a mystical prodigy of human sanctification commenced at the invocation of the regal Queen of Heaven and Earth. The loving Mother of Jesus Christ has been allowed by the Omnipotent God of Creation to come to the spiritual aid of a horribly reckless and irreligious humankind. This utterly unthinkable, and certainly unanticipated, intercession of the Immaculate Virgin Mary into the American culture at its ignominious pinnacle of moral dereliction is a glorious blessing of righteous renewal that is sounding the apocalyptic knell in the parlours of immorality and secular abomination. My childhood friend and I are witnesses to the Divine Love who owns the fields upon which we will play-out our lives and which renders our grandest national successes to be just a few scattered droplets of rain before the gushing torrents of immortal victory are beleaguered like a hurricane around our unsuspecting consciences. Our Lady's miraculous appearances to us on the heartland plains of Illinois during these modern times are the embodiment of God's emissarial Mercy extended to each of us in anticipation of the convincing administration of His perfect Justice, which spares no mortal in its cleansing wave. For those of you who have never listened to the authentic voice of God, cared about His elevated intentions for the unfolding of our world, or considered your fate before the eternal ages, now is the most opportune moment of your entire lives. For anyone who has found it difficult to accept the Wisdom of our Creator issuing from the lips of sinful human evangelists or surrender to the moral precepts from priests, pastors, or pundits, the sinless Mother of the Messiah, the Virgin of Nazareth, wishes to speak with you. This benign Matriarch is without peer in the supernal Wisdom of what is true and real. The passionate desires of Her Immaculate Heart originate in the effervescent Love of Her Son, who is tireless in His longing to teach our lost world the Universal Truth that will never change through heresy, hatred, havoc or horror. Our Blessed Lady has proven Her unimpeachable authority to articulate the prescriptions for Redemption when, in Her finest hour, She became one in the Passion of Her Son and cooperated in the inscription of the sanguinary legacy of the Calvarian mountaintop into historical being. No one can fail by extending their humble deference to this Immaculate Queen and Veridical Benefactress. Even if one was to heroically advance the courage to throw their entire material existence onto the trash heap of society as being so much bad rubbish, they would become infinitely richer than their wildest imaginings for their sound decision to finally abandon their worn-out thoughts, understandings, and careers to move into union with the redeeming transformation of life as it comes into alignment with its most prestigious reflection of the Almighty Father. As I have stated before, *...I can tell you how to become holy, but it is you who must make the transformation. I can tell you that I have seen the meadow, but it is you who must travel there. I can speak of commitment, but it is you who must become committed. I can reveal the Truth, but it is you who must accept it. I can ask you to believe, but it is you who must summon the courage that escorts that faith to the surface of your life (Morning Star Over America, 1999).* Faith is not only a capacity to believe in the unseen that is solely dispensed by the Holy Spirit. It is also a willed extinction of our old selves that we sacrifice to make way for the new. While we decide *to* believe, the Holy Spirit tells us *what* to believe. Therefore, we come together as one heart in these pages, seeking to remedy the failings in the darker corridors of our past by cultivating springtime rows of a new season of grace, and heralding the hopes of generations of our forebears who held to the revelations of God through the cyclical ages of moral transgression and faithless indifference.

There are thousands upon millions of human beings who have never encountered a sincere witness or an authentic testimonial to the mystically Divine as my brother and I are extending through our works. Yet, this holy collection of days which has been manifested by the supernatural intervention of the unseen Hosts of Paradise is accelerating the transformation of an irrefutably wayward humankind into the pristine image of unified Love that our Creator has wished us to emulate since He first cast our frames onto the exilic plains of this mortal Earth and encased our souls within them at the Paradisian Fall. Whether one might wish to characterize the past 14 years of our lives as a supernatural odyssey, a metaphysical trek, a private revelation, a prophetic warning, or merely a simple blessing, there has undoubtedly grown a horn of impeccable spiritual fruit which is granting a fuller realization to everyone within earshot that the God of Creation is real, alive, and has been completely engaged with His created humanity and the universe that we providentially inhabit since the moment of its terrestrial conception at His Divine Hand, notwithstanding whether the original six days incorporated a big bang and millions of years or a mere 144 solar hours. The Most Holy Trinity has been communicating Divine Wisdom and guidance across every age of human existence in the dispensation of infinitely merciful graces to throngs of ordinary people. Throughout the evolution of our civilizations, the development of our cranial intellects, and the maturation of our cohesive interactions, the Pentecostal Spirit has revealed His nurturing care in multitudes of vastly differing manifestations encompassing as many variant magnitudes of insightful depth of the Heavenly Kingdom as can be envisioned by the infant faith of sinful mortals. Yet, God has always beneficently unveiled His celestial designs, reverent commands, and stern admonishments according to the times in the most prolific and fluent means that each generation would faithfully embrace as we collectively move as one bassinet of divine children ever closer to the fullness of time and our eternal judgment. Therefore, during this fortunate generation and from this blessed place, the unyielding continuity of miraculous legitimacy processes forth with crystalline clarity, generous humility, anointed authority, unalterable resilience, steadfast certitude, and ultimate victory. Our postmodern era is not bereft of the beatific intercession of our Lord God. The question remains, ***Will we believe His Heavenly Messenger who also happens to be His Mother and Queen?***

Sunday, July 11, 1999 (excerpt)   *3:00 p.m.*
  "Dear little children of Mine, you are the offspring of   i(192)
your Savior, Most High! I have come again to bless your
prayers and help you regain the millions of souls who have
collectively slipped into the oblivion of indifference and
outright wanton hatred. I have told you many times that
Love is natural to My children, and only Love. Hatred is a
manifestation of evil and an attribute of the lost souls who
follow Satan. I ask the world, I beseech humanity—May I
have your hearts as the new property of Salvation? Can
Heaven be so bold as to implore you to reside there for the   x
sake of your own Eternal Life? I hold the destiny of human
fulfillment in My Immaculate Heart. There is no way for
you to turn back now! Redemption is at hand and God is
ready to dispense it. These are the times that will determine
when enough prayers have been lifted to completely vacate
Purgatory of its last suffering soul. The weeks and months
ahead are the direction that all humanity must take, not
backward into the illicit pits of destruction and despair. I
assure you that the many celebrative Feast-days that are
coming will ring with a renewed resonance because all for   xx
whom those Feasts are offered are now on their feet to watch
your souls scamper across the finish-line to reach your place
among their ranks. I must tell you that if Creation were to be
measured as the size of a cloud, the Earth is but the
circumference of one raindrop inside it. But, it is that tiny

droplet of moisture that is soothing the parched lips of everyone who has fought with such valiant courage to claim it for the Kingdom of God. Yes, Jesus has transformed the Earth into a massive flood of victory and righteousness, a waterfall and cool-running brook which swirls as the delight of millions of souls who bask in the shadows of her beaches. These are the reasons that the heavens rejoice! I am the Immaculate Queen whose happy duty it is to tell you that you have all been saved! By scourge, by sorrow, by Blood of the Cross, and by the steel of the blade, you have been renewed into a paradisial people, a chosen race, and a royal priesthood; never more can despair and guilt hold you hostage. No more will you weep because you cannot see the Light! My little children, the flurry of this ripe happiness is blooming in your midst during these summer days as the rest of the world brawls in the foyers and precincts of secular indifference. They will turn-about, take notice, and their eyes will peel in awe as they first-look at the monumental gift that you are about to give them! Can you feel the joy of that anticipation? But, remember to be patient as God reveals His purposes in time. Do not count the hours, days, weeks or months. Allow your souls to ponder much larger dimensions than that! Set your sights on the last goal, the day to come when all humanity will gather at your feet to hear the endless story of how all of this began to unfold and they were none the wiser."

xxx

xl

l

Without a healthful dose of trust in the Holy Spirit, one could probably surrender to the hopeless belief that it is impossible to generate the anticipatory vision required to compose a comprehensive treatise that will initiate the spontaneous conversion of sizeable portions of humankind to the Gospel Truth in one unified step, realizing the diverse antagonism generated by arrogant human intellectuals who are self-buttressed by pluralistic religiosity and politically-correct ideologies. Everyone must henceforth realize that I have no politics to please, and the so-called religious will only be recognized as such by their personal display of faith; for the parable of wolves in sheep's clothing teaches us quite apropos wisdom at the beginning of this twenty-first century. There is a wide chasm between theological knowledge of the Faith and actually invoking it. Faith means fearlessly trusting in the Voice of the Holy Spirit; and it is characterized by an abandoned, kinetic responsiveness to the One who inscribed its indelible, multi-faceted definition into seeable Creation. The Sacred Scriptures, themselves, cast great light in their literary testament to the requirement of humble subordination to the revelations of Christ, especially in the stories of Jesus' appearances after His Resurrection to people who were themselves penitent sinners. The spiritually exacting summons of faith, the spontaneous acceptance and instantaneous obedience wrought through the loving power of the human heart, is precisely the same today as it was during those difficult days nearly two-thousand years ago. The Apostles did not believe Mary Magdalene after she reported her personal encounter with the Risen Christ (Mark 16:9-11). Neither did they believe two other disciples to whom Our Lord appeared when they subsequently witnessed before them to the great happening (Mark 16:12-14). But, when Jesus thereafter appeared to the remaining Eleven, He rebuked them for their stubborn unbelief and hardness of heart, *since they had put no faith in those who had seen Him after He had been raised.* You see, they lacked the humility to accept and correspond with the earnest witness of another mortal being, just as the remaining faithless world refused to embrace the declarations of Almighty God because His Word was emanating from a human body. Christ said, *"Do not persist in your unbelief, but believe"* (John 20:27). And, to this moment, Our Lord and Savior has never issued a "bye" to anyone to place toward the obfuscation of their responsibility to trust and submit to the unfolding course of our Redemption and our participation in His Holy Cross. The authentic, evangelic messages that witness to Jesus Christ alive and working in the world deserve to be accepted, elevated, and propagated before mankind as light and proof to the faithless, lest rebuke be the culmination of our legacy. Woe to those who have been the prideful impediment to the ascension and flowering of Our Lady's grace in the course of history! They are on the downward spiraling path and slippery slope of their impending humiliation. I tell you with all seriousness that there have been more authentic heavenly intercessions condemned by intentionally-erroneous witnesses and blinded ecclesiastical interrogators than have ever been faithfully accepted and obeyed. And, why? For the same reason that the Apostles did not believe the witnesses that the Lord chose to send to them in His grand Providence. My soul can hear the crying of "foul" as I write these words from those who worship at the inflated altar of their own educated egos. Let every one of them now hear this: *The fool ignores the Truth to salvage the illusion of his own autonomy, for we are all morally bound as brothers and sisters to the Grace of the Holy Spirit wherever and to whomever He should so deign to reveal and dispense it on the Earth!*

The grand sense of legendary morality that has been secured as the underpinning of our contemporary world by the heroic sacrifices of our bygone Saints is being eclipsed by a great darkness whose infernal signs of decadence, degradation, and death are proliferating through the most willful and creative manners. We watch as one immoral abomination after another rears its hissing head, screaming for legitimacy with their creators profiting both socially and financially, but certainly never eternally. Christians numbering in the tens of millions are gathered in their sequestered congregations listening for the faintest hint of reveille from their secularly-embattled leaders, the slightest breeze of exhortation arising from an indomitable faith that we yet espouse an invincible conviction of superpower dimensions, that we are a sacrificial contingent of gestating saints who have the perseverance to outlast the most malevolent opponent, and who own the divine authority to amend every hopeless situation, even unto our death. Alas, Love's ancient Sacrifice has been unduly squelched inside the muted throats of those with sound venue in this, our most propitious hour. But, not anymore! Let it be known that the Most Blessed Virgin of the City of David has transcended the mortal veil and entered our earthen valley like a seasoned Conqueress, wielding the immortal prowess to slaughter an entire pack of famished lions with a single swipe of Her inviolate sword; yet, She possesses the taming grace to tranquilize them at Her feet as though they were hapless kittens huddled around a saucer of milk. If you are pining for a rallying cry or are wearied in search of an instrument of victory; if you have ever envisioned the moment when all good people will simultaneously rise to their arches with the conquering roar of divine acclamation unleashed from the depths of their souls; or if there lives but one steadfast person who still dreams of that day when the tides of irrepressible good fortune will inundate the shores of mankind with gracefulness and purity, now is that monumental day! Our Lady is the Immaculate means to the ultimate Triumph of humankind redeemed! It is Her ageless cry of jubilation in union with the trumpeting witness of Her children that is bringing the walls of evil crashing to the ground like the horns that blasted against the ramparts of Jericho! The Mother of God declares from the paramount rafters of Heaven that the authoritative righteousness of Catholic Christianity is the ultimate wealth of God's Universal Power, which is beyond impeachment by any worldly pontificators. We are witnessing the repeating days of darkness come to their inevitable culmination with the heinous stampede over Eternal Truth finally delivered to a face-to-face engagement with its abysmal end. So, to *you,* the sinister legions of this vanquished age who stand either obstinately or ignorantly in the face of your divine obliteration, I declare by the holy power of Jesus Christ and the ominous intercession of Saint Joan of Arc: *Surrender your faithlessness and raise your hands and hearts to the Love that shines so high above you! Your world is* conquered by the Son of God on the Cross of Calvary! And, your Reckoning is hereby announced, confirmed, and sealed by the sun-clad Woman of Revelation, the Immaculate Virgin Mary!

Sunday, May 30, 1999   *3:58 p.m.*

"Oh, My sweet children, how I love you! Never in   *i(150)*
the boundless history of Creation have you ever been loved as does this Mother love you in reflection of God! You are a very fortunate faithful because He is about to reward those who have decided for Him. These are the times that Jesus has been standing in patience to embrace. While the world seems to be moving swiftly out of control, it is truly going nowhere that it has not been before. Generations of mortals have led their lives in anticipation of a material victory that they could never keep. My children, material wealth will   *x*
slip through your fingers when your hands fall open in death. You can grasp an Eternity of happiness only with the clutches of your soul. You are My children whom I have come to guide back to your good senses. Thank you for responding to My call. You are about to enter a new month which is dedicated to the Sacred Heart of Jesus. In Him, you are enjoined by a timeless victory that will pale before no enemy. Please be assured that I am telling you the Truth. You are still being deceived by the concept of time because daily life keeps lashing-out to draw you away from God.   *xx*
Remember that His Love is your timeless elevation away from the pangs of mortal life. Nowhere else in any other universe can you find such freedom. You are worthy of this grace and Salvation because you have found favor with the Creator of souls. If this were not so, I would have told you. This is why you are living in the Light of imminent Triumph. You are poised and composed because you cannot be defeated by the stench of the world. Just as it was a matter of time before your messages began in 1991, it is only a matter of time before the entire world will see your diarist-   *xxx*
collection of them. This is why you must be patient, all the while knowing that your victory is assured. Remember, we

have something they all want. It will be their big surprise. God does everything for a purpose and allows what you see to foster the need for that purpose. While it may seem that you are now moving in fractions, you are actually achieving the goals of Jesus in the measurement of galactic light-years. Only in your heart have you known this in the past. However, before this year is out, you will see it with your eyes. My children, the world is ready to hear what I have to say. America is poised to receive the Good News that I bring to such a sorrowful land. I assure you that the message will be heard! You must be patient while I prepare the hearts who need to know My Son for such a startling revelation. This is what My intercession is all about! I am bringing the revelation of holy conversion to a people who are lost in the dark! Be My Light! Be My little beacons who usher My message of Love into the urban culturalization of a truly primitive people, a helpless lot, a community of hearts who know no better. I have told you how helpless is a humanity without God. You are seeing the running amok of a world that has always been helpless, a world that despises justice, and a Creation which is fighting its hardest in this modern age to reject the Salvation that is free for the taking. Peace is at hand, but humanity has its collective hands jammed into its pockets. If all the warring nations will look toward Love as one dignified people, their flight will be toward the Holy Altar, rather than the killing fields of hatred and disrespect. Human hunger is not so much a corporeal deprivation as it is a spiritual bankruptcy. All of this is mitigated in the Heart of Christ! I am the Mother of the Greatest News ever known to man! The Earth rests in the fingertips of a Child who is perched in My arms. His Crown is one of perfect assurance and absolution. This little King pours-out His Blood upon the people He has died to save. You have known this since you were old enough to comprehend. That same Holy Spirit lives in you to this day. My children, if a maiden can be fair, then I am Fairness Incarnate. And, if Mercy can take to the flesh, Jesus is your

xl

l

lx

walking Forgiveness who was nailed to a Cross to prove it.   lxx
Be the angels of Light which He called you to be on that dark
hilltop of Redemption! Live the message of hope, faith,
pardon, and peace before all the world! That is what He has
commissioned you to do! A day at a time, walk toward the
redemptive horizon in confidence, knowing that millions will
follow in your shadow. While it seems like you should be
flying by now, you are still walking a day at a time toward
the end of the ages, inexorably passing with this age into the
courtesy of the coming midnight of your mortality and your
leap across the chasm of time into the dawn of Eternity.   lxxx
There can be no less than the high spirits and charming grace
left under your feet before you fall into the arms of the
Redeemer of every soul who has employed the great faith and
obedient conscience to seek Him in the Love that has grown
from the center of your hearts. My children, this is the time
of the Great Reckoning of Creation. This is not only your
time, but the arrival of Eternity for all the ages. Please come
to that horizon in assurance that this eleventh hour is your
procession toward unity with all that is of God. I am
awaiting that grand reunion with all the Angels and Saints,   xc
looking all humanity in the face! I beseech your smiles as you
rise and continue that grand march toward Eternal Life!
Give God every fiber of your heart as you continue in your
stately stride toward the Light of Love who is calling you
from beyond western summits. Your heart and soul know
that you are going Home, despite what your eyes can see! It
has been said by opthamologists that the ability of the retina
to cast a vision from it to the human brain is the macular
enhancement. That is, there has to be a stain on the retina in
order for the eye to see. When someone begins to go blind,   c
they are said to have macular degeneration. But, God knows
that the eyes of your soul can see Him only through an
Immaculate vision, free from the stains that have so
tormented humanity since the Fall of Adam and Eve. My
children, I am your Immaculate Vision! See Heaven through
My eyes! Allow Me to cast the majestic hues of Divinity upon

*your very souls! That is the rainbow that you can truly see
through your tears. The immortal vision of God is the reason
for Love and for Life, the purpose for which Jesus was
begotten and conceived in My womb, the reason He taught   cx
the righteousness of the redeemed, and the reason He died on
the Cross to take you to that chasm and take that leap back
into the arms of Almighty God. I am your Mother of Hope
because I have seen the reason for your hope! I gave Him to
the world under a bright star on a cold night in Bethlehem!
This hope will never disappoint you, He will not forsake you,
and He will do everything He promised from the moment He
was able to utter His first words... You are My hope, and I
realize that God trusts you. That is why I am speaking to
you today.   cxx
        My Special son, this has been a month of joy for you
and your brother, but of sorrow in the awful world. We will
continue to pray together to bring healing and peace to those
who suffer at the hands of others who will not love. I have
come today to share My hope and ask you to remember that
the future is now. These are the days that will usher the End
of Times. This is the Last Age of man. God has provided the
venue. This is a very special blessing in reflection of the
celebration of the Holy Trinity. + Please remember to be of
high spirits and peaceful heart. I will speak to you again   cxxx
very soon. Be My loves! I love you. Goodnight!"*

The manuscript you hold in your hands right now, wedded to the
collection of writings that have been published in succession, beginning with
the comprehensive Diary entitled *Morning Star Over America,* compose a single
gift of Divine hope from the heavens and a lightning rod of timely opportunity
for the transformation of millions of hearts who have been unable to discover
their way to authentic Love through any other venue. Although these written
pages are not the verbatim recitation of the definitive and all-encompassing
Deposit of Catholic Faith that the Christian universe rests upon, they are
nonetheless the particular flowering from that same Fertile Divinity which has
been cultivated for these latter times by the Most Blessed Virgin Mary, who
wishes to reveal great manifestations of Her Son's Original Love to our post-
modern civilization in order to bring "fullness" to His salvific work before

Jesus comes again in majestic Glory. The Catechism of the Roman Catholic Church states clearly, *"...even if Revelation is already complete, it has not been made completely explicit; it remains for Christian faith gradually to grasp its full significance over the course of the centuries... Throughout the ages, there have been so-called 'private' revelations,... It is not their role to improve or complete Christ's definitive Revelation, but to help live more fully by it in a certain period of history"* (CC. 66-67). Although Jesus Christ heroically succeeded in His Impeccable Revelation of God upon the Earth and single-handedly effectuated the Deliverance of humankind 2,000 years ago, even the most knowing theological minds of today must concede that they have yet to fluently grasp the panoramic explication of its transforming significance and the unimaginable power it renders to the progeny of God through our personal and communal declaration of faith and the invocation of our prayers, especially during the Holy Sacrifice of the Mass. The Definitive Revelation of Christ is that we, a bonafide nation, are liberated from our justifiable punishment, redefined in personal essence, recreated through our evolving spirit, restored in purposeful allegiance, rescued from the pyres of Gehenna, purified of every stain, pleasing before the eyes of the Father, empowered by celestial Grace, predisposed to beatific heights, melded with heavenly divinity, advanced in saintly benison, clothed in reciprocal Light, commissioned with the Hosts and Saints, as impenetrable as a marble fortress, stronger than the most oppressive legions, more intelligent than the proverbial last whit of mortal genius, and capable of leaping in a single bound the tallest, babbling netherworld of scrupulous naysayers who refuse to lay their arrogance and hand-wringing insecurities aside long enough to realize that the Immaculate Conception is assisting their paltry Christian evangelization through Her long-suffering intercession. Thus, Mary is gracing humanity in every miraculous way to manifest the fullness of the Definitive Revelation of Her Crucified Son and bringing His Kingdom to come and His Will to be done on Earth as it is in Heaven. If anyone claims to own the unilateral authority or the superior venue to remain indifferent to this heart-rending Love and gut-wrenching power to pigeon-hole such overwhelming beatitude into an obscure corner of anyone else's purview, *let him stand forward before the judgment of history and his Divine Creator, too!* I tell you—it is these dilatory modern-day inn-keepers who will prepare no room for God and His flushing spiritual manifestations, and who again relegate Jesus to the stark, barren stables where His Maiden Mother will someday ignite the greatest prodigies of humanity converted—revelations that will burn with the brilliance of a billion suns before the celestial backdrop of angelic choirs and flaming stars in the heavens.

Sunday, December 30, 2001 (excerpt)   *2:59 p.m*
      "If ever there was a time when any one society of k(364)
people was blessed more than in the history of mortal
humanity, this is assuredly the moment. I have offered My
consoling Immaculate Heart to My children of the Americas
because you live in places where lauding the King of Justice
is your right, responsibility, and honor. Today, I am pleased
to tell you that all sovereignty is bestowed upon you to even
a further degree through the Divine Mercy of the Sacred
Heart of My Son. We are a Holy Family that espouses the
virtues of Love, duty, servitude, and honor; and this is the   x
moral excellence which we seek in Christians everywhere.
As I have appeared in this place once again during the
recorded year of 2001, I ask all who hear My messages to
know that it has been a time of reckoning in many quarters
and neighborhoods; the Truth of human conversion can be
heard ringing all throughout your land, and the Cross on the
Hill of Mount Calvary continues to be paramount to
anything you will ever endure inside the parameters of time.
I ask you never to be afraid of change because the constancy
of the Passion, Crucifixion, and Resurrection of Jesus is   xx
always your Standard and Compass for your continuing
journey through life. There are many weak members of the
human family who need your attention, and I ask you to
humbly focus upon their needs, as they are growing quickly
older by the hour. Those who have the means to live in
surplus should subject themselves to the tendering of those
who have little means at all. Why in America is this so
important? Because there is no mandate for sharing like
there is in many other institutionally communal societies;
those who are in need depend on the generosity of others who   xxx
have plenty as their wares.
      I have come today to speak to My little children, My
Special one and My Chosen one, who have been quietly
moving countless mountains of opposition from within the
path of righteousness in your land. There are noblemen who
are born into great fortune, and others who have inherited

treasures untold, but theirs is nothing like the cache you are now building-up in Heaven. Jesus knows that you are not people who pursue material wealth or personal fame, but I assure you that the end of the mortal world is near and everything for which you ever dreamed is nigh at hand. Who could have prophesied the matter of only ten years ago that you would still be kneeling before My presence, listening to the Will of God for His world, eagerly savoring every morsel of My Wisdom, and working like little slaves to take the Word of God to the masses. Not only has your Morning Star already converted the hearts of tens-of-thousands, and 'At the Water's Edge' has taken the souls of as many by great surprise, but now, your next tremendous work, 'When Legends Rise Again,' is only a matter of ten days away from its completion. I ask you to believe Me when I tell you that those who are reading your works know that their origin is the center of My Immaculate Heart, that their strength is the power of the Cross, and their Divine nature is derived from the Holy Spirit. Please do not be ashamed to be proud of the work you are doing for My Son because He is quite pleased by the offering of your daily lives and mortal souls to His Kingdom; your minds, hearts, and every intention to the Love who has taken refuge in your spirits, and you in His. You live in a world of great imagining, and there are few dreamers who remain open to the powerful influences of God. Heaven seems like an unattainable place to many of them because they have not the faculties to seek it with an open attitude. These things have no bearing on the efforts of My children because your sights have been set anew on a Kingdom for which there is no comparing.

My little children, I have not the words to express the deep appreciation that Jesus holds for you as you enter another year of service to humanity in His Name. Yes, you are still running together through the element of time, hand-in-hand, with your vision trained keenly on the prospect that the rest of Creation will follow you to the Arms of God. This is a dream that will come true because the

xl

l

lx

lxx

Almighty Father is Love, a Love that cannot fail, a Peace which cannot wane, and a future of Everlasting Life that will never end. You are the provocative children of the age of Christ's Dominion, 2,000 years strong and counting, like the many legends whom you have hailed so appropriately in your books. Someday, your names will be situated among them as having not only the profile of courageous Love, but an entire multi-dimensional genius by which you have altered the world and the course of human history forever to come. The Apostles and Disciples of the earliest days are pleased for you to be in their company, these who lead the Communion of Saints in prayer for the mortal world, for they know that you are aligned with the dignified Truth of service for which Jesus has called from the very first Word of the Sacred Scriptures to the very last. Saint Paul has been weeping tears of joy to the point that he is lost for words in describing the means by which you have joined in His message of freedom for the captives, food for the starving, shelter for the homeless, healing for the sick, and guidance for the wicked. He knows that all these things are found in the Son of Man, the Savior whom you praise today before a globe which is inhabited by no less than six-billion people strong. Each new soul you gain for Christianity is another candle lighted in the darkness. There is no doubt that, little by little, you are setting the entire world afire in the flames of righteousness. This, too, is what Jesus said would happen near the end of time.

  My Special son, this is particularly a pleasing time for Me to speak to you because you have been the host to My intercession for nearly eleven years. I can see as you are reading your present manuscript that you can detect how momentous it really is. This is the power of your personal writing and the profound way that you have in moving humanity all together beneath the umbrella of God's Grace, one and the same as My Mantle. God will forever employ your works toward the advancement of His Kingdom. Every single sliver of manual effort will be pronounced as though it

lxxx

xc

c

cx

is being magnified a thousand-fold by the beaming light of the sun beneath a glass. No measure of time can contain the strength you are garnering to continue in your effort to assist the lost in regaining their identity again. Should all of your actions ever try to contain themselves in the confines of an hourglass, it would burst wide-open in a millisecond. You have power that has not been proffered to many other men because of your commitment to succeed in the Name of the Lord. There is no substituting the fact that you have never surrendered the mission that you accepted when I first came speaking to you. Your potency is in your faith, your Light is in your Love, and your Victory is in the Triumph of My Immaculate Heart, heretofore present and ongoing to this date, and to be capitalized very soon upon the Return of Jesus to take the redeemed souls who are given to Him to the Glory of their seeking. I ask you to be happy for them and pleased that you have afforded your Holy Savior the opportunity to remake the face of the Earth through the conviction from your heart.

cxx

      I will be speaking to you again next week as the new year of 2002 ensues. It will be another period of great tribulation for many, spiritual progress for thousands more, and a time of great enlightenment for everyone alive... As I say, these are very special times for you, and you can even sense inside that they are in a new and remarkable way even more special than were the days in 1991 when I first came to speak to you. You are savoring many of the fruits of harvest now from the seeds that we planted back then. This is why Jesus is so happy with you; your life as a prophet is allowing many things for which millions are praying to come true in their lifetime. Without your service and dedication, this would never have come to pass. Thank you for an entire lifetime of saying 'yes' to God."

cxxx

cxl

An additionally-fruitful point of holy contemplation can be entertained when considering the Deposit of Faith and the articulation of its "closure" with the untimely death of the last Apostle in relation to the many charisms which have arisen within the Church, especially those of miraculous and supernatural origin. Although "closure" confirms the completion of the salvific Revelation of the Second Person of the Most Holy Trinity in crucified human flesh, it is a misapplication of meaning to accept any definition that in any way maligns, impedes, or attempts to downplay Our Savior's presence, power, authority, interaction, mystical Beatitude, and continuing desire for our faithful obedience to His Immaculate Mother in any series or concurrent moments of time. If anyone is in perfect union with the Holy Spirit who emanates from the Gospel of Jesus Christ and the Catholic Church as revealed in the Deposit of Faith, their spirit will spontaneously rejoice in thanksgiving to the heights of Heaven that Our Lord would so bless us with miraculous charisms to fortify our faith and dispense to us the evidence needed to win the hardest of hearts for His Divine Kingdom. Our Lord Jesus Christ is not dead, neither is His mystical guidance and miraculous power "closed" behind some historical door in time, nor has the requirement of our obedience to His Plan for the unfolding of Redemption been suddenly rescinded, circumvented, or overshadowed. Our Lady has said in Her private dialogues with me that the heavens do not share the same disconnected overemphasis on physical death that we harbor as an effect of the frailty or infancy of our faith. No one's mortal passing is an impenetrable demarcation of separation between Heaven and Earth, as if the two are mutually exclusive realms, nor does it impede the interaction of the Heavenly Hosts with those still here in exile. The Catholic Church recognizes as a matter of Faith that the intercession of the Angels and Saints is a real, reciprocal friendship founded in the revelatory Love of Christ through the working of the Holy Spirit. The Saints who are presently living at the Throne of God are altogether functioning in our world in union with His power and authority in much the same way they did while their souls were embedded in mortal flesh. Their transition into celestial realms did not change who they are, how they desire the peaceful culmination of Creation, or why they still work for the Kingdom of God to eclipse the Earth in preparation for Jesus' Return. The faith-wielding priests who have passed through the veil have lived beyond their own necrology and bask in a perpetual state of Christological renewal at the Altar in Heaven, where they worthily mirror the Sacrifice offered upon the Catholic altars by their brother-priests yet in exile. These bygone, heroic evangelizers are still trumpeting the ages of Our Lord, just as they did while walking the agonizing paths of their own mortal militance. Such legendary healers are yet bestowing recuperative wholeness upon the sick, dying, and broken which their easement of mortal hours could not allow them to encounter or bestow. These brilliant, departed conquerors reside in oneness now with Saint Michael the Archangel and his pious legions, dispensing untold moral victories greater in frequency than the milliseconds of their earthly days combined. There is neither a mother nor father who was called to leave their children seemingly too soon who is not now tendering benefactoral discretion and loving care upon their offspring from the strains of Paradise. Every means of dispensational grace is being robustly applied to the mortal Earth from every venue and through all sanctified participation from our newly immortalized legends as we speak. And, to this day, Our Lady continues to be the grand Intercessor whom She has always been to Her Son, even prior to Jesus' performing His Father's scrupulous gift of the vessel-changing miracle of water into wine at a Cana wedding feast nearly twenty centuries ago. This, too, is an immutable fact contained within the Deposit of Christian Revelation. Hence, we must re-approach the Light which beams from our renewed understanding of authentic "private revelations," realizing anew that they are undoubtedly the potent work of many-a-Saint still acting in devotional intercession for the children of God, the same brothers and sisters whom they love in perpetuity as they did on Earth through their toils, labors, sufferings, and sacrifices. It is nothing less than an act of the highest wisdom to respond to the interactive presence of the Holy Spirit in these miraculous charisms; for it is none other than God Himself who is extending His divine beatitude to animate the personal faith that is so vital for the explication, sustenance, and propagation of the Deposit of Faith. The Catechism states ever so clearly a truth that no man has the authority to deny, *"...(so) that the submission of our faith might nevertheless be in accordance with reason, God willed that external proofs of his Revelation should be joined to the internal helps of the Holy Spirit. Thus, the miracles of Christ and the saints, prophecies, the Church's growth and holiness, and her fruitfulness and stability are the most certain signs of divine Revelation, adapted to the intelligence of all; they are the 'motives of credibility' (motiva credibilitatis), which show that the assent of faith is by no means a blind impulse of the mind"* (CC 156). And, the great Saint Augustine further said, *"Next you [God] set special lights to burn in the firmament. These were your Saints who are possessed of the Word that gives Life. In them, there shines the sublime authority that is conferred upon them by their spiritual gifts. After this, from corporeal matter, you produced sacraments, miracles that men could see, and voices to carry our message according to the firmament of your Book. These were meant for the initiation of unbelievers, and also for the blessing of the faithful."* If this living interconnection between the natural and supernatural, the temporal and mystical, and the seen and unseen is ever obscured or denied in the present reality of the Church, we sever ourselves from the successive graces of *motiva credibilitatis*, which henceforth cripples the power of our evangelical commission to courageously witness to a hyper-skeptical world the many providential facts concerning the sacred intercession begotten through the sacrificial lives of the Communion of Saints. It is our foolish declaration to God, independently and arrogantly, to say that we can scale the mountain of life alone, which is an utter absurdity. When we reject the miraculous intercession of the Mother of God and of the Saints, are we not advertently declaring that our Catholic belief in divine assistance from the Heavenly Hosts is only a tepid mantra in the void our minds? Our present refusal to respond to the obvious intercession of the Blessed Virgin Mary creates a pallid dissonance within the dogmatic soul of the Faith-Church on Earth. There have been thousands upon millions of unchurched faithless secularists, non-denominationalists, and atheists whose hearts have been blossomed by the supernatural perseverance of the Queen of Heaven. The eyes of their spirits spontaneously turned toward the Original Apostolic Church because they knew such apparitions of the Mother of Jesus Christ were predominantly a phenomenon associated with the Roman Catholic faith. Oh, how they have pined for validation of what we have professed all along! Sadly, untold thousands have turned away with their hopes in bludgeoned dismay, scoffing at the true-to-life witness of our Faith because so many theologians and leaders of the Church have failed to wrap their mantles of ecclesial authority around gestating charisms when called to ratify their truth. How large a miracle does it require to burn such indifference to cinders and force a response of more courageous witness to the intercessions of God? Will the world be converted any other way? In all honesty, we do not appear able to effect a powerful enough witness against any particular sin within our modern society to turn our Ship of State around, onto a more righteous course. And, what does it say of our pious declarations concerning the Communion of Saints when we lack the assertiveness to believe their manifestation ourselves?—not to mention what the Saints must be thinking while watching in wonderment the exercise of our willful rejection of the graces they sacrificed their entire lives to procure on our behalf. We must perform an immediate retraction and instead invoke the functional, living faith required to elevate the divine actions of the Saints presently living in Heaven, slamming their legacies with joy upon the earthen tabletop of the world before God's enemies as though we are playing the ultimate winning hand in the game of life, because their sainthood is the best wager for humanity's spiritually broken souls! The transforming power required to convert every hemisphere, hearth, and hamlet is tucked carefully within each catechetical imprint under the Saints' miraculous control. I herein declare that Our Divine Lord expects our unbridled response to His Queen; and it is Catholic Christianity which will be held most accountable for any hindrance of Our Lady's success, either intentional or absent aforethought, in retrieving Her children from the wiles of this world. If ever there was an opportunity, a moment, or an assemblage of factual impression in the public fora of Christianity issuing from the lips of our unseen God, He is standing at the lectern now! Our Lady's urgent intercession is the pinnacle and grand exclamation defining that outpouring of grace! Our Christian "L-A-B-O-R" must be actualized by *Listening, Accepting, Believing, Obeying,* and *Responding* to the miraculous intercession of the Queen of Heaven and Earth, no matter how many enemies it garners or barriers it creates for somebody's model of religious ecumenism.

Friday, December 5, 1997

"My blessed little holy ones, welcome into the comfort g(339) *of My Immaculate Heart. You are worthy of great praise when you yield your lives and tender your hearts to Me. As you see, My children, this commitment is not without its responsibilities. You are asked to remember that prayer is obedient. Your days continue to be blessed in spite of ever-present dangers and difficulties. Many are the moments when you feel defeated and forgotten. You feel these things only when you forget the Passion of Jesus. You are wholly remembered and always victorious in the only Son of God.* x *You are, therefore, asked to invoke the power in His Cross during times of distress. I have been recently reading and recalling the most beautiful diary of this generation, your own. I have been touched by its call for prayer and human beauty. I am brought to tears by its poetic means of describing the heart and the bliss of human suffering. Its words describe a flippant thing and many other colorful images that pull upon the heartstrings of all called to those words. How could your lives have been more beneficial to the lost world? How else could such grace be yours? My time* xx *has come! It is time for the great Triumph of My Immaculate Heart. I will bring the Savior of humankind into this world once again, and for the final time. But, this time will be different. This time, all will bow! This time, the King will be King, indeed! He came as a Child and will now return for His children. This time, He will bring with Him the room He called-for on Christmas eve, a mighty mansion and many mansions in which His children will reside forever. My little*

ones, do not give-up on this hope. Do not be afraid in your patience to ask Jesus to hasten His return! Call upon Him to finally bring His Kingdom and actuate the demise of the already fallen darkness of the world. Jesus is the Light of the world who is now temporarily hidden under the bushel baskets of human materialism, greed, impurity, indifference, and sin. It is the choice of humanity to call upon the Light, to magnify the Light, and to savor the Light like millions of hungry butterflies hovering about the brightness and warmth that draws them in. You have described My hundreds of messages with power, passion, and perfection in your diary. It will be completed in a few months, and I will hand it to My Son, a gift from you, so that He can wield it as a mighty saber against all it portends to destroy! It is you who have made this new weapon against evil possible, you who have procured and produced for God a powerful force to allow the Second Coming of Jesus to be magnified by endless proportions. Thank you! You must stop thanking Me for your work. I have not done your work, you have. You are My mighty foot-soldiers at the front of the battle against evil and for the conversion of humanity. You must know that it is you who help God do His work on Earth. If it were Mine to call, Jesus would have already returned, and all souls would be with Me in Heaven. But, God has awaited the stirring of human participation in the great plan of Salvation. That is why I am here tonight. We are waiting for the total response of humankind, for hearts to become alight through the Holy Spirit instead of the distracting world. And, despite what you see, we are much-winning that battle. Each day, new eyes are being drawn to the call, the means, and the effort of the children of God. Each new sun brings a most contemporary revelation in the collective human soul that God is about to end the world as you know it. Millions are learning anew each day to live in anticipation, but they do not yet know what to expect. People see a line forming behind a new front, a new beginning, a clarion of the ages. They know not yet who is

xxx

xl

l

lx

calling, but they know they are being called. You know why you are in line for the succession of Saints. Others are forming behind you because you are yourself standing firm in your hope for God. They see your faith by your example and see your anticipation by the skyward turn of your face in joy. All of these beautiful occurrences are now unfolding in the real world of God, one day and one soul at a time. And, like a candle, time has now burned near its base. And, as God would ironically have it, the smaller the candle of time, the greater is the Light in Creation, and brought by the Rectifier and Reconciler of the ages, Jesus Christ.

My children, this is a special age in time for Me. I have yearned prayerfully for centuries for the coming of the final one at hand. I did not know if Jesus would return in Glory in the first century after His Ascension, or the second, or which. And, though I know not the day or the hour, I know that we have arrived at the last century. I will not have to wait another hundred years. All except a handful of those born before 1890 are with Me now. Jesus is about to return for the rest of you, still mortal and still frail and afraid. My children, this is a happy time. You should observe your days, your actions, and your seasons with great joy. The ride you have been awaiting is nearing your door, and your passage has been paid. The lights of the new day are being ushered to you with each stroke of this pen, which has been like a paintbrush in My hands to yours. My children, I know this God you seek. I know His Heart and His Plan. He could not have conceived or perpetuated a more beautiful finish to the mortal world. He could not have imagined a more brilliant culmination to the efforts and sacrifices of all His Saints. And, yes, that is what He calls you. No production, no desire of a heart could compete with the salvific flourish of Jesus' Return to Earth to bring His Kingdom to the blessed and simultaneously crown those who desire it. If you were to strike every beautiful chord that you have ever heard at one moment, you could not match the beauty that your hearts are about to know. Men will fatally

lxx

lxxx

xc

c

fall in ecstasy. I have seen the Glory of the coming of the Lord! So, let not your hearts be troubled or dismayed. I have already seen the jubilation of My children, but not yet. That is why you must know to live that Truth in confidence. All your actions and prayers are bringing that Kingdom of which I speak.

My Special son, do you recall seeing My blessed A__ upon her deathbed in 1984? And, do you recall seeing your   cx *beloved little J__? You were seeing Christ yet incarnate, from which you must draw your strength. Therein lies strength for all humanity, the humble example left by the Saints now in Heaven. That is the true reason that you were given a capacity of memory. Thank you for the days you attended the Novena. This is also a special night of prayer. I again remind you of the noon-hour on Monday. I give you now My holy blessing. + I will speak to you soon! I love you. Goodnight!"*

We must come to understand that the mystical phenomena of the Holy Paraclete are essentially the overpowering promulgation of the King of Creation inundating our lives in a genuine attempt by the collective architectures of Heaven to bring us to heroic acceptance of the realities of all that is unseen. The facts that speak to spiritual absolutes and reconfirm the omnipresent compassion of our Almighty Father overwhelmingly outweigh the intermingled fallacies perpetuated by renegade sinners whose obstinate blindness prohibits them from seeing past their own noses. There are many misguided people who crassly mock the power of the Holy Spirit by dampening the fervor that Jesus ignites within His children's hearts through so-defined private revelations. Miracles do not diminish faith, they complement it, inspiring our virtuous passions to become as exemplary and indomitable as our Crucified Savior. So, we should allow the Spirit of Christ to bring about a combustible ignition of awareness that the divine intercession of the Virgin Mary is not *too good to be true*, but Her presence is *too Good not to be the Truth*. Only a casual perusal of our postmodern culture in the United States and around the globe is required to make the case for our continuing need for divine intercession. What else but mystical revelations are going to save us from ourselves? It could not be made any clearer why the miraculous Wisdom of the Most Holy Virgin of Bethlehem is of such crucial importance as the world teeters on the edge of contingent, countless and nameless holocausts waiting in the wings to be unleashed upon humanity. What politico or secular leader has the vision to become the knight in shining armor, galloping forth to rescue our future from the callous darkness rampaging across our cultures? Who but the Supreme Pontiff in Rome has uttered more than a whimper of moral Truth loud enough for evil forces to understand that they have been put on notice before the trial of the Eternal Ages? Have we truly placed our collective trust in secular relativists who claim that if we close our eyes and click our heels together three times while repeating, *everything is wonderful,* our country will be suddenly transformed into social benignity before our eyelids have time to bat a second time? Only America's greedy corporate marketeers flanked by their hired advertising henchmen can generate such a propagandized fallacy, albeit with a deficient consumer product and paid broadcast rhetoric claiming that their wares are already sweeping the nation before the first unit ever leaves the shelf. What capitalist possesses the spiritual regalia to accomplish the planetary task of reconfiguring a self-possessed humanity into the loving shape of the Cross in advance of the Second Coming of Jesus Christ? None! And, since we have thus far declined to respond to the Blessed Virgin Mary, the Woman sent by God to effect this enlightenment, isn't the answer to the question of why we are seeing the world slide ever downward toward the hellish abyss coming into clearer focus? You see, those who have the power to stop our descent often shy away from the Cross by refusing to recognize the apocalyptic nature of the times, denying the collective invocation of faith needed to abandon themselves to our Heavenly Mother and Her supernatural intercession, and forwarding an outright, public rejection of the humility required to defer to and obey the intercessory guidance offered by the Almighty Father to help them make things better. The Lady who lifts our ship of courageous souls high-enough to be loosed from our false perceptions is mystically present now! The only hope for our deliverance rests beneath the Mantle of the Immaculate Virgin Mary, where we must confidently raise our conjoined hearts into an arbor of holiness in the vineyard that has been left to our custodial care. The royal essence of humankind must be purged of apathy and indifference because they are the lifeless carcasses of our lost hopes and dreams, the dead weight of a coward's fate.

Christians everywhere pine for the miraculous redressing of human life, or in the Biblical vernacular, the spiritual conversion of the world, but do not consciously encounter the fulfillment of their visions in the present because the *explication* of the liberating Wisdom of Christ has been nailed to a modern-day Cross by insidious people who have intellectualized something so beautiful as our spontaneous, faithful Love for our resurrected Messiah. We are witnessing on too many occasions the mystical adjectives of our full-fledged description of the Universal Truth being suppressed by people who believe in parabolic terms that the Christian Deposit of Faith is fully-encompassed by the statement, *Jesus planted a tree.* This, to them, is the unabridged totality of the Revelation of Christ; and they often fight like pit bulls guarding their supper bowls against anything more than those four words, believing they are doing it all for the Glory of God. And, this poignant description does not begin to take into account the Manna-less protestors who have reduced nearly every passage down to a single word. Therefore, God's benevolent desires are justifiably inflamed; and He dispatches His Immaculate Queen to widen everyone's vision of "fullness," allowing Her to communicate heavenly Wisdom through the mystical conduit of our faith with such messages as, *The Perfect Master, the Christ, My Beloved Son is the Arborist of the Beatific Order of Saints, the Architect of an Infinite Kingdom so high above the meandering visions of fallen men. He has turned the blade into the soil of the hearts of human beings, laid the fertile ground open to the vaulting skies. It is He who is cultivating the world like I wish to draw pretty combs through the silken hair of My little girls. The King I bore has bound every wound and wrapped them in miraculous bandages of delight, supporting and sustaining the seemingly endless ages and ever-recurring convolutions of developing civilizations. This Giant of men carried the seed of Human Redemption into a dark and broken world, a Love so profound that the Angels of His Paradise shielded their eyes on His most triumphant day. With His undying and unyielding Love, He rooted the sapling of Divinity into the fields of Creation; and with His indomitable Will steadied the winds and gauged the rains in order to secure the Mighty Oak of Righteousness on the barren plains of your failing netherworld. And, from its soaring branches has blossomed the propagation of every truthful sentiment of humankind, a veritable forest of inspiring flashes of purposeful contemplation, infusions of courageous sacrifice, and flaming convictions of heroic witness that have appeared toweringly prolific in every vestibule of mortal exile. The charismatic buds of revelation are blowing across the acreage of souls through the advancement of the personal declarations of those who evangelize for My Son, borne by the uplifting Breath of the Holy Spirit, past epochs, eons, and eternities. The Eternal Harvester stands now at His Father's side awaiting the Trumpet of the Ages and the faith of His children, filled with anticipation that the Feast of Heaven and Earth will ensue with a fanfare that will make Creation new.* But, these theological pickers-of-nit oftentimes cloak themselves with their vainglorious scholastics and say, *the Church simply teaches that Jesus planted a tree.* Sadly, the Church Militant is thus deprived of the "full explication" of the Deposit of Faith; the Church Suffering must endure their precarious plight with greater awareness of the faithlessness that first took them to such a reparatorial predicament; and the Church Triumphant must patiently await a more valid faith to be cultivated upon the Earth through the providential suffering allowed by the Most Holy Trinity. Yes, human suffering is exacerbated in the world as a result of our collective refusal to hail Our Lady's intercession from one corner of this cosmic sphere to the other. And, our banal excuses can never purge this glaring omission from our souls.

I certainly hope no one mistakenly presumes that my somewhat writhing candor is anything less than a merciful exhortation of the Wisdom that our Heavenly Mother has transmitted during our mystical conversations. It has always been a Work of Mercy to instruct the spiritually ignorant, no matter how educated they may be. It is an operative manifestation of heroic evangelization to enter into Pauline engagements with those who try to impede the work of the Holy Spirit through the Immaculate Virgin Mary. The judgment of our souls hangs in the balance. Salt must never be allowed to lose its flavor. There have been multitudes of innocent people in generations passed, most significantly little children, who have lain too long in the excruciating agony of destitution, infirmity, and poverty atoning for the sins and omissions of the faithless, the haughty, the arrogant, the self-centered, and the worldlings who are only now clutching more desperately the arms of their self-appointed thrones with each indicting word Our Lady levels at them. The triumphant elimination of this sacrificial reparation is in the invocation of faith from the rest of us, we who have necessitated their suffering in order to bring us to greater Light. The supernatural power of the Most Blessed Trinity has always been present, without diminishment or dilution. Every miraculous grace we encounter throughout our lives has been purchased with grueling tribulation, galling distress, and waves of personal hatred directed at the most tender lairs in which a child of God could ever take refuge. In union with our ecclesiastical brethren, we are mandated to forge our trust in God and magnify His abundant blessings so these horrors can finally be eradicated, once and for all. Our refusal to act due to collegial apathy is a malfeasant product of human pride and our outright cowardice in the face of moral warfare, both of which spring from our fear of the sacrifice required at the unleashing of God's grace from our intellectual shackles and our confounding lack of vision about the facts of the suffering of such innocents! Faithlessness, itself, has been lying to humanity under the guise of prudence over twenty centuries and counting, and has been the rationale of prevaricating cowards since time immemorial. Jesus speaks sternly in the Sacred Scriptures while admonishing His people who refuse to enter the door, and who keep it locked for all who wish to pass through. It will always be vexing to Christians how such anxious trepidation is generated by the mystical intervention of God to the darker quarters of the world; but nary a figment of reservation seems warranted concerning the contemporary visions of worldliness that spew from the minds of people whose supernatural faith died so many years ago. The peace of Christ does not rest amidst the numbing fraternity of pluralistic morasses caused by blind moral ignorance. The Catholic Church must always be allowed to stand as the stately Lady She is. Yet, if our response to date is any measure, there will surely be more than a few money-changers' tables overturned by Our Lord before that eternal apportionment is finally secured.

"Do you desire to study to your advantage?   Let devotion accompany all your studies, and study less to make yourself learned than to become a saint."
- Saint Vincent Ferrer

Sunday, March 28, 1999   5:03 p.m
     "This is the home to which all of the Heavenly Hosts   i(087)
follow Me, to see and pray with the two children of God who
are making such an eternal difference in the elevation of so
many souls. It is your faith, My children, that tells you this
is true. Yes, you have seen many miraculous signs of grace,
but these supernatural gifts satisfy only your mortal
inquisitions. The Love in your heart is the true source of
faith, not only for you, but for all of mankind. You are living
proof that God is real. Your testament of faith is God's
validation that He wields complete power and authority   x
over Creation. His Wisdom is the source of your undaunted
trust that Jesus Christ holds in His possession the destiny of
every soul that the Almighty Father has given life. My
children, your Savior is elated that millions have chosen to
return to His side. He is as happy that His people have
chosen to come Home as are the very souls who have gone
there. That is why the tombs and graves of the deceased are
empty. Your Jesus could not wait until the end of time to
bring them back to His embrace. You have learned to not be
deceived by the element of time. You are the living proof   xx
that righteousness is the source of all mortal strength and that
Love is the origin of all immortal life. I have had the
pleasure of watching you grow and learn. I know the
expanse of your anticipation and what makes you happy.
Your hearts are mended, healed, and consoled because I am
comforting them. Jesus is the mainstay of your courage and
determination. I offer Him to you with pride because I know
that He will soon bring you back Home to My side. You
must always remember that the Holy Family that you so

admire has walked the same Earth that you now tread. We   *xxx*
have suffered the same wounds and grieved the same
sorrows. Humanity lives within the circumference of our
joined hands as we circle the globe, seeking-out hearts who
will step forward in faith, face the bantering world, give the
charge of conversion to the many hidden valleys and aloof
peaks, and suffer gladly anything that befalls you, all for the
sake of being poised at the end of time on the plateau of
Salvation. That, My little children, is why I come to bless, to
teach, to petition, to invite, to share, to love, to pray and to
partake in the most living and brilliant faith to be found   *xl*
anywhere in this American nation. I am the Morning Star of
your Lord! I have come to this heartland prairie of the most
affluent country in the world, just to seek you out. You know
that wealth is truly not everlasting power. You know that
justice is not brought through a gavel, a jury, or a system of
penal ethics. You know that justice is a child of peace, a
peace that can bloom only from the seed of Love in the heart.
I have seen the world that you will one-day see as the New
Earth. It is the Holy Spirit in you who is making it new, this
Love who has died so that all mortal life can live again. You   *l*
have become the incarnation of the original Love who has
created the very soil on which you tread. I have Good News
for you on top of even greater news. Your souls are saved,
and your faith and servitude are the origin of the conversion
of millions more who will know the Light of endless Glory at
the end of time. When you see the world in looking back at
it when time is done, you will not have to look down at the
ring on your finger or the automobile you are driving and
cry-out that you could have purchased the Salvation of just
one more soul. You are the Oskar Schindlers of the immortal   *lx*
ages, the lineage of the fruits that begot the foundation of
faith, charity, and good works that has been profoundly
absent since the early centuries. The souls of your brothers
and sisters have already been purchased by Jesus Christ. You
are the holy stenographers and clerks who are reminding
Him who to include in the manifest of the children of God

*who will all join in Heaven. That is the list that you are
compiling for God in this, the world's darkest hour, for
affirmation and deliverance to Mercy by the Morning Star
Over America. That, My children, is why I have come to*   lxx
*this holy place. I come for the lost and lame, the pitiful and
aggrieved, those who cannot stand on their own, the weak
and alone. I come to you because you care more about the
Salvation of humankind than your standard of living. You
hear the Voice of God and know the essence of His tone. You
add harmony and tenor to the meaning of human existence,
you give the deposed reason to stand and be counted again,
you breathe life into the quarters of the Earth that have been
dead in sin for countless generations; and most of all, My
little angels, you are God's instruments in repairing the*   lxxx
*breach that befell the collective body of humankind under
the Cross from a sixteenth century gone awry. The
Reformation was not the beginning of freedom for the
faithless, it was their start toward an errant path that your
work will now reverse. You may invoke all the symbolism
that you wish—the gauntlet has been thrown, the glove has
slapped the cheek, or whatever metaphor you choose to
employ. But, the fact is, the battle is begun to re-unite the
Church under the dominion of Saint Peter. The time has
come! This is the hour! No other age will be able to bear-out*   xc
*the truths that are to be revealed in the next months. I do not
tell you this to raise your ire or your anger. There will be no
vengeance in this battle. There is only victory in the offing,
a victory that was given flight from the mountaintop that
saved the world, from the Cross that shed Light on every
error, and from the skies that still billow with grace-shaped
clouds that make Palm Sunday one for all ages. This, My
children, is why I visit this place. You are the reasons why
your sweet Jesus in Heaven and on Earth has hope. He*
knows your willingness to serve and your capacity to succeed   c
*in Him. I would never bring you to a hope that is false. I
am telling you the Truth that springs from the incomparable
integrity of the Infinite and Sacred Heart of My Son. Your*

hearts and souls know that all of this is true. That is why you will never grow too weary to continue in your work. That is why the Angels come running to you like honey bees around a flower, that is why Jesus falls to one knee and places His Face in His palms in thanksgiving while looking at you and says 'Thank God! My brothers are standing for Me! They are living for Love! They have dignified My Death through the faith in their lives.'   cx

My special little children, this is also the reason why I come to this home. You are a blessed people who have a holy direction. You are proving it in delineating your faith by-laws. Please be confident in God's assurance of your success, come enemy, opponent, plight, suffering, or even death. Keep the Truth in your hearts that this is the last age, and your Father in Heaven has not depleted His supply of miracles. There are plentiful weapons in store, many more lasers of Light, flashes of Truth, and the searing bolts of   cxx
lightning to awaken the slumbering souls who now only recognize you as two people who ride around in a white pick-up truck. Time is not through, and neither is your Father. I will never allow you to go to rest without full-proof that you will have none-other than complete victory when all is through. Thank you for listening to My words of hope and victory on this Passion Sunday. It is now Holy Week. I wish for you to pray the Stations of the Cross on Good Friday. You are both serving the Stations as you live each day. Thank you... Thank you for your holy prayers. I give you   cxxx
now a very special blessing. + That is especially why I have come to this place! I will speak to you soon. I love you. Goodnight!"

This is why the Blessed Virgin Mary has furled Her guiding presence around my brother and me, and ultimately before everyone else who has the decency of heart and humility to listen, embrace and obey Her. I have been conscientiously recording all that She has spoken to me since those most auspicious predawn hours of February 22, 1991. The eternal consequences of Her intercession cannot be overstated if anyone honestly inventories the immorality of this post-modern age and anticipates the logical repercussions which lie on the course that many have chosen to travel toward cultural and moral oblivion. You see, the Church in two of Her grand dimensions already approves and witnesses to the authority and intercessory powers of the Queen of Heaven over the Earth. The Church Triumphant in Heaven is in complete union and acclamation with the motherly work of Our Lady wherever God has deigned to send Her throughout the ages of history. And, the Church Suffering in Purgatory passionately yearns for us to mitigate the damage they inflicted by similar lives of wilful denial of heavenly grace. This leaves us here in this world, the Church Militant, as the third dimension to be converted into beatific union with these two celestial domains at the pinnacle of Truth so that all may be triumphant inside the Kingdom of God. Therefore, let us lend our hearts to Our Lady's tenderizing admonishments, and accept Her spiritual guidance through every venue across the globe where our Almighty Father is allowing Her to intercede for us. We must raise Her Matriarchal Standard before the nations for the sake of the Salvation of men! The glaring inconsistencies generated by our intentional denial of Her supernatural grace must be eradicated through the invocation of our most resilient faith, here and now, lest the chastising antidote be applied to us by the sure Hand of God! If we force the justifiable resurgence of His Wrath, it is going to take far more than a spoon full of sugar to make the medicine go down.

Through the sublime demeanor of God, the Immaculate Virgin has procured my solemn oath to fashion the thoughts and meditations She has engendered in my heart into scripted artifacts. I realize it is Her speaking to humanity from the vantage point and perspective of the unimpeachable vision I have come to recognize as the sacred imprint of the regal Queen of Heaven. For well beyond a decade now, I have never harbored any illusions that I am expounding a spiritual masterpiece that yet-anonymous theologians may eventually hail in time. The Virgin Mother's intentions, and mine by reflection, have always been more duly modest than that. I care not a single whit about the accolades of mortal men because I know how the most sincere high praises and human honors can evaporate as rapidly as Palm Sunday devolved into Good Friday. Furthermore, no one is more aware than me that if I had been left to negotiate life according to my own paltry accords, none of these writings would have been conceived in a thousand years. Both my brother and I are fully aware of the stupendous gift we have been living, and of its impact in the deliverance of souls to the foundation of the Cross of Jesus Christ for merciful Absolution. The weight of our responsibility to the Holy Spirit rests upon the faith-filled uniformity that Our Lady daily sustains in us. There is no spiritual benefactor or compatriot on Earth who is of the same impenetrable strength, incalculable wisdom, transcending vision, unyielding hope, or cogent persuasion as the Mystical Queen of Paradise. We have received no prerequisite ecclesial training which would "taint" the innocuous vision that the Most Blessed Virgin Mary has impressed into our hearts, nor have we tried to mutter or soft-sell Her miraculous messages into esoteric, orthodox perspectives that might be more readily accepted by those with a tendency to be harshly hyper-scrupulous toward privately revealed works of the Holy Spirit from the cloud-piercing purview of their university towers. She explicitly warns us against allowing others to grasp our poor works, assigning to them a different meaning based on their own failed, misguided interpretations, and handing them back to us as hostages before our denial of the Truth in an altered state from the way She first bestowed them. This Blessed Queen did not come to instruct us in the finer nuances of theological debate just to satisfy our hunger for acceptance among our critics or to awestrike intellectuals in the likes of Saint Thomas Aquinas, nor did She confer any advanced scholastics that would extract from us the impeccable simplicity of Love. Yet, we know Jesus Christ and Our Lady in ways that most moral sanctioners have not the headiness to dream. There is neither pride nor arrogance in that, rather the simple truth spoken for the sake of understanding mankind's lucid mortification. Our only wish is that everyone will finally realize one day just how much they are loved. When that shining eternity comes to pass—as it assuredly approaches with each elapsing second—the world will be transformed before our very eyes, and we will see the sweet stars of Heaven sparkling through our briny tears. My writings are a concerted effort in the repertoire of the Most Blessed Trinity to inspire that beatific vision which is vested in Catholicizing our already extraordinary Christian faith. My humble treatises are a simple manifestation of the immeasurable success of Divine Light I have witnessed, past the forlorn, while hoping against hope for the sacred consequence of reorienting the better discernment of men toward a higher order of Love. This inner-conversion is strengthened through a seemingly stringent process of cultivation in each human soul, one that is advanced to an exponential degree in hearts which utterly sacrifice the desire to hail their ofttimes unkempt personal views, no matter how elevated or conformed they believe them to be. I submit that the greatest secret for our spiritual advancement divulged from the years of my relationship with the Mother of God resides in the meaning of self-denial and our absolute obedience to the Hosts of Heaven through the Providence of the Holy Spirit. Saint Vincent Ferrer once said rather effectually, *For whosoever will proudly dispute or contradict will always stand without the door. Christ, the master of humility, manifests His truth only to the humble and hides Himself from the proud.* I have never seen written so clearly what my heart wanted to say.

Friday, January 15, 1999 (excerpt)   *7:03 p.m.*

"You are learning more with each passing day   i(015)
because the angels are teaching you as a part of the extension
of your work. I tell you again that it is ready for the world.
Those who are used to reading lofty manuscripts will
embrace it as a work of art, those who rarely read such
nobility will be proud to make it a part of their library for
something to aspire to become, and those who read very little
and are relatively poor will closely embrace the way you
have approached the indignance and arrogance of the rich.
Theologians and Priests will be exhilarated by its   x
ecclesiastical authority, and cloistered servants will find it a
great source of meditational aesthetics. The words have
power and authority, admonition, compassion, poetical
construction, and alliteration. All in all, it is being prepared
for the entire spectrum and cross-section of the human race,
for people of all walks of life and many faiths. I tell you that
your reward will be great. The proof is in your living Fiat.
The heavens know what you are both doing for Jesus. Can
you see the authority of God in a way that even you did not
expect? That is the tone that must be used in these Last   xx
Times. The days of a feeble, 'will you please be holy?' are
gone! It is now time for the unequivocal Truth! That is why
your Diary will succeed. No one is beyond reproach, short of
the Holy Father and the Deity Itself! This is now your holy
blessing. + Thank you very much for your prayers. I will
speak to you again very soon. I love you. Goodnight!"

Before our Holy Mother first began Her charismatic reshaping of my heart and soul, I believed I was reasonably well read in the writings of many of the Saints, including SS Augustine, Aquinas, John of the Cross, Louis de Montfort, Alphonsus Liguori, and of Bishop Fulton Sheen, the bourgeoning 1960s Second Vatican Council, the Catholic Catechism, and a host of collateral writings from various religious, laity and mystics, much of which has now paled from my more immediate recollection. Although I never received any formal theological instruction other than the basic Catechism as a youth, most of the thoughts contained in such writings were logically revelatory to me; and their mystical scents were pleasing to my budding faith. I cannot recall ever reading something penned by these timeless visionaries that I could not embrace outright or through the backdrop of nurtured reason. I was even willing to forego my penchant for rudimentary orthodoxy to follow the dimensioned complexities of scholastics like Thomas Aquinas because I was stimulated by his views of epistemology and consequential reflections about humanity's relationship with God. Notwithstanding this early, structured foundation, the Wisdom of Our Lady and Her radiant presence overwhelmed my entire intellectual constitution, circumcising it to crystalline clarity focused solely upon the titanic, majestic Love that streamed like a laser beam from the mountaintop of Calvary past every barrier of time and temperament. A divine flamethrower of celestial Wisdom and understanding was directed at my heart and mind, incinerating everything that could not withstand the fires of simple Truth. The Catechism of the Catholic Church states, *Faith is certain...revealed truths can seem obscure to human reason and experience, but the certainty that the divine light gives is greater than that which the light of natural reason gives. Ten thousand difficulties do not make one doubt...The grace of faith opens the eyes of your heart to a lively understanding of the contents of Revelation: that is, of the totality of God's plan and the mysteries of faith, of their connection with each other and with Christ, the center of the revealed mystery.* (CC. 157, 158) What I have seen, I shall never doubt. On February 22, 1991, I willingly immolated the worldview by which I believed almost everything. Every wall of obstinance came crashing down before the countenance of the overwhelming love, beauty and tenderness of the Mother of Jesus Christ because I had finally confronted someone for whom I would gladly sacrifice my very existence. In the presence of such breathtaking majesty, I lacked the arrogance to accede to the contemporary mantras leveled at me to challenge the Woman who was talking to me or to "test the spirit" that was approaching my being, although I did encourage my brother to ask specifically who She was. I did so to help him sustain the initial shock, just as John the Baptist instructed his followers to ask Jesus whether He was the Christ. The Baptizer already knew the Lamb of God; and I likewise recognized His Mother. No, I did not test the Queen of Heaven, because my heart somehow "remembered" Her from the very first moments as though it was a transcending liberation from estrangement for which I had pined since I was born from my mother's womb. The only spirits I submitted to rigorous exam in the first few years were those emanating ferociously, and sometimes convincingly, from our dubious peers who descended upon my brother and me with overt, grotesque personal attacks against our tenacity and our characters, undoubtedly generated from their fears wrought by their own faithlessness. I even leveled a challenge against the quirks within my own soul that attempted to frighten me or call me back into the dark thickness of this finite world. I rejected the baleful contusions of pragmatic men by battling their defamatory slander because my heart vividly saw the stark distinction between the acts of Zechariah, who was struck mute for his lack of belief in the face of heavenly intercession, and Our Lady who displayed such graceful spontaneity in Her salutatory compliance to the commendation of the Archangel Gabriel. I chose to reflect Her Fiat and emulate Her pristine faith to the most magnanimous degree, evincing my love for Christ as if I was standing in Her sacred shoes. From the first moments, my soul knew to its core that the Mother of the Savior of the world had entered our midst. And, that conviction has never waned or faltered, even though it has been kilned and seasoned by Our Lord to sustain the purity of my flesh with the devotions of my heart. I have rhetorically pondered who could summon the audacity to gainsay a Love so great? What kind of a person does that? My heart knew Love that first day, just as the tiniest child knows its biological mother. Thereafter, I set my unflinching determination upon a path of the most selfless submission I could muster and maintain. I have never been at odds or argued any point with Our Lady in all these years; but such is not to imply that I have not been asked to step forward on a number of occasions beyond my immediate comprehension in complete abandonment, not knowing at first where we were going. If I have ever been tempted to believe something that was not in complete harmony with Her mandates, I punctured my own will so as to begin anew alongside the ebullience of Hers. My intentions are to discard my own birth-name if it pleases Her more to summon me by another. There is no question about Her motivations, direction, and wise approbations. Therefore, I have immediately accepted every concept and viewpoint She has graciously dispensed to my awaiting ears. If She declares something to be true—hereafter it is! The passionate yearning to unite my thoughts and perspectives with Her enlightened visions in an absolute way is truly living inside me. God alone will someday judge how precisely I have succeeded in pursuing these lofty goals. The overall effect of my compliant disposition has literally been the manifestation of celestial blessings. It is stated far and wide that our Heavenly Father cannot be outdone in generosity; and my own life witnesses to this Truth. In every instance where I have subdued my interior druthers in faithful submission to Mary, allowing another seemingly logical precept to be expunged by the heel of Her Wisdom, miraculous grace compounded with supernatural sign has been heaped into my lap to further enlighten the world. These have not always been simple, juvenile victories of self-denial or success in basic emotional control, but a profuse spiritual rending pouring through the aortae of human discernment during the heated battle for souls. I have been taken to what I believe to be the precipice of my very being where life meets death, where the grace of God is the only living alternative. Imagine navigating a field of spiritual cultivation where you are subjected to trial and torment for the sake of enhancing the limits of your own trust in God and your abandonment to His Will, knowing that each step is voluntary and that the unpalatable lessons will cease at your next uttered concession. Would you voluntarily go to the Cross in Love for humankind? How about offering one's livelihood and future familial bonds as a sacrifice to God with as much consecration as Abraham conceded to execute Isaac, his own beloved progeny? Will you suffer unjustly by the adversity of those you love and admire the most? It is in these strapping mortifications, borne through the power of the human spirit, where a body truly comprehends the perseverance of our Crucified Lord and the Wisdom of His indomitable Sacrifice. All our crosses endured in union with the Passion and Death of the Messiah are the mystical portals in which our parched souls are submerged in the Divine Love shared between Jesus and His Mother. This meadowspread of Infinitude—Infinite Beatitude—is the final bastion for our dull and exasperated hearts. We must reorient the extremity of our difficulties and temporary agonies, and consign them to the eternal context of God's Divine Love; for the pleasing significance of our lives before the graciousness of the Father is beyond all understanding, although not outside the grasp of humankind's spiritual domain.

Authentic claims of supernatural intercession and paranormal voices from heavenly realms might be of little consequence if not for the fact that the passing of Resurrection and Judgment to Eternal Life or unending Death is a vital choice presented to each living being over the course of time. It is the sole opportunity each of us will be accorded to finally convince ourselves and the personages of Heaven that we wish to unite with them in the personification of Love within the presence of the Holy Trinity, forever to come. Ignore the fallacy of physical reincarnation, whatever it is supposed to be! We are now experiencing the only dichotomy whose end product is final. No soul must be allowed to decide wrongfully before the grave vestiges of human sacrifice and forgiveness, especially toward themselves. For people who reject this Truth and the forgiveness of God to the bitter end, their day of Reckoning within this Deific Absolute will arrive anyway without their foreknowledge, solicitation or approval, and apparently without sufficient preparation. The tawdry exposition of their lives of wanton belligerence and rejection against everything good will be a steaming caldron in which they shall not survive without accepting the Merciful Christ who will save them all from Hell. You see, ignorance is not always bliss, for only the Heaven of Jesus Christ provides this sacred beatitude. And, it is obtained through believing in the power of the Holy Cross, which is merciful forgiveness for every spiritual and corporeal malfeasance we have ever perpetrated against the Kingdom of God. I often anticipate the world's predictable rebuttals, having heard them before, ...*It is different for you because the Holy Mother speaks directly with you. Why doesn't She talk to me?...then I will believe all of it and change my life.* My response to such twisted logic is an assuring one. The Virgin Mary is readily apparent to Her earthly children, even those who decline to accept Her motherly assistance. This book, itself, is Her outstretched arms, extended to caress our hearts. Her soothing words recorded in this grace-filled manuscript emanate a majestically acoustical resonance that anyone, even the weakest in faith, can succinctly hear. The greater issue is our acceptance of Her intercession without requiring a miracle to prove it. The sacred transformation from intellectual sightlessness into perfect spiritual vision occurs within the heart and soul of Christians who pray the Holy Rosary from the nucleus of their own humility. These are the imminent saints who embrace Mary's miraculous assistance "... across the chasm of the ages," as She is prone to say, and as if they were all one timeless revelation. The children of Mary know with eager confidence that the modern world is being inundated with Her Immaculate Grace through every passing moment. I truly believe that Our Lady dispenses signs, wonders, and even discernable miracles and supernatural intercession into the lives of anyone who surrenders themselves, heart and soul, *permanently* into Her hands. The harvest is rich, but the workers are few. God will never ask His heavenly proletariat to enter the foyers of human affairs unequipped for total success. Our labors in the vineyard of eternal Truth are a sacrificial whirlpool we blindly forge by sustaining our religious pact with the Victim on the Cross, brought to spiritual perfection by Him, to which the Heavenly Hosts respond with grace atop of blessing. Pray for miracles of the Love of God, but do not wait for them to occur before extending your professions of belief. The abandonment always precedes the miracle. The repose of our hope in the benevolence of the Almighty Father is a tribute we offer Creation from our storehouse of allegiance to Jesus in loving devotion to His people. The world needs believers, lest it never see the glorious reflection of Christ again.

Sunday, July 15, 2001   6:47 p.m.
*   "Somewhere amidst the cohesion of the thunderheads,   k(196)*
you can see and hear the placidness of the more simple lives
of Love to which you are called and the riddance of the
callousness which has been the subdivision of humanity in
too many places around the globe for seemingly endless ages
in the past. This is a new day! My children, the broader
scope of your spiritual awakening has taken you to a new
land of happiness and opportunity, one which can bring the
consolation that so many of My children are seeking from the
rest of the world.   There are so many who would ask 'why   x

now? Why not heretofore or after this generation has passed away?' The answer to any such interrogatory is that the Will of God is the provision of Life for every man, that all may come to comprehend the unity of all peoples and nations under the Cross of Salvation which Jesus suffered for the Redemption of all. Is it a matter of redundancy for a child of God to stand aright every day of his life and proclaim that he is waiting in joyful hope for the coming of His Kingdom, even if that soul shall die before the Arrival of Jesus in Glory? The answer is no, there is no redundancy, because all life is one. The days are only an alliteration of a poetic existence of peace and joy in the faith to which you have been given, the faith that has been dispensed to your hearts from the Love of Almighty God!

xx

There are so many proximities and parameters to which humankind responds! But, God is never subject to such incarceration! His is immortal Life in an endless Kingdom of happiness, Love, fulfillment; a land where there is no death or threat of death, no danger or reason to fear, and nothing to ever set a soul's sights on anything other than the perfection of endless Glory! I ask you to always remember that I have come to be with you as a portion of God's Plan for the imminent sovereignty to which all who are blessed will bow! Yes, and this too will be done of the free will of man! So, today, we are together again in prayer for the restoration of the decency that humanity seeks. We are called to prayer inside the loveliness of My Immaculate Heart, where Jesus has placed the world for the preparation of His final Return. These days are suddenly now being transformed into your own portion of enlightenment, for the dispensation of knowledge which will lead you to the foyer in which you will continue to be wrapped in the Grace that will make you all saints!

xxx

xl

My children, I ask you to remember that the maturity of the continents is never a function of time, but the process of understanding God in your own days. While the hills and meadows sing of their lofty stature in His sight, it is you that *they truly envy! Theirs is the joy of knowing that their inhabitants are journeying toward a great reward, to the Land of Plentiful Peace! You have been told that there will be no more room for crying, no tears, no sorrow, and no grief in the Heaven you will soon possess. If you must cry, please do it now, My little children, for there is no reason to shed a tear beyond the breach which is the veil between Paradise and the mortal Earth! If there is weeping in your consciousness, weep with the power of the Cross in your hearts, both in sorrow for the sins of the world and in complete jubilation that they have been wiped from the face of Creation! If you must dance, step forward and take the Hands of the Christ who is your Groom, He who is so powerful and strong, He who is at last your deliverance over the threshold of death into the Life anew for which there is no parting. If you wish to stand upon the ground during your starry nights and hide the moon beneath your thumb, let that thumb point also to Heaven with the affirmation in your souls that you are alright, that you have accepted! * Yes, indeed, that you will soon be boarding that celestial ship of Godly Absolution which will rocket you to the shores of the New Jerusalem."*

l

lx

* a parable of the movie *Apollo 13* where Commander Jim Lovell was standing in his backyard obscuring the moon beneath his thumb as he was contemplating his journey to the moon.

"My children, I have given My oath and honor to this same God, answering to a humble little Angel asking Me whether I would bear His Son for the purpose of remaking the face of the Earth and filling Heaven with the souls He came to save. I have said 'yes' in the likeness of that same Angel Gabriel. When you are united in Love, there is only 'yes,' there is only the affirmation of your gratitude that you have been chosen by Jesus to accompany Him Home. Indeed, who am I that the Lord would call on such a simple Maiden to give birth to the Holy Christ-Child! I will tell you

lxx

that it is God, Himself, who knew that My success would be   lxxx
ensured because He knew to give Me these children of the
latter times—you! The prophecies of old are now coming to
pass because you are all just like that little Angel and the
Love inside My Immaculate Heart who met on that fateful
Feast we now call the Annunciation. There are no litanies
in the world which cannot be made real if only My children
will recite them! There is no such thing as an unanswered
prayer because there are no people of God who are unloved!
Yes, I call you to the celebration which is about to ensue
because so many of My children are reconsidering their role   xc
in the purpose of life. How happy I am that the greatest
awakening of humankind is now unfolding before your eyes.
And, just in time! Just in time!

Just like a little child who has wandered too close to
an uncovered well-shaft, humanity has ventured so very close
to losing all that was gained by the generations past! Too
many transgressions are being ignored, too much suffering is
being left unattended, too many prayers are being left unsaid;
and, oh what a waste! But, I have come running to take your
hands before you fall into the Abyss! I have come in the   c
Name of the Lord to tell you to reverse course, to plead with
you to pray, to beseech your understanding of the higher
graces of life, and to implore you to allow God to lead you,
and to leave your own errant courses behind. I wish to tell
you very clearly today, My children, that in My Immaculate
Heart, you cannot fall! You assuredly cannot fall! This is
why I have come! No more will Heaven stand by and watch
you weep without responding anymore! We can see the
response which is coming from all corners of the globe, from
those little children in the former Socialists Republic who are   cx
*bound by ropes and wires to their beds. * Jesus hears their*
cries because you are praying for them! He sees the little
babies in their mothers' wombs in the nations of Africa who
have been stricken by fatal diseases, even before they have
passed into the hands of those who will deliver them to birth
in a hospital room. By your prayerful hopes and

contributions, these little babies will finally have the chance to stand tall in Creation, once and for all, and proclaim that it was the supplications of the living that preserved them from so quickly joining the dead!"

cxx

* referring to a recent news program documenting the conditions of orphanages in the former Soviet Union.

"There is no shame in the dignity of being called a Christian; there is no cowering in the corners of the continents anymore! You are living the time which has been the blossoming of your new beginning in the Resurrection of My Son! Hereafter and beyond, you are now the strong ones, those who have humbled yourselves to lift high the Cross and tell the rest of the world that Jesus is the standard to be met for the measure of perfection! There is no inherent arrogance in telling the world that you will be saved and taken to the Mansion on High! Yes, be proud of your humility, even if this sounds like a contradiction in terms! When your Blessed Mother tells you that I am proud of you, it is wholly different from the pride which fell Adam from the Garden of Eden. This is a joyful acknowledgment of your Victory over the grave! No one knows better than I the sorrow which was brought onto the Earth to make this Triumph known. We weep now over the sorrows of those who do not yet understand, not because we have given-up on ever converting them! If ever there was a time when I need to assure you that the conquering of evil has been completed, this is the time, now is the moment; these are the days during which you should rise from your sleepy naps and say, 'Indeed, the world is one step closer to Salvation today because the Reign of God is at hand!' Although I continue to admonish you to get your rest, it is almost too bad that you require it because the fireworks of Victory are still ongoing all around the world and at every second that is ticking from the clock! You will see all of this someday!

cxxx

cxl

*If you speak of the alignment of the planets as being
a sign of things to come, get ready for the awesome day when*   cl
*they are bobbled with joy as though they have fishes on their
lines because the Son of Man is just around the turn of the
distant Universe, waiting to usher His children to the City of
Light, the Divine Station before which those celestial stars
are only footlights in the sands. These are not solely some
quaint poetic images of an imaginary world, they are the real
Truth about the fruitful lineage of the Sacred Mysteries
which you already observe! God is about to take you to live
in Heaven, little ones! Do you really know what this means?
Can you cease the motion of the tangible Earth for only the*   clx
*briefest of instants to understand that the world that you
know is passing away? Should time continue to pass, you are
only a short series of months away from 2002, a time that
seemed like a miraculous temple to fear not so long ago, but
is really only a skeleton in a closet to the millions of souls
who can see it already from the other side of time. Humanity
upon the Earth has come to an intersection and a fork in the
road at the same unique moment; that is to say, you need not
choose to turn away or decide for one over the other. Your
only direction is upward, skyward toward the forgiveness*   clxx
*that is continuing to fall from the skies like the showers
which grow your fields.*

*It is midday and, simultaneously, the pit of the night
for the world these days, but the Dawn of your Resurrection
is only a breath of the Almighty Father away. If this seems
urgent in nature, then your hearts have finally decided for
Him. If your conscience is telling you to fear what you have
done and failed to do, then the Holy Spirit is alive and well
in your hearts. But, if your faith is strong and your Love is
committed to Jesus, Wisdom will tell you that all is right*   clxxx
*from within. The stars are in alignment, indeed! And, why
do they move? What makes them glitter in the yonder skies
so that your eyes squint to see what they will eventually do
next? Because the God who resides within you begs to see
His own reflection in your lives. I have told you early and*

often that you cannot seek the Kingdom of Heaven on your own, that it is Jesus who is living within your heart that makes you yearn for the Light of Eternal Day. I am the Mother of this Light! You have been given to Me! This is the resplendent perfection to which you are called, to walk in the   cxc *Truth of the Love who first came to ask Me for the Fiat which has given birth to the Savior of the world, the same Love which took Me to the bedside of Elizabeth, the very same Love which leapt her little boy in her womb, the same Love which has blossomed from a Trinity of Three, now waiting for your own Love to make your conversion complete. What is all of this that I am hearing about signs? With all due respect to the dignity of man, how many more signs do you need? How much more evidence of God do you*   cc *need?*

      Cannot a perfect Child in a Manger be raised and persuade a world of people to accept that He is now seated at the Right Hand of the Father, but had to go through Hell to get there? Can the men, women, and children of the Earth not understand that He had to suffer a shame which is nearly beyond comprehension to set them all free from the bonds of their sins? Does not the world understand that He was impaled to a Cross and ridiculed before He surrendered His Spirit back to Heaven in order to remake the Creation that was set into place from the first? Is it too much to ask that   ccx *you believe that this Holy Son, the Messiah of God, was raised from the Dead by His Father in Heaven to spite those who hated Him on Earth? I ask that none of you fall prey to the doubt that befell Saint Thomas! Believe all of this that I am telling you before it is too late! Believe without having seen! Pray like there is no tomorrow! Fall to your knees and pray to My Son for the strength to unite in His Cross by taking-up your own for His sake! I beg you to believe that what I am telling you is true!*

      Then, there are those who continue to refuse to pass   ccxx *beyond the blessings of the Mosaic Law. These are the truly special people of God! They are His chosen race, those who held-on for so many centuries before. I ask you to be kind to them, to feed and nurture their faith, to accept the convictions to which they hold about the Psalms, the Proverbs, and the Ecclesiastical Truth! Do not cast them aside, for these are the pretty souls who have so consoled the Earth with their suffering and plight. Do not hold them at arms length because they are different from you. Before My work with the globe has been concluded, you may have to* ccxxx *compete with them in the race for the blessings of the Cross! Peace is the answer, and Love has posed the question. What will you do with your days? There is an entire evangelism which lives in the power of your prayers! Please ask Jesus for whatever you desire, and He will respond in-kind.*

My Special son, I trust that you will eventually deliver these words to the rest of the world. I will tell you when the time is most opportune. Can you not see with what Love your Mother is looking at the little ones who have been placed under My Mantle? Can you not see the patience with ccxl *which you must live? I am thankful and grateful that you are continuing to pray with Me, and to pray for the world which is so in need of your petitions. I would hope to someday come to speak to you and begin a message with 'This will be My last, because Jesus will be returning before we have the chance to speak in faith once more.' As soon as I know that to be true, you will be amongst the first to know. I again implore you to believe that the power of your Victory need not wait until then. We will continue to work through the cluttered world so that everyone will come to understand* ccl *what we have been doing for all of these years. You can, indeed, see many signs unfolding already... I say the things in My messages because I have such tremendous Love for you! This is My blessing for you now! + I will speak to you again very soon! I Love you, Goodnight!"*

Our Lady has erected a firewall of meticulous Truth to protect Her children against the erosion of their popular piety; and its arching expanse is augmented by measurements of eternities with the addition of each little voice who is heard to say, "*I will stand with My Mother from this second in time, through the end of my days, and beyond eternity. Nothing will take me from Her side. No force, no suffering, no challenge, no persecution, no worldly enticements, and surely not the voice of any faithless mortal, no matter how influential he may be. Nothing and no one will separate me from the Love of God through His Immaculate Queen!*" If God could ever be accused of invoking the musings of the world's most transcendent romantics, He has assuredly done so through the spiritual rapprochement of His Mother and me. She is His heavenly Pied Piper, leading Her children to the Promised Land on a pathway illuminated by Her brilliant Love bathing our souls, as our eyes feast upon the messages She has given me for more than a decade. Let us together enkindle the torch to full flame and run with the athleticism of the Summer Olympiads, igniting the braided fibers of hope within the heart of every good man. The wick shall never smoulder, but burn ever more inexorably toward the Armageddon of the Earth. The Virgin Mary is launching the beatific salvo of prefigured Light across the bow of the material world—a vision piercing the darkness of human corruption like lightning out of the night, beyond the gates of ivory towered estates, thundering across the skies above our corporate echelons, past the jam-packed stadia of competitive vitriol, squalling the eyes of every soul still breathing, hammering heretics with mind-melding Wisdom, wresting away the wealth of faithless nations from their cold, dead hands; exhausting a trail of Divinity en route to the most pitiable valleys of human despair to light-up the simplest dreams of impoverished men, and resurrecting their share of Life which we, ourselves, will bestow in abundance upon their broken hearts. The Morning Star yet flies over America in stately magnitude, higher than any U2 rocket could ever soar, seated with infinitely greater Powers, and light-years above any satanical artillery that might wish to bring Her down. She's not just a traveler , but a Destiny whose perpetuity has fully arrived; a Legacy that will not go down in history, but will *be* the History in which we shall revel forever to come. Our Lady is stationing Her cause for the sanctification of man upon such a lofty pedestal of Deific ascription that even the love-starved heart of the most incredulous atheist will soon break wide open, their lips pleading for merciful pardon under the Mantle of Her supernatural protection.

Indeed, protection from what? From the prevaricating disquietude that has pummeled our people's faith since centuries past and left us a lesser flock than God intends, in spiritual limbo where individual fears and interpersonal hatred have all but stripped the glorious countenance from our best intentions and consigned us to fight shivery battles of ill-wills at the dark, shadowy edges of uncivilized ignobleness. I remember one day when I was traveling in my car with a high school classmate some years after graduation, before our Holy Mother began Her miraculous messages to my brother and me; and we were reminiscing about the many highs and lows that we experienced from the time we were in kindergarten. I particularly recalled my days as a prep school basketball player and the strange sensation of confidence that welled-up in me at the beginning of some of our most important games during my senior year. I knew deep in my soul before the opening tip-off of these contests that the outcome had already been decided, and our impending victory was only 32 short minutes away. Oh, what similar anticipation St. Michael the Archangel must feel knowing He is about to be dispatched into the world to close out the ages! I told my childhood friend that day as we drove unnoticed down the paint-striped highway that I longed to feel this premonition of triumph again, and to escort it to its fullest crescendo with all the passionate devotion I could stoke. Well, I have discovered this overwhelming vision once again! We, the children of Mary, are situated arm-in-arm with the Hosts of Paradise and our heroic contingents of dearly departed friends, anxiously waiting with intrepid righteousness and Rosaries in hand for the tip of the Almighty Father's assent and the charging report of trumpets to sound the matrimonial nuptials of our transfigured souls between their Heaven and our Earth through the reciprocal intercession of the Most Blessed Virgin Mary. Nothing can impede, impugn, hinder, prevent, or forestall the royal procession of Her Immaculate Triumph! Heaven's Hosts are on the move from beyond the ramparts of the celestial firmament, spreading virtuosity across the hallowed hills and rolling plains of the indelible human spirit with eternal benisons written all over their hearts. They are collectively trained for the beatific conquest and final conquering of the beleaguered wastelands of hapless imprisonment that seek to dash our ecstatic dreams and skew our perception of perfect Love. Why? Because the enemies of human Salvation harbor the vainest hope of exterminating the miraculous proliferation of everything good that is unbounded between the uninfringed reigns of the Alpha and the Omega. Never before has there been a campaign of Providence so prepared for battle or finely attuned to such a perfect culmination.

Communist dictator Josef Stalin opined one day while contemplating the expansion of the Soviet empire, saying that if he had twelve men with the conviction of the beloved Saint Francis of Assisi, he could have conquered any civilization on the globe. Well, his visions of grandeur were an accidental prophecy for the whole human race because the truth he spoke that day proffers a visionary hallmark that lends transparent perspective to the timely Victory of God in the Triumph of the Immaculate Heart of Mary. The Saints of *every* age are standing upright at Her side, each one sporting an heroic spiritual martyrdom that would make the great Saint Francis' earthly devotion seem like the feckless dawdling of a little child. Indeed, with Francis and the rest, Our Lady will conquer! The prevailing of goodness over evil will be complete in the bombastic onslaught of that initial annihilation. This is why we must heed Her supernatural call, pretypify our spiritual preparation, and chaperone the entire world to the foot of the Cross for Christ's Absolution, because no one will want to find themselves located on the wrong side of history on that fateful day. The subdued consciences of mortal men require a wholesale reorientation and new enlightenment for our spiritual success to be realized in its most prolific form. And, that is the context of the life my brother and I have shared and the codices we have produced under Our Lady's mentoring since February of 1991. We are living witnesses to the Divine!—Heralds of a far more glorious future than the world could ever portend, an age of Light that is blessedly moving within our reach! It matters not by what criteria sinful men might deploy to disparage our work. Oh, there have been multitudes to date; and countless more will doubtlessly appear. We will outlast them all because our fervor shall never die! The hagridden judgments that such perverse minions use only rail against the prospects of their own uncertain future. They wish to keep humankind shackled in chains, but we desire to set men free. The failed attempts by which their kind have historically mocked the works of Jesus Christ are but the obtuse psychobabble of befuddled mortals, cringing at the prospect of losing their intellectual designs and the pupils to whom they condescend, groveling in blind adulation at their feet. They believe the world will plummet to ashes if they do not remain the piece-mealing custodians of the Wisdom of God, as if He were somehow judgmentally challenged by reason of deficient mind and unable to venture beyond their dictatorial care. In the enlightened Truth of Paradise, Jesus Christ Himself would never have been able to satisfy their contemptuous scrutinies, even if He suddenly decided to walk across the crest of the Atlantic today. Our Lady has told me that there has not been a significant change in the ill-mannered disposition of anti-Christians in the past twenty centuries; but this, too, is about to change!

Sunday, October 21, 2001   *4:02 p.m.*
   "I appear here in the mortal world while never leaving   k(294)
the infinite beauty of Heaven and, on this day in your lives,
to ask you to accept the everlasting ages which is the Divine
Realm of Perfect Love in the Glory of God the Father. My
call is for you to not only be holy, but to also become Sacred

in the sight of Jesus, that your perfected souls will find a lasting home in His Sacred Heart, and so that your happiness may always be complete by your station at His side. There is no greater Light known to humankind or to the fullness of Creation than that which is the Love of the Almighty Father,   x *manifested equally as Divine by His Son on the Cross. My children, can you not see that the generations in which you live are only a portion of the life which has been allotted to you, that death is not the end of life, but its transformation into your complete awakening? These October skies into which you peer are the solemnity of the harvest which your souls know to be imminent for all the world! The warring continues to be protracted around the Earth, and those who participate know not the day nor the hour when the Son of Man will call it all to a sudden end. Should He deem it to be*   xx *in the next hours or days, will any wars that are waged not in His Name or toward the advancement of His Kingdom be of any circumstance? I plead with those who will listen to My words to heed the call of Jesus to be His evangelists for the entire globe, to take the message of Eternal Love to the streets and the mountaintops where every heart can see and all eyes will become trained upon the real purpose for human existence.*

    We pray together; all of the flock of Jesus works toward the goal of christening humankind into a new   xxx *vestment of Justice inside the Sacred Mysteries of His loving purpose. I seek those who will utter the profound blessings that will make all mortals turn unto Love, who will beseech every man of conscience and good will to speak out loudly and clearly, to remold the morality of everyone alive about the inevitable conversion which must come to humanity before the expiration of time. Cannot the people of God agree that Paradise contains this jubilation for everyone? Therefore, My appearance here today is His confirmation that this can still be accomplished in your day. The darkness*   xl *of the world is contagious to those who refuse to escape its grasp, so much that a global pandemic of apathy and indifference has taken hold of the masses. My continuing summons is for this to end both swiftly and permanently, for My Son has plans for Creation that must be placed into being inside the hearts of those who will eventually go to Heaven. Yes, The Divine Mercy of God is Jesus; but every mind, heart, eye, and ear must be lent to the reason for Mercy; and this is a product of the allegiance of humankind to complete and infinite Love. If all the Heavens were to approach the Earth lower than any sinner could imagine, please know that I have brought them here now, to plead with you to finally understand that God is a Divine Creator of ultimate destiny, that there is no other way to the Redemption of your souls than through the Crucifixion of Jesus on the Cross. There are no substantive ointments that can remove your transgressions from existence; only the Blood of the Son of God can do so, a Blood that you must willingly accept in order to be saved! Is this a difficult decision to make or a defiant process? Only if you have not yet let go of the material world in favor of the transformation of your lives into Grace, which is the reason for your newborn righteousness. Whereabout can you travel to retrieve the expiation of your sins in this modern-day of deception and fear? It is not the Earth, dear children, where this journey must be taken, but rather the voyage toward goodness which begins at the center of your hearts! While you trek the many passageways on the land, seeking to uncover the secrets of human life, you shall not find them unless you accept Jesus Christ as the Loving Savior of your souls.*

When you ponder the Paschal Mysteries of Holy Week, culminating in the Easter Resurrection of Jesus from the Tomb, this is your beginning to be earnest about the destiny of your own souls and the purpose of your lives. Did Jesus not tell you that the road would be perilous on the way back to Heaven? Has He not asked you to pray to His Father in the words that He has given you? Therefore, be the likeness of the Son, and you will please the Father. Give your entire lovingness to the service of His people, and you

l

lx

lxx

will be named as being among the Saints. Offer your bread lxxx
to your brethren, and you will be fed the nourishment of
everlasting Life. Carry the burdens of those who are weak,
and the giant rewards you seek will be given unto you! My
little ones, these are not just some hopeless musings of vitriol
that you might read in the marketplace somewhere, this is
the Truth as it has been dispensed by the King of the World
through the lessons and teachings of His Life and by His
Holy Spirit as He has been advising and admonishing
throughout all the centuries since. Living as Jesus has asked
you to live may not be a pretty sight because you will be xc
assaulted and assailed by those who are His enemies. In this,
however, is your joy complete and your mission anointed.
Through the giving of your entire lives to the Kingdom of
God, you will inherit what no man of material wealth can
bestow upon you. Be not afraid that the foes of Love can
destroy you because you have already been vested with the
Triumph of human Salvation within the beauty of My
Immaculate Heart. Despite those who continue to protest
this, the Cross on which your Savior died can be reached
most prolifically through My benevolent intercession. I have c
been provided the means to take your souls directly to the
Mercy of God through My Holy Son, a Son to whom I would
say 'yes' again and again. As He has asked Me to be your
Mother, too, I am here today to establish the following which
He has requested Me to seek, an entire Blue Army of holy
people who know how to live in the image of Him.

Did He come to save the sinners? Indeed, He has
come to save them and more; His purpose is to ask every
sinner to take his brother by the hand and tell what he
knows about the end of the world. I implore you to accept cx
everything I am telling you as the Eternal Word because I
have been commissioned by the Savior of your souls to effect
the conversion of those who will live happily with Him in
Heaven when the time is ripe. As I have reminded you
before, I will not fail in this duty to which I have been
assigned, the one that I have gladly accepted in Love for My

children. *I continue to call upon everyone to seek the holiness which is found in the storied sanctity that the Most Blessed Sacrament provides and reveals, indeed, by enlisting the noble causes of the many apostolates on the Earth such as the Eucharistic Fidellites. There is a destined purpose in every one of them, all to the advancement of the entire world to the Sacrifice of Jesus on the Cross.*   cxx

My precious little Special son, I have offered the statements that I wish for the world to know today. They will receive them at the appointed time. Thank you for offering them to the entire world for Me! I come today not in brevity, but in profoundness that you will know that everything I have told you has unique, Eternal power! I continue to seek from you your trust that the world is unfolding according to the Plan of the Almighty Father, one through which millions are being changed by your participation. I am allowed to heap as many accolades upon you as I wish, for I am your loving Mother, and this is My purpose... You have had a very good week during the last seven days, and the forthcoming one will be a grace-filled one as well. I know that you are in a state of awe by the pages that My angels are giving to you. The ensuing chapters of your next book will be so profound that it will bring scores of people to their knees in thankfulness... I thank you for your humble service and sacrifices. Please know that they will live well-beyond the elements of time and space... Remember My words for you of October 17th, when your soul traveled so deeply into the heart of your little nephew... It was an awful moment for his little 'being.' Thank you for remembering to God what he endured... Thank you for all the work you have done! This is now My holy blessing for you and your brother. + I Love you. Goodnight!"   cxxx   cxl

An additional perspective might be useful in capturing complete unity under Our Lady's protective Mantle as a prerequisite for the abundant success She so passionately desires for us. *We must realize that matters on the Earth occur sequentially and intermittently, while the things of Heaven are simultaneous and perpetual.* This is no less true in the limited paradigms of human communication that we often employ, and in our honest efforts to transmit our heartfelt visions of love inside the parenthetical confines of this ego-stricken world. We live at the behest of a new sound-bite culture, shallow thoughts, unfounded and biased criticism, opportunistic libel and sedition, and compartmentalized slander where unscrupulous people serve as the devil's advocates by refusing to expand their vision to realize that the perpetual acclamation of our Eternal Redemption in Jesus Christ is of infinitely greater dimensions and sits atop a far more solid foundation than the scrawny antagonism they level at the sequentially-unveiled perfections that have appeared before the limited purview of the world over the past 2000 years. God's "Universal Whole" is a Divine Kingdom supported by the infinite super-realties that have permeated the hearts and minds of faithful Christians throughout the ages. It would be good to place our understanding, acceptance, and mobilization of the evangelical works of the Holy Spirit within this wider context. Thus far, I have found it virtually impossible to sufficiently articulate the universal, multi-dimensional facets of the Divine Wisdom that the Mother of God emanates without offending the sensibilities of at least some circles within my immediate midst. If we humbly submit that our vision is not yet perfected, why should we be offended if it is revealed to us on occasion where our faith may be less than adequate, especially since the purpose is to secure our ultimate happiness and bond us more interpersonally as brothers and sisters in Christ? Should pagan spiritual apoplexy impede our advancing the message of the Queen of the Universe? It seems to me that far too many people have succumbed to the fallacy that the supreme elevations of Christianity cannot be captured by mortal men. And, in failing to recognize this, they errantly conclude that their anemic paralysis is the clearest standard for spiritual comprehension available during these modern times, only exacerbating their hunger for the mystically sublime. *...if your eye is bad, your whole body will be in darkness. And, if the light in you is darkness, how great will the darkness be.* (Matthew 6:23). I am reminded of a neighbor I once had who was prone to overindulgence in the spirits of aqua vitae, saying he liked to drink, and that it was actually some strange exterior, parasitic influence imbibing in him. Such is the similar human denial in which the world now finds itself precariously juxtaposed outside any laudable spiritual legitimacy, rather than fashioned by the Holy Spirit inside the inebriating grace of God.

Ironically, and in the absence of the plausibility of anyone attaining a deific vision about the meaning of human life without faith in Jesus Christ, they believe no one else owns the right to intuitively posit moral ethics that in any way slights their schemata of principled conduct either. And, the darkness dives to even more temporal fathoms. Many of these individuals mistakenly equate and intertwine their sense of precocious human "dignity" with self-aggrandizing thoughts and expectations about the actualization of the "self," an impression they have construed to offset their disoriented egos—back to the alcoholic again. Henceforth, when anybody attempts to redress this scandal, it is seen by them as an attack on their present status as children of God, rather than realizing that perhaps they have their wagons hitched to the wrong star and their souls are being julienned beneath their own churning wheels. Each of them must understand that they are of infinite worthiness to Almighty God, along with every Angel and Saint who inhabits His heavenly Kingdom, no matter what ideas, truthful or false, adhere to their consciousness in the course of a given day. The Verity of the Holy Spirit is above and beyond humanity's linguistic reproach or any intellectual, psychological, or pathological models we may choose to deploy in our often nondescript attempts to illustrate the Truth that must be allowed to infiltrate, infuse, eclipse and overtake this world. Yet, God transmits the impeccable vision of moral absolutes about His Kingdom to His children through the conduit of our religious faith that enlightens our hearts and souls to all things everlasting. And, no spirited debate or impassioned oratory in defense or advancement of this righteous clarity is without foundation and blessing in the Trinitarian Spirit. Therefore, anyone wishing to discern whether the proclamations and admonishments issuing from the fiery lips of a child of God flow from the Wisdom and Providence of the Holy Spirit must position the entire spectrum of communication into the timeless intentions of the Immaculate Heart of Mary, because She convenes the diastolic influx and enlightenment of the human heart through the Paschal Paraclete, defined and contexted in these end times for the revelation of and opportune momentum for the conversion of human souls. Need there be any odds placed in there being at least one member of the Sanhedrin who heard Our Lord preach about how the meek would inherit the Earth who chided Him to remember His own teaching when He was thundering rebukes at their hypocrisy and irreligious behavior? Was our courageous Messiah guilty at any time of being anything less than meek? Not for a moment was He; and neither is any spirit-filled child of Immaculate Mary who appropriately re-echoes those admonishments in modern times. We must ask ourselves: Meekness to what and to whom? Satan pines for a world that is clueless of adverse opposition; and the most diabolically effective artifice he uses is the baseless indictment that the outwardly righteous are not being sufficiently meek in the image of

Jesus Christ, an attempt by evil to ply the righteous into lowering their spiritual sabers and allowing Satan's haggards to proceed unchallenged and unencumbered. It is always someone with the most aggressive and dispersive agendum tucked beneath his lapel who wails the loudest at the sight of the slightest whiff of moral rectitude because he knows the reign of his domination is near its end. His soul can sense that his future has been focused in the cross-hairs of the righteous scope of God. Seductive lies like his will live no more!

So, when you see the loneliest warrior standing at the peak of the most ferocious hill, rise to your feet as well and proclaim your name before recorded history as having stood steadfast in Jesus Christ. The harsh epitaphs that are barged against the forces of the world who are opposed to our Savior, His Mother, and all that is good in Creation are oil for the lighted lamps to Christians disposed to need it. Their enemies' legacies shall burn in infamy to enlighten their unwary prey about the peril they are in. Verbal assaults against Christians by the adversaries of Salvation are neutralized like a puff of wind blowing-out the flames of Hell when an orphaned child asks Jesus for help. Their collective call to Mary is one simultaneous declaration of the Holy Gospel issuing from the lips of the same Christ who has long administered grace and blessings in perpetual sequence to humanity, dictated by the needs of the times. Hereafter, let nobody trivialize or sound-bite the works of the Holy Spirit or retreat from the guidance of the Queen of Heaven simply because unbelievers require Her to invoke us as His disciplinarians on rare occasions instead of being deferential "cult members" whom obstinate sinners bypass without incident on their journey to final perdition. Every one of them should realize that there is a Cross standing between themselves and the bowels of Hell—the crux of their extraordinary fate; and it is better that they encounter it while still in this life. The Face of Jesus Christ is as potently multi-spectral as the Gospel accounts to this day. It is both inevitable and appropriate to acknowledge that the dynamic potential of human conversion is often divergently complex; and the confrontations manifested in directing our brothers and sisters to higher stations of grace is a product of the collision between two different worlds; a pluralistic one dominated by error, mistaken identity, misunderstanding and sin; and the other, the prudent, singular, and absolute Paradise of Love through Eden's conceivable venues. We truly *are* our brothers' keepers within the framework of eternal deliverance. This is why the genius contained in the Spiritual Works of Mercy is so profound. Humans who wittingly stake-out parametric boundaries of interior autonomy ultimately realize through discordant lives that the Holy Spirit does not recognize any Will other than His own when choosing to separate the sheep from the goats in the collation before our Eternal Redemption. Our Lady told me that Her divine purposes are far more grand and of greater consequence than to preserve anyone's illicit feelings when it serves to elevate the seriousness of these times and the priority of the salvation of mortal souls. Hence, let us be unsurprised that the warnings from the Most Holy Trinity can be sometimes outlandish, brash and scripturally foreboding. The intentions of the Hosts of Paradise are to liberate us through the process of casting unyielding Light through the translucent perceptions of our feeble hearts. The children of God are called to be all good things to all people in the hope that at least some of them will garner a renewed strength to respond to the call to unequivocal holiness. We know that some people sow, others reap, and still others turn the soil in preparation for human life to be lived in abundance. If the soil is rocky, let us begin sifting the earth. Should we find thistles and thickets, we shall now strike them at their roots. And, for the hard-baked clays of dead valley floors, God help us to call upon the Angels to make them all supple once again. The farmer becomes a scant when he performs his duties out-of-season. But, now is the season; this is the time for eradicating evil and making loving disciples of all nations. Yes, all races, peoples and tongues! Therefore, embrace Our Lady's expansive vision and realize the immense power resting within the grace-filled spectrum of our evangelic composure, where the most gruesome plotting is annihilated with a simple thought, irascible storms calmed in a single prayer, and the broadband sanctification of human souls bursts-forth like lilies of the fields.

Much Madness is divinest Sense —

Much Madness is divinest Sense —
To a discerning Eye —
Much Sense — the starkest Madness —
'Tis the Majority
In this, as All, prevail —
Assent — and you are sane —
Demur — you're straightaway dangerous —
And handled with a Chain —

Emily Dickinson
c. 1862

Section Two
Synchronizing the Obvious with the Mystical
Transcending Discernment into Obedience

When I Heard the Learn'd Astronomer

When I heard the learn'd astronomer,
When the proofs, the figures,
* were ranged in columns before me,*
When I was shown the charts and diagrams,
* to add, divide, and measure them,*
When I sitting heard the astronomer where he lectured
* with much applause in the lecture room,*
How soon unaccountable I became tired and sick,
Till rising and gliding out I wander'd off by myself,
In the mystical moist night-air, and from time to time,
Look'd up in perfect silence at the stars.

Walt Whitman - 1865
From a collection titled Drum-Taps

Like the stars in the heavens, we are a mystical improvisation of souls whom, when seen from beyond the aftermath of Eternity, compose a stellar constellation burning in the celestial vaults to the elation of everyone who has passed into history and into the Hands of the Handsome, the Crucified Progeny of the Thrice-Blessed Vestal of the New Jerusalem. Humanity is chastised by the Chaste through Mary's foreboding Wisdom, reminiscing about the predicament we were in before Her Son was Crucified. And, if ever a time appeared before the purview of the ages when the world's centrifugal spirit had shifted past its most delicate equilibrium than any leaning Tuscan tower could ever stand, these are those ominous days. Should we but engage a silent christening of the intangible attributes of outer Creation, it is certain that everyone here would suddenly realize the glaring disparity between our overemphasis on mundane flesh and our uncontrollable penchant to see the unbounded "pre-realities" of God's floriferous domain. What about the conceptual hopes which men often dream to realize, those that sprout from the genius of the contemplative human heart? The critical mass of our prudent awareness has been fraudulently transferred onto more fragile foundations that are utterly incapable of bearing the titanic forces that, thus far, lie mercifully restrained within their sardonic lairs by the wiser application of honest discipleship and the visionary insight that has been allowed its venues in our much enlightened past. This intentional adulteration of everything normatively virtuous is the byproduct of a clandestine waning of the mystically profound, coupled with the rancid wantonness of a people who are blinded to the beatitudes of the heart by worldly ostentation, pompous circumstance, and the unparalleled material pretentiousness of our age. A stunning expungement of sanctity has ensued, causing our social conscience to expire, spreading untold obscurity across the conspicuous moral intelligence of the true heroes of our righteous shores and the sacramental dignity of the highest religious confessions. Have Purity and Truth finally died within us, or somehow been allowed to lapse in the planned obsolescence of the ages? These towering pylons of ethics and authority are the girding pillars of the Golden Gate Bridge connecting the Church's redemptive evangelization and God's recurring bounty of Christological Absolution through the spores of civilized man. How can it be true that blind men and women whose souls are as dead as the corpses in our cemetery rows are allowed to ascribe a new meaning to the great miracle of human existence that is excised from the divine substance of eternal Truth? By what authority do anti-Christians claim levels of personal commendation they can neither protract nor sustain in their amputated state, separated from both deific grace and knowledge of the Wisdom imparted by the Holy Spirit of Jesus Christ? When anyone becomes sightless of the nobler qualities enshrined by the Slain Son of Man, with His benison and Being present in every human soul, and abandons the Mother of all Virtues, they concurrently restrict themselves to adjudicating the themes of life locked inside the finely-nuanced contexts of their ego driven self-righteousness. Why don't they instead scope their existence through the prism of God's good graces, He who indemnifies their progress and thrusts their purposes onto more prolific thoroughfares, whose sacrificial inclinations raise them to a new actuarial role, offering the children of Light the clearest outlook of human life with their feet up on their desks? It is beyond prophetic that the late Supreme Pontiff, Pope John Paul II, launched his Papacy with the exclamation...*Be not afraid!* in his inaugural ecclesial orations. The visionary order of pious works the Holy Father has implanted in us is being expropriated by self-serving charlatans everywhere who are mass-marketing their hysterical wares and exploiting our lives through every distraction they can possibly conceive, whipping both our apprehensions and impassioned idiosyncrasies into near uncontrollable frenzies, inciting fear and paranoia about the security of our lands, and herding our children's moral values into a corral of carnal corruption where the gate of their hopelessness about the love of our Almighty Father is quickly slammed behind them with a sedentary thud. Thereafter, these same profiteers presenting themselves on the supply-side of goodness demand incalculably high fortunes from their scare-mongering rituals of deceptively reframing the world as it is. There are no boundaries of decency to which they will submit before advancing the obsessions from our past in order to create new questions about the future, knowing full well that they can be successful beyond their wildest imagining if only they can elicit a critical "want" or create a hypothetical "need" that would never have burdened us before, had we but trusted in our benevolent God. Pope John Paul II was absolutely right; the fearlessness bestowed as a gift from the Holy Spirit sets us free from the total darkness that is peddled through the rancorous musings of lesser men.

Let us consider a parable. Suppose a stranger approached your table while you were enjoying an appetizing dinner and placed three playing cards on the tablecloth before you, then covered two of them with your silk napkin. If he was to subsequently ask how many cards were on the table, you would blurt out the obvious answer of three; one that you could see, and the second and third lying beneath the sculpted linen. But, upon lifting the napkin and to your surprise, the concealed cards had somehow disappeared, yielding only one remaining on the tabletop. You realize that the apparency of your thoughts has just been snatched away. Now, imagine dining in a second restaurant with your spouse and toddlers on another day, and someone else approaches your table saying he is not a man of sleight-of-hand, but truly an honest individual. He spreads three playing cards before you and covers two with your napkin, just as the trickster had done before. Upon his inquiring about the number of cards on the table and hearing your children's giggle-stifling answers of "three!" just as you had done the first time, you respond by saying there is only one of them there to avoid being duped again. Now, however, the person lifts the napkin revealing the two hidden playing cards resting next to the one that never left your sight. This story describes how our perception of the "obvious" is often skewed from the factual Truth that resides in its triumphant completion in the unseen world. What stood within the realms of the obvious, even to the unsuspecting view of little children, had now become an unknown quantity because of your guarded recollection of the previous ruse. In effect, the deceiver impeded your vision with an act of simple deception, tempting you to disbelieve something not openly apparent to your senses, be it cards on a table or two yet unseeable Persons of the Trinity of God. Consider further anyone who has never encountered that honest man, those people who have never been given the visual effects of the truth evident in the latter spread of cards, but who only witness the magician's deception. How would each of them counsel individuals they might meet who are faced with the same decision? They would doubtlessly tell them, down to the person, that the answer is "one," and would believe in their heart of hearts that they were telling the truth. They would maintain they were again witnessing the disappearance of the other two cards because their logical deductions are focused upon an unreliable "slice" of reality. Thus, when masses of people within a given culture are never exposed to, or who outrightly reject, the sublime realities that live and work in the mystically unseen, their perspectives become disoriented; their conclusions arrive without foundation, their perception of the obvious becomes an illusion, and their power of judgment becomes so lax before the Light of Truth that they are utterly incapable of counseling, guiding, or participating in any capacity that might positively influence the events of a society aspiring to achieve the truer pinnacles of greatness. In fact, they become the very impediment that detracts from civilization's ascension in the succession of divine reason.

The overtones of this allegory reveal a spiritually pratfallen humanity with a breach situated between us and the novas of our nobler achievements. Our thoughts are clouded by an opaque dumbfoundedness, somewhat like a debilitating fog obstructing the sextants of our guiding wisdom, rendering them to be less than corrective lenses in humanity's ever-widening continuum of metaphysical sight. The collective judgment of many cultures is being tarnished through the obtuse mind-set of those being deceived by their own naivete. Sadly and problematically, these are the lucky people who always seem to inherit positions of influence to wilfully distribute their misgivings to the detriment of more conducive moral principles. It is true that the cognitive abilities of the human brain are a gratuitous gift from God. Millions of people around the globe testify with profound personal pride about their superior mental capacities and enhanced aptitudes of logical reasoning and collative powers of deduction. What they regularly fail to realize is that such cerebral apologia when left abandoned and bereft of Messianic Wisdom is inherently imprisoned within the menial tasks of their rather rigid identities, rendering their spiritual prowess no more lofty than the occasional glance of a captive bird who has never once strode beyond the wiry walls of a pet store cage, let alone flown to freedom to the advancement of his kind. People who refuse to know God can only warehouse their wishes; and their constant resolving is no more visionary than the rantings of a Canadian goose. How sorrowful to be standing in the postdiluvian crowd who earlier, and too quickly retorted, *Only seeing is believing!* I do not subscribe to such pragmatic doubts because I know with outright certainty that there are much larger dimensions to human life than the ones impressing my retinas everyday; and the scope of our faith is significantly diminished when confined to the trammeled spectrum of anyone's psycho-optic conjecture, because there is always *more than meets the eye* in everything we see. Consider why a toddler shivers with a mixture of emotion, anticipation and trepidation while standing on the edge of a diving board as his mother beckons him with open arms to jump toward her into the pool on the first day of his swimming lessons. Every child who has stood with his toes curled-up at that position, scanning his heart for the courage to sheer his desires from the shackles of his fears, is a metaphor from Almighty God to revel the valor of the human soul that is missing in those who will not believe anything other than their own routine lamentations. How many times have those infants shown more unbridled daring than their adult counterparts? It is the rational deists who proclaim that there is probably a Supreme Being who created the universe, but they thus far decline to allow that He has revealed Himself within Creation in any miraculous way or through any organized religious faith. Those who practice this misappropriation of the meaning of human life base their entire dowry upon the observable actions of Nature, the rationale they develop from their laboratorical observations, and the corollaries in which they wane. Incidentally, the only reason deists concede to the existence of a Supreme Being at all is because their steely minds are so overwhelmed by the grandeur of the universe and the undeniable genius that forces its motion, from the nuclear to the galactic, that they would look like certifiable lunatics to anyone with an ounce of good judgment and a little common sense.

So, it is rhetorically apparent where this puts professed atheists. If either of these groups had been present at the parting of the Red Sea in the likes of Cecil B. DeMille, they would have run over to the wall of water to the right and back across the dry seabed to the left, inspecting the tension of the vertical waves so they could breathe a sigh of relief at finding a theory to explain away God to the rest of us who know better. And, where would that have left them? Indeed, drowning in company with Pharaoh's flailing armies, helplessly surrendering their salutes to the head honcho of the day. But, isn't this exactly what we are talking about when positing the argument for the necessity of synchronizing the obvious with the mystical? There can be no credible intelligentsia, rational observation, or reasonable probability without giving every facet of Creation, both seen and unseen, its apportioned value of importance upon the collective weight of our judgment. Would any curious scientist wishing to critically analyze a peculiar substance to determine its innate properties and categorical composition begin and end his evaluation only with a simple microscope, or perhaps a stethoscope to listen for discernable sounds? Without doubt, each of these trained observers would employ every instrument at their disposal to yield the fullest body of evidence that could be gleaned from each application. And, should we not use an equally comprehensive approach in the illumination of knowledge pertaining to the intangible aspects which influence human life to an oftentimes magnanimous degree? Where is the valid consideration given to the gargantuan impetuses of passion and devotion, honor and sacrifice, and the ultimate universal power of Love in the schema of our logistical models? The question we must ask ourselves is whether our immediate sight is truly without precedent. Something must surely be lying in the archives of the human psyche we can utilize to procure more ethical alternatives to the selfish artifice that worldwide cadres of millionaires use for enhancing their monetary gain. Or, are our consciences vacillating because of our own self-interest and social apathy, too, hoping someday to sit among the material elite? Paraphrasing popular legalese, why don't we enter into evidence the vast cache of artifacts produced by the supernatural powers imbued upon our hearts through the gracious benevolence of the Holy Paraclete? Bring to the fore the breathtaking rhythms of the poets, the sky-rocketing oratory of the evangelists, the immemorial visions of the prophets, the dramatic romances of the playwrights, and the ancient Psalters of the lyricists! Saunter through a gallery of the works by the late, great painter Bob Ross and feast your eyes upon his picture perfect windows of bristling divinity, depicting in miraculous overtones scenes that seemed to leap from the landscapes of Heaven into his impressionable heart, and stroke by stroke filled the hungry canvas of a saint who was as humble as anyone who ever lived. Imagine the moment he arrived in Paradise after enduring his final agony on the Earth, and his Almighty Father rendering before him every mountain range he ever pined to extol to the weary eyes of the world; each one a spiring, glistening wonderment comprising the lost horizons of the Divine Kingdom in which he just landed like a child jumping off a merry-go-round.

Let us burden the scales of the obvious with the salvaged grace of the nameless paupers who have long struggled through the stark oppression of their ephemeral bonds and triumphantly tossed their mortal remains upon the earthbound alleyfields of reparation. They have bequeathed to the world their glad departing, enshrining the reliquaries of their sanctified essence as honorary relics in the hallowed halls of history, thrusting their sacrificial legacies into the portals of Eternity as poignant reminders of the highest elicitation of our Messiah's Ghost. We must prepare a seat at the table of discernment and summon the sincerity of the simple, the vision of the virtuous, the humility of the honest, and the faith of the righteous so their counterweight of divinity will balance the world on the fulcrum of its Crucified Savior; for never has there lived an equal to the Son of Man in power, grace, Wisdom, servitude, strength, beatitude, perfection, and holiness. Should we decline to trim the tender vessel of the collective human heart, turning her battened sails into the irresistible winds of change, and with the heroic intention of charting a newer course for the sky-harbored Heart of Jesus Christ, we will remain hopelessly indulged in the decadence of this Earth. We shall yet be enchained by the wayward ideologies of mutinous lots of materialists whose heinous flapdoodling has driven the majestic galleon of our stately intentions onto the shoals of sin and dereliction. Western capitalism and secular pragmatism have aimed us toward a diabolically-plotted destiny that will eventually leave us foundering in those long, rotting lines of moral turpitude, becoming little more than another shipwrecked generation, littering the composting graveyard of human desecration with the death-rattling angst of once courageous men, sharing a berth with Satan's discarded minions, and bearing a yoke of defiled dreams. It is in this nexus of venal disaster that the potential of our glorious race will slowly disappear below the evolutionary tides of history. There, it will lay buried and forgotten beneath the obscuring silt of the scrolling ages, left to be entombed within a solitary crypt of corruption that is sealed only with the arrogance of our unmitigated shame. Sadly, lying helpless and hopeless, we will await the blessed day when our unmarked grave is finally exhumed by a visionary contingent of curious saints, a garrison of uncompromising conquistadors of spiritual perfection who, through divine ordination and the strength of their invincible volition, will singlehandedly resurrect the deftness of our aching human hearts from their posthumous internment and reinstate our lost piety and civility to their rightful station on the sacred tripod of paradisial Truth, mystical grace, and valorous beatitude. There, they will christen her bounty and set her theocentric compass for recommissioned shores to again gracefully waft with ecclesial comportment through the irreverent waves of heresy, hatred and horror; propelling humanity onward to the only Redemption ever to breach the final horizon of encapsulated time. Lest we someday be duly condemned as the scuttlers of America's last smidgen of sanctity, we must gulp down the irrational pride that beguiles our spiritual sense, and part the indiscreet veil of arrogance that exiles us from the dreams that greet the heart of every child and the contemplative prayers to our Heavenly Father which, we know, ushers them into being. The active Presence of the Holy Spirit through the inseparable charisms of His Triune Divinity must thence be allowed to eclipse every vernacular of rational human expression so the transposition of our founding awareness may be hurtled with confidence into the stellar regions of Wisdom where the Truth burns with the incontestable illumination of the very first day of the world.

No one can accuse me of exaggerating any facet of faith through the aesthetic parables I humbly compose, for my intentions are simply to embellish the human spirit to heights worthy of the Immaculate Queen of Paradise and the Throne She so applicably deserves. If anyone wishes to hold me in contempt or deride these solemn strains, then convict me of the whole; for I plead guilty to tenderness, for aiding and abetting Justice, and of being woefully inept at fulfilling an Herculean task that every creature must concede to be far and away above the columns of any mythical mountain, Olympus. Just as we have yet to fathom the loftiness of the holy tenets in the Sacred Heart of Christ, so too are we unaware of the pitiable desolation awaiting us should we refuse to bind those inspiring dreams. Evocative poetics, illustrious artworks, demonstrative exhibitions and eloquent orations are never without their critics. The sullen call of these worldlings who peddle their soul-dampening pragmatics is nothing more than a vile invitation for us to wallow along with them in the soiled praxes of Creation where they wile away their lives, elevating their spiritedness no higher than the soles of their wing-tip shoes. It is fair for my Christian counterparts to question why I oftentimes strike such impassioned contrasts that might be mistakenly described as excessively hyperbolic or imprudently inflammatory. My response is that the expanse of my hyperbola is only the distance a pocket watch travels to and fro before a hypnotized spectator in a carnival sideshow compared to the trajectory of Halley's comet parading from intergalactic space across the center of our solar system and into the stark beyond again, roughly every seventy years. And, my purportedly insolent remarks toward the proud and arrogant people who are causing so much suffering in the world will look like a kitchen match next to the sun's flaring solar-dynamic when Jesus Christ decides to reign-in their haughty pompousness and boldface, putrescent error. I am confident He will soon unleash the fires of Heaven and Hell against the adversaries of His Church; for it takes no clairvoyant's mystical premonition or sage's omen to read the signs in the air. Faithful Christians everywhere hold this Truth to be self-evident! Again, it concerns how one defines "obvious." The term *hyperbola* is derived from the Greek word *huperbole*, meaning *"a throwing beyond."* This is exactly what Our Lady is hoping to accomplish through the ameliorative power of the Holy Spirit inside the human heart. She seeks to bombard our spiritual consciences with images and ideas so superbly profound and stunningly genuine that our natural inquisitiveness is compelled to search high and low, mountaintop to canyon floor, and in every nook and cranny in the expectation of discovering that our beloved God has been watching and guiding humanity since the moment He first said, *...Let it be!*

Sunday, January 9, 2000 (excerpt)   *4:45 p.m.*
"*Your Heavenly Mother is with you to help you*   *j(009)*
destroy every facade that should attempt to distract My children from knowing perfect Love. Therein rests the reason that we pray together and ask all continents in every hemisphere to hear the voice of their Redemption, the Holy Spirit of My Son, Jesus Christ. There are no more reasons for My children to decline because every alternative has been buried beneath the ages by the Blood of the Cross. We rest in the comfort that the union of the highest Heaven and the most forsaken soul is found in the recitation of just one 'Our   *x*
Father.' That is more than a simple wish or whim, it is the

holy invitation to Jesus to reach well below the tabletops of the affluent to claim the souls who truly love Him with power. And, this Man of giant Divinity stoops to conquer the sorrow of anyone who is so humble to call-out His Name! This Gallant Star will shine with rays of Love so profound that the dungeons beneath the Earth are blindingly bright to the conquerors being held there. Yes, these holy men and women are the sunken vessels who await their resurrection from beneath the crest of the teeming seas! These little ones who cry in loneliness are causing the Angels on High to come running to their aid, and bringing the singing Saints to cup their ears in hope that they can hear the most faint of uttered words. My children, these are our people! These are the pious hearts who sparkle at the brim of Jesus' drink of consolation, waiting to be consumed by one who cares to the death that they again become whole and dignified in the likeness of Eden. When will they come to where the fruits are harvested every month? When God turns to you and tells you that you can stop praying now, time is done. Oh, what a glorious day that will be! The Son I call Jesus is on His feet now and is shuffling His vestments around His shoulders, looking across all the heavens in the joy and anticipation that the approaching moment has nearly come. He has trained His eyes on the inclement world and has told Me that it is time for Me to accompany Him on the journey of Life, of Everlasting Life for all who live and have died in His grace. My children, I cannot tell you the hour that He will come, but I can tell you that He was still seated before Pope John Paul II opened the Jubilee Door. And, now, He is standing to bring us all to the realization and reconciliation that His every prophecy is about to be fulfilled. How He shines in this Glory! How He knows that this victory is real and as new at this moment as twenty centuries before! How I come now in new anticipation because I see the new glow in His eyes! We wait for the word, the single most important utterance ever to come-forth in Creation, that of the Almighty Father: MY SON AND MY MOTHER, BRING ME

xx

xxx

xl

MY PEOPLE! These lofty truths are real and alive. This is factual Salvation and everlasting Glory! And, it is all for you! The parables are correct and the Gospel still breathes! This, My children, is why I come to you donned in happiness and peace. I come to implore you to pray for the weak, for those millions with crippling disease, for the millions begging to be born, and for the wretched lot who do not care why. This is the dawn of the new hour, and I have come to celebrate it with you." *1*

The entire discussion about aligning our sensible vision with the more concise realities that are flooding our world from beyond the veil between Heaven and Earth is a benevolent attempt to synchronize our hearts with the fasting purposes of our Divine Creator for the redemption of our souls. Only faith in what is absolute and truthful produces this peace, cohesion, creative spontaneity, joyful success, and idyllic advancement. It is long passed the time in mortal history for those seeking Paradise to enshrine a consensus of pious obedience to the prowess of Heaven now proceeding before our obstinate willfulness like a swan gliding across the glossy surface of a Swiss millpond. The Most Holy Virgin once lamented to me that actions from the Divine Hand of God, including the highest-echelon miracles themselves, do not seem to mean much to most people in this morbidly secular age. How many statues must shed copious puddles of crimson tears before we are shaken from our spiritual apprehension? And, what of the thousands of mirthful people returning home from Shrines dedicated to our Blessed Mother's peremptory intercession with testimonies of miraculous conversion who are treated like religious psychopaths by their fellow parishioners; and what of those bleeding Eucharistic Hosts being consumed or secretly discarded because today's ecclesial authorities tremble before these miracles and the thought of such converting command; and baffling icons of Our Lady and Her Son appearing on windows, walls, and trees dismissed by faith leaders as having no discernable significance; or inexplicable images of Our Savior in His Passion and haloed silhouettes of His Mother implanted upon rose petals being given no more than incredulous glances; and the mystical oratory from the Hosts of Paradise more evocative than the collective insights of the homilies and sermons of the past twenty centuries combined being strewn across vast minefields of human skepticism? It is obvious that there are far too many people with puny faith, malformed judgment, and misguided intentions who hold sway over the impressions of God's children. How recurrent is the theme where a sigh of relief is exhausted by pragmatic religious skeptics upon being temporally "rescued" from the sacrifice of their self-possessed dispositions by the scrawniest scientific explanation from researchers, intellectuals, and even our clergy by the rendering of their faithless verdict against the aforementioned gifts of the Holy Spirit: *We find nothing miraculous or supernatural in these events.* Our Lady describes it as two people witnessing the supernatural Miracle of the Sun at Fatima in 1917, after which one turns to the other and says, "Did you see that?" And, the other replies, "Yes!" The first then retorts, "Neither did I!" Heaven says that withholding spiritual food from a starving nation is a crime against humanity entire. And, there is an Eternal court much like The Hague in the Netherlands anxiously awaiting the opportunity to exact divine justice on behalf of the Kingdom of God. The moisture that formed into droplets, naturally or otherwise, on the eyes of the very first statue of the weeping Mother of Jesus Christ should have induced humanity to wail in agony beneath the oppression of our sins. Instead, some people will allow the first faithless wretch within earshot who has an obtuse opinion to cast doubt on them all, striking our God-fearing resolve from the skies and scattering the shards of His hope across the barren continents like a doomed shuttle dissecting a February morn. Is it any wonder that spiritually famished people who are searching for their truest identities cannot bring themselves to accept their essential dignity and the work Christ performs in their lives when faced with the excuses these malcontents concoct? How is it possible for anyone who offers an aromatic sermon about witnessing the florid beauties of the Almighty in evening sunsets and fields of gold to evade the charges of duplicity and hypocrisy when they refuse to humbly accede to the direct works of God in the configuration of condensed water molecules having stained a glass window that distinctly matches an overlay of the miraculous tilma of Guadalupe with uncanny precision; or astounding declarations from ill-educated little children producing some of the most profound ecclesial advice anyone has ever heard; or crowds praying the Holy Rosary being gently pummeled by flower petals from the clouds; or a living rose growing in minutes from the chest of a female mystic in the presence of third-party witnesses; or a stigmatic Roman Catholic priest living fifty years bearing the excruciating wounds of Christ's Crucifixion as witness to the authenticity of the Holy Mass and in reparation for the sins of other men; or photographs showing doors of light opening in the firmament, or letters of fire igniting in the heavens spelling-out the word *peace* in a soon-to-be war-torn country, or Rosaries turning gold, or invalids rising from their wheelchairs at the imposition of a visionary's hand; or thousands of people simultaneously seeing the Queen of Heaven hovering above church domes, in the hollows and clefts of rocky cliffs, in the vaulting welkin next to an ominously spinning sun, from mountaintops to canyons, from nomads roaming the arid deserts to the boatsmen waking the musty seas; and even to a U.S. astronaut gazing from the portal of his fragile spaceship upon the beautiful jewel of the Earth, not to mention one prophecy after another coming true; and, nearly all of these mystical gifts happening to dutiful Christians who live in conformity to the teachings of the Roman Catholic Church, and who receive the Holy Sacrament of the Eucharist with death-defying devotion and uncompromising faith. We have already seen that one superordinary, authentic manifestation of our Heavenly Father's converting care; and there will be many more to come because He is alive and well, on the move, and engaged with His Creation, fulfilling the promise that He will never abandon us as unfostered orphans in the wild.

Since the Devil can tempt us to fall into the sludge pits of desolation, we must assuredly believe that God conversely inspires us to reach for the heights of exuberance. The Holy Spirit will enliven any soul owning an ounce of humility toward complete abandonment to Our Savior in faith. Love is a power wrought through trust and filial devotion to the Omnipotent Creator who surrendered Life so we will have Love eternally. The heavens cannot fail us in anything! When we finally step to the plate of obedience, pine our abandonment with a healthy dose of bravery, rub a little sacrificial charity into our palms, and take a swing at the darkness enveloping this world, the exilic linen of human mortality that has been obscuring our spiritual vision will be ripped from before our eyes like the jacket of a baseball helicoptering to the ground, revealing the core of our very being as our intertwined essence rockets out and beyond the highest decks bordering the earth's rolling fields. And, like the honest man who approaches our table to initiate the revelation of the Truth, our beloved Father will snatch away the veil between Heaven and Earth and thunder the apocalyptic "Ta-Da" to close out these dark ages while bending down to brush the soiled plate of His Creation of the final stain left there by the foot of the last mortal creature. Until we garner the courage to invoke a collective response that will make the heavens weep in joy, we must entertain as much thoughtful soul-searching as our consciences can endure, becoming like inquisitive little children about the finer things of life, yet righteously honest before the mystical facts which are penetrating ever more mysteriously into the purview of our sensibly obvious impressions. There is not a leader in his chosen field who has done anything less than extend his contemplative soul, pondering the greater reaches of his vestigial genius. All we need do is realize that there is a Kingdom above all cerebral realms, a Paradise of communicable Grace, eternally sustained by an Eternity of Truth and the Wisdom before any age was ever called into being. Every saint who blesses the rainbow arbors of God's Eternal Vineyard triumphed over the coarse altercations that mark the parameters and surfaces of this life, the table of the Earth where our dignities have borne abrasion atop of contusion. They did so through the staid friction of their souls and the grit of their holy determination, polishing a stately boldness that shall forever illuminate the sparkling perfection of man. Wherever true fishers of men have come to the fore in the history of Salvation, the bobbers of Mystical Grace have danced on the waters of our awareness, sending-out concentric ripples of rejuvenated hope, offering the repeating announcement to the eager longing of every soul that bounty resides beneath and beyond the glistening reflection we see peering back at ourselves at each recurring dawn.

We must never allow the despondence generated by those who have cunningly mastered the damning artifices of material collusion and spiritual incarceration to persuade us to abandon the all-powerful, innate propensities of the human heart married to the Wisdom of God; mystically divine, potently dominant, overwhelmingly superior in form, grace, sustenance, and deliverance, and ultimately therapeutic and generative in all things everlasting. If worldly influence and intellectual force seem to be as impenetrable as the steel of a hammer's head and honed to the fineness of a razor's blade, let everyone know that the human heart is a divine diamond more spectacular than any crowning jewels of kings, set for perfection in the diadem of Divinity, imposing in its ofttimes silent grandeur, possessing the valorous mettle to entice the aspirations of brutes to moral heights, capable of whetting the appetence of holiness in the most derelict beasts, discharged to sheer away every impediment to salvific grace, impervious to affliction, long-standing in beauty past the vision of scandalous mortals, worthy in the sight of the ageless Saints, identified without reproach in the royal courts of Paradise, and permanently triumphant over every mental influence that ever reared its ugly head to stifle the childlike hopes innocently huddling in the heart of every man. All living things must become inspirited with the genius of Love Incarnate, who is Christ, and begin to sense the viable harmony that exists in the universe through the pulsating Dominion of the Triune God, He who has benevolently revealed Himself as Father, Son, and Holy Spirit. The dimensions of unity and the possibilities that flourish from sacramental devotion and abandonment to the spiritual voices from the Hosts of Heaven are consuming our every existing perception and fiber of being, from the ink that forms the letters transcribed upon these solemn pages to every solar exclamation point penned by the Hand of God that has blazed across the storied horizons since His Son destroyed the captivating boundaries of time with the final Earth-confined beat of His Sacred Heart. But, where is the world's attention being focused compared to this? And, who are the guilty parties perpetuating such blindness? Do you believe for a moment that these words are the rantings of a deranged zealot who is not in touch with the realities of life? Or, is the echo of the thundering voice of Truth rattling off the canyon walls of your precious soul, raising it majestically over the mountaintops of human sin, burning away the fog of corrupt rationales, and lifting the tear-filled eyes of any humane decency-seekers? The authentic history of human civilization is presently arriving at its predestined conclusion amidst the succoring spray of sacrificial seasoning being applied by humble Christian souls who have unceremoniously accented the generational bounty of each redemptive millennium; a seemingly clandestine occurrence that has reaffirmed the intentions of our loving Creator, a hair's-breadth below the arrogance of the disoriented magnates of worldly sensual pleasure, but just as apparent and predetermined as two playing cards laying stealthily beneath a silk cloth on a dinner table, and imminently more ominous and foreboding than two aces concealed in the cuff of a crafty gambler. The Lord of Creation is by far the most adept cardsman to ever stare Creation in the face. He has already announced the winning suit, dealt to Him by the Father of Destiny, which He promises to play at the close of the ages; yet mercifully suspending His Hand, allowing time for each soul in attendance to cast their fortune along with the rubescent, Royal Blood-Red Flush of His Most Sacred Heart.

Yet, it seems almost too unimaginable that we witness innumerable people possessing arrogance abreast who dare to burn a gaze upon a God who never bluffs, faithlessly calling Him for a show of New Providence instead of surrendering into the folds of victory which were prophetically impressed into the stars before the universe ever received its exquisite frame. Oh, yes, the celestial wallclock is but a few hallowed ticks from intoning the hour of Eternal Deliverance, a reckoning that will thunder the just Fist of God onto the green fields of Creation with the Revelation of a Queenly Triumph and a King's Second Return. The chips of our souls will be jarred into an end-dance of near incomprehensible delight as our earthly existence is finally raked-in as His sole possession with His embrace of Glory revealed, pulling us into the Paradise He created alone. Imagine the utter horror on the faces of those who expended their lives opposing everything faith reveals and advancing their blasphemous wiles with presumptuous impunity from cradle to grave, driving our fledgling societies and moments of opportunity into a decimated wreck of spiritual ruin, perishing in subtle increments of selfishness, inebriated by an ignorance which provoked their refusal of the mystical signs of Salvation that Jesus Christ placed before them like bread-crumbs upon their meandering paths of haplessness. There will be no posthumous, *I told you so*, once the champagne of Paradise is seen popping its effervescent Light upon the newly Redeemed because Final Judgment will have already been fully pronounced from the Alpha of man to his Omega as Saint, with dignity and justification conferred upon each evangelic soul. However, it can be done with the prophetic command, *I tell you so now*, on this side of mortality too, during these merciful hours, and with more certainty than any hustling odds-maker bearing a trifectionary tip on the final race at Pimlico or the probabilities of a blackjack table on a Las Vegas mall. The Trinity of Father, Son, and Holy Spirit bears the only profits of a man whose sanctified entry and perfect submission within the human soul occurs in communion with the Most Blessed Sacrament from the Altars of the Roman Catholic Church, whereby the original, Apostolic, and Triune Bread of Eternal Life is dispensed to the whole of Christianity. Only thence are we freed from the stalls of sinfulness which have all-too-often fenced the stallion surges of virtuosity that stampede from the noble of heart. The progeny of Christian conversion are spiritual thoroughbreds of a divine pedigree who have been recreated to inhale the salient winds of grace and the scent of roses waffing upon those breezes; high-stepping, confident, and free upon the fields of absolution; not constricted or relegated to repetitively retrace the oval paranoia of materialistic propriety, societal mediocrity, and indentured servitude which is selfishly officiated by lording classes straining for a victory tape that is no farther toward divinity than the line from which they began. Our Lady declares that our hearts need not be inexorably hitched to the exhausted ploddings of inordinate flesh and the delusions of the walking dead masquerading as the obvious terminus of human discernment. We can instead foresee the arrival of a newer era, one not unlike the sun evicting our cabin fever on the first budding days of spring. The cerebral antics of slick tricksters and mind benders are about to come to an end, along with the arrogance inevitably accompanying such pompous anti-beatitude.

Sunday, June 25, 2000 (excerpt)   *4:45 p.m.*

"My little ones, this is the day that celebrates the   j(177)
single-most powerful grace which God has bestowed upon
mankind since Jesus woke from among the dead. The
Eucharist is that which mends everything that is broken. In
another tongue, you know the Most Blessed Sacrament as the
Corpus Christi, the Body of Christ. Perhaps if there were a
different Creation in which humanity did not exist, that
would not mean much. But, in real Creation, the one which
God has chosen to create, the Body, Blood, Soul, and
Divinity of His Son is the difference between Life and death,   x
between sickness and health, and between Salvation and
condemnation. The Holy Eucharist is your life, health, and
Salvation. I am pleased to know that you have accepted the
call of the Holy Spirit to join the ranks of the vindicated, and

to bring as many lost souls to Jesus as you possibly can. That is what makes you true warriors and heroes, not whether you can succeed in public office or win a great sports contest. My children, I have told you repeatedly about the Kingdom of God, and that He wishes the Earth to be transposed into that eternal joy. The Blessed Sacrament is your Food for that   xx *journey, your vision and enlightenment, your strength, compassion, humility, and wisdom. That is why it is imperative that you continue to attend Daily Mass and live constantly in the Light of Christian charity. If there is to be hope in the human heart, let it be founded upon that holy order. I wish you could know how deeply I pray for all of My little children. I wish each of you could see through eyes of faith that Jesus is perpetually with you. If you muster thoughts of fondness for God, it is His Spirit guiding you there. Should you choose to help your neighbor in any*   xxx *benevolent way, know that it is the Son of the Most High working through you. And, if this land of America ever brings itself to again proclaim the dignity of life for those yet to be born, it will finally have opened the door of Grace given it from the hand of the Almighty Father wide enough for His Son to walk-in and say 'You are truly worthy to be blessed!' This, too, is a gift from the Eucharistic Sacrament, if only the citizens of these western hills and rolling lands will humble themselves to receive."*

I am absolutely convinced, to the credit of our Heavenly Mother's assurance, that thousands upon millions of anonymous people yearn for a reliable direction to turn; and I have been commissioned by Her to offer them a promising first step. The abominably scandalous constrictions perpetrated by radical theologians and the moral cowards who succumb to them regarding the academic definitions of the miraculous things that serve only to give the world better perspective about the interaction between God and man must come to an end! People must stop listening to the lukewarm snake froth spewing from the mouths of these lost souls who make it their dismal profession to minimize, lampoon, and misconstrue the supernatural intercession of the Heavenly Hosts and the mystical graces being dispensed by the Holy Spirit. They are living an existence defined by the lowest common denominator of spiritual mediocrity in which their tepid faith stoops to grovel, never rising to the glorious display of a personal commitment to God, while cackling like a thousand Chicken Littles, reminding everyone else what we are not required to believe. Obedience to the supernatural, maternal guidance of the Mother of Redemption is a mere afterthought in their whimsical ideologies and sectarian themes. They are not in communion with the Holy Spirit when they dissect the dogmatic Universal Queenship of the Ever-Blessed Virgin to whose conditions and consequences they must eventually defer. To most of them, supernatural manifestations from God are no more than ecumenical, cerebral stumbling blocks they just wish would simply go away. If this is the grand staircase by which they are carrying humanity to the heavens, then let them remember the legacy of a tower once plagued by the multiplication of languages. In the scrupulous eyes of too many religious intellectuals, there is no such thing as a miraculous phenomenon or supernatural intercession worthy of anyone's belief, no matter whether they witness it for themselves or are threatened to be struck by a bolt of lightning if they decline. Our Lady asks, *"what kind of faith is that?"* It is not the skies that are being brought to the ground by the great Love of Our Lady, but rather the rickety edifices constructed upon foundations not worthy of Her bearing. None of the great Saints who loved the Blessed Virgin Mary would tell humankind to ignore Her authentic apparitions we have witnessed in the past two centuries, especially the unprecedented manifestations of recent years. Therefore, let the days of cross-examining the works of the Holy Spirit and hiding beneath endless reams of scholarly treatises cease. We must respect what this Divine Matriarch will ultimately accomplish, should humanity choose to comply. We must harbor no vain justifications for our faithless disobedience to the incontestible requests from the Heavenly Hosts. The Redemption of souls hangs in the balance, beginning with that of our own. I certify with all the experiences with which I have been blessed, it would take only a single glimpse of the majestic Queen of Paradise to induce a wholesale reorientation of their dimmed perception, and some might even become Christian evangelists, too. It could be reasonably argued that theological intellectualism has generated a paralyzing stoicism today whereby multitudes in authority have peeled the charismatic guidance of the Holy Spirit into so many layers of nonsensical discernment and lulled themselves into such indifference and inaction that their judgment has become no more potent than that of all the king's horses and all the king's men standing beside a critically injured omelet, diagnosing the damage. And, as a result, we have collectively forsaken our responsiveness to the Will of Jesus through Our Lady's Dogmatic and Revelatory Queenship. Diabolical smoke is blinding our good senses through the subtle injection of impudent fears by people with fancy letters behind their names who simply refuse to tender their trust to the redemptive agendum of

Almighty God. Evidently, *Fiat* is not in their faith vocabulary. How did we descend from the celestial perch of the personified revelation of the Heavenly Hosts? After all, Christ walked across the earthen landscape and through the hearts of men, preaching freedom from sin and displaying the power of His Kingdom, conscripting a brethren of followers who knew almost nothing of scholarly thought. These humble disciples reveled in one Messianic miracle after another, believing in Love and that the Reign of God was at hand. They trekked with exuberance into cities and towns in advance of the Anointed One, calling forth the sick and infirm to prepare for their healing at His Holy Word; new Christians themselves who convoked inexplicable miracles while wielding a faith so profound that all, save one, would die at the hands of executioners with their Master's words on their lips. How has humanity gone from this to becoming so terrified of miracles, mystical charisms, prophetic warnings, and supernatural callings that we allow them to be defined in such temporal terms, ones that only spiritually-senseless and pragmatic mortals could devise? Consider the biblical witness of our early fathers, those closest to the Revelation of our Savior, in regards to the wondrous works of our Paschal King. *At that the whole assembly fell silent. They listened to Barnabas and Paul as the two described all the signs and wonders God had worked among the Gentiles through them* (Acts 15:12). Instead, we entertain the strange rantings of a doctoral head of theological studies at a major American university, a Catholic, who recently professed that it was perfectly alright for someone to believe that the three young visionaries from Fatima, Portugal were likely the victims of hallucinations. Now, there's some demonic babbling for you! I tell you here that the professor's declaration is an outright affront to the Dominion of God and Divine Wisdom, itself. We must be cautious that the flowers of our faith do not become wilted by way of such dark vanity, rendering us like a fish thrown onto the banks of blind agnosticism with no trust in God or our brothers and sisters with whom He has vested the evangelic lapels of His graceful intent for the mysterious fashioning of the conclusion of the world. What does the Holy Sacrament of Confirmation do if it does not make us all seers of the miraculous realms? I am convinced that Saint John of the Cross, himself, is pining for the moment of setting the record straight on our final Day of Deliverance. It is completely baffling to encounter the shortsighted musings of some people who fear the unlikely possibility of diabolic infiltration and corruption in spiritual manifestations when the Son of Man initiates a mystical dialogue with one or more of His children. To the contrary, they refuse to even acknowledge the high probability that the Evil One has far more success exacerbating their own ill-tempered and inept conclusions into outright chronic disbelief by intentionally misrepresenting the ecclesial teachings of the Saints. Notwithstanding both cases, I have come to realize that evil spirits are given occasional latitude in winnowing our thoughts and conclusions, but rarely in the presence of the Holy Spirit united with the Most Blessed Sacrament of Holy Christendom. Humanity must stop believing that God and Satan are coequals balancing opposite ends of a teeter-totter. Wherein Christ reigns, evil is dead! Our Lord already owns the Triumph during every moment of life. I tell you, there is greater danger of unchecked diabolical apprehension in the scrupulous doubts of overly cautious critics than has ever influenced a child of God nestled within a miraculous charism of the Blessed Virgin Mary. Yes, the process can sometimes be fraught with deception, but not from the source most people suspect. Human reasoning is only a badly cluttered mind stream without the enlightenment of the Holy Spirit. Yet, this does not preclude the need for prudent discernment by pious individuals, especially Roman Catholic priests with high regard for orthodoxy and an openness to the multi-faceted aspects engendered in God's miraculous gifts. Although one's vision may be clear, the process still involves invoking the Light of the Cross before the Truth can be magnified without undue impediment.

We should remember that every extraordinary grace dispensed by the heavens offers us the challenge of being delivered to the extreme boundaries of our spiritual faith. What did God tell humanity through the life of Saint Bernadette of Lourdes when multitudes of scoffers walked away from the Grotto after witnessing what seemed to be a deluded young woman rooting in the mud while speaking to an image no one else there could see? The Holy Spirit took our Christian predecessors to the precipice of disbelief; and they slithered off the edge like reptiles. Now, every succeeding generation can see by their example the true measure of their own trust. Where will we bail out? How will we deny the redemptive works of Jesus Christ? And, what flaws in our spiritual abandonment may eventually bring our rejection of human Salvation altogether? If we could not have remained open to the possibility of the Divine and stood with that innocent French girl in those crucial moments in the shadows of a stark, cruddy grotto, how can we presume to have accompanied our Savior to His Sorrowful Crucifixion on Good Friday? Or, that we are not at the brink of selling Him out at the jingling of two silver coins today? The illusion of the status quo can be awfully appealing sometimes. But, it was Bernadette who emulated in angel-like form the personified humility of Our Lady, whose inextirpable faith transcended into miraculous realms on Mount Calvary one day; that bound communion with the will of God that only few have humbled themselves to avow. Does this not highlight the beatific dimensions of the Grace of the Ever Blessed Virgin Mary? What does it say about the courage of the diocesan cleric who defended Bernadette while she was being impugned and pursued by local authorities? Said he, *Load well your weapons, for your path lies over my dead body!* What a manifest declaration of allegiance to the Crucified Christ and stunning rebuke to secular powers and pragmatic judgment! No cynical intellectual can compete with this kind of holy perfection; and in the minds of far too many theologians, it is of little value because it has nothing to do with the Deposit of Faith. What utter nonsense! That Catholic priest will be stationed in Paradise a thousand years before their shadows are ever allowed to darken the door. Just as in the field of Physics there arose a philosophical genius named Albert Einstein who redefined man's understanding of matter and light without amending our age-old physical theorems, and introducing the globe to a power as blinding as the sun and as destructive as impending Armageddon, likewise will the kingdom halls of theological intellectualism be shaken to the core by the personification of God's Love so surprisingly simple that human thought will be whittled to the likeness of the cooing voices of little children to be utilized for religious instruction by every future generation.

How many people in today's world would seriously entertain a mystical charism such as Saint Peter's vision of the great sheet descending from Heaven containing the different animals and birds, and subsequently respond as he did? (Acts 10:9-43) Can the point be made any clearer? Peter's vision of the obvious was in harmony with the mysterious powers of the Holy Spirit; and He responded affirmatively, transforming the thought of the Early Church with a Gospel inscription of their overtly sublime obedience to God's miraculous intercession which is still being read by Christians 2,000 years hence. Thank goodness the curiosity of the first Pontiff of the Roman Catholic Church was not driven by what he thought a miracle ought to be or the hair-splitting, palaverous dissection of the supernatural, preternatural, and natural. It is far too easy for someone's responsiveness to be submerged in that pitiable morass. Do we realize that searching every possible technological and scientific avenue for the rational explanation for each manifestation of the Holy Spirit with the intention of disqualifying it as an authentic sign of God's presence is gravely offensive to Christ, who is at liberty to command our obedience through any means He might choose to employ? Therefore, in light of these end times, we must conscientiously reevaluate the sacred attributes of Jesus' faithful flock who embodied filial obedience at its best while following the Messiah during the first days of the evangelization of the world. And, by so doing, we shall comprehend how to proceed in these latter ones. They were simple and humble, ill-bred in the eyes of educated men; yet, they were more than willing to be taught a perfect Wisdom that would place them at odds with the lauded aristocrats of their time. They probably knew little about ancient theologies, scholastics, intellectualism, or any other faith-defying facts. They were not obliged or justified by any other voice than the Holy Spirit. They did not become feckless mind-crunchers who spent the remainder of their lives parsing the words of Our Lord, nor were they even remotely well-read in the linguistic rubrics or polled hypotheses of their learned contemporaries. Yet, they were among the most uniquely well-prepared, prolifically capable, and personally endearing men ever culled to lead the conversion of humanity in the tenets of Jesus Christ. Why? Because for a mere three years, they were formed in piety by drinking from a Supernatural Font of Love that was so overwhelmingly pristine that it literally dumbfounded their earthly senses and previous perceptions of logic. Upon witnessing the crowning triumph of their Master's eternal power through His Paschal Death and Resurrection, a climactical detonation of sacrificial Love burst upon their souls, rendering them shed in everything but tears. They fell prostrate in awesome wonder before the Revelation of God who had so painstakingly pulled them into His confidence. Thereafter, what message could they have possibly embraced than announcing an inconceivable relationship with our unseen Father through the confession of our sins and the consumption of the Bread of Life; the Body, Blood, Soul and Divinity of His Son Jesus in the Eucharistic Species? From the Most Blessed Sacrament flows every conceivable blessing and gift, virtue and grace, hope and Beatitude, true vision and venue, sign and wonder, charism and conversation; whether requiring exilic ordinances to be suspended, planetary paths to be reset, suns wrested from the skies, diseases eradicated, ignorance suppressed, pretenses destroyed, human wills humiliated, opponents felled, mortality endured, crosses mounted, deceased souls raised, angels appearing, Saints interceding, miracles flashing, or the Queen of Heaven Herself speaking to Her children beneath the thatched roofs of each hovel in every borough and hamlet of the globe! I tell you now—sinners with derisive mentalities who are spiritually incapacitated by the cerebral inebriety of their secular works would have doubtlessly stood in limbo twenty centuries ago, unwilling to cooperate in the unfolding of Redemption until it was too late. And, their likenesses are still doing it now. But, when it is aimed with arrogant disdain and callous disregard toward the miraculous intercession of the Queen of Heaven, it is an egregiousness grounded in hatred, a prideful indifference reeking of the stench of Hell; and no crowing clarion of canonical jurisprudence is ever going to save them.

Sunday, May 1, 2005 (excerpt)   *5:03 p.m.*
Feast of Saint Joseph the Worker
     "...And, to My Special and Chosen ones, I have never   *o(121)*
doubted that you have never doubted that I love you with
overwhelming power. I understand that you discuss and

contrast the messages and images I give you with the conditions of the world. You must be strong of heart so you will not become embittered by the world. No one alive understands more your exasperation about the wrongs and evils in the world than Me. Imagine the sorrows of My Immaculate Heart as I witnessed the Passion and Crucifixion of Jesus. O' how difficult it was for Me to receive His Body in My lap on Good Friday. I made it through, dear children, for the same reasons you will survive and prevail over your enemies on the Earth. I knew that Jesus told us the Truth about His Resurrection from the Tomb. I ask you to remember the sense of impending victory that I embraced as I saw My sacrificed Son that day. I knew that the sinners of the world would not have the last word. By all means, I knew that The Word, the Son of Man to whom I gave Birth in Bethlehem, would emerge on Easter Morning to the shame and chagrin of everyone who hated Him, to the people who crucified Him, and to the pitiable sinners who knew not what they were doing. He forgave them all because they were bringing the Salvation of humankind to Creation, even in the error of their ways. Their intentions were not benign; their work was the work of evil. But, God turned this evil into good."

x

xx

Those departed individuals who were responsible for Our Savior's Crucifixion 2,000 years ago have never whimpered a single syllable of ex post facto jubilation in all Eternity that they saved the world by crucifying the Messiah; for as Pope Benedict XVI proclaimed in one of his inaugural homilies, *"...(the world) has been saved by the Crucified One, and not by the crucifiers."* At best, they asked for Mercy and received it abundantly. It would be a revisionist's nightmare to believe that human redemption is the response of the Father to their heinous crimes; for their sins were already extracted from His Divine Mind and needed no further redress. God, it seems, never gloats over His own sworn enemies. Quite the contrary, our Eternal Salvation only underscores the Almighty Father's Love for His Only Begotten Son who had just completed what had never previously been done. Humanity killed Him; and He woke up two days later to tell us how badly it hurt. And, strangely enough, we are the beneficiaries of it all! The cruel acts of His betrayers and torturers were wrought by evil works, even if their only transgression was indifference toward the deliberate offenses against the just cause of the Moral Taskmaster, Himself. In like manner, the Triumph of the Immaculate Heart of Mary does not bloom through theological virtuosos who refuse to trumpet Her intercession because their faith is too famished by their intellectual pride, apathy, indifference, outright obstinate imprudence, rendering their right to any legitimate claim or inheritance of the dignity of the Matriarch of Paradise null and void, even though they will see Jesus Christ utilize their sad omissions for the elevation of Her Triumph to heights never before seen by the human eye. Woe to those who hold-out in disobedience to the Immaculate Queen of Heaven until the strike of Her triumphant Glory! At that juncture, every one of these helpless pragmatics will suddenly realize that the majestic vessel of Deliverance has fully departed Her berth; and they are not footed on Her promenade decks. We will see some Olympic swimming records broken that day as they dive headlong into the waters of their own conversion, flailing like guppies to outrun the flames!

Sunday, December 5, 1999 (excerpt)   *3:12 p.m.*

"Through My intercession, you are becoming more i(339) *than messengers and examples. You are now participants in both the Teaching and Passion of My Beloved Son. His Teaching and Crucifixion cannot be spoken about as being mutually exclusive gifts to the Earth. No better lesson was delivered to mankind about forgiveness than that which was taught on Good Friday when Jesus was killed for the Salvation of all. I ask you to remember that no righteous act or phrase of Jesus can be dichotomized into individual slivers of human understanding. There can be no paring-away of* x *the totality in which Jesus lived in My womb through the present day as He is seated at God's right hand. Those Angels and Elders who pay such homage to Jesus as He stands proudly as the Eucharist in the Monstrance are the first who will tell you 'Do not ever say that Jesus Christ is anything not related to sanctity, perfection, divinity, humanness, and love.' Hair-splitting theology is no match for the universal goodness that no man has the power to dissect. That goodness is the singular Love of God for His people, present as the Messiah, the Holy Spirit, and the Most* xx

Blessed Sacrament. Jesus is truly alive and dwelling in and among you only because I have borne Him to humanity, a solemn rite that I still confer upon My children, especially those who pray. This is not My will, but the Divine Will of the Creator of the Universe who has told Me in undeniable terms that I am the Mediatrix of all Graces, the New Eve, and the Queen of Heaven and Earth. Anyone who would approach the King of all Creation should bear this in mind, lest He sends them away with shame written across their faces..."

xxx

I dare say that human history has never before had thrust upon its brow such an incessant barrage of contradictory philosophies, licentious acts, lewd practices, unsubstantiated beliefs, diabolic proclamations, rancorous protestations, erroneous postulates, unorthodox dogmas, and prevaricating platitudes than is being witnessed in our age, and whose collective disharmony has infested the hearts of men with seeds of discord and disunity, fomenting wars and insurrections, grievances and disputes, tyranny and tantrums, revelry, reformation, and revolution. If the Messiah's command is for His followers to make disciples out of everyone in Creation by helping them understand their divine identity as children of God, why do mortal intellects believe this to be accomplished by tedious indoctrination in sophisticated human thought and historical repetition, when their spirit-worn brothers and sisters flee to visions of the setting sun seeking solace and peaceful rest? Why do their battle-scarred siblings not dive headlong into a discourse of hermeneutics or treatises of scholastic theory? Consider the patrons of the arts who walk from the doors of great orchestral halls with welling souls after hearing the musical oratory of angelic choirs, translated from the trebles and staffs of inspirited composers, and launched from symphony and shell to their berth in the chambers of the heart. For those few sanctified moments, such works of the Holy Spirit buoyed their afflicted souls above the mundane diablerie that they know is soon to be inflicted upon them with increasing intensity. None of them exit those artistic thresholds with symphonies of ethical logic at the ready, prepared for the first altercation of whimsical minds and the eventual battle of titanic wills. Nary a patron rushes to the composer with anxious inadequacy, asking for sheets displaying the signature clefs of treble, alto, tenor and bass, and the decoding-genius that transforms the notation into the uplifting strains for their famished souls to hear. Those scores are factually dead until transposed into a medium that is recognizable by the human spirit. There has never been a person in history who has gazed at a piece of sheet music and had their eyes well with tears because their heart was touched by what they saw. Only when the scripted masterpiece resounds through the winds and into the fibers of our being, from sinew of the bow and the breath of the lips, to the brawn of our loving essence is the transfiguration of the spirit enhanced. And, so it is with the intellectual works of the academicians. Still further, why are tiny children captivated in rapt wonderment by the gently pulsing wings of a big rainbow butterfly—natural or supernatural, who decides?—but could not care less about the cerebral antics of those who dissect their beautiful existence so as to testify to the rest of us that they are not really a miracle? Because there is not enough child left in these folks' hearts for the little ones to play and dream with, and hope with, and accompany them in their mystically-inherent desire to build-up the Kingdom of God on Earth. And, how do they respond when these precious youngsters innocuously ask why their butterfly's wings have such pretty colors? You will never hear these stuffed-shirts respond; *Because Jesus wanted you to know how the wings of His Dominion Angels shine while standing in the presence of His Immaculate Mother.* I have the gift at this moment of hearing the voice of these crass individuals pontificating in their stoic, collegiate, window-dressed reply, *You don't know that answer to be true.* I say, *Stand back and watch from the purview of your dead souls; the day of Truth is coming! And, you are on the wrong side of immortal history.* All of the saintly reason that has been heretofore developed to complement the spiritual understanding of men most assuredly possesses individual degrees, reflections, and gradations of the Truth, at least in its initial inspirations; but the collective scope of its transforming potential is relegated to no more elevation than the bottom rung of a ladder that could reach higher than the stars if only we allowed our intellects to soar beyond the galactic, interior dimensions of the heart. Our Lord asks us to climb toward Him with as much innocence and anticipation as when we scampered to the top of our swing-set slide in the evening of our late summer's childhood. Only pride is satisfied by the answers to our selfish queries. Saint Padre Pio once said, *The habit of asking "why" has ruined the world.* It is the antecedent that reveals the stubbornness of an ego that has yet to die in Christ, absent of the capacity to accede to the Divine, and burrowing heels more subterranean in excuses than a donkey's hooves on his most intemperate day. All too often we forget that our curiosities about God's motivations are only the distracting seductions of a mortality-stricken angel whose spirit refuses to glide among the highest beatitudes.

Sunday, August 22, 1999 (excerpt)   *4:29 p.m.*
        "My children, you are blessed to be among that   i(234)
happy number of souls who know the Truth first-hand. I
have guided you forward with courage and joy so that, as
you march in time toward the 10ᵗʰ celebration of the Feast of
My Queenship, you will also know yourselves as truly holy
people whose 'yes' to My Son still resounds with crispness and
clarity, with the same solemnity as it rang-out on February
22, 1991. You know very well what the rest of humanity
must come to know, that the Jesus who is acclaimed as the
Alpha is the same Christ who lives in Heaven and on Earth   x
as the Omega. Your Savior has not changed, despite the
popular sentiments of contemporary theologians, sociologists,
and liberal opportunists who have drifted from their faith in
the Gospel as it has been handed-down for twenty centuries.
This same Truth is the Deity that so very many refuse to
accept because the Mystery of the Holy Trinity will not be
confined by their mathematical logic."

The human heart possesses a penchant for raw genius that the mind will never know. There are likewise expanses to the soul that worldly reason cannot procure. And, there is a freedom revealed to the spirit only after the psyche is exhausted, beingness is transfigured into lovingness, and all things mystical are ratified by our worthiness in unity with God. Within this unequivocal Divinity, the soul explodes past the mind, charring the gantry of mortal logic it leaves behind in the stark loneliness of the realms of exile, standing in wonderment with its arms outstretched like the doors of a cage ripped from their hinges, allowing freedom to the celestial dove who was always meant to fly higher than the stars. The heart soars like an eagle in these passionate times, toward dreams that lay beyond the grasp of mortal reason, fueled by an unquenchable hope that endures the derisive elements of scholars and scandal-makers, and drives to the pinnacle of Paradise on a plume of Divinity spread across the firmament of every age. Doctoral degrees and educational accolades mean very little in the eyes of Almighty God! They neither confirm virtue nor corroborate Grace; but they most assuredly remove any excuses from their conferees for not having both in the completion of their perfection. *You say that you see, therefore your sins remain!* The most audacious erosion of faith in the history of man has occurred on their watch, without so much as a whimpering of resistance being issued from the clock towers of modern academe against the forces that are ravaging Christian goodness. Holiness, purity, and sanctity cannot be measured by the biological capacities of the human mind, nor by its trained tendency to regurgitate facts—historical, religious, and otherwise. There is no inherent virtue in cerebrally synaptic aptitudes based on the frail physiology of sinful mortals. The temporal nature of the elusive human memory testifies to this truth. The smartest people do not always know God best, even when they are instructing others about whom they believe Him to be. The associative mental capacities of the mind, coupled with the gift of our memories, is neither the determiner nor the benchmark of full sanctity or holiness. Love alone is perfect piety, a simple perfection implanted by the Bread of Life that radiates from the human heart! It is the luminary pulse of a transcending Divinity that sustains the Life of God within us! It is rather ironic that the proof of my point came to me through my own grandmother who succumbed to the debilitating effects of Alzheimer's disease in April of 1997. In the late stages of her illness, she fell into the all too familiar phase of failing to recognize the relationships anyone enjoyed with her, including myself as her grandson. However, she always acknowledged and remembered the love that I gave her with all the intensity I could muster. She could not even remember my name or the nature of our interpersonal relationship; but upon seeing my face, she would light-up with a smile, point and say, "you!" Her brain lay in ruins, but her heart retained a cognition for the consistency of Love that could not be expunged, even during the moments of her final agony.

Never before in the annals of time has it been more prudent within the bounds of the Spiritual Works of Mercy for us to admonish sinners so unyieldingly, and severely, along with those who too often remand their faith and that of others to the rote recital of rhetorical riddles and spirit-numbing theological exegeses, leaving the voice of God to compete with the obscuring flurry generated by their thought-mincing pride. They destroy and rebuild at their own authoritarian whims and in their own image, as if seeing themselves as the custodial curators of all that is of God. Too many of them have been deceived into believing that knowledge marks their stature in holiness, when every true Christian knows that it is really the passion of our loving sacrifices. What if they were asked to carry the debilitating cross that my grandmother endured in the closing days of her life? While there is little doubt that their compendium of academic success and the anecdotal jurisdiction their degrees procured would evaporate, is it necessarily true that their holiness would leave them by the same door as their diminishing body of facts? Of course not. Then, why would anyone believe that holiness and Wisdom come only by quantity and quality in proportion to academic relief? Our Lady told me,

Wisdom is in the loving, and wise only are those who do. Are today's theologians more enlightened than our ancient Faith Fathers who knew nothing of the scholastics and exegetical parsing that the past 2,000 years have yielded? Yet, it is those same Original Apostles who would have accepted a message from the Immaculate Mother of Jesus Christ, and faithfully obeyed Her in a microsecond, without even knowing what a microsecond is, or questioning why they were being asked. Can the same be said of our religious leaders today, no matter their particular stripe? Not through the greatest stretch of the imagination. Thus, the obvious has become amputated from the mystical; the composers can no longer hear the ethereal scores; and the true knowledge of God in action that would serve to transform the world has become lifeless and dormant. Our moral leaders have been charged by Jesus Christ to be the first to believe everything the Holy Spirit initiates and dictates, not the last. But, where do we find most of them—yes, skulking in the shadows of faithless uncertainty! I am indicting the preposterous propositions leveled by those who claim a truthful view of life, then turn and use that sanctified intelligence to generate excuses for ignoring Heaven's Queen as She intercedes around the globe. I am a witness to their colossal error; and I will speak-out against their vanities until their hypnotic hopelessness is finally supplanted by more faithful obedience. The great Saint Louis de Montfort stated it rather succinctly in his work "True Devotion to Mary," when he wrote:

> *Critical devotees are for the most part proud scholars, people of independent and self-satisfied minds, who deep down in their hearts have a vague sort of devotion to Mary. However, they criticize nearly all forms of devotion to Her which simple and pious people use to honor their good Mother just because such practices do not appeal to them. They question all miracles and stories which testify to the mercy and power of the Blessed Virgin, even those recorded by trustworthy authors or taken from the chronicles of religious orders. They cannot bear to see simple and humble people on their knees before an altar or statue of Our Lady, or at prayer before some outdoor shrine. They even accuse them of idolatry as if they were adoring the wood or the stone. They say that as far as they are concerned, they do not care for such outward display of devotion, and that they are not so gullible as to believe all the fairytales and stories told of our Blessed Lady. When you tell them how admirably the Fathers of the Church praised Our Lady, they reply that the Fathers were exaggerating as orators do, or that their words are misinterpreted. These false devotees, these proud worldly people, are greatly to be feared. They do untold harm to devotion to Our Lady. While pretending to correct abuses, they succeed only too well in turning people away from this devotion.*

Bookshelves, libraries, archives, and lecterns are centuries-deep with the apologetics of speakers and writers who wish to confine the Truth behind the iron bars of their eager intellects; each believing the world should defer to their propositions, thinking human reason somehow begins with them. It was within the One, Universal, Apostolic Church led by the near-invincible Pope John Paul II that I was brought to my mystical awakening. I am furthermore charged to never apologize to any created being for a single scintilla of my belief in everything the Church teaches, attests, proclaims, and reveals about the Kingdom of God and Our Crucified Lord. Neither am I obliged to respond to anybody who generates rationales, queries, and debates that promote their scandalous agendas in an attempt to discredit and destroy what is left of their limp faith and that of everyone with whom they come into contact, basing their arguments on distorted interpretations of Sacred Scripture. Their twisted renditions of history cannot dilute my faith in the Roman Catholic Church. My message to every theologian and apologist, Protestant or Catholic is to become humble once again! Realize that the summary effects of your revisionist history have done very little to decrease the suffering of millions around the world. Far too many illusions are conceived through the cerebral fray, men sparing over the annals of Christianity, wasting time crafting rebuttal after argument, and ignoring the Good Friday Deicide that has wiped-away the distress of God's chosen people. Realize anew that millions are still agonizing in pain, you bickering fools! The most destructive byproduct of this disturbing neo-theology is the exacerbation of selfish human pride! We are tempted to assume ourselves to be wise beyond reproach, when our study should instead help us realize our puniness before the Wisdom of the Almighty Father and our helplessness to predict His Divine intentions. He always reserves His greatest vision for people with unassuming hearts. Indeed, self-abandonment in religious discourse is required of all Christians! There is an innate difference between knowing our Faith and having sufficient faith to allow us to advance into the exterior world, altering future events by our sheer reflection of Christ's Light. What good is there in deciphering unknown mysteries if it does nothing to help us love humanity as Our Lord loved us while hanging on the Cross atop Mount Calvary? It was not His command of the Holy Scriptures or the recorded history of men that kept Him transfixed there, but His invincible Love for His tormented people. Few men are converted to Christianity by theological debate or grandiose empirical methods. Their hearts change because they suffer greatly, and are loved because they do. And, no one knows how to love more profoundly than those who sacrifice their wills to reflect the Wisdom of God.

The greatest proof of the Supremacy of the Roman Catholic Church is found in the trained intellects who are impelled to hate Her. But, why waste time trying to defeat Her? Is this what Our Lord charged them to do? Their very lives attest to the insuperable preeminence of the Catholic Church. They bash themselves to spiritual death against the Jubilee doors of this great Christian Bastion in vain attempts to vanquish Her mystical foundations. And, these poor souls would have neither the power nor the wisdom to wield it if it was ever given to them. Yet, see the vanity of their ills! Indeed, what are they fighting against? Every heretic in history claimed to be defending the truth. Those who confront Christianity with such derangement know that the Church is always immune to human slander, staunchly confronting their errant pathways and impeding them from addling humanity into accepting their misguided beliefs. They live submerged by a defeat that has already overcome them, not realizing that it is Christ they are crucifying. Thus, the Messianic prophecy is already fulfilled. And, if instant success would greet them come the morning, by evening their great jubilation would be wiped from their faces as the Immaculate Triumph would arise before their horror-filled eyes. As a Roman Catholic, I am not fighting against any one man. Instead, I proclaim what the countless, selfless, obedient Saints for the last 2,000 years have been declaring with urgency. Jesus Christ is alive again! And, the Holy Eucharist is the Communion which unites us all! Come to the Eucharist if you seek Eternal Life! Yearn to participate in the Universal Church, and receive the Most Blessed Sacrament! Indeed, what evidence can be lent to ease the suspicion of anyone not willing to invoke this faith? In all truth, it is not written on the back of their eyelids, yet it still exists within the purview of their faith. How can we teach them? They can remain in their cold, dark hatred against the Catholic Church, haunted by their plundering reaves and gnawing discontent, while God awaits their hapless whimpers to readmit them into His beatific Grace. The icy fisticuffs of our barren human condition will ultimately tender their desires for the benisons of peace and reassurance offered through the Seven Sacraments of the Original Universal Apostolic Church. There is no solid refutation or legitimate compromise that can be invoked by sinful mortals because the damage intended by those who have rebelled against the Catholic Church is truly of little worth. To their demise, these heretics are about to witness their deceived proselytes stolen from them in the blinking of an eye. Then, they will realize that they are as helpless as anyone's newborn progeny. In solitude for the first time, they will stand alone before their lecterns, gazing across a slew of empty pews, newly fallowed by the call of the Queen they have simply refused to love. And, the only thing left to hear will be the discordant echoes of their impotent legacies bouncing off the cavern walls and empty prisons cells they built for forsaken men, long since liberated by Jesus on Mount Calvary. The centuries of loathing they have heaped against the Mother of God will be consumed in one Heartbeat of the Crucified Lamb. By then, the Triumphant

Fruits of Amnesty will have never tasted so sweet. I say to you, ye adversaries and compatriots alike, no man can stop this imposing day from arriving out of the blue. It is already approaching with cataclysmic joy and hoof-beats of thunder. The Saints of the Eucharist have risen to their feet! We soon shall see worldly egos stricken like cordwood, heaved into a blast furnace, and history lanced and laid wide-open, exposing 2,000 years of the awesome bloodshed of Catholic Martyrs, reverberating the same Christian oath of allegiance that first took them to the Throne of Life. Horrified will stand the adversaries of Holy Christendom as they realize for the first time that their errors and omissions felled the hammer that nailed their Savior to the Cross. They will finally comprehend the suffering that should never have visited the innocents, the wars that would have never turned the countrysides into crimson battlefields, the diseases that would have been repelled by miraculous belief, the desperation that could have been peeled like onion skin from the faces of the lost, the consternation that should have been displaced by moral certitude, the hopes that would have supplanted their moribund doubts, the effervescent comradery that would have convalesced pitch-black despondence into daylight Easter joy, and the unity that would have triumphantly poised us for entrance into Paradise long ages before today.

Too many factions argue about things they fail to fully understand and consequences they have mercifully not yet been allowed to see. People come nearly to verbal blows about whether the Virgin Mary is the Mediatrix, Co-Redemptrix and Mother of God. If only they saw Her one time, their pitiably presumptuous arguments would be cauterized from their newly enlightened knowledge—Game-Set-and-Match! Mighty Casey may have failed at the plate during his final at bat, but the Virgin Queen of Heaven is fashioned with a poise of dignified power that will cut a swath completely across Creation, emptying the bases, much to the chagrin of those still too far away to see who has been summoned from the on-deck circle. Their first inclination that something stupendous has occurred is when they hear the heavenly stadium roar and the Communion of Saints rise to their feet in ecstatic jubilation, raising a strain of hosannas more grand than a million Mormon Tabernacle Choirs. They will then feel the pitch She just struck clocking them upside the back of the head in the deep center-field bleachers while they were gawking over the fence, yearning for an easier way for such an ill-gotten crew as themselves to get to Heaven. Yes, I have seen this Woman; and this is why I marvel in my own quandary at the sheer audacity of people who do not even know who She is or what She represents spouting blasphemous profanities against Her miraculous intercession. She has come to convert our wanting souls into the state of grace required for admittance into Paradise. She knows what God sees, that human arrogance has come to a crescendo in our day. It seems that collective humankind does not wish to take seriously the many apparitions and interior locutions of the Blessed Virgin Mary throughout the world. And, for what reason? Why manifest all the rhetorical disbelief when there is real, Pentecostal conversion now ongoing before the eyes of every man, woman and child? Where is the earth-shattering faith of our most popular theologians? Are too many of them guilty of the old charge of not seeing the forest for the trees? It would seem that they do not know they are standing deep in the woods because they are nose-to-trunk with one tree, scanning its bark with microscopic curiosity, trying to find a maverick gene that is somehow displaced in the structural DNA so they can conclude with all the misconception of sinful mortals, "This is not a real tree; and therefore, there is no forest." What utter nonsense! They think human Salvation is located under the bark where little mites live instead of realizing they are standing amidst the towering sequoias of Christian faith having been planted there throughout the ages by countless holy Martyrs, all the while being drenched by monsoons of exculpating Grace from Heaven.

The followers of Christendom are multiply divided by a vast intellectual, scholastic, theological pride and the smoke of its sophistry, especially from people who reject the Holy Roman Catholic Church and the Divine Truth that sustains Her sevenfold bulwark of Sacraments. Everyone must realize that the miraculous intercession of the Blessed Virgin Mary is the providential cure for this lamenting disease. She is the Clarity of Christianity, a spiritual doctor who cares not whether any child of God likes the taste of Her medicine, and before whose Grace and at whose feet every Pontiff in history has laid his papacy, authority and allegiance. We must match Her Immaculate Virtue with an heroic obedience of our own, dismantling the incessant debate, the arrogant fracas, and the battle of wits. To fail in this task would be the legacy of the timorous theologians who have intellectualized the Grace of Jesus Christ, stumbled helplessly over questions they did not have the faculties to ask, rent the purpose of Catholic unity, and obscured the only possibility for the peaceful evangelization of this planet. The Holy Eucharist from the Altars of the Original Apostolic Church is the pinnacle and summit of humanity-redeemed; there is no doubt in that before God or the judgment of the ages. Unless one eats the Flesh of the Son of Man and drinks His Blood, he will not have the fullness of Life within him. The Blessed Host is a living Man! Acceptance of this immutable fact is no more absurd than for men to believe that Jesus was God in human flesh standing before them 2,000 years ago. Many could not make that leap of faith back then; and we see the same today, twenty centuries later. If humanity entire stood concurrently in communion with that Perfection, every mystical charism would be resting with the bourgeoning of its presence in each of us now. But, the world is conspicuously not yet in this blessed alignment. Hence, the lightning of Divine Intercession strikes Glory amongst the children of men at the discretion of the Merciful Deliverer of Humankind. There are far too many thinkers who have allowed their curiosity about the hows and whys of God's omnipotent providence to lure them into the clutches of religious indifference, trapping them in an obstinate refusal to obey the Holy Spirit unless God personally grants them the knowledge of His means so they can organize their response at their own discretion. They are like little children sitting cross-legged on the floor of the Sistine Chapel with small boxes of eight crayons at their feet, consumed by their meticulous efforts to apply the octadic hues inside the outlined caricatures contained in their coloring books, unwitting to the fact they are being overshadowed by Michelangelo's ornate masterpiece on the ceiling quietly pining for their attention. Which do we suppose inspires the greater faith?—someone reframing what a miracle is to the last vowel and consonant, or a child of God who can actually evoke one, caring not about the how, and always trusting in the why? Intellectuals will rarely concede to the conclusions of anyone other than their peers who are birthed from their same streams of consciousness. Their personal views and shared perspectives usually determine their level of conformity. They often trumpet the need for more ecumenical cooperation, but only within the framework of their social designs, while failing to realize that filial trust comes to perfection when someone submits himself to the Will of the Holy Spirit through an abandonment founded in Jesus Christ, complying without being handed the tethers of reason which only tarnish their faith and force them to proceed on a path that has acceded to their comfort zone of compliance. Is this not the submission that a bride should proffer her groom? The true detriment to Christian faith is not witnessing a miracle that surpasses the realms of the obvious, but whether the mind will grant easement to the heart to confer with every place faith will lead. I doubt there is an intellectual alive who would have remained steadfast beneath our Savior's Cross drinking-in the Salvation of the world. That is not necessarily a value judgment, but simply a calculated, reasoned deduction based upon the analysis of present trends of empirical evidence extrapolated to the percentage of liberal academics who stand at odds with the Dogmas of the Roman Catholic Church. What does this sound like? If some of the most ill-educated people in the world have been declared the greatest Saints in the history of Christianity, how can it be true that many of those acclaimed as having advanced theological knowledge are the first to throw their weight against Our Lady's miraculous intercession in the life of a simple child who is relating paradisial genius to the best of his ability? Is fear the reason for their apprehension? Or, perhaps plenary doubts? Probably the negative exists in both cases. Why? Because arrogance is rarely afraid of anything. I believe there to be three alternative reasons.

First, most of them have spent their entire adult lives generating batteries of nuanced postulates about every spiritual perspective that they can dream up, save the enlightening focus of the Holy Spirit rendering things so mystical and miraculous. Therein, they have effectively shielded themselves from acknowledging the Truth. The weight of their pragmatic arguments and evidentiary judgments is predisposed against realms requiring their personal abandonment and highest degrees of faith. Second, they see the recipients of these charisms as being pitifully deluded victims who are not consecrated in religious disciplines, in essence in a state of abject inferiority in relation to the scope of the former's discerning intellects. This leaves God's messengers no more capable of appeasing the cerebral minefields of His adversaries than Jesus Christ, Himself. They are then left only the option of mounting the Cross in the image of their Savior. Third, and most regrettably, naysayers simply refuse to generate the love in their hearts for our Holy Mother and their brothers and sisters that would suspend the two previous excuses altogether and allow them to wholeheartedly embrace the mystical prodigies occurring before their eyes across this earthen landscape and inside nearly every culture. Is it not the depths of hypocrisy to maintain that faith is not founded upon supernatural things, yet require God to burn our suspicion to the ground with His most astounding miracles before we will believe in the august guidance bequeathed by His Immaculate Queen? There are too many highly educated people these days who are mind-deep in a crisis of faith that their souls have not even begun to fathom. And, the light inside them is concealed beneath an entire trainload of bushel baskets. They simply lack trust in the mystical powers of the Roman Catholic Church. Such are false apostles and materialistic worldlings craving the temporal spoils of their personal prestige because it is where they wield their most influence, attempting to disarm the inspirited innocents with mind-piercing queries and theological obfuscation by inundation, and pushing passive aggressive agendas that stand in diametric opposition to the Queen of Paradise. The Most Holy Virgin is their consummate superior who is readily prepared to crush every vain thought they have ever allowed to wisp through their minds. But, it seems likely they will be required to stand stark naked before the power of the Crucifixion first because their humility is not mature enough to allow them to surrender without being tossed like buckshot from their thrones. I tell you, they have already been rebuffed and decommissioned, and their tarnished crowns are bouncing like tin cans down the staircase now, rattling haphazardly across the floor of the abyss. They just feign not knowing it, hoping that somehow Our Lady's intercession is not really true. When the realization finally bursts upon them, they will wish they had taken their Rosaries in-hand and kept their egos at bay.

Sunday, March 5, 2000 (excerpt)   *5:40 p.m.*

     "I must tell you, My little children, about the caution   j(065)
*that I wish you to take in reading and listening to lengthy
dissertations from such intellectuals as social theologians and
journal-artists. Words come very easily for these people
because their vocabulary is so large. This allows them to
draw many mental images that are oftentimes not contextual
in the sense of sacrificial Christianity or of the Traditions
and Dogmas of the Original Apostolic Church. Jesus is never
difficult to perceive where He is present because Love cannot
be concealed by intellectual architecture. Therefore, please*   x
*continue to seek-out the simplicity in the writings and
expressions of others, lest you find yourself grappling for the
understanding of all the Doctors of the Church combined,
including the holy works of Saint Thomas Aquinas. The
metaphors, mental images, and poetic works must never
make you have to decipher an equation or examine a
corollary in order to discover the intrinsic Gospel message in
a particular work. Had it been the decision of God, for
example, your book could have been 1,600 pages of text with
such difficult terms and expressions that only the most highly*   xx
*intellectual could have translated its message. But, in that
sense, how could we have reached those who are still lost in
pragmatism and the superstructure of grammatical
quandaries? I again ask the world for the same simplicity
that is apparent in your Diary, not for a course in
quantitative analysis or arithmetic methods. The simple
Truth is just that—easy for the little hearts to recognize. I am
not impressed by high-flying theologies that try to render the
understanding of Love, of God, nearly unattainable to those
who need to understand the most. Remember that My*   xxx
*answer was not a rhetorical qualitative affirmation, it was
a loving 'Yes,' unconditional Love that still lives to this day.
My affirmation is a simple Fiat—Let it be done! My
children, the rest is a matter of prayer, contemplation, good
works, and public example of the service, teachings, and
Wisdom of Jesus."*

I have arrived at the conclusion over the past several years that delving into the mystical complexities of God is utterly impossible unless we master our dutiful humility and the simple virtue of surrendering ourselves to Jesus in faith, sustaining an absolute trust, and yielding to the power of the Holy Spirit within our souls. It is going to take a good deal more than offering simple lip-service to the Blessed Virgin Mary to wrest the fate of the world from the jowls of human narcissism. We must deploy an earnest devotion to Her of the magnitude of the Saints, and invoke and convoke near-stratospheric virtues for the sublime intentions of Jesus Christ to be crystalized in any meaningful way. I was somewhat worried as I transcribed my thoughts into this chapter, thinking my comments may not be accepted too charitably by my critics. However, my perspective became instantly ratified when Our Lady told me, *"Do not worry that your tone is negative. For My part, I do not believe that your writings are reprimanding enough!"* So, newly emboldened by our Blessed Mother, I continue hoping to provide an appreciation for the necessity of our obedience to the Queen of Heaven. The only redemptive response to the Virgin Mary's call is *Yes* because it reaffirms the indoctrination of our faith. The passionate conviction that vets our proclamations portends and seasons the virtuosity of our righteousness. And, our responsorial sacrifices are the outward expressions of our Christian Love. Human civilization is undergoing a modern crisis of identity right now because we are refusing to comply with the mystical purposes of God or draw upon them to capture the spiritual origins that establish us as a revolutionary lot of gestating saints atop this earthen biosphere and in the Messianic realms of the unseen world. Our Blessed Lady is the Pantheon of Mystical Grace standing at the intersection of time and Eternity, a threshold better known by the children of God as the converted human heart. And, if we pursue that universal cynosure with the simplicity and honesty of our most sanctified predecessors, we will undergo a spiritual transfiguration that will leave both the heavens and the heathens breathless in awe and tearful in thanksgiving. It is to the goal of crispening the courage of the brave-hearted warriors of Jesus Christ that I declare that we must begin to transcend the discernment of particulars through a baby step of gallant faith, recognize the potential for human conversion, embrace the authenticity of mystical charisms, sanction the sacrifice of obedience to the all-encompassing macro-revelation of the intercession of the Woman clothed with the Sun, hand the reigns of Creation back to the Savior of the world, and call humanity into formation for the triumphant culmination of our Eternal Redemption. Amidst this unfolding drama of the Book of Revelation, it would be both imprudent and unjustifiable for us to stumble around incapacitated in hand-wringing conjecture about the intentions of certain individuals and become paralyzed by the honest mistakes they might make, especially when human evangelization occurs only through our faithful submission to the Hosts of Heaven whom no mortal should question if they wish to be embraced by the Lord of Creation. Mortals will always do battle with the theoretics of other people because the latter seem to be no more than ordinary human beings who always appear overly fallible to their counterparts. But, the introduction of supernatural phenomena renders some critics and observers rather speechless at times. The miraculous Triumph of the Immaculate Heart of Mary is a manifestation that no man can simply pluck from midair. She bears a Matriarchal Divinity they cannot fully comprehend, a visionary legitimacy poised beyond reproach, a celestial authority that squelches their denials, and a paradisial beauty that can rescind the final heartbeat of any dying man. The battle of wills and surplus opinions is irrevocably denied before Her Royal Presence because She supercedes everything that has been prescribed about Her Divine Nature. She is God's Clarion Beauty bearing peace and prescience to any curious soul, and the Annunciative Surrender who towers above all that has been consigned to the volumes of literary works describing Her. And, everyone will realize it once they see this Queen in Her splendorous glory. She is the Standard-Bearer who has borne the Standard Himself into this weary world, Christ the Lord. No one needs to stand in the humiliation of defeat if only they will resign without prejudice to the Immaculate Conception who dispatches Her children as emissaries of spiritual deliverance, as we are all through the Holy Sacrament of Confirmation.

Sunday, February 18, 2001 (excerpt)   *4:17 p.m.*
   "I offer you My humble appreciation for lifting Me   k(049)
up before humankind in such a powerful way. Everything
you have said about the indifference of the theologians is
true; and all the rest of the facts which you have defined will
be equally as well received by the rest of the world. Please
allow Me to provide you a short example of how the reaction
will be. As with most anything else which touches the
human conscience, many of those about whom you have
spoken will respond with outright denial and anger at the
outset. But, in an extremely short span of time, they will   x
know that you have accurately described the world as it is.
While you have given them a simple glass of water about the
righteousness which they should be seeking, you are actually

quenching their thirst for the Truth about life. As I say, they will cry 'foul' as being accused of being part of those who deny My Queenship over the Universe for a brief period of months. They will scatter all over the Earth, claiming that you are trying to poison them. They will use terms to misconstrue your intentions, claiming that you have given them a rancid mixture of di-hydrogen oxide. And, what is that? H_2O. Yes, the very waters of holiness that they need to know their Lord and Savior in the way that He wishes them to know Him. ...Why will they describe your intentions in such a tone so that the lay-people of the Earth will not be able to understand them? Why will they accuse you of employing chemical warfare instead of humbling to their prepositions of what Love is all about? Because they are not in communion with Love when they refuse to manifest My presence throughout the world, and they know it. Do you understand what I have told you here today? ...Your character is as clean as crystal glass. That 'flapping' of which you speak is only their diversion which they will have to deploy because they will see a chasm between their position and the Truth of God's Divine Providence."

xx

xxx

We see indistinctly

How hard we try
In the world we race,
To find Life's meaning
In the troubles we face.

To define our peace
We kick and scream,
Forgetting to pray
And ceasing to dream.

In hopeless despair
Days come to us,
Their heavy facade
We mistakenly trust.

We do not see
The Guiding Love,
The Tailor of Morning,
Or the gentle Dove.

Only the dust
Of the mistrust and greed,
Entertain our vision
And make us all bleed.

For the things above
A countenance gleams,
The lightness of Spirit
And a beacon that beams.

In purpose renewed
We see these things,
Broken chains from creation
And a freedom that rings.

-Original

Section Three
The Spiritual Kingdom vs. The Secular Empire
Reestablishing the Celestial Order

"Is Rome worth one good man's life? We believed
it once. Make us believe it again. He was a soldier
of Rome. Honor him."
-from *"The Gladiator"*

The Mother of God asks whether the inhabitants of the Earth can retreat from their inordinate pursuit of material things and their insatiable desire for personal power to a stance that allows the genuine intentions of their benevolent Creator—to whom we will all someday answer—to be waxed of the eclipse their licentious shadows are casting upon them. Human egoism is feeding the imperial duplicity of contemporary societies that are tenaciously warring against one another for possession of the Earth across cultural lines, disparate traditions, genealogical heritages; and nations, religions, kingdoms, and the primitive battles for control of the streets. The solemn Truth, seismic values, ecclesial virtues, and strength of faith that gushes from the Wisdom of the Sacred Heart of Jesus Christ; that same might that has restrained history's barbaric lords of war, recast the incivility of ancient worlds, and reconfigured the destiny of human souls has been besieged by a repugnant regurgitation of disrespect, rebellious arrogance, and blasphemous immorality that spews from the rostrums of our secular governments, our platforms of entertainment, the benches of our courts, the boardrooms of our corporations, the auditoria of our universities, the editorial desks of our mass-media, the storefronts of our businesses, the classrooms of our schools, the thoroughfares of our cities, the family rooms in our homes; and sorrowfully, even the pews in our churches, the chapels of our seminaries, the motherhouses of our convents, and the chanceries of our dioceses. Talk about a prime time for the Master of the house to return! Every Catholic who walks the face of the Earth must realize that the true surety of our faith does not rest in *holding the ball,* hoping the ticks of time will expire before evil eventually pervades the existence of every living thing in sight. Our apathy toward the works of Christian evangelization is an utter, outright sinful omission. It is not within the prospectus of our commission as God's children to relinquish the obligations of the Holy Cross, surrender our good works, or postpone our charitable sacrifices to a Returning King who will undoubtedly rebuke us for not showing greater buoyancy in the wake of His Infinite Grace. If a suitable depiction would ever descend from His Celestial Kingdom, the sight of a fiery, conflagrant fortress might be quite apropos; one which is burning to the ground while those who possess its keys seem only interested in salvaging its flag for some vacuous ritual of re-staffing it on the pile of ashes where they sold their lost souls into oblivion, placating the rancor of people whose only agenda was to convince the faithful to submit to their diabolical wiles. Mortal history has nary suffered a nation that has incubated and birthed such heinous human arrogance, matched to beastly immorality, as has become the sorrowful hallmark of our Western-American culture, despite the schmaltzy verses on the inside covers of our drugstores' fancy greeting cards. People in droves are destroying their souls in lecherous labyrinths of self-ingratiation, self-glorification, lustful wish-listing, and material asset building, all the while fraudulently claiming the right to gerrymander the lay of the land according to a temporal nightmare that only a true pagan can appreciate. Then, to add insult to injury, they declare with all the gusto they can muster that not even God Himself could hold them true to any sense of common decency. Oh, how wrong these poor souls are! It is time for the Voice of Celestial Thunder to shout-forth! Moral courage has never stood so tall! Our Lady fears no man!

Sunday, June 25, 2000 (excerpt)   *4:45 p.m.*
    "All over the world today, many were reveling the   j(177)
power of the Holy Eucharist. They were stating the words of
Truth that God wishes His people to hear every day. But,
they were not taking this important message into the streets,
the casinos, the brothels, or the houses where evildoers go.
The words were comforting the ears of parishioners, servers,
cantors, and lectors, but were not piercing the obstinance of
the 485 billionaires whose souls are dead, or those who hold
the keys to prisons, or those by whose command millions
could be set free from political corruption and social   x
oppression. These are the ones who need to hear and heed
the admonishment of the Gospel of Jesus, to inherit, avow,
and live-out the legacy of the Martyrs and Saints, and to shed
their spiritual darkness by living in the Light. Again, the
Body, Blood, Soul, and Divinity of Christ is their miracle
cure. It is their transference into the jurisdiction of the King
and Monarch of God, Jesus of the Cross, from whom they will
never flee and will defend to their death. In Him, they will
make themselves naked of the Earth so He will dress them in
the nobility of Salvation. In this Jesus, they will void their   xx
own commissions of dictatorial selfishness and fall to their

knees at the sight of the first pauper who happens to glance their way. Yes, through the Blessed Sacrament, they will proclaim that they are rich in Everlasting Life instead of steeped in the vast junkyard of temporary wealth. I come on this anniversary day of the Medjugorje messages, nineteen years advanced in time, to tell you again that your journeys there were not in vain. You are still the disciples that you learned there to be. You still reflect the Truth of the messages I have offered the world from such a diminutive spot on the   xxx *Earth. I am truly grateful that you have remained at My side and inside the Sacred Heart of Jesus. I truly wish you could know how grateful God is that you are still saying Yes."*

It is an interesting phenomenon of time and human nature that remands the historical architectures of bygone ages to the nondescript realms of simple legend, while obstinate critics and wilful rogues level vicious, yet surreptitious, discord against archived civilization like corporate timber-cutters laying waste to the giant redwood trees in our sprawling national parks. Is it possible for new generations of young Americans who are disconnected by the procession of years from the early remnants of our country's evolvement to reject them as having never happened at all? Will there come a time when such historical events as Washington's crossing the Delaware River during the Revolutionary War or the harsh winter they endured at Valley Forge might be considered simply romantic fables that were, "...conjured by period actors to secure a beneficial solidarity of weak-minded people within an infant American nationalism?" Although it is too preposterous for anyone to believe such a tale either here or a thousand years from now, does it seem plausible that if the United States were ever overcome by a foreign power hostile to our cause, the invading occupiers might respond in just such a way to aggressively dissuade anyone who wished to keep the heritage of America alive, hoping to expunge the record from human memory and inhibit their rekindling loyalties? It is a principle of obfuscation often used by people wishing to skew the perception of the facts. Now, if we straightaway direct our discernment toward the parameters of our modern cultural identity, one could defensibly hypothesize, based upon the revisionist misconceptions of secularly-minded people, that there is presently a deliberate agenda to stretch our societal conscience far enough from the truth of Jesus' Passion, Death and Resurrection (and the founding of His Catholic Church) to create a plurality of relativism whereby the most disoriented people are allowed to obliterate from memory the underpinnings of decency and civil propriety that confirms a sense of piousness upon our peoples. As a parable, it is not beyond the scope of someone to presume that Wisdom demands an individual involved with our space programs who is ignorant of the principles of momentum and acceleration, or who lacks the mettle of a tested veteran, to stand aside of any calculations of liftoff and clear the seats of every flight console that will guide the trajectory of the men and women encapsulated within the cockpits of their carefully staged orbiters. Should we ever adopt a latitude based upon anything other than this high competence, there would come disasters with such frequency that heroism would surely give way to ignorance in anyone donning a flight suit to try again. If we could only accept that there are spiritual laws governing the universe that are just as unalterable and precise as the physical laws dictating the movements of celestial spheres and the atoms by which they are composed, the seats of power would be immediately vacated by those realizing they are in way over their heads, lacking the capacity to even tread such perilous waters. Any person who relegates Spiritual Truth to the wisping vapors of unholy smoke should acquaint themselves with the power of prayer pluming from the hearts of God's Christians, commingled with their burning desire for Truth that ascends from the Catholic Altars of the world. The immutable facts of unseen reality will then reignite their sense of purpose in the Sacred Heart of Jesus Christ, freeing them from the secularly mundane and escaping the sensual ingratiation they inflame with each new fanciful whim.

For whatever reason, it seems extremely difficult for people without religious faith to believe that there is a sentient Wisdom in existence that will last beyond the final day of Creation, elucidating the Truth which yields to no man's fancies. Far too often, it is those who find the sacrifices of Love too demanding and demeaning who wish to alter the timeline of the world because they dislike the synopsis authored by Our Divine Lord. They become revelers in the flagrant rudeness of life and the insensibilities of other men, casting aspersions against our spiritual footings wherever they might find them shorn of superintendence, frantically and diabolically whitewashing the canvass of our mental perception with a derangement of priorities mimicking the drudgery of history's most notorious fiends. And, in these realms of faithlessness and iniquity, they wrestle the reigns of our social conscience from the grip of true Wisdom, knocking every sense of human discretion completely onto the ground. Lo, there is not a person alive with an ounce of piety who believes that mistakes cannot be forgiven of those who have sanctified their ways. But, the unrepentance of those who love neither God nor the human family must be demolished by the full-throated annunciation of the Truth. Any order of business that imposes the overshadowing suppression of a public declaration of the authentic Kingship of Jesus Christ within the panoramic view of the purple mountain's majesty is an immoral hijacking being piloted into the foundations of America's towering future by a collection of materialistic thugs and anti-Christian nitwits bent on driving us into the same heartless abyss engulfing their languishing hearts. The manifest spiritual dignity conferred upon the inhabitants of our inalienably sacred land by heroic Christians everywhere is the stabilizing bedrock supporting the fertility of our freedom to pursue all that is defined by goodness. This cosmic sphere is the earthly portion of an unseen spiritual Kingdom of "Divinity Maximus" whereby the United States of America was conceived as a mystical province endowed with the light-bearing blessings of liberty, human dignity, and deific intellectualism that have been unsurpassed in the flushing enlightenment of man. Yet, there are too many people seen by the heavens to be recklessly conspiring against Love and the aspirations and devotions of myriads of Angels and Saints whom they have yet to meet. They mindlessly forfeit their sacred identity for an ignoble caricature of epicurean conquest and capitalistic subjugation solely for the coffers and coffins of their personal estates and pungent futures—an autumn fortune whose leaves will be scattered by the inheritance of time as they pass from their grief-stricken posterity into the eternal purview of those who loved them the most. If anyone desires to begin the inscrutable journey of beholding knowledge, memory, and the simplest truths as sacred and sure, they need a clearer understanding that peace is a flower cultivated by God within the hearts of humanity who are suffering obscure injustice and indignity in their dark huts and hovels, and in the alleyways and tenements where they reside. These spiritual giants of life's daily holocaust discover the human perfection of Jesus Christ in their outward-turning of personal sacrifice while they weather the recurrent anguish and interior loneliness that pillories their best intentions to never surrender to luxury and comfort at the expense of their earthly siblings or their highest communal values. These are the true heroes who are undying in valor and loyal in allegiance to the indivisibility of our common good as brothers and sisters in the human family, courageously holding their breathtaking profile throughout their lives and into the vaults of heavenly bliss. America must accept and defend the docile, yet fragile, civility which flourishes from such spiritual elements, the marked genius of sound character that even now electrifies the filament of our cultural definition through the engendered respect we cultivate in the clear-minded strata of our higher institutions, the trust we maintain in the morality of our office-seeking citizens, the confidence we wield in the administration of social justice always flowing from the mercy of God, and the visions we hold as sacred, having been bequeathed to us through the hallowed victimhood of our forebears, many of whom perished on anonymous battlefields to sustain the continuance of these cartels of justice before the witnessing world. This all-consuming state of grace is a mystical gift of silent cohesion dispensed by the Divine Architect of our majestic union through the inspirited intercession of previous generations of selfless countrymen, a righteous stability providentially cordoned within the stately halls of time and the humane decency of those who answered the call of the Holy Spirit to profess the dignity of every man, woman, and child in the Sacred Heart of Christ in each historical epoch. Together, they unleashed the just thunder and lightning of His Divine Righteousness in the darkest hours of their most painful eras.

Sunday, December 5, 1999 (excerpt) 3:12 p.m.

"My dear children, always remember that perfection   i(339)
and light are one and the same Love. Therefore, perfect Light is your unity with the healing Spirit of Holiness that God places in your heart when you accept Him. To be in Jesus and He in you is to also be anointed as the chosen ones of His Father. Hence, you are the radiance of the Gospel of My Son on Earth, the souls who teach and admonish both the lost and arrogant. It is not only your decision to cause others to know humility, it is your commissioned responsibility. Thank you for acknowledging your role as doctors and   x
professors of righteousness and faith. The world will be a much better place if many would call themselves to this understanding instead of plundering those who know the whole Truth about Christian piety, who are scoffed-at as indignant snobs for proclaiming what others should already know for themselves in Christ. My dear children, I have told you many times during the last ten years that the season of Advent is one of spiritual joy, anticipation, preparation, and humility. I am afraid that millions in the world, especially in the capitalist countries, have yet to comply. There is a   xx
sorrowful greed that comes along with the celebration of the Nativity of Jesus which should not be there at all. Thousands of wealthy people expend fortunes for material goods to give to those who are significant to them and try to pass it off as Christian Love. What a contradictory state of affairs! What an ignoble hypocrisy! These precious days are meant to show the world the true significance in material selflessness and

raw spiritual charity. The Advent of Christmas is wholly equal to your humble wait for the Return of the Son of Man in Glory in that same sense. How can humankind reach for the blessings and graces of Heaven if his grasp is fasted to hoards of riches? How can sinners tell God that they love Him when their mouths are either stuffed to the throat with the finest of meals or groaning to claim the paltry share which lays on the plates of the poor? How can humankind call-out for heavenly aid when he is too busy blaspheming his neighbor as being an ignorant and gullible hayseed from whom his very shoes should be taken? Is this the Spirit of Christmas that these wretches will always espouse? If so, their souls are sorrowfully bound for the fires of Hell! My children, this is why our work is so important."   xxx

xl

Let us mortalize a brief, principled description of where the United States stands before the Vision of God in these cradle days of the 21st century so the disingenuous critics of the heroic virtues of traditional Christianity may be informed by the glaring mother lode of facts. We live in a society where comedians praise God for their professional careers and hail His charity in letting them survive the consequences of their deadbeat lives to see another day; yet, they strut proudly onto spotlighted stages, beating their chests before thousands of fans to pronounce one profanity after another as though they hold dividend contracts with Satan. Entertainment executives and motion picture producers use their pseudo-artistic talents and marketing ploys to create the most realistic depictions of Hell they can possibly generate—not even close to being authentic because no one will find enjoyment in the real horrors of Gehenna—while cloaking themselves in the garment of secular America's First Amendment when confronted about the negative impact their despicable works have upon the impressionable consciences of our adolescent children. Recording companies reap financial windfalls to the tune of billions of dollars a year marketing outright sorcery to their buyers, having all but destroyed the sense of decency of a rapacious "gangsta generation" of young people who see personal humility, corporeal chastity, and parental guidance as cruel and unusual punishment and socio-religious oppression. Such postmodern swagger and sensationalism is a reprehensible legacy of throat-slashing evil before which both Martin Luther King, Jr. and Bobby Kennedy would stand arm-in-arm to denounce. And, automobile companies scatter their henchmen from sea to shining sea building dealerships that are nothing more than fences for thieves, waiting to shakedown the citizens of our country with outright lying, cheating, and stealing, whether it be in the printed media, TV voice-overs, or from their own twinkling eyes with smiles across their faces—because they possess the mode of transportation every citizen needs to remain a productive member of society. And, some of these businessmen will not surrender a solitary unit unless we prostrate oursleves to make them filthy rich. Credit card companies swim like sharks around our university campuses, licking their chops at the new schools of minnows walking through the front doors every fall, solely for the purpose of hocking the future of the next generation of new consumers. Corporate shareholders of America's restaurants are allowed to compensate employees who are living one paycheck to the next barely $3.00 an hour, leaving servers and waitresses working two additional jobs to beg for alms from their customers with the sweat of their brows for money needed to care for themselves and their families. If this is not a miscarriage of social justice, nothing is!

Immoral mega-millionaires wield so much legislative lobbying power these days that they enslave hundreds-of-thousands of paupers waiting for tokens to fall from their oily money machines. And, wealthy entrepreneurs wail cries of injustice as if they are saints being burned at the stake when conscience-driven politicians call for a modest raise in the minimum wage. For this infraction against social justice alone, the Angels of God are going to draw and quarter the legions within the American right-wing conservative movement and their selfish, egocentric accomplices—that collusive group of heartless wretches who have gone on the Congressional Record as having relentlessly opposed decent minimum wage laws for decades now, howling they will somehow wreck the financial stability of the richest folks in town. Few of these people even know what social justice is, but they will soon realize it come the day of the Lord when their souls are thrust down before those who have languished in the ghettos and slums of Calcutta and Haiti, and the stunning awareness that respect for those under their stead was among the smaller steps they were required to take! Disingenuous monarchs of capitalist regimes appeal to elected leaders for preferential treatment with apparent empathy for the plight of the citizenry in their voices in order to build conglomerates to supply public utility and energy needs, but they then *manage* the exorbitant profits gained from the American people into their own pocketbooks at the expense of modernized, state-of-the-art infrastructure maintenance and capital improvements to keep these systems running. Whereupon catastrophic failures occur—the Great Blackout of 2003—for example, forcing these CEOs to appear before inquiry panels of elected leaders with incredulous smirks on their faces, stating that they simply needed more access to the public coffers to upgrade transmission systems—the same grids that fell into dilapidated disrepair while these poker-faced charlatans reaped the profits of those companies into their personal bank accounts. Likewise, the avant garde of the technological renaissance sit without compunction on their bastardized thrones after plagiarizing to the heights of disbelief the ideas of more intelligent men, ordering the subjects of their corporate fiefdoms to scramble with shrewdness, bereft of conscience, to the farthest reaches of the marketplace as if it was their private treasure trove waiting to be tapped. Thereafter, they move with the deftness of Anatoly Karpov to control and consolidate the capitalistic machinations of cutting-edge development, higher production, and swifter distribution through clandestine manipulation negotiated within their contractual agreements and with an intent that is none other than to lock-in every other creative opportunity under their greedy auspices. They extract the oxygen from free enterprise by ruthlessly thinning the herd of competition with cold calculation, crushing any credible opposition through hostile acquisition, asset strangulation, market manipulation, predatory pricing, tax dodging, and investment collusion. Their ultimate goal is to divide the creative arena between themselves and other materialistic co-combants of their trade, those they were prohibited from leveraging only because leaders of regulatory agencies needed a rhetorical alibi for allowing a true-to-life game of Monopoly to ensue. The battle still rages among these business goliaths, the same posh aristocrats who believe that Baltic and Mediterranean avenues are the scenic thoroughfares bordering the turquoise seas of the eastern hemisphere, rather than the unkempt streets where capitalists like themselves lord over broken shanties, shaking-down our impoverished countrymen for their last few coins in scams disguised as wealth-building real estate investments. So, let the rationing begin! The intellectual and creative gifts of God are being withheld from humanity until company and community are forced by necessity, survival, or lobbied legislation to bow to the extortion of millions upon millions of dollars for things that God, Himself, has given freely to everyone alive. Upon becoming financially independent through subduing gargantuan segments of the business community who have become technologically indentured, these same moguls are seen as icons of the American dream, entitling them to seats on every national and international commission, board, governmental council and social planning committee as if possessing some grand wisdom or miraculous vision about the solvency of the rest of the world whose population has been left unemployed, starving, or ravaged by pandemic diseases in the wake of their global domination.

This, my friends, is unrestrained capitalism run amuck that America is hailing as a model before the world! And, why do I say unrestrained? Because the elected and appointed officials of our state and federal legislative and judicial systems who are commissioned with the solemn duty of protecting and preserving some sense of decency, honesty, and fairness in the United States are foundering in a worldly, materialistic mindset of "survival of the financial fittest" while simultaneously rubbing elbows with millionaires at dinner clubs, thereafter refusing to dedicate themselves to the nobler part of America by returning to their chambers with a renewed commitment to lift-up the poor who own only their stooped postures and calloused hands. And, I also say unrestrained because far too many people in ecclesial authority compromise their sacred obligations to the diabolic chimera which is showing them the facade of comradery, remaining dead silent and beyond the stir that righteousness inaugurates so they can maintain the illusion of being influential principals in the secular world. However, the question begs to be asked, influencing what? I declare; those who are becoming exorbitantly wealthy by withholding medicine, healthcare, technological advancements and gainful employment from any needy race or people until the price is right—and those who shirk their responsibilities to check such atrocities—will see the flaming inferno of Gehenna unless they change for the better. They will never be able to sustain the self-condemnation they will level against their own souls when they see the record of their lives thrust before their arrogance and cowardice at the moment of Final Judgment. The instant a hospital is forced to close its doors because it could not withstand the leeches sucking the financial life from its veins, whether they be band-aid suppliers, trial lawyers, HMOs, insurance companies, or the doctors themselves is a day earmarked for the wrath of God upon the Eternal Reckoning of the Earth. Healing the sick is not just a business proposition or career building; it is a Divine mandate issued directly from the Throne of God; and woe to those who jeopardize the stability of any organization carrying-out such a sanctified decree. And, double woe to those who grow rich under the guise of compassion for the infirm or providing for the suffering! All who have purposely or inadvertently defined themselves by these atrocities are the same echelon of infidels winning repeated lotteries of windfall government tax cuts; and we are asked to trust them to lift-up America if we continue heaping such lavish advantages upon them. All the while, budgets to teach our children to build a better world are bleeding red ink and our church collection baskets tinkle with change. The philosophy of achieving a golden age where the wealth of this nation will be piled high-enough on the tabletops of the affluent that a surplus will fall over their finely-carved edges to care for the needs of the poor and less-educated is a diabolical absurdity concocted in the bowels of the selfish "politicorp" of Hell whose day will never come. These swashbuckling rogues are spending their last days trying to rig higher stock-racks on their tables to prevent even the most minuscule fraction of their fortunes from slipping from their grasp. Hucksters—all of them!—in this materialistic age, whose crippling flashes of blasphemy and greed will soon be swept cleanly into the incinerator of time to be consumed by the oblivion of their own humiliation. Naked shall they stand with the dead carcass of their life's folly hanging in effigy like an albatross around the necks of their grief-stricken souls. America's wealthiest people, along with those aspiring to enter their courts, have desecrated the parable of the widow, blessed above all for giving her last two copper coins to God, into a nightmare of undeserved accolades showered upon themselves as great humanitarians. They take front row seats at banquet tables served in their honor in the poshest dining halls because some Americans define heroic charity as the actions of moguls surrendering the barest fractions of their empires to the highest bidders of societal prestige. People who are frantically trying to outdistance sacrificial charity through their inane pursuit of unconscionable opulence are bound to the world by their haughty selfishness, and are driving toward the smouldering depressions of Hell with the grittiness of a Tour de France champion hurtling himself down the side of a mountain towering over the European landscape. They pop their affluence, amenities, and extravagant lifestyles like flash-bulbs before anyone they believe could enhance their social and financial stature, whether it be public officials granting them leniency in complying with social ordinances affecting the competitiveness of enterprises, the hypnotized fans whose wallets they target for pilfering with their commodities and circuses of darkness, or a few struggling charities to whom they toss a little change from their petty cash funds to convince the rest of us that they are not as doomed as we know them to be. Is this judging? I am simply citing the empirical principle that if something of enormous weight is released from great heights, it will plummet to the ground and be destroyed upon impact. And, Our Lady is no chicken little! Gravity is God's parable to the wicked. Worldlings with business itineraries focused on themselves have traditionally sold false bills of goods to unsuspecting consumers in the mindset they are inflicting upon today's culture. How often do we hear of win-win agreements? These flimsy accords are the new justice that is preached like a sacred mantra by the affluent minority seeking a greater portion of the Gross National Products of the United States and every other country, starting from our Californian shorelines and traveling westward until arriving at an opposite coast graced by a towering statue with a risen torch that stands for something they know absolutely nothing about. This very economic philosophy is their deception. Win-win. Compromise. Mutual benefit. Team players. Oh, how our passions tremble with excitement at these rousing platitudes of entrepreneurial advancement; all boats rising on the benevolent tide of the same bountiful sea! Notwithstanding the courageous few who are the sprinkling of sanctity amidst the obscene, the grace to sacrifice ourselves while gaining nothing in return is conspicuously absent, AWOL as it were, from both our secular life and the syllabi of ethics that prepare our children for adulthood. Is this sacrificial nature not the very definition of Divine Love embodied within the Crucifixion of Jesus Christ? Where is human redemption if not in Him? Has this salvific ingredient become extinct within our civil democracy?

Too many people have negotiated away the eternal longevity of their divine essence by becoming black art masters indoctrinated in business rigors. Their selfish retorts are always predicated by, *What do I get in return?* until the last ounce of profit is extorted from a given prey. The win-win scenario has been inculturated within our human interaction by opportunists successfully manipulating the American economic system. Tiny children learn very quickly from their parents to never surrender any toy unless a suitable replacement is promised to be immediately forthcoming. Powerful magnates are willing to relinquish only insignificant trifles to lower economic classes of people, provided they receive immense building blocks in exchange to further bolster their overshadowing empires. The average citizen is left to gamble his entire life savings away into the hands of those who will only give him enough rope to hang himself, after which the financial vultures cast lots for his family heirlooms and the precious mementoes of his life's work as spoils at bankruptcy auctions. But, what of the poor souls who have not a dime in their pockets, a place to lay their heads, or a reputation on which someone might wager their future? The disenfranchised have nothing power brokers want or need. They are a financial trove which the wealthy would lighten from the world if given the cloak-and-dagger to transmute the conscience of society into recognizing them as having no more dignity than a helpless child in the womb of its mother. How else can one explain a grotesque public policy where one-way bus tickets are given to a city's homeless people by council fathers as a gambit to solve the problem of paupers sleeping in their alleyways and on park benches? These politicians should have been tossed in their own pokies until they paid back every ounce of dignity they stripped from these oppressed children of God. I tell you that the Almighty Father is going to place them in just such confinement, but the bars surrounding them will be of their own shame. The wise can but conclude from the record of history that the affluent will not respond to their less fortunate brethren for anything less than an advantageous dividend in return. But, to soothe any pangs of guilt that have yet to be squelched, and to cook the books before anyone might have a chance to audit their characters, they offer little more than knowing nods at major charities and expect those who are doing the true works of God to see them as magnanimous benefactors for dispensing breadcrumbs from the factories they have built by hornswoggling every advantage possible from their capitalistic plans. Our American culture is indoctrinating droves of men and women to become nothing more than pathological liars in their marketing schemes, then setting them out to saturate the marketplace like leeches, fanatically consumed with surveying the nebulous reflections of worldly circumstances and plotting the demise of the perceptions of the masses to the advantage of their own financial and political prosperity, and to the detriment of those who would dare compete with them. They are thieves of the Truth who sell their chimerical fantasies as the prevailing vision of reality, and hide their true motivations behind claims that are as shorn of honesty as the novelties they are peddling. Snake oil, indeed! The foundations of their reasoning are so pervaded by self-interest, all to the obscurity of fraternal love, that absent of Christian admonishment, they have come to believe their haughty will and material prosperity proceeds from the divine ordination of God, Himself. As it currently exists in the United States, our capitalist democracy will function to the benefit of mankind *only* after those who are elected or installed to plot our courses, forward our ideals, and elevate our dreams are committed to an outspoken sense of decency and compassion toward the least among us. Yes, even at the expense of the rich, whether it be through taxing their hoarded caches of wealth, conscience-driven tithing of their own, or outright surrender of their talent, time, and treasure in a voluntary desire for the Kingdom of God to come to Earth; and even if they have to become beggars themselves for it to happen. You see, the Christianity that Jesus professes is the adversary of profiteering, materialism, and flesh-based addiction. The United States is articulating its definition before the eternal ages; yet, broken and naked in shame do we stand before the celestial Hosts.

At last count, some 74% of the wealth of the United States is owned by ten percent of the population, with the top one percent claiming 42% of the overall total. In other words, 90% of the people in our country are expected to survive, prosper, grow their own opportunities, and charitably help the rest of the impoverished world by dividing the remaining 26% percent of the entire wealth of the United States of America. Yet, some fiscal conservatives in our national government believed that the ten percent who already own 74% of this nation's assets are entitled to nearly a trillion dollars additional wealth through the restructuring of our tax system during the presidency of George W. Bush. And, do not make the mistake of concluding that I am a Democrat, as if there is only one other legitimate direction to look. I am a Roman Catholic, the highest and most noble of all persuasions before God! How much advantage and to what degree of absurd enrichment does the electorate of the United States have to heap upon this nation's cultural elite? Now hear this!—Jesus Christ says that we will be judged not by the amount we have given, but by the surplus we retain for ourselves. This alone is the meaning of Sacred Scripture and the Life of Wisdom Incarnate by which we will be weighed, measured and deemed worthy, and ultimately pronounce Eternity upon ourselves! There are homeless paupers who have given more to the Kingdom of God in one day than the entire lineage of this world's titans have deferred to the heavens during the last ten-thousand years. Anyone who is in communion with the wisdom of Jesus Christ knows to the depths of their soul what Saint James said in AD 1: *As for you, you rich, weep and wail over your impending miseries. Your wealth has rotted, your fine wardrobe has grown moth-eaten, your gold and silver have corroded, and their corrosion will be a testament against you; it will devour your flesh like a fire. See what you have stored up for yourselves against the last days. Here, crying aloud, are the wages you withheld from the farmhands who harvested your fields. The cries of the harvesters have reached the ears of the Lord of hosts. You lived in wanton luxury on the earth; you fattened yourselves for the day of slaughter. You condemned, even killed, the just man; he does not resist you* (James 5:1-6). And, this brief montage of outright moral depravity is only the beginning! Why are these indignities and outrages still flourishing in America and around the globe? Because humanity is rejecting the intercession of the Crucified Messiah and every palpable scenario of Eternal Wisdom He taught, leaving our culture more worse for the wear by the day. Need I risk being labeled an eccentric zealot should I continue for several dozen more pages, delving further into the facts and effects of the sins that are ravaging the lives of our countrymen and flying in the face of our Almighty God? Let me add a couple more *shining examples*—as my father would say. I recently went in search of a newer "used" car because the one I was driving had accrued well over 100,000 miles and was becoming somewhat undependable and too expensive to repair. I located one that suited my purposes through an advertisement on the world wide web that stated a given price in bold relief. Upon contacting the dealer and making arrangements to purchase the car, I traveled nearly 400 miles to the site and sifted through the minefield of documents to affix my signature, most of which were for the purpose of freeing the dealer from any reasonable liability for any illicit conduct he could possibly perpetrate in his business affairs. Then, with the deftness of a swindler—and a smile on his face—the dealer's finance officer casually demanded the addition of a 10% add-back atop the original price listed in bold print on their online advertisement. I immediately challenged the man about his brazen fraud and deception. He left the room and returned with the used car manager who, in a moment of strange honesty and without embarrassment, tried to justify himself by saying that these types of marketing techniques are the industry's standard—"*I personally wrote the ad, and I admit that it is deceptive. And, it is probably immoral and unethical; but it is not illegal. Everybody is doing it, so we have to do it to stay in business.*" When speaking later with the owner of the business, he admitted to being a millionaire and that he had been sued before for this very practice, and had won every case—saved by fine print verbiage and number juggling that neither a Philadelphia barrister nor an Einsteinian physicist could have deciphered. I am not singling-out for derision those who sell modes of transportation to this country's citizens; rather, I am defining what is presently ongoing at nearly every level of our capitalist society, where profits are being made at the expense of morality and ethics. Why have the attorneys general of the sovereign states allowed such predators to define our cultural landscape? Why must the buyer always beware? Why have our legislators permitted our land to be cannibalized by shameless businessmen and women who are seeking only self-enrichment? Why?—Because they also lack the vision of the Truth and the courage to fight the good fight for the sake of personal honesty. I ask rhetorically—*how did* the ten percent of the population of the United States end up stuffing 74% of the assets of our nation into their own bank accounts? As the former governor from New York State, Mario Cuomo, said in 1992 on a podium beneath the glaring lights of the nation's prime-time television cameras and cheering throngs—*How did it happen?!*

In another case in point, an elected representative of the 2004 Illinois General Assembly was approached by one of his constituents and asked to sponsor legislation against the onslaught of outrageous credit card fees and the deception by which financial institutions are reducing grace periods and altering business practices to the public he represents. He responded with a rhetorical reminder to his gentleman caller that the banking lobby is very powerful in the state, and there was very little he could do. I wish now to read to you the "fine-print" captioning his character—*there is nothing that I am willing to do because my sense of ethical decency was purchased by the rich a long time ago, and I am willing to crucify the Truth in order to be allowed to maintain my seat in a representative's office of the State of Illinois.* As some of our less polished citizens might say, "Now THAT is po' leadership." However, with a municipal water tower thrown-in as a consolation prize, the machine roles on to syphon the sweat of even more poor people's brows. The rich and powerful have created the near perfect storm in the vacuous atmosphere of their gaunt moral ethics. And, wealthy media giants have all but purged themselves of any Christian conscience that might be construed as a virtuous element in their broadcast reports. They are quick to pontificate that they are a secular medium, as if in doing so they can recuse themselves of any social or moral obligation. In truthful terms, they simply mean that they are no more than modern-day procurators washing their hands of the Truth of the same Jesus Christ whom they continue to crucify, admittedly scorning high-principled rectitude by choosing instead to become inebriated by the baselessness of relativism, the domain of every wretched abomination that has reared its hissing head in past generations. They effectuate scant standards of spiritual justice and moral attribution among their partisan ranks. All that remains is their chronic desire for the arousal of rancorous social drama for the sole purpose of selling their commodity to the common masses, peddling in daily increments the pretense that they are augmenting healthful public debate—a discussion in which they rarely allow Jesus Christ and over 2,000 years of His moral Wisdom to have a voice. In the course of human history, media reporting has descended into a pitiable state of "yellow journalism," whereby people of journalistic influence abused their God-given venue by manipulating the public through illicit rhetoric for personal, financial and institutional gain. Very little seems to have changed today as we watch the morality of their literary successors plummet into a dismal abyss that will long be remembered as the days of "Black Journalism." These lost men and women are defining and inflicting a condemning, immoral vision upon the American culture that is undeniably absent of beatific Light, entirely vacant of virtue, and wholly disinterested in becoming a unifying catalyst for a worldwide population of righteous people. And, the future of our blessed nation stands directly in the path of their blathering torrent. Their self-subscribed legacy will be a telling one henceforth because there can be no hiding behind the self-proclaimed, self-aggrandizing title of "guardians of the public discourse" or the alleged inoculating expressive liberties of the First Amendment of the United States Constitution. Politics is their god, sensationalism is their passion, and money is their motivation. They are exhibiting nary a single value with the power and resiliency to advance the greatest days of a truly unified American democracy seated on the throne of sound moral principles. Some media conglomerates and the staffers who pack their newsrooms are co-conspirators of immorality, are amoral at best, and are imposters before the rigors of social virtue. They are lying to themselves for allowing the hallowed standards of journalistic ethics and common decency to slide into such dire corruption and be pilfered by a carefully crafted campaign of loathing toward the magnanimous faith and spiritual super-dynamics of a republic as great as the United States of America, leaving men and women of their ilk helpless before the moral conflict that is still ravaging the sublimity of our national cohesion. Let there be no mistake about it—righteousness based upon the foundations of religious sanctity and personal piety which have been hewn into the bedrock of human civilization by the sacrificial sweat and blood of the recurring generations of moral giants will come into season again in the veins of the progenies of our time and space; and they will rise and condemn with full-throated acclamation this miserable epoch of prickly derision. The moral vision of our countrymen will come into clearer focus, and the minions of these days will be convicted based upon the horrific fruits that fall with a splat from the trees of their life's work, the daily historical record published by their literary sleight-of-hand, a self-inscribed legacy of damnation to serve as the stenographer's proof in the Eternal Court, finally indicting them for who they really are. No one has yet been able to bring to the fore the glaring conflicts-of-interest by which they work, prosper and flourish—profiting financially with utter self-interest, sensationalizing for the sake of a neoteric Pulitzer prize, consciously tailoring the public discourse with personal biases absent of moral Truth, according to whatever stories will titillate their readership, while hiding behind the outrageous claim that they could not possibly be accused of overt bias in their recounting of factual events. Their delusion and hypocrisy know no bounds because, in all truth, if they were to be presented with a public servant attempting to sell such a fabrication, they would indignantly and unilaterally decide that he was no longer worthy of public credibility and would effect their sworn duty of impugning his character through every venue at their disposal. And, this by the way, happens to be a collation of multi-million dollar data collection machines owned by corporate elitists who canvass the households of specific regions to "scientifically" coerce everyone else to see the status of the world as they envision it. They pose sound-bite questions out-of-context and reframe existing conditions to suit their headlines, and then ask an ill-informed public to provide knee-jerk reactions to them. If any public politician were to begin functioning by their model of business or methodology of social science, his character would be shredded to pieces before the sun set that day for the very inconsistencies of which they are equally as guilty. Irony has it that they not only own the venue by which they should be reciprocally pilloried, but they also control the public discourse of the citizenry who could provide an ethical check-and-balance to their maverick propaganda, if only they really understood the balance of power. The American media are a renegade monstrosity of duplicitous evil and sinister works. Yet, it is the honorable servants of ages past who will soon rise in union with the laudable defenders of our sanctified future to crush their tawdry repugnance from both ends of history like a vise, expunging their memories and futile works from the finished choreography of the newly created Earth.

Indeed, the days of "Black Journalism" are here! The darkness of an entire profession's bequest has brought the midnight trauma of illegitimacy upon the character of our nation. And, from this eclipsed station, those who aspire to serve the public trust must procure the only platform available for communicating with the people enmasse. Outlandish profits are extorted during every election cycle from these candidates by media corporations that are hostile to moral Truth and social fairness. Such fortunes are demanded in order to obtain the simplest opportunity to appeal to a collective nation of people with the hope of inspiring them to follow a better course. The presidents of these media giants believe they own the airwaves of the people, and thus our private consciences, too! And, as the storm rages—where does one secure the resources for such an opportunity? Yes, from the wealthy again, those who are themselves lost in the same darkness and mad pursuit of blind materialism, and who refuse to bestow any monetary blessing upon someone else without the latter compromising his priorities, and promising future surpluses to his benefactors. Does anybody really believe that a candidate is going to receive substantial funds from an institution if they promise to sponsor formal legislation to stop the corruption spewing from those same corporations chaired by the very executives beside whom they are seated at country clubs and the head tables of civic events? As I say, it is a perfect storm because the high-flying fiscal stewards who are subjugating the poor more seductively every day will cede to nothing short of wide-scale public insurgence against them, which seems unlikely, because the media watchdogs have been thrown a juicy steak by those who butter their bread to distract them from the tenets of true nobility and the spirit of the public law. Media conglomerates will not defend the moral interests of ordinary people because the Truth conflicts with the personal worldview they adopted from the segment of society that abandoned popular piety ages ago, and from whom they continue to receive financial windfalls. In concert with them, government officials have surrendered their own nobility and propriety by climbing into bed with unfettered evil for the sake of capturing funds for transfer into the pockets of the mass media in order to get themselves elected. And, strangely enough, our religious leaders simply don't want to become involved for fear of creating a stir that would cause the reprobates to retaliate by revoking their tax-exempt status! Can we finally understand why our Lord and Savior stood in the midst of them all, bellowing of white-washed tombs? My friends, just as a hurricane gains strength from the ocean's waters as it proceeds across its surface, this unabashed onslaught which is always demeaning to our national character fuels the surge against the fabric of our lands! Moral truth is rarely given a voice because it does not ensure a profit, either financially or in social prestige! The only result yielded by compromising with evil is the loss of that portion of our dignity we surrender to placate it. And, this daily diminution which has been ongoing for the past 50 years has rendered the whole of humanity more impoverished, and headed without recourse toward certain destruction.

Sunday, November 14, 2004   *3:28 p.m.*
Saint Lawrence O'Toole of Ireland [1128-1180]
        "Jesus sees every microscopic fiber of morality and   *n(319)*
goodness inside your mortal souls, little children; and like the
mustard seed, He helps them grow in you so that you become
the giants of sainthood that God has always wished you to

*be. I speak to you today with great hope that humanity
everywhere will heed the call of the Holy Spirit to receive
openly and willfully the Grace which has become your
sustenance on the Earth and the Love of Jesus that is your
strength during times of trouble. We pray together that the
righteousness about which you speak on occasion will also
continue to flourish on a societal basis so that nations and
continents will accept that transformation which is the call
of holiness. I ask you to never surrender to the grudgingly
pale babbling of relativism that is trying to take your faith
away. Ignore the call for allegiance to any persuasion of
politics because you owe no loyalty to any authority other
than God. Remember that there are many seasons in the
world that historically come and go—a time to live and a
time to die, a time to reap and a time to sow, a time for
mourning and a time for dancing. You must know that the
Mother of God is telling you now that this is the crucial time
in human history when pious people everywhere must band
together beneath the Holy Cross and defend the Sacred
Scriptures, even unto your deaths. Pay no mind to the
radicals who say that a certain gender is worthy of a pagan
movement of equal rights. Denounce those who proclaim
that abortion is not a mortal sin. Heap much pressure on
public figures who are calling for the social acceptance of
lesbianism and homosexuality—for these are the workings of
evil. Collect your consciences inside the Most Sacred Heart
of Jesus and He will protect them there, He will give you the
Wisdom you need to see past the prevailing winds of
sacrilege that are attempting to keep your piety down. Jesus
has given you to Me as My holy children. I will not abandon
My children to the wretches who are trying to take you down
errant pathways, away from the purity and sanctity that you
have gained in Jesus. I will protect you from harm if you
will remain steadfast in prayer with Me for the conversion of
lost sinners, for even these sinners must be told the Truth
before the last day is done. I wish for you to accomplish this,
My children, lest they be lost! Remain in prayer and
meditation. Pray the Holy Rosary every day.*

x

xx

xxx

xl

Today, I wish to also set your sights on the great Saints who have gone before you. This is the month of November, a time when you should especially call upon the deceased who have risen again in Jesus to be your intercessors. Soon, you will enter the Season of Advent once again and the arrival of another new year. Can you not see that time is passing-by very quickly now? It is inexorably marching toward that Final Battle that will end the ages and present to humanity that most crucial opportunity for everyone to return to the fold of the blessed. These are not just passing days in a perpetual world of endless time, they are critical times during which you must pray for God's help. Ponder the contributions of the generations before you, those who have continued to build-up the Mystical Body of Christ on the Earth. Give yourselves the opportunity to be one with them across the chasm between time and Eternity by remaining in unity with the Apostolic Church. You already know that mortality does not end human life, it only changes it. The continuation of the goodness and propriety that you begin here will not conclude here. Therefore, be careful to choose the pathways of righteous accord. Never mind how you may be chastised by those who do not believe in God. Ignore the crowds who scoff at you for your allegiance to Jesus Christ. Lend no ear to the enemies of the Holy Cross in which humanity has gained Eternal Salvation. You are the people of God now! You are the maintainers of Justice around the globe. You are the visionaries who have blazed new pathways of peace where pagans everywhere have denounced your faith as a signal of weakness. Your faith has already destroyed them! By that same faith, you have already been saved. And, through your suffering, so have the souls of the enemies of God been bleached and cleansed of the corruption that would have otherwise kept them from seeing the Face of God and the Light of Paradise.

Your Mother is asking you to give the millions who do not know God an opportunity to greet Him and know Him in you. Walk with your spirits so aloft that the many

l

lx

lxx

who pine for a morsel of your righteousness will need to look   lxxx
upward for their reward. Be the peacemakers that Jesus has
asked you to be by defeating His enemies with your kindness.
Hold your souls next to the Flame of Righteousness and see
that Good Grace emanating from you. Do you remember
that your Immaculate Mother has promised that, someday,
all those who wonder why you are so happy to be Christians
will eventually envy you? This time has come. Yes, the
world is changing by virtue of the demand for change that
has grown from the conscience of Christians around the
world. I assure you that you hear of change for the sake of   xc
holiness because new voices are being heard for the
recapturing of purity and Light. This has nothing to do with
borders of nations, politics, elections or who is fortunate to
live in the most prominent white house. It is the inner-spirit
of a collective humanity who has decided that it has seen
enough of the perversion of the Gospel of Jesus Christ.
Roman Catholics around the globe must lift-up the Papacy
to the nations as the example of human perfection on the
Earth. All Revelation and Truth comes from the Roman
Catholic Church. When God says 'Be now My vision,' He is   c
saying 'Be now My Roman Catholics!' Strength for your
journey comes from the Most Blessed Sacrament. Wisdom
and power are given to you when you receive the Holy
Eucharist in Communion. It has been said that no state or
people own the Truth of God. However, the Truth of God is
revealed to humanity through the Roman Catholic Church.
Should anyone on the Earth wish to place their soul closest to
the hearth and Heart of their Living God, they must come to
the Roman Catholic Church. There, they will be warmed in
spirit and given the Wisdom to know that miracle of Vision   cx
which was given to humanity when Jesus Ascended into
Heaven. Do not shy away from proclaiming everything I
have told you today to anyone who will hear. To those who
will not, pray that God will have Mercy upon their wretched
souls..."

And, lastly, this example describing why we have yet to become our truest selves, while apologizing to my readers' good patience. The books I have written do not arrive on the bookshelf unscathed by the unmitigated greed bred within our capitalistic democracy or the pallid censorship of modern critics who believe they know God better than anyone else. Both of these forces serve to the detriment of the pious prospering of the Truth of the Holy Gospel of Christianity, especially through the intercession of the Most Blessed Virgin Mary. In what ways (?), one might ponder. Most of you were asked to donate a sum upwards of sixteen to eighteen dollars for any one of the books heretofore published by The Morning Star of Our Lord, Inc., even though neither the Heavenly Hosts who dispensed them nor the authors who inscribed the words have garnered any financial compensation or benefit. Over 80% of the cover price is expended to finance the private interests of companies who are motivated by factors other than the spiritual renewal of humanity. And, if publishing services were to have been contracted from a secular corporation, over 95% of the cost would have been transferred into the coffers of people who have absolutely no interest in Jesus Christ whatsoever, and then only after their employees made advance editorial revisions to the content of our manuscripts to enhance their profit margins. The Christological Gospel is not materially profitable, nor will the Christian message be changed through the existence of time. Therefore, it will always be shunned by opportunists who spree toward a lesser destiny for humankind. And, to add insult to injury, it has too often been discovered that when the Holy Spirit deigns to deliver an authentic message to the people of the Earth, especially through the prophetically miraculous intercession of the Queen of Paradise, God rarely finds any response when He knocks on the doors of religious newspapers, sectarian publications, local chanceries, retail bookstores, media outlets, local parish councils, or private devotional centers, not to mention facing the unapologetic rejection by most Protestant-affiliated stationers who often cringe at the mere utterance of the Blessed Virgin Mary's name because it sounds too Roman Catholic. Oh, the number of times I have heard, *"We don't do Mary here!"* Yet, God still asks His Queen of Peace to extend direct supernatural assistance through avenues such as the book, *White Collar Witch Hunt - The Catholic Priesthood Under Siege*, which was placed in print at the Catholic Church's critical hours of derision during the clergy crisis of 2002-2003, a manuscript provided through the intercession of the angels at Our Lady's behest. I must modestly say that it is a work filled with the awesome enlightenment of the Spirit of the Almighty Father which was petitioned, envisioned, crafted, dictated, penned, published and printed in a mere eight week period as a conscience-rousing clarion meant to bolster and defend the dignity of the Roman Catholic priesthood and stem the tide of the enemies of the Church who provoked the historically unprecedented onslaught against our sacramentally-robed benefactors. The Queen of Heaven desired to quell the disingenuous hostilities of raw secular exploitation toward the foundational Hierarchy of Christianity. But, alas, while She called over 300 such religious institutions across the United States for support in defending the priesthood through this work, the number of respondents was pitiable! Entertaining angels unaware, indeed! Does God see this missed opportunity as being caused by the same temporal intellectuals who have drummed our hearts almost spiritless with the tired mantra that it makes little difference whether we respond to the miraculous intercession of the Queen of Heaven? Conversely, a shining glimmer came from the body of Cardinals, Bishops and parish priests who received complimentary copies. Dozens upon dozens of them responded, many in handwriting, which is a prudent measure in itself, because if they had personally done anything more, they would have been accused of being in selfish denial for supporting a work written in unabashed defense of their dignity at such a crucial period of perceived culpability. Our Lady asked, *"Where were the rest?"*

Sunday, June 20, 1999   *2:39 p.m.*

"My dear beautiful children, the greatest joy that a   *i(171)*
soul can ever know is found in the Sacred depths of the Holy Mysteries; Father, Son, and Holy Spirit, and the fruits they bear your spirit upon your acceptance of them in your heart. If the world is, indeed, to be made anew, the grainy sands of mortal indifference must become replaced by the glistening nobility of a new Creation in perfection. No other generation has held the countless folds of opportunities for conversion than does this one. You are a modern-day society, indeed, an impressionable world who is at the brink of leaping into a   *x*
new millennium with only a sparse amount of human dignity remaining. The sadness lies herein because the human family has procured this awful status on its own. God has come-down from Heaven to rescue you, the Christ has died for your Redemption! My children, My Special one, this is the news that you are reveling throughout the mountain valleys and hilltops as this Twentieth Century approaches its terrible end. Peace does not come from bombs blasting in air, but Love infused into hearts! The sound of

peace is Peace, itself! It can never be forced or coerced.   xx
Suffering can still continue under an artificial peace, the
horrors of oppression driven underground. But, if the true
Peace of Divinity is allowed a chance to blossom from the
same bowels which grow the wretchedness, the cultivation of
change will come from within. That is why the Paraclete is
not detectible to the human eye. Only His fruits can be
physically discerned! The Spirit of God is the Maker of true
Peace because it is a change that emits from the core of the
human soul. That is what My Son meant when He first
spoke of the new Creation on Earth, the rebirth of holiness   xxx
and perfection in a humanity who has already been born.
Your fall from Paradise was not so cumbersome that it would
impede your ability to take Jesus' hand and climb back to the
top. God has known all along that your souls are too
precious to remain as fodder for the grave. Your Savior has
told you that personally. If any single child of Christian
faith will honestly accept the Promise of Salvation, their life
will immediately become a new beginning instead of a
wayward end. Light is the vision of your souls! The
darkness on Earth is not God, but where the Son of God has   xl
found you. The Holy Cross is your first and last step toward
Paradise. They exist simultaneously in one Crucified Savior!
The only Begotten Son of God is, likewise, the same Son of
Man who has lived and died to retract, destroy, expunge, and
erase human sins! How can anyone live more perfectly than
that? How can benevolence and Mercy be more clearly
defined? I am the Blessed Virgin Mary, your Immaculate
Mother and Queen of Love. I have brought you to the joy of
recognizing your new life in My Son because My Love for
you is as large as Creation, itself. Jesus is the reason for your   l
anticipation and ecstasy! Give Him your joy! Show Him
how happy you are to be one in Him! He is standing at the
doorway of your own Redemption to receive you, ready to
acknowledge the ways that you are pouring-out your love
upon the Earth in His Holy Name. This is Father's Day on
the Earth and in Heaven. Your Almighty God is your

resplendent Father every day!   The Son who is your Salvation is the Host from the Altar who has invited you to the Eternal Banquet Table in Heaven. Please, allow no one to decline this offer! Make kings of all men and warriors of cowards by leading them to the Altar of perfect contrition! That is where true power lies, upon the holy and sacred Altar of Sacrifice, not in missile silos or on projection screens, not in sartorial beauty or in financial success. The first will be last, and many who are last will be first! This day is one of recollection and prophecy, one of fulfillment and new direction. My Special son, this is the hope with which your Father in Heaven wishes mankind to live! Thank you for allowing Me to share it with you!"

lx

There is not a creature, commonwealth, company or camaraderie that can be recklessly gutted of its Christian spiritual identity and remain standing to any benefactoral use or lasting legacy. Secular societies foster no religious tenets or ethical values, and nothing principled, sacred or spiritual; and certainly no tenor in which one might enshrine the stabilizing virtues through the diversity of life. But, this is exactly what is being manifested in the oligarchic menagerie of our elected government, the mass-media, and the incumbency of corporate kings; a treble conjunction of insanity who adroitly sacrifice the sacred Truth to the financial deity on the altars of materialistic capitalism. If the Communist-Socialist atheism that God so disdains was one horn of the beast, secular Capitalism is another. When there exists a lacking in conviction for moral goodness, there is downright anti-conviction. Where there are no spiritual values, there flourishes turbulent anti-values. Should there be no religious faith, there will be anti-religion and anti-faith. And, where there is no Christ, there will arise the Antichrist. No one should ever believe that a peaceful void exists between these diametric poles or a buffer zone where someone's conscience can rest in a fainthearted malaise to wait out the clash of Heaven and Earth. Those who refuse to ensoul Love as the motivating power of their existence have no love at all, and certainly no eternal being, which renders them incapable of passing through the Gate of Paradise until they do. The secular architects of modern democracy whose hedonist mindset festers in our lecture halls of higher education and the law schools of our republic, those who have altogether abandoned their measured faith and personal nobility to the ghastly license of ill-will, are fashioning historical epilogues that are godless and undignified; defined by greed, perversion, agony, and death, along with a clandestine hellbroth of immorality that is simmering in the brewing pot of their collective angst, a potion they hope to serve to humankind in crystal champagne glasses, giddily beckoning us to toast their sophisticated "enlightenment." Vast and widespread are the venues from whence the Universal Truth would have otherwise flourished, having instead been mortally stricken mid-bound in their fairest moment of grace, fatally field-dressed for the devouring contagium of hellish perdition, their once elegant purposes disemboweled of their noble essence, quartered and flung into the remote dungeons of self-interest, plundered by an imposter named *relativism* whose fluctuating darkness has draped an insidious pall of glaring blindness across the barren fields where our pious inspirations once grew, never again proffering the warming solace or guiding light that would awaken the slumbering human spirit, inescapably bestowing no redemptive absolution upon any wearied or broken soul. In the vile social excrement of the spiritual wasteland evacuated by the worldly potentates of the secular American empire lies the consecrated breastpins of holiness that we once pined to affix to the lapels of their beatific achievements and benign comportment. History's room of tears presented a sartorial vestment of American liberty to a legion of visionary conventioners who saw fit to clad our blooming chrysalis of diverse origins with a hope the ancients had never conceived, paternally knitting us into their dreams of a common destiny despite their monarchial subjugators. But, God's expansive raiment that was woven for the christening of a new nation conceived with righteousness and endowed with the indispensable gifts of its Divine Creator has been all but rent from the bearing of her contemporary constitution, monomaniacally tossed to the material, the mediocre and the mundane with flagrant disregard for the moral trust; in horror wallowing, the pristine image of our sacred birthright lays like a tattered rag in the septic latrine where our timeless honor has been passed from our consciences to the outright profane. Witness the supernal banner of our holy race heaved face-down into the noxious effluent of freedom shorn of compunction, licensed to licentiousness, choosing death over life and lust above chastity, perverted in defiance with ignominy prevailing over a luminous prosperity bestowed degrees above any other age, left there to endure the plundering abuse of an irreligious band of moral cowards and profiteering vagabonds whose spiritual chambers whistle the winter nightmare of an interior greatness that never materialized in their futile pursuit of tangible possessions, frozen in time and relegated to death, locked in an oblivion bereft of Eternity, a stricken fatality of triumphant nature lost without ambulatory grace, terrified in the shadow of the Cross, much too blind to bask in Creation's Original Light, in retreat before the heroic demands of a bedazzling faith, abdicating the formidable responsibility of their imperial thrones, and snubbing the humble conquest of the inspiring peaks of charitable grandeur that would ratify their reason for being. Yes, these imperialists are far too busy numbing their senses, enchained as prisoners to their fleshy passions, utterly unfazed by the stipulations of mercy and forgiveness, ignorant of the Eternal Reckoning, pursuing profits in the deceitful mastery of their hollow domains, awash in insidious guile, perpetrating a mockery of the venerable course the Holy Spirit pleads for them to entrain, codifying abhorrent self-serving ethics into the societal order, and clawing like wild beasts to every summit of power, prestige, and perversity that a rogue capitalistic state could generate to assuage their luxuria and greed for dominion over their fellow man. And, their pinnacle defiance of honesty at each tick of the clock in every jet-setting time zone of the Earth is the tolling extermination of any august moral sense they might have ever hoped to achieve, an ominous death knell of their inevitable judgment before the Throne of God—were it not for the miraculous intercession of Heaven's Queen which is about to reach the heart of the child She knows each of them to truly be. What a revealing day this is!

Sunday, June 27, 1999 (excerpt)   *3:20 p.m.*

    "My very precious little children, since this is the age   i(178)
of the spiritual enlightenment of man, Holy is the Spirit, and you are the men! I bring you the Divine embrace of Heaven to cause your souls to stir in victory and peace. Indeed, through all you have seen from God and have done for Jesus, can victory be far behind? The offing is brimming with shouts of gladness and affirmation. Yours is the Wisdom to know the Face of Almighty God in Heaven. The justice for which you seek rests not on the mortal road, but in the Holy Spirit of purity and redemption. I have told you on many   x
occasions that your holiness is a fruit of your obedience to your Mother. My little children, that same obedience is a fruit of your desire for the Salvation of all souls. That, My children, is true nobility. That is the essence of your lives, the intentions of your prayers, and the thesis of your Diary. How can a nation and world be so blessed as to receive the good works of your hands? Because the Mother of all humanity has given you the opportunity to be transformed into the image and likeness of My perfect Son. You are living amidst the days of a beautiful summer season. The   xx
Earth is abloom and the colors abound with the genius of

God. You find yourselves in that same growth of freshness.
Your souls are not wintery still or tethered to the bitterness of
plight or dissension. You have knowledge of these things
because it is natural for you to be 'little christs' on the Earth.
In Him, you have the capacity to grow to unparalleled
heights of divinity. The perfection of Heaven is, indeed, as
immeasurable and invincible as Love, itself. Where are your
hearts? Like the Father, the Son, and the Holy Spirit, they
are in Heaven and on Earth, beseeching the sleeping world
to awaken from their hibernative slumber, seeking them to
rise to the occasion of this modern-day opportunity to be
transported with you into the miraculous Grace heretofore
known only to the Saints. This is an age that knows no
boundaries. This is the time during which every man and
woman should place that blooming spring in their step and
walk with both pride and confidence to the corridor of
conversion. As has been made clear to the world, the time
for perfect piety is now, for all the gold in the world could
not purchase a day lost without the blessing of the Christian
conscience. My children, the world-over is restless, but is still
asleep in sin! The excruciating pain of rebellion is rocking
societies to the foundations of their heritage. Hatred is
pillaging the most innocent of hearts. And yet, they do not
dare to dream of a Paradise to come because they cannot
seem to wake from the nightmare that they call mortal life.
This does not have to remain as it is. The twenty-first
century world cannot bear the strain that has come only from
its own plundering. Human hearts are vast, barren
wastelands instead of blooming flowerbeds of justice and
reconciliation. Together, we have set-out to change this
terrible course of sadness, despair and desolation. Then, the
guilty will be filled with a new regret that will be difficult
for them to overcome. I tell you today, My children, that
simple forgiveness can conquer any guilt or regret. When
you pardon the transgressions of the penitent, all of the
hard-rock walls of impudence will come crashing to the
ground and, when the dust of holy cultivation clears, will

xxx

xl

l

reveal the wide-open skies that give-way to the horizon of a seamless union between the Son of your Almighty Father and the children whom He has come to redeem. Indifference is an unwholesome virus that has congested the thinking of an otherwise piously intelligent people. They know to love, but do not know well enough to do it better. Your Lord and Savior, Jesus, is your medicinal Grace who can restore the health of any soul who is lying in the sickbed of indifference. The Holy Spirit is about to raise the dignity of millions of infirm hearts who have succumbed to the bantering temptations of the world. Your Wisdom awaits you, O' humanity! My Grace is of that same Holy Spirit. I have come to share it with you, to dispense the great and mighty Commons of Light that will keep you from stumbling on your journey to Salvation! My Special son, these are My hopes for this modern-day world. Like millions before, you and your brother have embarked on the day of the Lord, to write, protect, profess, enjoin, and to teach. I am with you, and I will always give you a guiding hand to see you to the Triumph in which untold millions upon millions will share. These are the heady days of summer, as they are called, when men are posturing for a greater social advancement. I am telling you that this is, instead, the day of the growth of the immortal spirit of humanity, a time to be self-extracted from the shell of indignance and impropriety. I hold the Good News for anyone who will place their ear next to My Immaculate Heart to listen. That, My children, is what you are doing here today..."

lx

lxx

lxxx

A terrible tragedy has befallen the children of God in that we do not comprehend that it is not only our flesh, but also our mental constitution that has been penetrated and immersed in the vision and consequences of broken humanity. In the absence of the Light brought by higher Wisdom, we have no more perception of the Truth than our forefather Adam after he was evicted from the beatific realm of the sight of his Creator; and we are conjoined in this soul-spurning exile, rendering us mere journeymen on a subcelestial carousel that neither charts a more heroic path beyond the splints of the boardwalk nor produces any higher elevation than was wrought through the grievous transgression of the estranged patriarch who was the first to bear the lands below the heavens. The souls of God's children throughout every aching generation have yearned to fill the cavernous void within themselves with the mystical apparency of the God of Eden, pleading together for a solace their hearts know must have once existed because, "...how can such heartfelt dreams be conceived within our beings without an evident Greatness placing them there?" In the course of world history, our siblings and friends have engaged sorrows of soul-wrenching proportions, battled loneliness like travelers marooned in space, shed copious tears rivaling the seas, and endured the acidic vileness of generational hatreds that would pale a cyclonic front rolling over an Oklahoma prairie; and yet, they continued to search for deliverance to a "home" that the innate impulses of their hearts urged them to believe is real. Honest reason compels us to trust the logical prospect that if a child has never been imparted a particular body of knowledge, there is—barring the miraculous influx of grace by God—very little hope that he will fully manifest any outward proficiency in those realms without facing unimaginable odds. It is the same regarding the highest perfections that have attended humankind through the evolutionary phases of self-immolation. Although the soul of every person instinctively knows that there are universal precepts and transcending ideals residing within the possibilities of our integrated human potential, it is through the loving vehicles of heroic conviction, wise religious counsel, and impenetrable unity emanating from preceding generations who sacrificed their wills, fortunes, and honor that we might enjoy the fruit from the orchards of their purifying lives. All of these virtues ultimately come to everyone, whether it be through humble submission or by way of the desolation brought by prefigured agony. But, why is it true that those who sit at the temporal pinnacles of human existence require the horrors of devastation to realize that God exists above and beneath their fleeting reigns? And, what is "Wisdom" if it does not refer to a soulful grasp of the highest unseen orders? Even the articulation of its venerable definition presupposes the existence of the unalterable Truth standing beyond human abridgement like a majestic castle impervious to siege. There are spiritual realities upon which the mortal realm is founded that were revealed twenty centuries ago and more; but it is the innocent hearts of each age, while immersed in their hours of horrific suffering, whom God has elevated to the panoramic mountaintop of His Paradisial Reign so our exiled world would neither revolve nor evolve hidden from His Omnipotent Light. The revelatory genius of life that comforts these desolate souls when the Earth provides little consolation to soothe such grievous torment is the jewel that transfigures Creation. These eternally sacred perfections are uncompromising in the obligations they impose and are justifiably responsive to their senseless violation. Our hearts can easily understand that true peace preexisted before humankind first learned to destroy it, and that war is the tractable judgment for breaching that same serenity. Love has been the ultimate and most explosively motivating power the universe has ever experienced since before the initial composite of physical form was ejected from the primordial soup on its trajectory to frame the first mortal creature and bear the fruits of the first holy soul. Our respect for the dignity of the human person, while blind before their color or creed, and notwithstanding their incidental complicities or corruption, is as much an inescapable requirement as our life-sustaining blood trafficking through the thoroughfares of our veins. It is a deference which inspires the virtues of merciful restraint and honest forgiveness as they process from this auspicious acknowledgment. The universal tide of ideals flows with priority and duty as clearly and simply as an arithmetic problem yields the result of four from the adding of two and two more. Every person who has ever been recognized within the leagues of sound judgment has celebrated, defended, and nurtured the sacredness of the beginning of life and the union of a man and woman for the propagation of the human species and its imminent evolution. These luminaries were wise because their spirits articulated the Sacred Eternal as their hearts came into communion with the Glory of Heaven. This leads us to the inevitable conclusion that clinical facilities where our unborn offspring are obstetrically slaughtered—no!, slaughtered is not a sufficiently inflammatory word—by their being pureed into prenatal bits and prematurely purloined from their mothers' wombs, are dark crypts of Hell on Earth of the same ruthless magnitude as the "showers" and crematoria of Auschwitz, Dachau, or Ravensbruck. Let there be no doubt that these abortion mills will have their hideous legacies razed from human existence in irrevocable defeat, just as the foundations of those death chambers of World War II lay now in disgraced piles of rubble for their survivors to pore over in triumphant prayer. Humankind enmasse is infinitely poorer for the wilful encroachment of our lesser misconceptions upon the sacred domain of the heart where God inscribes His immutable laws of Eternal Life.

After all these centuries of the revealing of Christian goodness focused in the suffering of its finest hours, can there still be a debate about the highest values and premiere ethical norms, or even a remote alternative presented to the just and equitable precepts comprising the sanctified dimensions of Divine Love? Yet, here we are, our noses flat against the realization of an entourage of civic leaders who knowingly forfeit these sacred principles for the sake of secular expediency and their own advancement, blinding themselves before the charge of the ages, thinking in the midst of their commissions that their delinquencies have no consequences, dulling their spiritual senses, and ultimately self-assassinating their enlightened souls through the rapid-fire strafing of Truth for personal worldly gain; and then in miraculous moments of conscience stubbornly fight away repentance, lash-out in defiance at courageous religious men and women, shed their wisdom in its infinitude, redefine a renegade reality, and invoke a more palatable orientation which flounders in the proclivities of the secular order; all because they cannot bear the just condemnation that they have crucified the Son of God for the hollowness of stock options, quarterly bonuses, fleeting moments of prestige, or a few votes from some atheists and agnostics who would spit in the face of the Christ who would save them if ever He was allowed into their presence. Amen, I say to you; what does it profit a man to gain the whole world and suffer the loss of living forever in Paradise? If lists recording the names of endangered species can be generated for the many animals that populate the wilder regions of this planet, is it possible to create one denoting the near-extinction of heroically-virtuous public servants so we can go about protecting them with a little more conviction? We may yet be able to find a precious few amidst the public thickets who might qualify for inclusion, ones that could be nurtured back to thriving numbers. How profound are the Gospels which clearly prophesy that the sacred principles of the Savior of the world would be regarded as merely insane propositions to people who are perishing by hands over fists of serial greenbacks. Those who make it their avocation to argue are asking, *What about the principles of all the other religions?* Although I realize that God has left nobody orphaned, I can only reply in the way Wisdom should encourage every human being to evaluate their existence—Show me a man who is the equal of Jesus Christ in what he taught, how he lived, the wonders he wrought, and especially whether he allowed himself to be killed because he believed in the dignity of all humankind to the point of death, thereafter rising from his tomb triumphant by the power of his own omnipotent will as an evidentiary exclamation point for the skeptical ages! Christ the King is the undeniable, undisputed, and unchallenged Perfection of the human person to whom every man, woman, and child must consecrate their allegiance to the alabaster doorway of their graves, because it is He alone who will draw us up from them to live again; for He is the Love who cannot die! It is imperative that we stand together arm-in-arm and follow this God-Man who is Greatness Incarnate. There is no other Savior or Messiah!

Sunday, February 2, 2003 (excerpt)   *3:57e/2:57c*
Feast of the Presentation of the Lord
        "My dear little children, Jesus has asked Me to tell *m(033)*
you that on this day of the Commemoration of a Sword
which has pierced My Immaculate Heart, as America's

*culture of death is still doing; that during the sixteenth hour
along its eastern seaboard and to an obedient messenger who
has knelt to pray within a few hundred yards of the tomb of
its sixteenth President, Heaven is confirming after a space
vehicle was launched on the sixteenth day of 2003, completed
a mission of sixteen days, and that perished within sixteen
minutes of its return to the ground, God has decided that if*   x
*the United States of America wishes to continue to inject
poison into penitent sinners' veins to execute them in the
name of secular justice and strew their corpses in dark graves
all across its breadth and length—if you wish this retribution
to be the legacy of your nation—then God has been moved to
complement your wishes by allowing even more corpses from
the heights of the skies to be strewn across the expanse of your
vast and vengeful acreage. They are more innocent victims
of a republic of unmitigated hatred. When He commissioned
you to be fruitful and multiply, He did not intend for you to*   xx
*do so corruptly or with the same pride and vengeance that
has brought such evil into the lives of the suffering. Were it
not for the Grace of His Almighty Love, He would have
heretofore allowed the destruction of many more of your
institutions and social cliques. Why are these things
occurring? Because the people of America are still too far
from holiness. Your designs are always to the advancement
of the self and rarely for the care, teaching, and nourishment
of the helpless. Be sure to remember that Jesus had
proclaimed that vengeance belongs to Him, and He is on the*   xxx
*brink of claiming it on behalf of the billions throughout
history who have been forced to agonize in other parts of the
world because the USA has been so absorbed in garnering as
much materiality as possible. These are perilous times, not
because of the wrongful things that foreign legions might do,
but by virtue of the Divine Justice that has made the
Kingdom of God the place of blessing and exaltation to the
followers of Christian Truth.*

*I have spoken at length to you before about Truth
and Love because too many among you have mistaken them*   xl
for posterity and patriotism. The ways that the Western

world has skewed the meaning of Love has brought devastation upon the entire globe—so much so that the errors of Russia which had been put down at My intercession pale by comparison. The Soviet republics embraced atheism in an outward way, while the United States of America has espoused Christianity while deceivingly living in a way that despises its very tenets. This, My children, is why the American republic must be humbled, and humbled it will become! How far? Completely to its knees and flat on its   *l*
belly so it can crawl around like the Reptile it has so egregiously embraced! You must know that this process has already begun. When hundreds-of-thousands of American people turn their heads to the skies and ask God why such torment is being brought upon their nation, He is silently but assuredly responding that it is because the United States has become a companion of evil! The way your impressionable youth are being scandalized is an outright abomination! Could it be true that the Mother of God would come before you through the kindness of a humble messenger and tell you   *lx*
that your God is not pleased? Yes! As surely as the Son of Man died on the Cross to save you from the fires of Hell, I am telling you that masses of your citizens are unfit and undeserving of such an absolution. These are difficult things for Me to tell you because you know that I am the Patron Saint of America and your Protectress from harm. I wish to protect you by asking you to avoid the perils of your own error! In its simplicity, is this too difficult for you to understand? Those who claim to be fair upholders of the public law are as corrupt as the criminals they are   *lxx*
attempting to capture. Their discriminatory practices, vices, hatred, and outright sorcery in the name of some blind civility that has nothing to do with the Love of the Son of God will make for a great fire in which the chaff will burn! Indeed, such error and corruption are more fuel for this inferno of Justice. If anyone whose eyes fall upon the text of My messages should become afraid that they are among the guilty, then let them convert to the Sacred Heart of Jesus before it is too late!"

Notwithstanding the posthumous accolades undeservedly heaped by partisans upon their own kind, it is apparent that the wellborn leaders of our republic can likewise be nothing but ashamed of their collective vitae before Almighty God for all the previous illegitimacies mentioned above that they have allowed to clandestinely infest our great nation while being stationed at the honorary watches of decency during their elected tenures. It is furthermore breathtaking to consider the dimensions of dignity of the children who are conceived into this world in their mothers' wombs, a gestating new civilization of Earth-shattering possibility for the transformation and elevation of the sacred esteem and storied ideals of the human species. Yet, the career political elite of our federalist system, the 535 representatives of Congress from every state in the Union; a president, vice-president, one disenfranchised senator from the District of Columbia, nine Supreme Court justices, thousands of notorious jurists in the appellate courts, along with multitudes of ancillary decision-makers, negotiators, and policy consultants in concert with a pathetic media empire that would give voice to the most hideous opponent of decency should they whimper from their dungeon of immorality, cannot see their way clear at any level to muster the courage to impede a ruthless band of self-possessed, renegade American women from advancing the agenda of murdering the children of their wombs and exterminating a prolific portion of this great nation's future while posturing themselves for eternal damnation in the process. This glaring mortal omission is simply the first line item on their docket of egregiousness before God! Two hundred and twenty-nine years ago in the cradle of human liberty, muskets would have already been brandished and blazing. And, remember, the pregnant mothers themselves are oftentimes the least guilty of the entire hideous lot when considering the momentary anguish that has been diabolically thrust upon their discerning constitution. For those who would rebuke me by saying that I am not their judge, the Queen of Heaven told me to respond, *No, I am not your judge, but I am to warn you how you will soon be judged!* I hear the vain objections cascading through time and impacting my spirit from those who wish to defend the integrity of their supposedly pro-life partisans. Even though I ascribe to no political affiliation whatsoever other than to recognize even the smallest good work that anyone can perform, I will still petition your conscience: Why is it true that the so-called pro-life, majority political party dominating this republic can somehow find the moral justification—when there was none—to hackle our fears, incite our paranoia, and foment a war of death, destabilization, and destruction against another sovereign nation under the guise of patriotic self-defense, despite the negative consensus of nearly the entire international community, including the Supreme Pontiff in Rome, but previously and thereafter refuse to rally the heroic will of righteous Americans to launch the single most virtuous battle that Creation will ever know against those who are murdering millions of our nation's unborn children? You, nefarious cowards, all! The Holy Spirit has a message for you: *You may stand in defiance of the Truth today, but history will hunt you down and expose you with undeniable certainty as having colluded with the ravages of hatred and injustice, revealing your shallow hypocrisy and paltry cynicism, and how you brought great suffering to bear upon the virtues of peace, decency, hope, and light!* It is beyond dignified imagining that the governing parties of our nation are inscribing the following epitaph on their mystical tombs by the historical legacy they are perpetrating: *"The deliverance of the unborn was not our priority; we had to reek vengeance and kill while the political season was good."* And, so it shall be written. How could any of these people claim to be enlightened by the living Spirit of Jesus Christ or consider themselves or be labeled by others as honestly being on the side of protecting the children of God, dedicated to the preservation of the sanctity of human life, or devoted to securing authentic peace around the world? The abounding title of *Peacemaker* is not earned through the false virtue of appeasing one's partisan priors with prevaricating rhetoric during an election cycle, nor is it gained by waging war while trying to hoodwink the appalled gallery of global spectators into believing that we possess a rectifiable vision before the Face of the Almighty. Our Lady would like to sincerely inquire as to when the season of deliverance will come for this world's tiny progeny. I, on the other hand, standing proudly beside Christ, wearing a breastplate of righteousness, would like to ask our leaders: *What does it feel like to be such cowards seated in dead consciences so far from Divine Truth while plunging toward the floor of the Eternal Abyss like asteroids streaking toward impact with an orbiting planet? Is there any chance that you will choose to move closely enough to the Hearth of Jesus' Love to thaw your hearts and end the macabre seasons of militarism, materialism, and infanticide, so that we may begin the springtime of His command to love, and to teach, and to evangelize the only Redemption that will ever be offered from On High?* If we do not swiftly heed the admonishments of the Most Blessed Virgin Mary, God will bring the Era of Righteousness through the infinite power of His own Divine Judgment. The days of *will you please be holy?* have come to an end!

Sunday, February 24, 2002 (excerpt)   3:47 p.m.
        "When you pray the Holy Rosary, little ones, you   l(055)
mitigate the horrible errors that make so many among you unhappy and impure. I ask that you continue to recite the Sacred Mysteries so that those who are in need of your petitions will turn to the Sacred Way of the Cross. I have

been beseeching the Almighty Father on their behalf, and yours, that you might gain the strength and vision you need to see the journey of faith through its destined end. How happy I am that you have given over your lives to the beauty of Love, that you realize that only the Divine Perfection of Jesus should be your goal, and that you will indeed reside forever in Heaven as a result of your spiritual conversion. There are many souls who are still suffering, My children! Too many are poor and hungry, alone, naked, grieving, and abandoned. I have spoken most recently to you about those who have no one to call their friends. These are the poor children of God who often walk through life as though their entire mortality is a mission through the desert of despair. Please remember them to God, and ask Him to bless their hearts in a special way. I know full-well what it means to be rejected, and My Son knows the feelings which haunt His followers who are despised among men. This is a time of reconciliation between all peoples, especially those who have been cast aside by the lot of humanity. It is true that you cannot know where each of them resides, but it is imperative that you realize their existence in many places around the world. They are children who are hiding in the dark corners of orphanages and in caves to escape the explosion of rockets of war. These are the innocent ones who are suffering the plight of being threaded amidst the scourge of battle with no way to fight for themselves. The horrid aggression of the arsenals of the United States of America is causing the deaths of many of these innocent children and their mothers and fathers. This is a senseless and selfish infiltration of evil against poor indigenous peoples from foreign lands for the sole purpose of vengeance and public pride.

When you see placards in the hands of your foreign neighbors which call for the death of America, they are actually seeking the end of this horrible warfare which is causing such destruction in their homelands. They wish not to spread the error that is only to be blamed on a few thousand renegades. All they wish is to live in peace upon

x

xx

xxx

xl

the soil where their ancestors gave their fathers birth. I am the Immaculate Mother of God and the Patroness Saint of the United States of America. I am ashamed of the government of your nation and the arsenals of war by which she is spreading her error. Please be assured that the justified Wrath of God will make the world a better place when such error is brought to conclusion... My children, I do not tell you these things as a matter of an idle warning; My words are the facts as they are being dispensed from the Throne of Our God! He wishes not for the destruction of America, but it seems that the United States continuously invites others to attack her by being so obstinate in the face of such global unrest. I ask My holy people in your homeland to pray for peace, and not make war! In the midst of the sacrificial season of Lent when Christians are called to reconcile between themselves and those of other faiths, the warring is only being escalated by those who so hypocritically received the imposition of Ashes upon their foreheads on Ash Wednesday. How can any public leader receive such a penitential rite and walk away harboring even greater plans to annihilate his enemies? I assure you that God is not going to allow this type of misconduct to go unchastised. I have told you that the Cup is filled and running-over, but now it is about to be pushed completely off its base!

It is for these reasons that I have come to speak to you today, and to pray that all of My children in the Americas will pray for the conversion of the Western Hemisphere to the Peace which is dispensed through the power of the Holy Spirit. You must remember how filled were the churches after the events of September 11, 2001; and now, most everyone has abandoned their faith again and forgotten what punishment this was for America. What else must God allow to ensure the permanent conversion of such a materialistic society? Does the awakening of the American people require the destruction of the entire continent of North America? I implore those who know Me as their Mother to warn the rest about the peril of the days to come. Is it wrong

l

lx

lxx

for those who believe in God to state that He is allowing the   lxxx
slow undoing of the United States because the American
people have embraced such a culture of death as to allow the
systematic abortion of 45 million little children in the wombs
of their mothers? Indeed, anyone who might allow such a
proclamation to pass their lips would be speaking through
the power of the Holy Spirit, Himself! For those who are
seeking omens and signs, for prophecies and premonitions,
they should prepare to take cover. Of all the abominations
for which the United States is going to have to pay a heavy
price, and there are multitudes of them, the sin of abortion is   xc
the single one that will ensure the certain destruction of such
a misguided nation of indifferent people. I assure you that
this is coming, it is in the offing, it is imminent, and it is
inevitable. Were it not for the suffering and sacrifices of so
many who serve Jesus so well already during these days, it
would have occurred forthrightly heretofore.

*   I do not bring you messages of doom and disaster, I*
bring you the Gospel Truth which has been given to you
through the Holy Paraclete and the lives of the First Apostles.
These are the modern times about which Saint Louis de   c
Montfort spoke. I am traveling from nation to hamlet,
calling 'Where are My children?' It is time for us to bring the
rich and powerful to their knees, to force them into contrition
by the smell of their own souls rotting before their eyes. The
moment has come for them to see the flash of Eternity and be
unable to find themselves anywhere in it! I know where My
children are located. You are the quiet ones who have been
standing-in-wait while those who are powerful and wealthy
have had their day. My holy followers, the fulcrum of
modern history has finally come! While the children of God   cx
have had to maintain the shoring of their strength by
defensive measures for so long, the time has now come for the
movement of the Army of the Children of Mary to take the
field. You are now enlisted in the most noble ranks of souls
who ever walked the face of the globe. You have now
become the aggressors who are on the offensive! Your God in

Paradise has finally given the command for you to take this world back from the wretches who have been trying to steal it from the grasp of His Son for the past thousand years! This Victory will come in your day! This Triumph will occur on   cxx *your watch! When you assail those who have been lukewarm in the face of the righteousness of Jesus, please drive the dagger of their own death a little deeper for the Saints of old! Breathe the flames of Justice upon their arrogance and burn their heathen souls back into the fires of Hell! Speak the words of the Son of God, and they will go running back into the dark for cover, where the Christ of all has placed His garrison of back-up Saints to keep them from getting away. The flames that will consume the chaff are leaping for them now! Love is this power and might!*   cxxx *Holiness is this giant movement! Yes! Those millions of legends from the past are just now rubbing their palms together for this day to have finally come! I ask everyone alive today to be a part of this culmination to the only Kingdom of Love that can withstand the final battle between good and evil—those who are the children of Light, warriors for the Cross, lenders of their sights and ears to the cause of Truth in a world that has been lying to God since the first dawn of its exile ever broke!*

     I ask you to place Creation on notice that the Queen   cxl *of Heaven and Earth is claiming the Triumph of Her Immaculate Heart now! This is the 2,000ᵗʰ year that I told the humble Marian Movement of Priests to prepare for! It has finally arrived, and it is ongoing!... Let those who stand aside in pride and atheism prepare for their demise at the hands of the Lady with the Crown of Twelve Stars! Thank you! Thank you to the children I love, to the little souls of God who obey and understand, to the treasures of the Sacred Heart of My Son whom He is now placing into motion to conquer the wicked! The snarling despots who have been*   cl *trying to pilfer the Victory of Love away from those who are helpless could never have anticipated the defeat they are about to suffer! They miscalculated the power of their enemies! They misjudged the Divine Omnipotence of the Cross! I say to them today 'You did not think that you would be caught and brought to Justice, but you are just as wrong now as you were when you first began.' My children on the Earth are as bright-shining as the sun overhead, and no darkness shall prevail over them anymore! I have given them the Resurrected Christ! With all the power of God and the strength of His Love, these are the Last Times; and those who oppose Him can already feel their demise creeping up their spines. Indeed! Fire and brimstone, indeed! This is a Mother who never once said 'no' to Her children, and She is not about to forsake them now! Why? Because I bear in My Arms the Son of the Almighty God who has created Heaven and Earth. No Hell can prevail against His Church, His Kingdom, His Justice, His Wrath, or His Divine Mercy! Prepare the enemies of Love for their defeat, for defeat is assuredly theirs!"*

clx

Our Lady has every intention of upbraiding human arrogance and rattling the foundations of men who have spent far too much time on holiday away from their interior mansions. Inflammatory? God willing, indeed! Our purposes are to spark the flames that Jesus so passionately desired to be raised upon the lands. How blessed Flint, Michigan would be to find its name to be a mystical parable where its incorporated boundaries would one day be seen as the actual stone of Truth which God could strike to set spiritual fire upon the Earth. Humanity is required to listen to God or perish. That is why a little more deferential humility from the reprobates is in order. No one of these works has yet been directed toward the saint still in the flesh. I write from the position of the commanding presence of the Immaculate Virgin regarding the spiritual facts emanating from the Truth of the Almighty. All men will one day bow at Her feet, and the sooner the better. Let's face it; we are mercifully fortunate that the Most Holy Trinity has not incinerated this planet in justifiable wrath for the mocking indifference we have arrogantly launched toward the Queen of Heaven, paying no mind to Her miraculous intercession throughout the global centuries, but most especially in today's prolific era. The human race is going to ask, "what Twin Towers?" once the Heavenly Father commences exacting the Justice which flows from His Throne. There is no line that can withstand our breaching courage if our efforts are to impress the vision of the truest reality into another soul who yet knows not to walk the

Earth in the itinerant freedom that comes through the Holy Spirit. I ask emphatically, *who had the authority to create any line and then tell a child of God that he could not cross it in the service of the Heavenly Hosts? Who has the audacity to proclaim that the Truth of God is not allowed here? Who has the right to oppose the Lord of lords and King of kings? I say in unison with the boy-champion David—Let this goliath of an ego step forward; and bring his armies with him! They will never withstand the hail of Rosary fire!* How many marks in the sand did the Messiah storm past without a hint of conscience or remorse at the devastation inflicted upon the egos of men and the obsolete renderings of their practical worldly power? Who owns the vineyard? If the Earth is the potter's field, it is time for the plow to incise the cultivation of man. It is the wish of every holy Angel and Saint for us to sit in rapt wonderment before the factual witness of the miraculous intercession of the Queen of Paradise with new thoughts and clearer perspectives spinning in our minds as we try to imbibe the boldness and beauty which has become our mystical lot. If only the masses who do not know God would be forced into astonishment by the refreshing enlightenment of a new order of discipleship and the prophetic declarations that storm against the malaise and anemic ideals of their materialistic worldliness as in the days of old! I want them to consider whether they are going to claim the Truth that is being miraculously revealed as their own, or watch it shrink in the distance as their only chance for a better world marches resolutely toward the morning dawn. How blessed would those souls be who found themselves flat on their backs in the ashes and staring at the sky upon opening their eyes with thoughts of being steam-rolled pealing in their brains and righteous terror rattling the racks of their bones. Let them hold their wagging heads between their hands with their palms covering their ears, and with newfound revelation echo a redeemed Quasi Moto—*The Truth! The Truth!*—licking their obstinate wounds that were self-inflicted long before Our Lady's words ever graced their ears, contemplating how they ever surrendered their sacred lives to the shadows of a flock of carnal vultures. I tell you that Saint Joan of Arc was a heavenly premonition of critical things to come, far greater than mortal minds have been humble enough to envision. It is not a rogue band of Englishmen who have laid siege to the spiritual landscapes of our countrymen; rather, it is the age-old nature of godlessness in its most rapacious and pinnacled forms. Presently, our souls are as atrophied as those of the French before the arrival of The Maid. Imagine what the enemies of Christ and His Church will face at the rising of the children of God upon the Earth. Inflammatory, I say again! Before Jesus Christ is finished, there is going to be a spiritual battlefield littered with the decadent remains of every human animosity and defiance that ever reared its ugly head against His Catholic Kingdom. Thy Kingdom come, indeed! I will irrationally beg no one, nor placate any arrogant human will. Salvation is real for the penitent, and damnation a certainty for those who refuse to embrace the virtues of Paradise through some haughty "show me the money first" attitude. I will repeat, *when His Majesty, Jesus Christ, finally returns to the Earth in Glory, one of His first bold acts of justice will be to reduce the public media's fallacious empire into a smoldering pile of rubble and ruins in a heap atop the ground.* The Blessed Virgin wishes us to be convinced that anyone who is vested with the Holy Spirit is obliged to challenge the children of men in a spirit of merciful honesty and courageous witness. And, before our lives burn-out as a holocaust to the Divine, respect for the Truth we are speaking and the conviction by which we display it will flower in every hearer of our words unto Eternal Life.

Sunday, May 16, 1999   *3:25 p.m.*
    "Essential to any child who must love is a Mother who   i(136)
can give him the Son of Love. Dear children, can you not
feel the Divinity which surrounds you? Can you not detect
the aura of anticipation as you prepare to begin the second of
holy testimonies that will convert your brother humanity?
We will pray that everyone will understand the measure of
God to convert and save His people, to employ the virtues of
the righteous, to expunge the opposition before you, and to
pursue the cultivation of a world which is still much too
lethargic to understand what it means to face the Justice of   x
God... My Special one, you have just completed a parable
about the human spirit and the reason that people become
leaders. As you know, the true leaders in the world have
been the Popes of the Roman Catholic Church... I cannot
make it too clear that you must always foster that hope in
your heart. Heaven is not only a place, My children, it is a
collection of all places and all times. The strength of all the
righteous armies in history is but a puff of wind in Heaven.
The crowning of every king and champion who served on
Earth is a simultaneous act of 'Well done' in two words from   xx
the Savior of the world. All of the tears that have ever
flowed since the fall of man from the Garden of Eden could
not fill a thimble in the everlasting expanse of Paradise.
Every drop of blood ever shed by humanity on Earth could
not equal the power of the Blood of Jesus that lives in one

chalice upon the Altar. No war or collection of wars has brought as sweet spoils to the feet of God as the Crucifixion of your Savior on Good Friday. And, the righteousness that now flows in your heart and in the lives and actions of all the Popes blooms from the Holy Spirit who is etching the words   xxx *you are hearing at this very moment upon the firmament of your soul. This is a momentous time for the Earth. You are standing before the world in a professorial role, and your Diary is your textbook. And, as you just witnessed, you never told anything about any number of popular or electoral college votes. It is not an issue. Likewise, you need not go into detail by the prodding questions of those who will scandalously ask how I have come to you and what exactly happened in this room. You must be poised and wise. Indeed, the time is now unfolding that will begin the changes*   xl *that you seek. This is My holy blessing for you. + Thank you for your prayers. I will speak to you soon. I love you. Goodnight!"*

We have transcended into this extremely precarious position because a critical mass of immorality has been achieved by the forces of wanton evil who have secured the image-making machines of our culture before which millions are hypnotically enthralled. Their seductive and sensual imagery are generating a trance of lifeless existence, an obscurity separating us from the hallowed vaults of spiritual potential where every grand achievement has found its inception. This country has birthed a culture of unmitigated death because our political and religious leaders refuse to stand in the breach of our moral integrity with their hearts pulsing blood and fire in their eyes in testament to their willingness to surrender every drop of their righteousness to this sacred soil with as much integrity as the King on the summit of Calvary. So, let the ages-old proclamation of Justice and Sacramental Absolution be renewed with its original clarity from the mountaintop of Calvary: *All of you who are immersed in the hideous cult of secular global domination, materialism, lust, and heretical dissent, come now forward and realize that it is the Divine Mercy of Jesus Christ the Redeemer alone that protects you from the onslaught of Divine Judgment and your just eviction from paradisial Creation for endless time. The breath still coming from your lungs is the proof of Jesus' Divine Mercy and that the Kingdom of God is not of this world. Never believe that it is weakness or lack of conviction on the part of Christians the world over that we obediently restrain our passion for righteousness beneath a meekness that will inherit the Earth. Know as an eternal fact that before the Judgment of the Ages, there is not a debate that we have not already won, a wage of war that has not fallen to our triumph, a defeat that has not been stripped from the clutches of our oppressors, or an inequity that has not been re-balanced on the scales to our favor; neither is there a broken heart that will remain uncaressed in our faithful wake, an injustice that we will refuse to address with our amending righteousness, or a good deed that is beyond the breadth of our heroic sacrifices. This is the gift that Christianity is for you! The world is ours! And, it is our Love for you which maintains and strengthens our capacity to endure your audacity as we plead peacefully in these times for the Almighty Father to forgive you and to provide you the undeserved grace of your conversion and submission to all that Love commands. It is our prayers, our sacrifices, and our patience that brings the extension of Christ's Mercy to your days. For without the holy millions that you mercilessly torture and mock, you—the unholy minions of this dying world—would have been flushed from Creation generations before this day; for each of us knows without doubt that when the Trumpet of the Ages sounds, the Archangel-Prince of the Seraphim, Saint Michael Himself and His Retinue of winged Righteousness will blast through the veil between Heaven and Earth and grab your rebellious nature by the throat, slamming your heathen, death-ridden souls against the wall of Eternity to the encore jubilation of all those who have patiently submitted to the sacrificial Cross of malignant, indifferent aggressiveness that you have so brazenly regurgitated upon this sacred domain of man. The Redemptive Epoch of Mercy will have expired and your time will have run out! You will be judged lacking with no recourse before the heavens but to lie face down on the floor of Abyss, breathing the sewage of your earthly legacies for all kingdoms to come! As it is written, so it shall come to pass!*

I warn you because I am a witness for the Queen of Heaven and have seen the just fire of the angelic powers. No one will be able to restrain their avenging allegiance to the Divine Majesty of the Most Holy Trinity when they commence the fulfillment of their purifying commission to restore God's Spiritual Kingdom upon this planet. Therefore, let the Virgin's words be your conscience-rousing bugle, Her voice a spiritual reveille warbling like a Dove from the hills of Paradise, down upon the haunting watch-fires of those poetic, hundred circling camps where this nation's greatest inhabitants are huddling in anticipation of the great Day of Reckoning. The mystical banner has been exhumed from its humiliation, and whipping in the breezes of the Holy Spirit does it fly above us now! A new deputation has been discharged from the Throne of God, a Saint de Monfort prophecy fulfilled, ignited in the souls of the children of Heaven's Magnificent Queen. And, although some may be patiently enduring the momentary atrocities of a few sinister men, I promise that injustice and immorality will be vanquished in all its forms! If a battle is to ensue for the souls of the children of God, know rightly and ominously that the Trumpet to sound-forth will be one which will never report again in retreat.

The Mantle of Deliverance has been conferred about the shoulders of those who call the Immaculate Virgin their Heavenly Mother. The breastplate of Righteousness has been dressed across the chests of those with the courage to raise their arms like toddlers and don it; and the garment of liberty has been unfurled as a red carpet beneath our feet extending to a crystalline Conception of Triumph. With the razor-sharp Sword of Divine Love by which we were first confirmed as inspirited children of the Only King, we shall impale the Truth into the soul of this sacred land with a quadruple attack of miracle, marvel, Mary and the Holy Mass, causing the sons of secular royalty to tremble at the imminent Return of Jesus Christ! There is a Lion poised to bellow the Justice of a High King, and He is from the Land of the Celestial Judah. If sentiments of indignance or even anger be detected in the voice of our welling dedication, know true that they reflect the restrained fury of a just God who would scorch the barren continents were it not for the righteous ten that Hope has placed among the irreverent cotillion of modern man. Dare we dream of the perfection of the human race? Or, do we defy our own destiny and cower in the ill-bound cry, "Let fate perfect us!" challenging its grueling impartiality with atrophied nerves mistaken for courage and faces sneered at the prospect of the sacrifices that would bring it more peacefully into being? Why must such foreboding terms about the future of mankind be brought to bear? Because the arrogant obsessiveness of the least of humans must be shredded and put-down by a more princely nobility so their benevolent spirits may rise again, lest they remain forever enslaved beneath the inordinate realms which will show no deference to their future happiness. They must begin the preparation for meeting Eternity Face-to-face, an emotive reality that expects an instantaneous composure of reciprocal holiness in order to be embraced.

Sunday, February 6, 2000 (excerpt)   *3:44 p.m.*

"You should pray that Jesus' Light will be the true   *j(037)*
dawn tomorrow. But, we should all pray that He will arrive to the cheers of believers, and not the wails of hundreds of millions who are unprepared. Thank God that the Reign of Justice did not fall upon the Earth today! Thank Him that He did not close the door on those who still have a chance to pass through! These are My grave concerns which keep Me moving about the world, seeking a more noble persistence in My children's hearts to know that Jesus will come in the fullness of time, and not before. And, what is that fullness of   *x*
time? It is when every message that I have given you for

nearly nine years is heard by every ear. It means that all on the Earth will eventually have the opportunity to turn a humble spirit toward their Lord instead of a defiant one. It means the time when the newborn cries of all the wholly innocent ones who have been aborted can be heard above the collective roar which ushered-in the 21st century around the world. I am telling you all of these things because all of this can happen in one day, one hour, or one moment! God knows when that instant will occur, and we yet do not.   xx
Would this miracle for which My children pray truly be believed to the depths of all hearts, the moment would be seized by the Savior of all Glory and the world would be ended at last. I will give you a better description. The world requires greater patience because Jesus is waiting for the likes of obstinate ones who pray the Rosary and claim to be My children, and then spit in the face of true warriors. He is waiting for people to deliver the gifts of bread and wine to the Altar who do not believe that radio hosts are the solution to western social problems. He is waiting for all priests to   xxx
rise-up and say that abortion is murder and marital infidelity and divorce are mortal sins. He is waiting to see His priests on Earth who do not drive Lincoln Continentals. He is waiting for humanity to help My little messengers to an audience with the Pope because they are believed, and not being pushed aside by millionaires who purchase their way into the Vatican with the wealth they have pilfered from others. He is waiting for national leaders who will guide them in the conscience of the Christian Gospel, rather than   xl
rallying around the most distracting product of the day. The design of modern culture is deplorable because all of these things are still in the way of Thy Kingdom come!"

The forces of evil have mercilessly taunted every age, crucifying the people of peace who were conscripted to hurl them from their thrones into the galleys of delivering reparation. For every legion of despots and overwhelming darkness in time, the heavenly estate has responded with new Saints, spiritually seasoned for victory, mysteriously tuned for deliverance, valorous before the Holy Cross, unintimidated by the wagging tongues of reprobates, flashing in paradisial Wisdom, soaring in conviction beyond the earthly principles of men, and faithful in allegiance to the Crucified Redeemer, even unto social banishment and violent death. Every king has his reverend sword, and with it he confirms honor and nobility upon those who rise to the dignity of his cause. Henceforth, let it be known to the ends of the Earth, the Divine Excalibur of the Supreme King of Creation is the Marian children of the Mystical Body of Christ, we who are about to be unsheathed from the Immaculate Heart of Mary, She whom eternal destiny pierced, the Magnificent Queen who is calling-up an army through Her miraculous intercession that is the *Esprit de Corps* of the Old Rugged Cross, a sacrificial legion clothed with the beatific reaches of Heaven. Whether America is to survive the grand ascent to perfection as a storied Kingdom of eternal ideals, or laid waste as a vanquished empire with her awe-inspiring appointments divided as spoils in the wake of the battle, is suspended in the balance of our collective invocation of the highest orders of convicted engagement we undertake with the marauding intellectuals who have infiltrated the sprawling acreage between our shores. In accompaniment with an humble grasp of the Sacred Mysteries of the Most Holy Rosary, each person must draw forth the realization that a Spiritual Kingdom sustains the ethereal precepts of our country's existence; for without this indomitable composition of passionate grace bolstered amongst the cardiac sinews of our divine progeny, the brutal bastions vacated of our sentinel-wisdom will undermine every cultural edifice, leaving them teetering in abandonment along with our unsupported hopes and dreams, offering no destiny but to topple like titanic dominos into catastrophic oblivion with as much shocking delirium as the Supreme Soviet president helplessly watched his individual socialist blocks tumbling one after another into a fertile new chaos, where the God of human sovereignty began anew the mysterious process of human sanctification.

Sunday, April 9, 2000 (excerpt)   *3:20 p.m.*
        "Can it be possible that a humanity which is so   *j(100)*
unprepared to meet its Maker is about to see Him Face-to-
face? Yes, indeed, is the answer to that query of holy
revelation! I have come again to pray with you because
there still lives the arrogant among the humble, the proud
who oppress the simple, and the wicked who persecute the
faithful. The world is yet fraught with peril and greed, and
tart in the very quarters where it must become the most
sanctified and sweet. My little children, your brothers and
sisters must become like you, knowledgeable in the ways of   *x*

the Holy Spirit, and willing to relinquish their lives to the advancement of the Kingdom of God on the Earth. The peril resides in the corners of Creation where the Blood of Salvation is rejected outright. My little ones, if I were to ask you to select a number that exists between 1 and 58,000, can you tell Me the number that would be the least among those selected? The number is, indeed, two. Do you know why? Not only is it the least obvious, those who respond would have an entire spectrum of 57,998 numbers from which to ponder, not knowing that the answer that God has provided is resting the closest to their soul, the reason for His inquisition of 'Will you come back to Me?' You may try this every day for the rest of your life, but you will rarely be given the answer of two.   To many, God seems that ambiguous in a body of undetermined creation, a small contingency in an endless pool, and an anonymous spirit among all those who seek their allegiance. My children, the vision of the world must be better defined. The criteria for the judgment of righteousness must be so focused upon Love, that the consciousness of man must wish to stray no further than the singular God who has put the question, present in the Trinity, which is concurrently and omnipresently the Deity of Divine Purpose. Can you see that the multiplication of words of which Jesus speaks is a product of this propensity of mankind to be so undefining? Yours is a God of the particulars of goodness, service, holiness, and peace! Your Salvation is the explicit and concise fruit of the Blood of the Cross, not the many errant theologies which try to explain it away! Your ever-knowable Creator is concealed in the grace you cannot see because of the blinding Light of the Love you can see! Dare any soul to turn a disavowing shoulder to this redeeming Truth, and he will be simultaneously saying 'no' to Everlasting Life! Would there be one who would refuse to taste of the cup of suffering, and I will show you the same one who shall never set foot on the streets of perfect gold! My children, if there is a soul in the universe who bears the audacity to scoff at Mercy, that same soul will grieve forever

xx

xxx

xl

in the charred remains of the creation which he has burned. There is no solace in rejecting the forgiveness of Jesus because that is where only Life can be found. So, those who will scan the continuum for any number but two cannot see the Hands of Divinity in front of their face. My pretty ones, I will not rest in My prayers and intercession until all of My children look directly where I point them, undistracted by the glittering world, whether it be material wealth, physical satisfaction, or promises from other mortals that have no chance of being kept. There is a charter of hope which hangs on the doorway of Salvation which reads 'Enter if your soul is well prepared!' That means only your soul, wrapped in the stately cleanliness of your baptismal gown and saturated in the Blood of My Son. The Angels who will escort you to His Throne will never approach someone who still holds fast to their wares or the stench of egoism, or the burdens of impurity. They will stand aside and allow these souls to see themselves as they really are, tethered to a weight so unbearable that they cannot escape their own fall. My children, Jesus is your profound release from these bonds! His Resurrection is the reason that Salvation will not let go! I am telling you today that there is hope for them all, there is perfection where there once lived corruption, there is sainthood where once stood sinfulness, and there is freedom to conquer any constraint which might snag your gown on your flight to your Celestial Home! This is the Truth that has conquered the bewilderment that keeps humankind asking the question 'Why?' This is the backdrop of all your dreams, the pedestal upon which the future rests, the pool from which the parched may drink, and the ultimate Eternity in which the wretched may finally escape the perils of time to once again take their heavenly seat of humility beside Forgiveness, Himself. All of this is inscribed upon that plaque which is posted at the doorway where the human conscience finally awakens to God. It is held there by the cohesion among men and crafted by hands of unity who have all come at last to understand what is written in the Gospels

l

lx

lxx

lxxx

for the whole world to see. It is a phonics of service and love, pronounced with a deafening roar of 'We win, because Jesus has set us all free!'

My little children, I speak of this consciousness because it is coming of age. All of the kittens are finally realizing that they belong in the box because it is their deliverance Home (ref. message of May 22, 1992). Your Mother has the joy of telling you today that these last days are meaningful to the point that My Son is about to bestow a blessing upon His people that is unprecedented since century number One. It is the Two, the Second Coming of this Valiant Warrior who is gleaming with joy that His followers are clearing His path. But this time, My children, He will not come alone! He will not warble in a Nativity cloth, but will roar with the power of the Cross! He will be accompanied by nobles and princes from every former age who dared to stand firm for His sake! He will usher-in servants and queens from under their habits which kept them in prayer in convents. This God of all Creation will shower upon the world the happy souls who have preceded you in death and have been raised from their graves!—your loved ones and leaders, fathers and Martyrs, and brothers and sisters of Light! All of them will come sailing into the land of New Liberty that you will know as Redemption! So, whenever someone asks you to pick a number, allow your heart to make the choice, and you will never, ever be wrong! Let Jesus be your Judge because He now holds your Judgment at bay! Let the Angels rejoice around you because I have ultimate victory beneath My Mantle, and I have already dispensed it to you. I give you Jesus! I give you peace and patience and love and pardon and Light! Thank you for allowing your Mother to love you this way!"

xc

c

cx

There have been cinema depictions whose actors have stumbled upon baby bear cubs and became enamored by their innocuous cuteness. It is none other than suspenseful to remember the complete lack of awareness the actors had for the full-grown command of the mother bear hovering precariously in the camouflage beneath the underbrush. Or, in like vein, a baby dinosaur being encountered in a fictional prehistoric epic, but all sensory composure being lost by its cinematic participants at the appearance of the behemoth creature who bore such an offspring. Out of the unknown vacuum they transcend, bearing soul-shattering revelation, sometimes inciting fear, but always administering a reorientation of priorities and purposes. Consider someone handing you a bouquet of the most beautiful lilies to ever touch your senses, then at hearing the words—*they are yours*—you turn to see a boundless meadow graced as far as your eyes can perceive with the same endless splendor residing within your leisurely grasp. Could there ever be a more exquisite replacement of perception or magnification of vision? Regress in time with me and consider the people of an ancient city in the land of Greece who gazed in satisfaction and confidence after erecting a symbolic god whose statuesque bearing straddled the harbor of their great port. Amid pomp and pageantry, they must have christened it the Colossus of Rhodes and basked in the honor of its imposing presence before the purview of their pagan world. But, as advanced as the culture of these primitive peoples surely was for their time, could any one of their number have been so visionary to imagine the legendary advancement of a newer world in the distant future, one that would sparkle in the visions of their successor centuries upon centuries later, a land bearing the title, The United States of America? Could they have possibly conceived a commonwealth materializing from the idyllic Heart of a living God that would be given the breath of existence and the sublime responsibility to advance a towering liberty enmeshed with sanctified dignity and rightful legacy, a veritable splendor of God-fearing justice and equitable human rights? Would these chosen people not also have been equally inspired by the spectacular grandeur impersonated into the artful creation of our French brothers and sisters that we call the Statue of Liberty? And, inspired into even higher reaches of awe would their wonder have been launched upon seeing it placed high in glory upon its exalted base of freer ideals in the gateway seaport of the grandest city they would ever see, poised there as a lighthouse to the theretofore unknown potential of their children, mothers or men.

The New Colossus

Not like the brazen giant of Greek fame,
With conquering limbs astride from land to land;
Here at our sea-washed, sunset gates shall stand
A mighty Woman with a torch, whose flame
Is the imprisoned lightning, and Her name
Mother of Exiles. From Her beacon-hand
Glows world-wide welcome; Her mild eyes command
The air-bridged harbor that twin cities frame.
"Keep ancient lands, your storied pomp!" cries She
With silent lips. "Give Me your tired, your poor,
Your huddled masses yearning to breathe free,
The wretched refuse of your teeming shores.
Send these, the homeless, tempest-tost to Me,
I lift My lamp beside the golden door!"

    The poet Emma Lazarus honored the tremendous conception of our Grecian ancestors, an assured wonder of the ancient world, by penning these prophetic words in kind remembrance of their concerted efforts, although somewhat misplaced in reverence. Rightfully so, these splendid verses were affixed to the pedestal of the aforementioned Statue that accents our coveted freedom in the tide-battered harbor outside New York City, the new and greater colossus of the modern world, the unemotional feminine giant standing robed and maternal as the sentinel before the symbolic coastal gates of our homeland with her guiding torch thrust aloft in parental conviction, whose fixated gaze peers silently across the inhospitable seas, scanning the stormy eastern horizon far into another hemisphere, yearning for the first glimpse of that next ship of rejected humanity who would pine to become freedom's newest children, those who would dare the treacherous waves and harrowing fathoms, offering their lives to the face of death in a challenge of their icy depths, they who would toss their fate upon the nobler crests of the future, bobbing through the uncivilized fog of their times toward a blessed rendezvous with the union that is guarded by values personified within the trusses of a figure's stately engineering.

"It happened every time. Someone would look up and see her. It's difficult to understand; there'd be more than a thousand of us on that ship—travelin' rich folks, immigrants, and strange people, and us. Yet, there was always one, one guy alone, who would see her first. Maybe he was just sitting there eatin' or walkin' on the deck; maybe he was just fixin' his pants, he'd look up for a second, a quick glance out to sea, and he'd see her. Then, he'd just stand there, rooted to the spot, his heart racing; and every time, every time I swear, he'd turn to us, toward the ship, toward everybody and scream: America!"

- Giuseppe Tornatore

Everything this colossus divines beckons as an apparition penetrating the haze of unsuspecting hearts, in gleaming sunrise and shimmering twilight, before the dawn and after the night, parting the veil of the current moment and presiding over the future with her back against the errant past, whose purpose and presence chide her primitive companion to be of a greater valor, usurping his corroded stature and terminal legacy in time, and furthermore humbling his purposes for even broaching human existence. This honored image of our country's once-great soul poses erect at the gateway of our national embrace as if she was our Trojan gift from which all Americans would spring to the greeting decks of our eastern seaboard with a rectitude that would cause her metal lips to crease into a smile, her righteous offspring dancing at her feet, all the while knowing that we would gladly extend our riches and respect to any weathered remnant of man who might search-out her protective shadow in their trembling hours of hope and need. Alas, and in spite of all these heartfelt sentiments, there she so conspicuously stands, the finite corposant of stoic helplessness and inanimate being, ne'er to discharge the slightest tenderness, tolerance, or tears; frozen upon her pedestal at the doorstep of the recurring generations, existing only to contrast the whimpering heights that glaringly imperfect men have dared to contemplate for an ascension. Yes, there she stands misappropriating a humanness to which she shall never awaken, locked in a dream beyond her liberating abilities, advancing no offensive and bearing no deference but to be herself, overwhelmed by a larger destiny whose age has arrived, heeled in historical lineage beside her ancient predecessor, and forced to concede her sacred bearing and holy identity that has heretofore and ever after belonged to another. You see, there lives a Divine Lady who moves and breathes and has Her being from a full-bloom pedestal stationed for Her by God; One who is appearing through the border mists of Paradise to so many expectant hearts, a Benefactress of Exiles who has majestically stepped-out upon the mystical waters, and strides with dignity across the perilous waves; without fear She addresses the howling gales, piercing the murky veils that would separate any child of God from Her embrace. She instead greets Her children mid-journey, knowing too well the darkness out of which we are traveling, too in love with humanity to risk a midnight passing beyond the awareness of our trammeled nighttime vision. The Immaculate Queen of Heaven and Earth, the Most Blessed Virgin Mary, the Matriarch of Paradise's immigrating population, all of Creation's grandest Lady, the perfect Woman personified; it is She who has existed before and beyond, the One of truly delicate flesh and living royal blood, spiring visionary heart and solemnly courageous deed, the authentic Bearer of Immortal Grace and the extension of God's noble composure, the Spotless One before the scrutiny of Perfection who is always compassionate and gentle in the face of life's greatest storms; she, the Virgin Purity, who instead birthed the unbridled ocean of tear-drenched pardon and the stellar Divinity which pales the universal collection of stars that clothe the vaults of our spacious heavens from the solar setting of this day's wisest illumination to its potential rising to divinity once again. Mary is the Final Colossus of a Creation that will never need another, a Morning Star of benevolent grace, the Queen who shall never be overshadowed in time or Eternity by either the paltry imaginings of men or the conceptions of God, Himself. She is the Immaculate Conception! Where are the words to venerably describe Her unchallenged Beauty? Who would refuse to elevate Her Maternity to its most-deserved plateau of gasping awe before us all? Bring on the gallant Shakespeares and all their fictitious Romeos, and the thriving rest who have done better justice to Love than myself in either myth or manifesto! Yet, it is I—this seeking child—on this sacred voyage—during this apocalyptic passage—before the living and the dead—who stands and cries-out with passion and devotion—*Mother!*—for it is this title, overshadowed by none other, which reveals Her Grace most invitingly to us all. If a perfect flower comes from a field of a million stems, and the maternal instincts of a beast remove endangerment from their precious offspring, then just as assuredly and far more convincingly does the Immaculate Virgin Mary instantly develop our contemplations into surreal ecstasies of new deliverance, and transcend into beatific wonderment the creative consciences and poetic inspirations of all creatures possessing a magnanimous spirit or a hopeful sense, protecting our long-sought Eternal Redemption in the same fell swoop.

Sunday, July 8, 2001   *2:44 p.m.*

"My prayerful little ones, if God had not chosen to   k(189)
*fulfill His promise of Love at all, would there still be a
Creation? So many philosophers and theologians have been
so suspended in the midst of answering this question that they
have refused to know the need for their own Divine existence
inside the Providence of His Kingship. There is no other
food for life than the perfection which is gained in knowing
the Maker of all that is good! Toward this end, you and I are
gathered today to pray for a greater comprehension of the
family of man, that everyone who knows the Truth will turn*   x
*to those who do not with the intention of helping them
understand. The simplicity of the Most Blessed Trinity is a
Mystery to behold, but one that is never a stumbling block to
becoming one Love with our Singular God for they who are
united in His Son. Indeed, just because there exists the
Triune Deity to which all men are called, there is but one
Love; and that Love is the essence of becoming immortal and
being perfect again in the sight of the Omnipotent Father. I
call you then, little children, to continue the march toward
everlasting Salvation by never stopping the fight against*   xx
*those who refuse to believe, the many who are trying to hold
you back, those who would rather destroy your faith.*

       *These are the days of essential Being, the natural
course of events which are revealing the destiny of Heaven
to the children of Light, the many-faceted walkway of
righteousness upon which God is by your side and within the
strength of your hearts. Christians have professed the noble
and sacrificial cause of Love because this is why you have
been born! Life on the Earth is your acclamation that God
has created you, that He has given you the breath to speak*   xxx
*His praises throughout all the Universe! No enemy can
defeat you because their opposition is burned in the flames of
Holy Love inside your hearts! Yes, the Holy Paraclete has set
your very power into motion in an otherwise quite sedentary
world! I ask you to continue the journey back to Heaven,
just as the Sacred Scriptures has commanded in the Liturgy*

today! There is no cowardice which can ever stop you from succeeding because, believe it or not, time is now on your side, where it has been since the Resurrection of Jesus from the Grave. All the stars in the Heavens are in alignment now, not for the purpose of predicting the future, but to sparkle in the midst of your own awareness that it has already come! The Kingdom of God is at hand!

These are the reasons why I have asked so profoundly in many places around the world that My children be both bold and beautiful in the midst of your piety and service to humanity at large. Indeed, the Angels have instructed that there is no fear in those who Love with the greatest power, except to realize that God is the Dominion and the Refuge over all with greater Wisdom. When decent men rise from their sleeping quarters at the break of another day, their purpose is to seek the God of Abraham and beseech Him for blessings anew. I have told you over and again that the Valor of the Cross is the expungement of all the transgressions of human souls from the beginning of time until the end. Your profession of faith is concurrently your confession that you are helpless alone, that you can know no Life without the Savior of Mount Calvary! My plea today is that all mortals on the Earth will prepare the way by which your predecessors have gone, that you will let go of the material world and join them at the intersection where they have passed into the Eternal Ages. One need not yet die to know the Truth in the fullness of day! Be Love! Thereafter, your soul is united with Heaven by the invocation of your intentioned destiny and the eradication of suffering from the globe.

If this were not the case, the Holy Spirit would have told you long ago. God would have wasted no more of your precious mortality if His Eternal Word was not meant to be passed-down to every generation since the Birth of His Son! I am the Immaculate Mother of this Love! Please accept that I have brought many miraculous signs and graces from Heaven so that the present age will know, and so that

xl

l

lx

lxx

anyone who is born in the flesh can walk upright in the fullness of peace, Grace, and Everlasting Life. I have spoken to you about Grace for many hours, indeed for a seeming Eternity, because it is only by the Grace of God that He has forgiven you! What does this truly mean? Is it possible that a debt so large as the one created by the sin of Adam could be erased by the Passion and Death of a single Man? Always   lxxx
remember that His Resurrection is the evidence! Eternal Redemption cannot lie in the grave, or it would be no new beginning at all! The First Fruit of the Holy Cross is the very One who bore it and died upon its horrible crux to save the world! Were He to have never walked again, what future would this have brought to those who were created in His image and likeness? Therefore, the Cross stands as the future of Life for all who accept it, for those who acknowledge its burden in their own lives, and then believe that it has absolved them! The Blood of Jesus which was let there is the   xc
acquisition of the forgiveness of every sinner who ever tread the face of the Earth.

      Dear children, My being here is, in itself, a fruitful factor in your Salvation because I have come to assist in the conversion of the lost to the Son I bore to save you. And, I am brought by that same Love, that equal devotion which is now resting inside your hearts from the Right Hand of the Father in Paradise. You are manifested inside this same capacity of Love, this same portion of the higher order of Creation which has called you blessed! Be not dismayed by   c
where you shall earn your next dollar or whether you will be entertained before the fall of the night; everything has been placed into Eternal order by the Son of the Most High God. The Mysteries about which you pray are revealed in your relationship with Him; and there is no other way to fully know God with this ultimate transformation of the human conscience and will. Yes, your communion with perfection is found inside this order of Love. Why are the Saints in Heaven already there, notwithstanding that the Final Judgment has yet to come to the Earth below? Because God   cx

has given you all the advocates that you will ever need, beginning with Me!

It is not simply a Catholic purpose to ask the Saints for help, it is a human involvement in the greater purpose of life for every soul who is still breathing the mortal air. I have come as the Mother of all humankind, not just those who belong to the Original Apostolic and Catholic Church. By all means, I am calling every soul to new Life in the Sacrament of the Eucharist, by conversion and prayer, and through the power of the instruction of the Holy Spirit in   cxx *those who realize that it is useless to protest against the Divine Nature of the Church anymore. The example is perfectly true—for those who are clinging to their lives while hanging on the cliff of their own weight in sin and error, only the Holy Eucharist is their anchor, lest they fall into the Abyss and be forgotten forever past the end of time. When the human soul makes contact with the Most Blessed Sacrament, it takes flight and lets-go of the temporal world altogether, toward the greater purpose of Love. If life on the Earth is to be perceived as collective humanity clinging to a*   cxxx *cliff, I ask you to hold on together! Never let a single one perish by allowing them to loosen their tether in the throes of temptation and error.*

This is an age during which the very perception of God by humankind will be made more keen to the eyes of the consciousness of all. Why? Because, as I have said, the Kingdom of God is at hand. One need not necessarily look to Nature for the answers or the signs, but around the Divine service of the Holy Father in Rome. He is your evidence that Jesus is about to enter His Reign on the face of the globe and   cxl *put the past to rest. The Vicar of Christ is, himself, a Signal of the Revelation which has been revealed by the New Covenant for your age, for all the ages combined. His pious words and sacred acts are the essence of reconciliation; and he is proving the fortitude of God on the Earth very well. Why should brother take-up arms against his brother, when everyone knows quite well that Love is the ultimate unifier*

in a world which reeks with such division. Jesus Christ is the only Savior of the wounded souls of men, and the End of Time will bring the encapsulation of this Truth to everyone.   cl
How can this Holy Pontiff fail when the Almighty Father is on his side, when the Morning Star is in his sights, when all the Angels and Saints are supporting his every move from the City of Light? He cannot fail! He will not fail! I implore the societies and nations of the Earth to listen to his command, to follow in his sacred steps of forgiveness and asking for forgiveness! This is the sweet Pontiff who is so dear to My Immaculate Heart that nothing in Creation could ever drive him away!

      Many are the hours and days when man and woman,   clx
alike, lay on their beds to ponder the purpose of life. The Holy Father in Rome is proving to the nations that the purpose is Love! Anyone with a sliver of hope can see it in his eyes and know from his words that the End of Time is near, and the God of all Ages will come to take them Home! I spend the precious time which God has allowed for Me to speak to those who will listen, telling all that human life does not need to be lent to agony, sorrow, and disease. Ask God to alleviate them all, and He will do it! He is just waiting for the many who will call His Holy Name to dispense the   clxx
Mercy and healing to the Earth that it so desperately needs! My prophecies and exclamations are not of some impending doom or inevitable chastisement from on High because God knows that His children have the ability to alter the unfolding of history and the curvature of the globe. I have told you this too, My children, that the answer is prayer! The Apostles who walked with Jesus on the Earth knew this with the greatest of intentions; and they are still praying for the world to this day in the company of the Holy Trinity to which their souls have been called. Can you not sense their   clxxx
yearning for the Salvation of the world, calling now through the ages for their millions of successors to accept the genius to which they have been drawn?

In all of this hope, My little ones, you still see a world of people who continue to say 'no.' But, that will not be the final response they will utter to God. Yes, the continuation of time will show you that each one will ultimately wield their own sense of responsible Love, because it is this Love who has given them life from the womb. I am a Mother who carries great joy today because I know these things to be true!   cxc
There is no doubt that I am sorrowful for many who are oppressed during the wait, but I know that the final outcome of the world will be a return to the mountaintop of happiness again. Here, too, if this were not so, My voice would have dropped into silence long ago. I cannot tell you the hour when the last moment of the mortal Earth will come, but I can tell you that it will eventually arrive. This is enough to keep Me going around the many cities and hidden hamlets of the Earth, seeking those who will look up again in faith that the Father's Will shall be done. I come to this humble home   cc
in America because you are being guided by the Morning Star to which you have tendered your lives for so long. You will never stumble on your way because you can see the reflection of your path in its glassy seas! Great is the purpose for which you are living! Mighty is the strength that you have been given by the God who has placed it there!

My children, the key prevalence for all those who live is 'respond!' It is not enough just to see and to know, the world must respond to the Living Christ who has asked you to live once again! 'Bring Me your tired and your poor'   ccx
indeed! This is no statue of a former god, this is the Living Life of Love who has said that HE HAS COME FOR YOUR TIRED AND YOUR POOR! He is walking, teaching, and breathing for the purpose of conquering the fathoms where sinners used to hide. He shall not wait for them to somehow wash upon His shores, or come sailing along in some accidental grace! This is Jesus! He is the Son of Justice who cannot be taken away, whose Light cannot grow dim in the face of rejection or disdain! This is your pro-active God who does not stand along the edge of an island and pretend to be   ccxx

freedom for all. He is the mainland shore who is already standing at the center of the Ocean of Love, in which He beckons all men to drown their sorrows and be lifted from the throes of despair. In My Arms rests the Light to which all humanity is drawn, from the perils of the globular seas, from the cities where they boast of their angels, to the rolling acres and towering peaks! I am asking you to hope again, dear children! I am asking for you to finally stand for once with a renewed strength upon your feet and turn your faces to the skies in relief and say 'My God, my God, I finally believe!' ccxxx

This is the reason that I continue to hold My hands of blessings over your little heads and pray that God Almighty will shower the delights of His Sacred Heart over you. I can lift you to the heights of His peace if only you will hold on to Me, if only you will not quit the fight again, and never, ever let go! I can see your troubled hearts and trembling hands in the night, those who are shivering in the cold of disbelief and painful regret. All those who feel like they have offended God too much to ever be absolved are absolutely wrong! There is a new beginning for everyone ccxl *who lives, those who are addicted to drugs, they who have given their past to the pleasures of the flesh, the many who cannot see because they choose to remain blind by their own callousness, hatred, and unmitigated arrogance and greed. Again, I say to you, the key to this change is 'response.' React to the intercession of God, and He will guide the lot of you to the peaceful ravines where you can be brave again, where you can draw a new breath, take a fresh drink, sit on your tired breeches and look into the skies with a wholly new arrival again! Respond! Respond! Is this not, too, the* ccl *essence of prayer? There are no endings to the countless years during which a homily would continue that reveals the newness of Life in the Love of My Son. There is only the unrivaled destiny of wholeness anew, a way to escape, a means of protection, a model for flight, and a change for the best! If it is only one 'I am sorry' away for those who cannot bring themselves to accept, please get down on your knees at the feet of your brother and beg his pardon in advance! Tell him that Jesus is alive in you, that the Holy Spirit is prostrate at his side and begging him to consider your soul as having been refreshed, absolved, and enlightened, and that you wish for him to join with you there!* cclx

Where are My children to whom I am calling, asking them all to fall in joyful reunion in front of the Cross in this very same way so that the reconciliation between God and man can begin? I am a Mother who is wearing a Mantle of protection for the lost and forsaken, a living devotion to those I inherited on the Hill where My Son was killed for the sake of your souls. I do not stand with spikes jutting from My head and the salty seas eating away at My pleats. I am the Mother of Love with the Living Crown of Glory atop My head! I am wearing the Immaculate laces of Satin and Love to which all those who yearn for Salvation in God still cling! There are no stony tablets in My arms for a secular proclamation that has long passed into the annals of history. I bear the Savior of the world who is calling out from His humble Manger throughout the portals of time for His people to finally know Him! There has never been a generation that needed to pass any further than the Love which He offers from the Cross! Let there be no mistake! The Son of God has made it clear that graves are for cowards! Only those with the bravest faith who accept Him as the Redeemer of the world are fitful warriors to fight in His stead! No hollow chamber or pit in the night can kill those who Love in His likeness! There is no defeat awaiting those who are scurrying about the Earth in His Name! cclxx cclxxx

So, let us go on together in peaceful accord; you, My children, the birds and the beasts, all who serve to the delight of the Lord! Be at rest in the knowledge that there is no stopping the Light of the World. Come to Me, all you who have chosen NOT to be weary anymore! Walk in the beam of Light who glows in My Arms, and never again shall you call yourselves poor! You will be rich in the Love of God! You will own the enemies who have finally been put down ccxc *by the purpose of your faith! This, My children, is Love at its best. This is the Glorious Crown which has already circled the globe, taking the waiting to the deliverance for which they have longed! High, above, and away they all now fly freely in the space of Divine Joy, never again surrendering to the walls that choose to discriminate against their hopes for* ccc *a better day to come! The soaring eagles are quite envious of those who are given to God! They sit on their lofty perches on high mountain ranges and look-out with generous glee while admiring the souls of the Saved. 'Where in the world did they come from?' they ask amongst themselves. 'We have never been able to fly like that!' And, these same eagles come from those towering peaks to join you in flight, all who have beckoned for My help. I will ensure that Jesus will take you back to your Heavenly reward. He will not say 'no' to Me, I promise you that! So, upon the occasion of the heated* cccx *summer days in America, as you ponder the hours that pass, the seasons which come, and the fortunes which might slip away, please never stop hoping for your Salvation in Jesus. He is more than any address that a Saint might deliver from the plateaus of the globe, higher than any summit which the Angels might ascend, and more peaceful than the solace that your hearts always gain when you find that you have won the race! You can 'be' this victory in your hearts! You can know that Heaven has predestined your success, and your competitors will be the first to come to a stop, run in the path* cccxx *of your tracks, pull you from the charge in which you have been engaged, pat you on the back, smile as though the end of the world has come and EVERYONE has been crowned its king, and embrace you with a touch of Love so profound that no one will ever let go, never, ever, ever.*

If you will only stay with Me, pray with Me, be patient in the face of rejection, continue your search for the Truth, be peace amongst the ravages of war, bring decency where there is only the impure; all of this will be yours, soon enough, and plentiful enough. Indeed, not a million speeches cccxxx *could ever capture the joy that is yours for the taking in My*

Son on the Cross.   No victory could ever catapult your jubilation to a greater degree. I ask you to 'respond.' This is the key. ...the ones who have left many courses in total despair because their hearts have been so aggrieved can return again and depart this time as the victors over all. God will make the world aright if only the world will give Him the chance. ...I have told you in the past that Heaven is beautiful because the children of God are beautiful. Hence, you are the lilies of the fields!"   *cccxl*

There is an almost forgotten Land of eternal reality staring point-blank Divinity into the soul of every living being. It remains the celestial Shangrila, existing forever before the wilful foundations of this age of Cain, independently subsisting in Eternity within the continual newness of its very first day, the Risen Perfection that has been pulsating with Love at the highest pinnacles of our prayers and all the edges of our mystical awareness surrounding them since before that first, ominous moment when time was loosed from Eternity and began its diminishing tailspin toward being consumed by Glory once again. This Spiritual Kingdom flourishes in unapproachable Light, glistening beyond our reproaches and encamped far above abridgement within the angelic realms of unimpeachable virtue; erecting walls too high for its anemic enemies to breach, but bending and beckoning, opening and inviting our contemporary existence to be transfigured into its everlasting purpose, that reign where Saints and Angels revel in the awakening of man from his nightmare of terminal being to grasp with flailing palms an irrevocable destiny, soaring without end above his ecstatic dreams. We reside upon the multiple plats of sanctified plains, made sacred by our heroic predecessors who launched their bold sacrifices upon the catapults of their devotion, the same holy legions who remain imperturbably fixed beneath the Mantle of the living and breathing Monument of our transfiguration, that Virgin Most Statuesque, with the uncompromising gates of their hearts flung to the wayside, greeting and drawing any beleaguered humanity who would seek and strive to bedrock their souls within the Absolution of Christ and the highest perfections any mortal could conceive, attempt, or desire. It is here, at this salvific Portal of Eternity, that God Himself has poised His Final Colossus of Revelation, the Co-Redemptress and Mediatrix of all Divine Graces, She who wields the flashing fire of Saint Elmo's intercessory deliverance, and who presents a torch of Love blazing in the spiritual darkness of our sorry nights, a redemptive Lamp from the Throne of every man's God—imprisoned Lightning, indeed! The Mystical Lintel supporting the Gate between Heaven and Earth, this Woman Clothed with the

Sun, stands with commanding Authority, impregnated with unyielding Power and bearing a solicitous demeanor, honorably assuming Her matriarchal station with as much conviction and determination as was let from Her Vestal Conception in the hour of Truth's steadfast Triumph beneath the Cross of humanity's worst calamity, the true ground-zero of Redemption where She inherited the Corpse of Life for the sake of our Eternity, in the stateliness of Her grand Divinity, cloaked with an Omnipotent Pallium of Protection, within the mystical reaches of our hearts and overshadowing the context by which a naive American democracy exists, projecting righteousness from a Kingdom of the Spirit which permeates the creation of things, the history of hearts and the dispositions of men, still enfolding and enrapturing and bearing a trust that no devices of fiends or pitting winds of indignity can strip from the frame of Her royal bearing. Within Her Immaculate Heart, the children of God reside, paying tithes and tribute to the Universal Truth, and praying for the Triumph of heavenly nature to soon descend and wipe the face of Creation of its ill-comportment as swiftly and adeptly as any mother has intercepted the last mouthful of strained peas before they were spate upon a freshly-washed bib. The ethereal gifts within the possession of this New Eve of Creation are the delicate qualities and immeasurable quantities we must seek. Only there will we rediscover the greatest sentiments and noblest successes—reminiscence-come-alive—the deliverance of the broken and the suppling of the wretched. Exclusively, in these heretofore unknown heights—*sui generis*—humanity will revel in its sacred purpose and devise bolder courses for unseen mountaintops of a more sanctified life where we can peer down in wholesome fraternity upon every other diminutive range of ages that has contested the face of this incubating planet and say with hope and with assuredness, *Let us go now to our lives, and in humility create the grandness of being wherein we will inscribe our God-given names into the everlasting ages beside the giants of the dignity of men, positing our legacy of goodness and life as a brilliance shining upon our progeny through the transoms of our blessed memory, traversing the remaining corridors of our sacrifice and marking instead these hallowed chambers with our divinity and grace, forthrightly announcing to both the posterity that we will nobly birth and the orthodox scrutinies of history, "You are the worthy heirs of an unending promise secured from that Calvarian mountaintop in the days of old! May the Reign of God be sustained in you until all be made forever One in Him!"* So, let our final age and its righteous battles commence through these earnest verses delivered by an Archangel who so honorably wished to hail again the crowning of Heaven's maternal Wisdom from the crashing shores of the Pacific to the lapping shelves and teeming banks of the Atlantic coast, Paradise's Final Colossus, the Easter Lily, God's Tabernacle Rose, the blossoming Revelation of the Most Benevolent Benefactress and Mother of the Consummate Epitome of Human Grace, *Jesus Christ the King!*

The Final Colossus

Basking, bathing, brilliant! Outpouring the Wisdom of God!
The Visage of Heaven, flowing freely the tears of pristine Glory.
Clothed in unerring, inevitable Light. The winds of change!
Eradicating, electrifying, compelling, beloved!
You teach the shedding of Earth amidst the corals of sin.
Go! Go into the world that knows no peace.
Greet, bless, call, embrace!
Heal, sanctify, purify, caress!

You, the Virginal Shores of Paradisial Love.
Monogram and Monument to the Triune God.
The Trident, the Benevolent, the Salvific, the Bold.
You, the Sunlit Matron of God's Holy Ones,
lost in the portals of bewildering Death.
O' Perfect Glory, Mother of Life Renewed.
You, the Hands of Grace.
The Fair Maiden who birthed the pacific Pardon of fallen souls.

You, the Beatific Dawn of a Boundless Age.
Bring the solstice of Ecstatic Light to heirs and orphans.
To the Well of corpus hearts brooding in hopeless Dusk.
Seek ancient tundras and mystical parlors
where mortals huddle amidst battle and waste.
You, the flawless Blessing and newfound Trust of generations lost!

You, Matriarch and Queen of the lifeless Daughter in the Harbor.
Your Son is the Torch of Life to the children of Earth.
His Light unifies the blessed, the grated, the wretched,
the lost, the timid, the damned.
You! Summoned by the outstretched arms of Hope!
Stationed high above the stillness of invincible Freedom.

You celebrate the Destiny of man and beast, alike,
with Your Immaculate Crown of Stars,
to which the little Child in the Bay bows in deference,
her spiked chapeau heeled near her humbled feet.

She welcomes Your cultivating Touch to the unwitting masses,
the hopeless chest of inordinate pawns
awaiting their passage to the Celestial Port,
while the Streams of Paradise reflect your glistening Mantle.

Yes, You step into the world to claim the Unknown.
Clasping errant palms that flail in the dark,
pulling to beat their breasts
in the vibrant New Groves of the Land of God.
You are the Parasol of Infinite Bliss.
Refined, Robust, impassioned Delight!
Where cities of angels moor to feast on placid temperaments.
Come this Day! Lift every age to Heaven's Door!

- Saint Gabriel the Archangel

Friday, June 26, 1998
　　"My dearly beloved and beautiful children, your　*h(177)*
souls are more precious than gold, and your hearts are sweet
as honey in the summertime breeze. I have come on this day
to remind you of the simple eloquence in which I have
dressed you for the coming days of Glory. I am confident
that you will know My Jesus when He comes to greet you at
the great wedding of Heaven and Earth. I am now
transforming your writing with the same stately eloquence so
that it simply portrays the beauty of the mansions of Heaven.
Those who read it will pine for the Grace it gives to the soul.　*x*
Be careful not to be possessed by a spirit of urgency when you
see that My work is often painstakingly slow. Yes, My
messages are urgent in nature, but they must be pretty and
articulate. That is what I am helping you accomplish as we
work weekly toward that goal. It is through this same
understanding that you continue to pray in reflection of My
desires. Your journeys to the hills of Croatia provided you
both with an awakening, but your true transformation has
taken place here in this hallowed house, blessed by a Bishop,

Myself, and Jesus. This has for the past eight years cultivated   xx
your own conscience, purity, and prayerfulness for the sake
of yourselves and many. I desire that you continue this
progress as I pray with you and for you. Your participation
in the Sacraments keeps you holy and feeds you the joy of the
Truth which God provides through them. He will give you
the opportunity to keep your promises when you proclaim
your life in Him. That Grace is of the power of Jesus to
manifest Himself through all good things. The greatness is in
Jesus' teaching and providing the opportunity for you to
display His Love. Please see this for all who come to Jesus for   xxx
strength and conversion. God is almighty, and yet so simple
in the life He gives to His people. He does not require you to
be a great statesman, but a simple messenger for His peace
and providence. I am sent to tell you, however, that the two
of you are simple messengers who are providing a
monumental message for the world in your pretty work. It
will be seen as the Final Colossus.

You have been displaying your happiness for which
God is entirely grateful. You are hearing My words with
obedience. It is through this obedience that I am able to   xl
dispense to you grace after grace, upon bountiful grace. I am
the Mother of the Catholic Church, the Original and True
Church of Jesus Christ. I am also the Mother of all people
everywhere, and I will see to it that everyone at last finds
their way back to the Sacraments. Pray for the homeless and
for those who do not know God. Pray for the end of abortion
and the poor souls in Purgatory. Thank you for lifting your
prayers to the heavens today. I will speak to you again very
soon. I love you. Goodnight!"

Dearest Virgin Queen and Mother of misguided Humanity, please turn your merciful gaze toward every heart that is lifted to you. All thanksgiving, praise and honor be to your Beloved Child for these beautiful days of mystical revelation. I intone this prayer to your Immaculate Heart which I know without doubt is filled with love for your children, honoring Your radiance and the mighty King you bore. I venerate the love You share with Your Sacrificed Son, and pine with all that is living to be found worthy of being embraced by the infinite mystery which exists between your two Hearts. Please extend this Eternal Life to us in the here and now, within these, our helpless bonds of mortal reparation. Help all who have been given breath to open their hearts and participate passionately in the divinity that humankind now witnesses so prolifically in Your Immaculate Being. Dispense to us the Wisdom to spur the potential that lies bridled and bewildered in our collective soul. Ignite hope for a better world so that we may rise to the occasion of your miraculous visitation, weeping not over our derelict past, but rising in persistence to address a nobler day. Since God desires our joy in Him, help us ring it across the lands with the clarity of tubular bells, pealing all Truth with potent abundance as prolific as the blades of grass and the leaves of the trees. Secure for us the holy atmosphere of caressing grace, and teach our hearts to swim effortlessly in the currents that wisp in Heaven's skies. Inspire every heart to look upward for their embodiment of true victory. O' let that day be today! Allow that future living in our dreams to descend from the heavens upon our present selves, forgetting not to mend the broken, heal the stricken, comfort the afflicted, strengthen the weak, regenerate the timeworn, enliven the despondent, humble the proud, and most of all, transfigure the evil. Remove the shades from righteousness and loose the glowing radiance which pulsates from the souls of Your little children. Permit us to advance upon the globe! Bestow the Power and grant the venue; give us authority over the world, the landscape of nations, and the souls of beasts. The armor is polished, courage stands at the ready, the plans have been drawn, and the bugle is kissing the lips of Destiny. Advance the cause of the Lamb of God into Creation! Lead the final victory of Your Almighty Son! Launch the heavenly offensive! Sound the charge!

Unleash the imprisoned lightning from Your sacred torch!

Friday, January 30, 1998

    "Hello, My precious children. I come in grace, and   *h(030)*
as Grace. Thank you for welcoming Me again, as together we pray to bring the mortality of man to closure. My message today is the same, and yet is always new. I am the Virgin of virgins in whom you will find all the power you need to reach the heights of your hopes and expectations. In Me, you are comforted and healed. You are made whole by My Son, who indeed exchanges your morning hopes for sunset realities. He transforms your mourning into morning,

filled with the newness of day and light. How can you come   x
to know such a benefactor? I give Him to you. And, I have
come to ask you to come with Me to be reciprocally presented
to Him. My beloved children, I hope that you can now feel
the Truth in the words I have been speaking to you that you
have always known to be true, but you were too fearful to
adopt. You have seen the healing of the Mother Angelica
because the reign of God is at hand. I have told you this
many times. It was told during the first recorded century.
That hand has reached to the Earth for twenty centuries, and
has now arrived. You will know more and see better in the   xx
coming months. I ask for your continuing patience and
prayers. The things I have told you are alive in your hearts
to set you free. I am the Lady of Liberty. The Light of My
torch is the Love of My Son—Yes, about to break free into the
mortal world and expose all, and to liberate all. No happier
will a collective humanity ever be. It is a time for both
reflection and anticipation. Remember always the goodness
God has shown, and that you always said 'yes' when God
asked you to serve. Remember the peaceful times that will
now be restored. Recall the happy times that you will soon   xxx
live again. You know that Jesus owns the world and is the
Ruler of your hearts. He will protect them as you continue
to serve. Now, My children, that dreaded word 'however.'
However, there is still a great battle ahead. There is a final
battle for souls that you have many times pondered, and for
which I have been preparing you. Yours is a great period of
tribulation because the world is being purified. But, to your
good fortune, you have the Mother of all on your side. You
have My Grace and prayers to give you strength. You do not
enter the battle alone. You do not serve Jesus anonymously.   xl
He knows your soul and where you are in time and space.
He knows also your love for Him and your commitment to
allow Him to succeed through you. All Creation is flowing
toward the moment when all is reconciled to God. And, you
have come to the bottom of the page. It is time for the
summation. Jesus will turn the page of human life to reveal

what is written in the epilogue. He will rip the page that you have yielded to Him from the book of time, and it will sail gleefully onto the Throne of God. Yes, God will pick it up and recognize the finest words ever written by His Son. l
Your name is on that page, along with all the new Saints, the last to enter the great Kingdom. My children, you have every reason to expect that moment of all time to come soon. You are seeing the conditions of the world now forming in revelation of the reconciliation of God and man. You are seeing occurrences never before witnessed, and many atrocities that Satan has never before dared to try. But, never before has the power of Jesus' Cross been so intense as it is in this last age. Jesus has met the challenge and once and for all destroyed the evil that you see now, not a permanent lx
ill, but a passing manifestation of an already-dead evil. Satan can still blow weak souls off their feet in despair, but he does not have enough breath to extinguish the Flame of Love that is Jesus in the world. Satan is on his deathbed and is trying to constrain souls beneath him. He will not succeed. And so, as these final times play-out, do not despair at what you will see, but rather be hopeful that the permanent beauty of God has arrived. Those who hear His call have raised their head to see Him. Others are still waiting to hear, to see, and to know. Many are too weary and afraid to look up. lxx
Others have covered the ears of their souls from the shell-shock they have come to know in a world that has so ravaged them. And, others are just too weak and worried to care. All must now have courage in this last age. Jesus has destroyed human fear and all that makes humans fear. This is the greatest time of hope since the Pentecost of the first century."

Section Four
The Geoglyphic Spiritual Kingdom

"Houston, Tranquility Base here. The Eagle has landed."
- Astronaut Neil A. Armstrong

There was an evening in the not-too-distant past when I heard one of the most acknowledged protestant evangelists state before thousands that he was bewildered by the enigmatic nature of human suffering, especially when innocent children have been called into the grips of its redemptive burden. He honestly professed not knowing why our loving God would allow so many people to suffer the hideous atrocities and glaring misfortunes that arise so often in the lives of our brothers and sisters. I somewhat marveled at his exalted stature as a leader of Christianity while failing to grasp the basic understanding of the sanctifying unity in the Mystical Body of Christ. Notwithstanding his admitted lack of Catholic vision, I admired him deeply when he pleaded with lion-hearted confidence for his listeners to invoke their own faith in the providential Will of God anyway, asking those in attendance to marshal their belief and proclaim that our Heavenly Father does everything perfectly, no matter whether we understand His benevolent intentions or not. He petitioned us all to take that intrepid leap of faith and bear the tragedies of life without seeing their specific purposes in advance, to bestride our doubts and reach for the comforting genius and soothing peace emanating from the seemingly veiled Wisdom that flows from the Throne of God. Consider the galvanizing act of allegiance that his many followers were honored to attend him at his revival beckoning, renewing their strength to blindly confide in a Providence few of them have ever understood. How so many struggle to make sense of each child born with infirmity, the lives of the soldiers who have encountered horrific misfortune and even death, or those good people whose hopes and dreams have been shattered by the accidental negligence of other human beings on many a reckless day? From where does the trust arise that inspires people to advance into unclarified acceptance without the empirical evidence to bolster them there, realizing and responding to a force much like the wind, although not knowing what composes the invisible substance that wisps their souls like the unseeable breezes blow the tufts of hair from their foreheads? Their response resembles a little child who knows nothing of the composition of air, but dances with glee when a contraption of colorful paper and sticks is lofted on a string into the cloud-strewn skies of early spring. And, even though for a brief moment this honorable spiritual leader was himself like a kite which had lost its own stabilizing tail, spinning dizzily in a disoriented trajectory, he still soared safely in the heights of Jesus' merciful Grace. My purpose is not to inordinately highlight any chasm in the righteous integrity of anyone's understanding of the Mysteries of Redemption, but to challenge each and all to consider the inexpressible fact that there are far grander plateaus of insightful knowledge that the King of Creation wishes to dispense to those who will humbly accept His Divine Wisdom without question or debate as did those congregants who nobly anteed-up their fealty on my television screen several weeks ago. I sincerely appreciate, honor and elevate their faithful invocation of filial commitment to Christ and extend to them the vast support charitably offered through the concise enlightenment that God dispenses through His Roman Catholic Church. It is just such courage, openness of heart, and selfless surrender that Our Lady is seeking from the entire body of humanity so we may move together into those enhanced realms of Divinity that are more precisely aligned with our collective deliverance and the clearer vision of the hallowed nature of our existence below the heavens. You see, the Truth will not go away. It shines as a star that pales the midday sun; and we are asked to toss aside any impediments, whether they be generational, familial or religious traditions, along with the outright sinister demagoguery, to embrace the bright revelations of the Holy Spirit with as much abandonment as that auditorium filled with our evangelical brothers and sisters who surrendered their trust to the words of their charismatic leader, even though he did not understand what the Original Apostolic Church has been teaching since those first auspicious days of its glorious inception. So, let us begin constructing an understanding in places where it may be lacking, and further the Light into the darker quarters of human sympathies so the full power of Catholic Christian unity will materialize for the transformation of our existence into a Kingdom on Earth beyond description.

Sunday, July 9, 2000   *3:33 p.m.*
    "Where are the omissions which are keeping   *j(191)*
righteousness and justice from overtaking the world?—In the
empty arms of humanity who collectively refuses to take up
their holy arms, whose material obstinance has left their
consciences numb, and whose rampant impurity is the
manifestation of deadly disease through all the continents.
My dear children, if the people and races of the Earth wish
to eradicate the suffering which engulfs every shore, they
must rid themselves of the sins and corruption of the flesh.
These corporeal errors have been the origin of carnal lust,   *x*
infidelity, and reprobation since mankind first walked the
surface of the globe. But, it does not have to be this way.

Jesus wishes His people to be whole, healthy, and pure in Him. The diminishment of the flesh should come through the spiritual uprising of Grace in His Holy and Sacred Heart. I ask My children to take heed of the teachings of the Epistles, and teach the world about the spirit by leading in the Holy Spirit. These are days of great terror and fear for many, like shadowy palms in the night which lurk so closely. No wonder so many lie in such reckless fright, they will not gain their strength and insight by approaching the Savior of the world. They will not repent, confess, and amend their lives. They refuse to accept the Thanksgiving Feast from the Throne of God and His Altar in Heaven, the Eucharistic Body, Blood, Soul, and Divinity of Jesus Christ. Why is their depression and disgust so profound? Because they will not avail themselves to receive these Sacraments and blessings. They will not submit their errors to the absolution of God. They will not allow their fractured mortality to be healed by the graces of the Church, whose power and unequivocal Wisdom can cure any malady and redeem any soul. In short, humankind only needs to give their hearts to the Messiah of Nazareth, their Emancipator on the Cross, and say—Heaven help me, God hear me, Jesus have mercy on my soul. Then will all that has perverted the lives of mortal men be expunged from Creation. Then will happiness reign over grief. Yes, only then will your land be healed. My dear little ones, too many have forgotten and many others never heard that I gently walked the pathways of the Earth. I have seen the same fear and indignation which still plagues the societies and ghettos that were apparent 2,000 years ago. Time has done little to ameliorate the horrors of human life because there is no compassion that time has to offer. Only the efforts of man, the complete conversion of the heart and soul of the inhabitants of the globe to Jesus Christ can bring that new beginning, despite the deafening passage of years which roars past like a thunderous herd in the night. Only the living testament of the Holy Gospel can restore humankind into the likeness of Paradise. It is in that New

xx

xxx

xl

Covenant where every sickness is healed and all wars will   l
cease. I have been bringing this same message of peace to
every nation on Earth for endless generations. I have offered
the reason why humanity must invoke faith, and that reason
is the Salvation of man. The Almighty Father dispenses
miracles and cures, but He also requires His Creation on the
Earth to read the signs, to live by faith, and to recognize His
Divine Presence in the visual world about you. Living
without this trust in Him is like continuously working
against the grain of His lofty woods and trying with dubious
failure to reverse the movement of the universe. Mankind   lx
will hold that power only when he becomes the likeness of
Jesus. This process begins the moment you receive the Most
Blessed Sacrament. As soon as the Eucharist makes contact
with your tongue, the ground beneath you rests in peace
because you are the new life in Christ standing upon it. The
angels weep in happiness because they know that you will
thereafter recognize them. And, the Saints in Heaven swell
with happiness because you are living-out the faith that God
dispensed to their own fathers many centuries before. The
power and majesty of the Eucharist is much more than the   lxx
union of your soul with Heaven on a given day. Your Holy
Communion is your commitment to God that you will
commence your efforts in assisting Him to close-out the ages
with courage and love amidst an awful world of people who
would rather destroy the world than hand it back to God in
one united piece. I cannot tell you sufficiently today how My
Son yearns for your unity in Him under the Cross when He
Returns to redeem you. He requires the participation of
everyone who will eventually arrive in the miracle of
Redemption in the arms of peace beneath My Immaculate   lxxx
Mantle. You may be both weary and scarred by the journey,
but I assure you that, by the time you have a Rosary in your
hand, you will be like the fortunate gladiator who has won
the favor of the King, the one who will be crowned with a
champion's nobility once the battle is through. My children,
this is the race to which Saint Paul has referred. It is not one

for which he who finishes first will be crowned, but for he who finishes best. That authentic achievement is claimed by the collective body of humankind whom Jesus will marry and claim as His Body at the end of time. This is the mystical matrimony between the Woman of the Earth—the Holy Church of faith—and the Bridegroom who now awaits in the paradisial chamber. I give you My assurance that you will understand these things with spotless distinction as the future continues to unfold. Collective humanity is filled with the Holy Spirit, and Jesus is coming to reclaim humanity in Himself. The fruit which He seeks is the souls of mankind. You are seeing firsthand why human redemption and purification are called the Sacred Mysteries. They are difficult to place into words because they are confined to linear time for those who have yet to pass across the threshold of death, back into life. I am pleased that you understand. How happy with you is the Son of God! This is why these are such special times. Thank you for your endless efforts to receive My messages, to have your Diary published and made available, and for building the system that is in place which makes the spirit of people come alive. Do you see the domino effect which has begun in Medjugorje? Thank you very sincerely from your very pleased Savior. My Special son, you help Me cry many tears of happiness and joy, like you shed in watching the 46 year-old see for the first time since he was only three. The principle is the same. You are seeing the Kingdom of Heaven now because I have been remaking your vision through the power of the Holy Spirit. I am unsure whether you are capable of realizing how happy that makes Me feel. You have said 'yes,' and the Kingdom of God on the Earth will long be the better advanced for your goodness. This is My holy blessing for you. + You have My Immaculate Heart in which you may always take solace. Therein rests My perfect gratitude for your life of Love! I will speak to you again very soon. I love you. Goodnight!"

l

lx

lxx

lxxx

I never fail to get a giggle out of that cantankerous lapin, Bugs Bunny, although an old-timer named Jack Smedley used to humourously contend that he was the meanest rabbit he had ever seen. Despite the fact that I could find agreement with him, I was particularly struck with this animated cartoon character when his creators decided to embellish the story of Jack and the Beanstalk. Most everyone knows how the tale progresses, where Jack trades the family cow for a hand-full of beans which, when planted, invariably grow into an enormous vine towering skyward into the kingdom of a tyrannical giant. Well, in this particular rendition of the fable, the beans end up being tossed into Bugs' rabbit hole where he is taking a nap. Of course, the beanstalk quickly grows like a ballistic missile being launched from an underground silo, transporting both Bugs and his bed, which is entangled in the branches, upward into the behemoth's domain. After waking and realizing that he is in a new land above the clouds and having several humorous altercations with Daffy Duck, who plays Jack in the story, Bugs Bunny is seen racing across the giant's estate unbeknownst to him that he is running in the cultivated furrows of the despot's planted garden. As ol' Bugs gradually becomes aware of his new surroundings, this perpetually composed, long-whiskered snob comes to a screeching halt with his eyes transfixed skyward, his long ears drooping to his sides and his mouth gaping in overwhelmed awe as he stares up at spiring rows of carrots that are as tall as skyscrapers stretching as far as his eyes can see. Truly a rabbit's heaven! In that instant, the interests he previously held were not as important as the new feast before him, which also happened to be the ultimate satisfaction of his fondest dreams. If God is allowed to use cartoon characters to expound mystical parables, surely this is one good example. As a rabbit, Bugs Bunny instinctively understood the delectable nature of his favorite food, but his composure was not prepared to assimilate the scale to which it was eventually revealed to him. The many cultures of the world are permeated through-and-through with vast throngs of people who are veritable Bugs Bunnies before being thrust aloft into the Light of Truth; unprepared, pompous, arrogant, self-possessed, insolent, vengeful, violent, and pseudo-experts about everything pertaining to the claim they stake over their societal domains. We are often like overconfident children who believe ourselves to be great mathematicians when we have only gained a modest command of our elementary tables of addition and subtraction, or great aircraft engineers after merely folding a paper airplane, yet much too afflicted by our prejudices and insecurities to look behind our thrown-back shoulders and realize that our superiors have mastered fluid dynamics and quantum theory, or that the backdrop of our wallpaper genius is a military squadron of multi-engine F-15 Eagle jet fighters whose cockpits are stationed with battle-hardened aviators who themselves are about to be taught firsthand by the seraphic angels what flying is all about. Yes, there is a celestial Garden for each of them also, one containing airy skylines of mystical castles they will thunder past while rocketing heavenward, blasting through the holes in the clouds as they race toward the Face of God. The remarkable clarity accidently fostered by a group of animators could no more clearly exhibit the instantaneous transposition of vision and the re-prioritizing of interests of one who is mystically exposed to the Christian Truth dispensed from the Throne of Wisdom on High, not to mention being rejuvenated and made to feel like a child who has just looped and tied the first bow in his new sneakers' shoelaces. Nor could they better differentiate between the knowledgeable state of those whose interior visual senses are supported by heavenly grace and the glaring contrast of those who are unmistakably adrift in spiritual blindness. There are two measures of sight within the human person. The first is our natural perception, which is an anemic function of the flesh that is incessantly diminished by the effects of original sin; and the other, our spiritually-oriented vision, the one we call "beatific," which is enlivened by our faith in the unseen genius of God who sustains it. When the Church speaks about the conflicting visions manifested within man's nature, those referred to clearly by Saint Paul, it is accentuating sublime precepts of reality that are deftly hidden by God beyond our sensual awareness, yet fully knowable through our noble capacity to believe in the spirit-motivated inclinations He inflames in our hearts. Indeed, what eye hath not seen, nor ear heard, nor even entered the mind of man has appeared to us through a mystical unveiling conferred by the Holy Spirit of God!

There are innumerable perspectives, perceptions, precepts, and even so-called facts themselves that are no more than unsalted musings issuing from the frail minds of lost individuals who have no sense of the grand mystery of human life because they either refuse to realize or have yet to accept that the ascension of the mountain of God is the only way they will ever see it from above. This brings to mind the geographic artistry imprinted upon the earth across the famous Nazca Plain. Centuries ago, primitive people undertook the labor to clear the top layer of darkened rock from vast areas of an arid plateau in the Peruvian desert, leaving the barren landscape littered with lighter-hued pathways resembling roads winding over the terrain and extending great distances, but which actually lead nowhere. Some of these "roads" stretch over 13 miles in a perfectly straight line, while others wrap around themselves almost endlessly like the mainspring of a humongous wristwatch. Their awe-inspiring magnitude renders it nearly impossible for anyone walking among them to recognize their features as anything more than random pathways that someone undertook great efforts to etch in the desert for no apparent reason or aesthetic value. It was not until the 1940s and the advent of air travel, almost two thousand years after their supposed creation, that their secret significance was divulged. Once the plain was seen from the height of an airplane passing overhead, it was revealed that the plateau was an enormous canvas and the lines were actually gargantuan images of spiders, hummingbirds, and other recognizable shapes called "geoglyphs" that had been planned and drawn-out on the ground by people who could never visually appreciate what they were because they would never see them from the sky. Think about it—those who walked along those cleared paths and among the maze of lines did not know that, by their steps, they were retracing something of far greater meaning, complying with an unapparent creation they would never fully see or comprehend in their mortal lives. If the population of those days had been told of their larger dimensions by the original artists, succeeding generations of their ancestors would have had to rely on a primitive faith to envision what the lines actually depicted.

The plains of Peru are simply another parable by which our Heavenly Father is catering to the growth of our awareness in His Divine choreography of human existence. He is revealing to us how our elevation, or lack thereof, can fundamentally alter the possibilities by which we exist, the foreknowledge by which we walk, and the fulfillment in which we may imbibe, contingent upon whether the realization occurs that we are participating in something on a scale that leaves the Saints and Angels in an awe greater than any long-eared rabbit hypnotized by some giant vegetables. The lesson of a cartoon and some curious lines in a desert lay open to us the delicate nature of our unity and the tempestuous conflicts flourishing through the rogue obscurities stoked by men who fail to invoke the higher reasoning of noble faith. However, become elevated they must! And, if they reject the faith to blindly obey the original artists and those in their custodial stead, then each of them must board the spiritual jetliner of the miraculous intercession of the Most Blessed Virgin Mary to see reality for themselves. Our Lady will bear them to new heights of the Truth to provide a vantage point that only God can evince. And, what is it that all of us will then see together?—the interconnectedness of our hearts, the universal fabric of our spiritual nature, the common bond engendered within our destiny, the unlimited powers of Divine Love, and the Hierarchical Church of human Salvation etched into history by a band of ordained Apostles and confirmed disciples whose artistic genius flowed from the Salvific Cross of one Perfect Man. The Original Apostolic Church of Christianity is the Messianic success-story, a constellation of recognizable providence upon the plains of the Earth stretching to Creation's end of days, and over which a successor of Saint Peter still presides in authority and dominion. Once humanity is caught-up amongst the clouds at the final appearance of Christ the Lord, we will look back upon the world and see all the disciplines and the dogmas, the rituals and liturgies, the sacraments and the shrines, the orders and the hierarchies, and the decrees and the teachings to be more than pathways excavated on a fertile sphere in the cosmos, but the exalted evidence and rarified substance where a geoglyphic Kingdom came to rest upon the Earth to imprint the masterful tranquility of the unseen world into real mortal existence like our spacecrafts impressed the lunar surface with their extended legs, never to be obscured. Mankind existed in a paradigm defined by every inflected form that could tend toward death. Yet, God restamped Creation with the impression of His Divine perspective by sending the Paragon, the Excellent One, His Only-Begotten Son to reestablish His impregnable Kingdom. The Most Blessed Trinity is the Almighty Definer who in Himself remains unlimited and unconfined by His own omnipotent definitions. Hereafter, He has laid claim to humanity and the ground upon which we walk by virtue of His indelible embossment of Redemption, never again to cede His testament of ownership which flowed from the veins of our Savior. We will ultimately realize from those elevations and with the awe of the raised hair on our heads that we were circumscribed within the bounds of Heaven all along. There before us will be the Roman Catholic Church with its timeless raiment of authority spread like the mantle of a gentleman upon the acerbic puddles over which human history had righteously walked, clad in the impeccable beauty of her devotions, the breathtaking testimonies of her Saints, and the monumental completeness of a Holy Mass that finished it all through a Covenant-Faith that was never broken, encompassing every plateau and plain of human existence, maintaining the pathways of grace in the cyclically-barren generations where God's faithful children obediently marked-step in a Triune unity beyond their times, their temperaments, and their means, hand-in-hand with Divine Providence who lighted their way with nothing more than the mystical bonds and manifold signatures of God to trust as their guide. All of this Truth is symbolically, parabolically, and factually what the Lord Jesus Christ is intent upon openly manifesting through the Roman Catholic Church to every person given the Breath of Life.

Friday, February 27, 1998

"My tender children with such innocent hearts, My   h(058)
Love is with you during this renewed Lenten season of prayer, and in union with Jesus as He denied Himself for forty days in the desert. This is a period of reflection and refinement, yet a time of anticipation. You must recall My previous Lenten messages, and how I wish you to call yourself especially to listen to God. Jesus' soul was never parched in the desert, neither was His Love diminished.

*Rather, His time in the desert parch was a time of inward
contemplation of His Love for God the Father and for
humankind. His forty days represents an invocation for you
to ponder likewise. You are the reason that God decided to
save humanity, all of you who are My children, because He
knew your potential to return to perfection. He recognized
in you the object of the Love of the Son He sent. And so,
during these days, you may pray humbly for pardon in union
with Jesus' upcoming Passion and know through it all that
God will give you nothing that you will not survive in union
with that same Passion. What is it that brings God to do
these things? His knowledge that, before Jesus, you will
ultimately judge your own soul. You will search-out your
soul for anything in you that might stain Heaven should you
be offered entrance there. You will shake yourself down in
search of any poison that would breach the perfect union
between yourselves and the Angels and Saints. Yes, God
wishes through these days to cleanse your garments and
render them perfectly pure, fit for a king to wear. And, this
He does because upon your passage from mortality, you will
look down to see if your clothes are fit to be presentable to a
perfect Lord. While Satan will be there to point at your
stains and laugh, Jesus will be there to tell you that they are
just echoes of former imperfections that your Virgin Mother
has washed away. Just as you now see stars in the night that
have long been extinguished, Satan will be fooled into
believing that you are not perfect. Your stains will be as
long-gone as those stars. In this great miracle of God, as you
go to Jesus to accept your holy crown, you may turn to Satan
and tell him that he terribly underestimated your ability to
see Truth given you through the Holy Spirit, that he failed to
know your obedience to the Virgin Mother who taught you
Grace, and most of all, he indicated his simple ignorance by
believing he could dilute the power of the Blood that made
you whole and a legitimate heir of Paradise. Indeed, you
may turn to Satan now and tell him that he may as well
return to the deathbed that he fully knows is his. With*

x

xx

xxx

xl

power and courage, you know that you belong to Jesus through Me, and thus, once again the perfect property of God. These are the holy meditations which you should enkindle both through these forty days and all through your life. Jesus anticipates with joy your contemplation of His time in the desert when He, too, refused to listen to the lies of Satan. It is not easy for you to dismiss all the temptation that confronts you, but you are inherently more weak than evil. So, I will make you strong, and in Jesus you will conquer the evil. That is the true majesty of Lent. That is the reason that you resolve to be righteous conquerors rather than indifferent followers of the flawed and lifeless world. The Earth is your temporary resting place, but you are now universal because you love. You are part of God's Creation again instead of an inanimate mortal. Through Jesus Christ, you live, breathe, and have life. This is the fortune that God wishes you to inherit. This is the future that is timeless and the perfection you already share in Jesus. You need not wait to be living Saints. In My arms and in God's sight, your soul has already arrived. You need to complete His work, also through Me, by being 'Jesus' for the world, His Body of Love; and I promise that He will soon return and take you to rest. I know that you are hungry for Jesus and thirsty for peace. God knows the pangs you feel deep within your soul. Therefore, to give you life until you are taken to Life Eternal, you are fed the Life-giving Eucharist, your thanksgiving that the only thing keeping you from seeing Heaven is time. In the Eucharist, that time is breached and you are already perfectly united in God. Through the Blessed Sacrament, you become an inner-visionary and the ecclesiastics of the mysteries revealed to mankind through the ages. You become the knower and revealer of God to the modern age by your unity with all former ages. This is the power of the Holy Eucharist. You consume and adore a portion of timeless perfection, a Body that is all Divine and a Soul that is perfect. Your humanness is given the gift of the immortal so that it travels through time like a butterfly over the lilies

l

lx

lxx

lxxx

in a field on a sunny day. That is why your heart is warm and your soul is at rest. Through the Eucharist, you are consoled in Jesus, and He in you. God is allowed the gift of your presence in Him before you ever draw near to sighing your last breath. So, to understand this Lenten season is to also understand God's fidelity to you through the Blessed Sacrament. Jesus' Body is God's ringing of your doorbell, asking you to come out to play in the fields of your fondest xc *dreams. The Eucharist is your formal invitation by God for you to vacate your mortal cell and return with Him to the land of your birth, to a mansion so magnificent that your soul cannot yet describe it to your heart. And, forget about your mind ever being able to conceive such a place. Jesus has prepared a mansion for your soul fit only for a newly perfected body. You will no longer wish to see the one you inhabit now again. For all of these images, Jesus wishes you to have a holy Lenten season. He wishes you to scoff-at the enticements of the devil and to remember the great* c *Resurrection of your soul which He provided on Easter morning. His Mercy is wide, indeed. Once, a soul came Home and told Jesus that he did not wish to steal his way into Heaven. Jesus told him that it was a gift He gives freely, and reminded him that the first Saint was also a thief. You cannot out-do the generosity of God, nor can you misconstrue the savvy of the means which Jesus will heal your soul and bring you Home as you are being tempted by evil to choose a different end. My son, these words and thoughts I have brought you tonight I hope you will one-day share with your* cx *brothers and sisters. I will tell you when is the time. You may now address the heavens who listen to your hopeful supplications... This is now your holy blessing from your loving Mother. + God is indeed very pleased. I will speak to you soon. I love you. Goodnight!"*

The Original Apostolic Church, collectively in the embodiment of the Dogmas She declares, the Traditions She propagates, the Faith She proclaims, the Sacraments She dispenses, and the unity She manifests is the seeable coalescence of Heaven on Earth, the concrete sanctum of the Kingdom of

God that is viewed from above through the power of loving abandonment to Her Canonical Vision. Still, there is a great difference in the perception and acceptance of the reality She emanates in relation to the dismal caricature fabricated by proud worldlings whose lack of faith and obedience, and whose historical revisionism precludes them from seeing what the Mystical Body of Christ really is and how our Crucified Messiah is in perpetual function until the end of time, bringing to pass the mysterious Triumph of Eternal Redemption. Only few of the blessed have been graced to openly see past the veil of faith and witness the finite nature of Creation magnified and transfigured into its authentic dimensions across the palatial infinitude of the heavenly scale. Yet, this Divine perspective is precisely what the Roman Catholic Church teaches, particularly when She speaks of the Eucharistic altars on the Earth mirroring the One Altar in Heaven, the Eternal Feast Table presided over by Jesus Christ which receives our sacrifices and offerings as they are transported into the purview of God during the Holy Sacrifice of the Mass. Can we intellectually contemplate the duality in the Moment of Consecration of the gifts of bread and wine at a Holy Mass previously celebrated in the musty catacombs of ancient Rome by a handful of the earliest Christians with the grandeur of that Sacred Instant of Eternity that occurs during an Easter celebration in Saint Peter's Basilica at the hands of Pope Benedict XVI with tens-of-thousands of faithful in attendance from around the world? Is it beyond our faith-borne meditations to imagine the soul-gripping profundity and deep humility that would have grasped the reverent hearts of those priests and communicants who cautiously, yet faithfully, memorialized the Death and Resurrection of our victimized Savior in their indecorous and inhospitable subterranean hideouts if they were to have been miraculously propelled through time and space from the caverns of the 2nd century to the present main-floor Altar of St. Peter's on the great Paschal morn of this modern day in the midst of Christianity's greatest liturgical celebration? Imagine the walls surrounding them and the ceiling above, the tunneled dirt, the formed plaster, the littering of rocks and chiseled stone, mystically fading away like a curtain being dropped to unveil a masterpiece; their eyes reopening to a boundless glory as they sense themselves rising into a Basilica that had yet to be built, to the exquisite marble and fine granite, and a sculpture of the most magnificent edifice glorifying Jesus Christ that the world has ever seen. Away roll the roughly hewn boulders, the finely honed crypts of their departed faithful, the cobweb strewn alcoves, and the rustic traveling chests upon which their bread was consecrated, disappearing and mysteriously replaced by the sanctified altar beneath the historic dome of the genuine Seat of Christianity. Imagine each of those precious souls finding themselves suddenly staring through their tears, out and over the sea of their brothers and sisters toward the vestibules and the balconies overflowing into the piazzas of Rome, and throughout the countrysides of time, the vision of their hearts falling upon the visible legacy of their belief, standing in majesty, vibrant, alive, thriving, and immense; and then humbly realizing that it was their unrelenting conviction in blind hope and steadfast identity beyond their persecution which sustained the bucket-brigade of faith brought throughout the ages to the thankful posterity of the Christianity they professed, all beneath the shadow of an architectural canopy that itself resembles the overarching protection of God, Himself. Let humanity entire share this universal vision of the one Church that Jesus Christ founded twenty centuries ago! Our Holy Church—the Roman Catholic Church—built on the blood of Apostles, Saints and Martyrs, indeed! The visible legacy of Love and devotion that cannot die! Let the vision of the transposition become fully apparent to every honest soul, for each of these great ones from former epochs are presently here, gazing upon this wonderment of timeless majesty in which we participate as Catholics, knowing straightaway how fully they participated to the selfless depths of their generous souls. And, shall we not in even higher beatitude contemplate that Altar residing in Heaven, the one before which each of our holy predecessors now stands, a sublime congregation unto whose company we shall someday be summoned in much the same way that I have just called upon the redemptive legacy of our saintly ancestors. You see, our departed brethren from those ancient Masses stand with us outside of time during each of our Eucharistic celebrations. The walls of mortality have ceased their binding, the veil between man and God has been rent, and the glories have been revealed, all in the same eternal breath as they perpetually worship at that very Altar in the Divine Kingdom—one and the same—awaiting our final deliverance from the fusty chambers of mortal conscription so that we, too, may be embraced by the realization that we have been in communion with them and in their presence all along. The absolved contingent of modern man will soon have thrust into his awareness the revelation of being released, unbounded, freed, elevated, enjoined, summoned, absorbed, bonded, commingled and united openly and magnanimously with the single Sacrifice which has been the reverberating Eternal Truth both directions through time since the moment Jesus Christ was crucified. Know true, each and all, that the entire history of Masses that have been offered daily from one corner of the globe to the next for the past 2,000 years is a single, great Pontifical Mass whose Altar is both in Heaven and on Earth—a never-ending eclipse of righteous Divinity that has passed before the face of Creation, receiving the Sacred Host and our lives at the miraculous words of Consecration uttered by our heroic Catholic priests for one hundred score of years and counting, each and every celebration emanating a brilliance upon renewed splendor, effecting a luminescence that makes the Earth look like the sun from the ever-watchful eye of the Almighty Father. If there be a beatific vision revealed, let it be thus: As the children of the Catholic Church have collectively gazed in faith and anticipation toward each of their individual altars of sacrifice before which they have knelt throughout time and the world, as a singular body of hope, people of the True Faith have peered in expectation and humility across the chasm between life and death to that one unseen Altar in Heaven which was manifested and consecrated on Mount Calvary through the Blood of the Lamb. And, then and there, and here and now, let us realize that when the Eternal High Priest, Jesus the Christ, looks down from the stead of His Sacrifice while reigning at His Altar in Heaven, the hallowed walls of Paradise have long ago given way to the penetrating gaze of His Sacred Heart, revealing to all the choirs of Heaven and every universe to be convened the glorious treasure for which He died—His loving people who were faithful to Him. And, in that ecstatic vision and embraced by His prayers to the Father, there materializes the chiseled tunnels of those catacombs; in full view appears every alcove, bay, nook, crypt, cranny and corner that for a hidden moment in time became the grandest of cathedrals, every remote place of the fearful and the persecuted nestled with breathtaking dignity alongside the elegance and majesty of the most expansive and impressive of our sanctified churches and basilicas, all those places where righteous praise has been given to Him in the Consecrations uttered by His humble priests. In these shining moments of Eternity, Our Lord and Savior sees into convents and brothels, castles and commons, hidden rooms and clandestine porticos, basements and root cellars, mountain passes and canyon shacks, caves and convention centers, keels and crows-nests, engine rooms and promenade decks, submarine bunks and airline cabins, rumble-seats and cabooses, teepees and pagodas, temples and towers, skyscrapers and hovels, shrines and taverns, mortuaries and delivery rooms, stables and dormitories, libraries and mess halls, soup kitchens and shopping malls, city halls and nations' capitols, bunkers and barracks, concentration camps and prison cells, foxholes and tents, troop transports and school buses, hospitals and orphanages, cemeteries and country churches, culverts and lofts, dirt roads and winding highways, quarries and country homes, construction sites and gated estates, ghettos and green valleys, forests and pastures, train stations and airports, fire houses and paddy wagons, council chambers and oval offices. He blesses and dedicates every makeshift altar of mortal time, the bulkheads and the baggage, folding chairs and pedestals, fence posts and workbenches, card tables and trestles, thrones and tabernacles, pasture walls and stumps, caissons and drawbridges, counter tops and piano benches, patio tables and clothes hampers, buckboards and mangers, oak mantles and cedar chests, operating tables and prison bunks, airplane wings and gun turrets. The Precious Eucharistic Body and Blood of Jesus Christ has been made present and laid in honor on catafalques and gallows, scaffolds and parapets, gang planks and mastheads, caskets and cornerstones, car hoods and tailgates, on tombstones and the slabs of pagan sacrifice, on the chests of His priests lying in prison confinement, at the equator and on the globular poles, on stages and center courts, in balconies and stadium boxes, on cardboard crates and stacked-up tires, from the grandest altars ever conceived by passionate men to the most wretched platforms ever given the opportunity to become sacred by the True Presence of God Almighty, at every place where evil once belittled the reign of greatness, the Eucharist Body of the Savior of the world has pierced its pitiable darkness, miraculously dispensing with the old and making all things new. And, the Roman Catholic world thunders—Thank you, Merci, Gracias, Faleminderit, Shenorhakal yem, Shukran, Dankschen, Sayol, Eskerrik asko, Dziakuju, Dhanyabad, Blagodaria, Do jie, Toa chie, Hvala, Dekuji, Tak, Dank je, Aitah, Tashakkur kiitos, Gmadlob, Dankeschoen, Efharistó, Danyavad, köszönöm, Go raibh maith agat, Grazie, Arigato, Go mop sum nee dah, Gratias ago, Paldies, Aciu, Nanhi, Takk, Dziekuje, Obrigado, Multumesc, Spasiba, Hvala, Tack, Tesekkur, Dyakuyu, Diolch unto every language known to humankind, as the Divine fire from the eternal Thanksgiving Feast plunges into our midst at the Holy Sacrifice of the Mass to obliterate the fanaticism of every heretic and false prophet. The Roman Catholic Church is the Kingdom of God upon the Earth, a fortress whose walls are the veils of faith, never to be scaled by anyone who mocks or impugns Her supremacy.

Sunday, August 19, 2001　　　　　　　　　　　*3:25 p.m.*
　　　"With endless Divine Love, I rock you gently in the　　*k(231)*
cradle of My Arms while assuring you passionately that Jesus
is your King and Salvation. My message to you today is that
yours is the Kingdom too, and the Power, and the Glory
forever to come because you have been regained within the
invincible beauty that is perfect Love at the Right Hand of
the Father. Jesus has taken you there timelessly, although
your voyage through the waters of the mortal Earth continues
at the pace of His Will. I ask you humbly to accept all that
He asks you to bear, to laud and praise His Holy Name　　　　*x*
without end, to strengthen the weak with the Wisdom of your
faith, to pacify the wailing through the counsel of your
allegiance to the Cross, and to be singularly one inside the
Sacred Heart which has become your salvific Vessel.
Kindness and Mercy assuredly await you during every day
of your life. It is true that God will never fail you, the

*Heavens shall not forsake you, the winds of Truth will
always prevail to be your ease of Grace back to the Land of
the Birth of the Saints. I continue in their presence to call
you to peace because there is no terror in knowing the King*   xx
*of Peace, that there shall no more be war inside the timeless
parameters of Everlasting Life, and gone are those horrific
memories that have too long made you weep in sorrow for
your sins. There is more than a beatific Dawn to greet you
in the Morning because God has placed an unending Day of
Gladness at the shores to where you are being led, gleefully
acrest of the Blood which Jesus so profoundly shed to Redeem
you from the lost who, at the end of time, will have their own
new plight to suffer. Can you not see this wonderful day in
the offing?*   xxx

*I am happy to speak to you today because these are
the continuing times during which the world is being
cultivated—mortified to expunge even the slightest veniality
from your breasts, and conditioned to be able to travel
through the perils that still haunt you to this day. God has
made it very clear that only perfection awaits you, and such
is your goal during your lives on the Earth. He asks you to
strive to achieve it in Love because all things are possible in
Him. He moreover beseeches your prayers for your brothers
and sisters who yet do not know Him. And, those who have*   xl
*already passed into the Light of the Pinnacle of Creation
look back to the world they left behind with sincere affection
for those who still struggle. As a blessing through the
intercession of one who has passed there seventeen years ago
on this Sunday morning, the following is a gift of Love for
your faith, the voice and Wisdom of the Savior of the
World."*

(Jesus speaks)

*"To My faithful lot of children whom I deem to call
My Own, can you not see that My Love has forged the
pathway that you are, indeed, continuing to blaze for those*   l
who still seek? Just like the world in your midst, that trail

must also be pruned and sheared so as to keep it clear for all succeeding generations. This is what makes you continue to search and call, to manifest, to repeat and pray. The Glory that I own, I give to you! Please take it freely of your Will to the perfection of humankind! With this Love, Peace, and gladness at the Center of My Sacred Heart, I promise that these days and your lives shall never pass in vain. I bless you with the strength to carry forward at the behest of My Father, who is in Heaven. You are My Honor and Grace; you are My humility and joy; you are the reason I Live. Come unto Me!"   lx

(Our Lady resumes speaking)

"My children, it is with these holy words that I commission you to live-out the happiness that you have gained through the Resurrection of My Son, He who came to be and who Is because God has so loved the world. If you truly try to comprehend that which is His Love, you will come to know Him concisely. How do you know what this daily search is for, and where, and why? The Holy Spirit, the Third Person of the Blessed Trinity, is this same Divine   lxx
Power in you to wield toward all understanding, knowledge, judicious temperament, and peace. If you seek these virtues in the Name of Jesus Christ, you shall become each of them and bear them to all the world. How could any soul be any more jubilant than this? I dare say that it would not be possible to be so on any other path. Outside the windows of this beautiful home is a world that is filled with error and regret, one that cannot yet know true peace because many who inhabit it have yet to accept the Cross as their reason for life. When many among you try to imagine what lies beyond   lxxx
the horizon, they are helpless to know because the weakness of their faith has yet to transcend the vision from their eyes. How can they imagine what lies just beyond the stars when their heads are hanging so low in despair from the ravages of their sins?

It is in the overcoming of sins, the transgressions against God, and the faults of the self that becoming holy is all about. This is not some unattainable mission that has been assigned to those who are somehow supernatural in essence, it is the struggle for everyday men to achieve.   xc
Indeed, it is the imperative charge that the Holy Gospel assigns to everyone who lives! Be now My good children of pious purpose and pursue all of this which is good! Take every step on the advancement of the righteousness of God to remake the face of the Earth! Remember to pray for the suffering who are making reparation for the wickedness you see! Whether you choose to accept it or not, there is always a greater purpose in the normalcy of your days than you can readily see with your eyes. These very messages of Mine are sufficient evidence of that! The nations and continents of the   c
world compose wholly more than a collection of capitals and states, they are the foundation from which many spiritual heroes have grown. Their lands have been the bounty to feed those who have traveled the globe for the purpose of evangelizing the Christian faith. These are the true warriors of Love, not those who have advanced the placement of a multi-colored banner on a political battlefield somewhere. You can engage this spiritual fight from where you reside, from inside the confines of your home and hearts, too! When I call you to prayer, especially for the conversion of all   cx
humankind, it is to the deliverance of the many who are held captive by all those vices which keep them from knowing their Savior at all.

So, when you see your brothers and sisters who ask you why God does not bless them, kindly remind them about Me! Implore them to stand upon the caption of faith and describe themselves to their friends and peers as belonging to the Handmaid of the Lord! Then, they will know what human life is for! Then, they will grasp that new beginning that they could never hold-to before, for I will lead and teach   cxx
them about becoming great Saints! I will ask for their concession to Jesus and for the entire origin of their being to

be placed inside the Cup of Eternal Redemption at the Holy Sacrifice of the Mass. There are no haughty protestors there! No mortal can place his lips to this suffering Cup and say that it is not of the Truth! Let Me tell you! I have been there! I have seen this compassionate beginning and the ultimate culmination of human life, itself. When the Crucifixion of the Son of Man rises inside the heart, there are no longer any roles for the liars and cheaters, no room for those who are cxxx *addicted to the sins of the flesh, and no desire to seek any other pathway but the Spirit of God. No neighbor who is truly in search of God will ever fail to find Him because it is He who has searched for them first. If they say that they will try and refuse to persist in the fight, they have failed both themselves and Him, alike.*

Time is wiling away, and there is no more room for trite excuses and lame expressions. The Kingdom of God is at hand! Let they who claim to own any higher dominion come to the fore and take their beating now! Let them fall at cxl *the feet of the Lamb of God who takes away the sins of the world and say with active submission in their hearts 'I had no way of knowing that the power of Your Truth was so profound!' Then, they will be glad that their suffering was the healing from their addictions, and the Love of the Almighty Father is the balm for the wounds they have inflicted upon themselves! Yes! All of this is in the near offing, just before they see with emblazoned embarrassment the pain and agony they have imposed upon those who loved them the most, who tried to get them to listen while they only* cl *wished to wander astray, those who cried in their beds at night because their loved ones would not listen to them! It is the same with those whose fathers have cast them aside because of their allegiance to God, and the sons who never took time to listen to the Christian witness of their God-given fathers. Jesus is assuredly setting the world aright, one relationship at a time. There is no need to worry anymore whether the faithful are on the straight course. The separation of the sheep from the goats is nigh, and I have the*

pleasure of telling Creation in advance. Yes! This is the   clx
reason for My appearance here today and for all the blessings
that I bestow on My children everywhere, and why I have
prayed in the sunlight of Heaven for 2,000 years to turn My
children around once and for all to see the Brother, Savior,
and Friend who is their Redeemer and God."

I agree with the detractors of Catholicism when they declare that it is
not our actions, conduct, or works that unilaterally establish our goodness and
thereby justify an eternal longevity upon our spirits. Jesus queried, "Why do
you call me good? Only God is good." He did not say that He was not good,
but refocused the attention of everyone upon the unseen Father of the Most
Holy Trinity in whose goodness He is hypostatically united, one in substance
and being. Everyone, including Jesus Himself, concedes that it is only through
a verifiable unity with the Divinity of Most Blessed Trinity who deigns to us
that we are inebriated with a sanctification wherein our restored perfection is
the product of heavenly justice. Therefore, if goodness comes from being
united with our unseen God, where does He descend and dispense His
unilateral beatitude of unification upon us? If none of our personal actions can
deliver us to perfection, where do those who refuse the Holy Eucharist receive
such blessedness? The answer is—nowhere! No one who rejects the One
Loaf from the One Feast Table, which is the altars of the Catholic Church, can
rest upon their feebly outward actions to come into full-fledged unity with
God, nor can their proclamations or incantations justify any goodness or
wisdom about themselves because it is only through humble submission and
acceptance of the Bread of Life that our communion with Goodness is initiated
to the fulness of the human potential, both in substance and being. The Sacred
Scriptures clearly state, *"Unless you eat the Flesh of the Son of Man and drink His*
Blood, you will not have life in you." Those who proclaim otherwise—crowing
about mere symbolism in this Bible passage—are simply motivated by their
own self-possession and rife anti-Catholic bigotry because, should they accept
this great declaration of Holy Scripture as it is clearly delineated, they know
they would be required to surrender to the Traditions of Roman Catholicism,
the Grand Lady of Christian Faith who has preserved their opportunity to be
embraced by God through the cyclical ages of ever-recurring mortal derision.
The universal unity for which Jesus pined when He prayed that all may be one
in Him is found in only one Communion from one Table of Faith! It is the
only Communion founded in angelic submission; all others were initiated in the
rebelliousness of their times. Thriving and booming in this seraphic vision is
the one Sacred Heart of Creation, beating a unifying chord in the mystical

corridor of every living soul who has come alive at the reception of the Bread of Life from the hands of Catholic priests. Our Lord Jesus sees His children through this transcending omnipresence from that Altar in Heaven and unites His desires with those prayerful petitions He sees flooding toward Him from the heart of anyone who humbles themselves and their sacrificial lives before His Sacred Altar. There is much Truth that has been obfuscated throughout the ages by knavish opportunists, themselves sinners, who needed a common enemy to maintain the fragile consensuses they were trying to construct without the Rock of St. Peter. But, let us be fair! Our contemporary siblings hold very little culpability for these sins wrought by their protesting forefathers. The spiritual cyclone of the 16th century swept Christian civilization with its millions strong into disunity and revolution because the braking influence on man's immorality was torn into factions who separated themselves from the only Bread which gives Life, peace, hope, and longevity. We are living in the obscuring cloud of theological dust, kicked-up by packs of feckless men, the hapless lot who rejected 1,500 years of spiritual genius that had been dispensed by the Holy Spirit to legions of Saints who suffered in the likeness of their Master to sustain a united Love at a single Table that men of the cloth would spread to the far-flung corners of the globe until the end of time. Everyone must return to the place from which they came! God cannot and will not validate any other communion as His life-giving Body because He will not justify the disunity created by those who willfully separated from Him at the onset of the disaster. It is the prodigal children and their progeny who must return! There are no other valid communions which unilaterally grant Eternal Life before the sight of our Heavenly Father. Those insolent facsimiles which have been raised are all imitations, much like the difference between a live cow and a picture of a cow. The portrait will never give milk; and it is to the land of milk and honey to which we are called. Jesus desires unity in Him because that is where Love flourishes, not in some shoddily negotiated truce, but in abandonment to the Truth.

"That citadel surrounding, the angry foe-man raves;
Upon that Rock resounding, dash high the sullen waves.
Still, still with light supernal those battlements shall gleam,
And Peter's rock, eternal, confront the restless stream."

O King of kings in Splendor
Fr. L. Camatari, SJ

When the Almighty Father decided to manifest the Most Holy Trinity within the mortal world, He did so in such a way that measures His eternal magnificence within temporal increments apprehendable by human beings whom He endows with the capacity of faith. Humanity was created as the vehicle for concealing and defining His omnipotence for revelation in the flesh of His creatures and providing for the possibility of faith. How can one have faith in something he has already seen? Jesus, who is God, came to us with a veil over His outward brilliance, but not without dispensing our capacity to witness His interior beauty beyond the sheerness of our mortality. Our Almighty Creator could have chosen never to fashion the first human being, desiring His Glory to be unique and never obscured by the impediments and limitations of our physical frame. He could have simply invoked the power and decision to appear in full raiment over the course of time at His own Divine Will, fully homo sapien from thin air, a supernatural prodigy that would have driven any mortal beast involuntarily to its knees. But, instead, He mysteriously inaugurated His Divine entrance within the parameters of time by creating a human race who would precede Him into the world, thereby necessitating our articles of faith and providing the opportunity for a reunion that would be wholly greater than a tyrant forcing his subjects to their immolation. Think about it—humanity was created to veil the miracle of the Savior's coming, thereby allowing Redemption to unfold before our very eyes. If we consider only the original universal premise that God has appeared on Earth as the Messiah, and that this substance of revelation has occurred, notwithstanding whether the motive was instantaneous from the ether or timely through the womb of the Immaculate Virgin, we realize the stupendous magnitude of His interaction with the tangible world and recognize that our profound awe should be of equal measure, no matter what circumstance He used to effect it, albeit the latter offers the blessed opportunity for us to kneel through a more solicitous posture. In like analogy, it must dawn upon us that the Body, Blood, Soul and Divinity of Jesus Christ as the Bread of Life from the altars of the Catholic Church is the miraculous appearance of God before our senses out of thin air. Indeed–out of thin air! Jesus instituted the action and function of His Sacramental Appearance before us by utilizing bread and wine to veil His instantaneous presence at the words of Consecration by our Catholic priests. Most certainly "Transubstantiation" actually takes place because the complete substance of the bread and wine is changed into the complete substance of the Body and Blood of Jesus Christ; but the change we realize is not an organic transformation of a substance, as if the latter required the previous. It is accomplished through a binary action performed on two separate entities, one the bread and wine, and the other the Sacred Body and Blood of Jesus Christ. At the intonation of the words, *"Take this, all of you, and eat it; this is My Body which will be given up for you,* " the common bread and wine are instantaneously expunged and removed from Creation—the true Divine Annihilation—and simultaneously supplanted in that instant by the Sacred Body and Blood of Jesus Christ as the Eucharistic Host, manifested without deference to earthly creation by God's own Divine power. Roman Catholic priests are unilaterally vested by God with the mystical vocation to create something from nothing in temporal terms, while God uses the bread and wine offered by His priests to veil the entrance of His Son into Creation to feed His children the salvific Body and Blood of our Messianic King. Our beloved priests manifest the "Everything" from nothing. You see, God does not need the bread and wine in order to appear on the Catholic Altar; it is the Eternal Salvation of men that caused Jesus to dictate such a requirement—solely for the purpose of the preservation of our faith and the opportunity to receive Divine Mercy instead of instant and irrevocable Judgment. If Jesus were to reveal the manifold dimensions of His instantaneous incarnation as the Bread of Life without the prerequisite gifts of finest wheat and fruit of the vine, justice would demand that all human sin be instantly punished before the Sacred because there would no longer be the dimmed understanding brought by the fall of our first parents, Adam and Eve. Culpability would remain in complete effect; and as Our Lady said, Fiat would be required to flow from our lips as immediately and flawlessly as the transformation. Perfect spiritual vision requires perfect submission, as imperfection is simultaneously and eternally wiped away through justice. The beasts would be driven to their knees. Simply for contemplation, because the Holy Mass will always require the bread and wine until the end of time, imagine attending the Eucharistic Celebration where there was no bread and wine offered, but at the intonation of the priest's words of Consecration, the Most Blessed Sacrament mystically appeared out of thin air. The world would be stunned and would flock to the Holy Altars, realizing that God had come with the profound desire to feed His sheep. This is essentially what is taking place now; humankind is witnessing this spectacular miracle right before their eyes, although Jesus instituted the Holy Eucharist using bread and wine as a precedent to this miraculous appearance so we would be required to believe it through faith. How could He have delivered Heavenly Bread and preserved our faith without preceding it by common bread? By providing the antecedent in the presentation of ordinary bread and wine, He has veiled our eyes to the reality of His True Sacramental Presence in an entirely revelatory way. Is this not the reason why God has allowed Sacred Hosts to miraculously appear on the tongues of visionaries? While we are stunned to the depths of our souls to see such private revelations, too many Catholics are totally indifferent during the ecclesial grandness of the Holy Mass, itself. Let us, therefore, be renewed by this revelation, and open our hearts to the Prince of Peace who appears before us in the Eucharistic Bread from the Altar of Sacrifice. Let the clarion bells of castles and cathedrals ring-out at the moment of Consecration! Peal them faithfully, one and all!

Sunday, January 16, 2000   *4:14 p.m.*
   "*To My very loving children who so seek the justice   j(016)
of your Divine Lord, I come again not because you do not
understand the Love of Jesus, but because you know Him full
well. You have accepted My Son for all that is good in
humanity, for the ease of all your sadness, for the Light of
Truth where there is darkness, and for the eradication of
your most errant impressions of what Salvation is all about.
Have I not told you that perfection and justice have already
laid waste to evil and indifference? How many Saints before
you have poured-out their lives seeking not the motivations   x
of God, but ways through which they can alleviate the
suffering of people for His sake? Humanity is crying-out from
the depths of all that is malignant, and you are answering
with kindness and service. If I were to reveal to you the
outcome of the genius of Love in the world today, as I have
told you before, you would lay down your hands in assurance
that the Son of Man can do it alone. But, the Holy Spirit
needs you as I need you, not to question and complain, but to
continue in faith. If there is a scoreboard to this last century
of the Earth, you would not be able to see it over the   xx
shoulders of the jubilant Saints jumping in ecstasy before you.
You are the Christian witnesses for the Holy Gospel of My
Son on the Earth. Love in your hearts tells you that you have
chosen the long and difficult path, one on which you will not
always be able to see for the buffeting of hatred against you.
It is not a lack of cooperation from the Kingdom on High
that is causing anyone frustration, but the lack of Love of
those around you. They have been given a will to employ as
they choose. If that collective will has not yet been
transformed into the perfect unity of all humankind under   xxx
the Cross, then war and dissension will continue, division
will linger, and human suffering will proceed. As long as*

there is one soul on the Earth whom God knows will convert at the last who is still giving-in to a renegade spirit, He will dispense the gift of asking the most noble in the world to suffer for his conversion. My children, you are listening and speaking to the Mother of that singular God, present in Three Divine Persons and Sacramentally-blessed on the Earth. I am the reflection of the Wisdom you need to grow to be like the Angels and Saints in Paradise. When you acknowledge an inequity or heresy on the Earth, that in itself is a prayer to God to change it and make the world more holy. Living for Jesus is not winning a game whose parameters will end before the mortal Earth comes to a close and then going on to something else. Seeking the Kingdom of Heaven to live as wholly on the Earth as it is in Heaven is an ongoing and perpetual process that will lead you all to everlasting Life from where you stand, sit, or kneel. Humanity will always need the grace-filled Sacraments; and God will always need you to defend them until the end of time, at which these Sacraments will be revealed in their true Light, their most clear Revelation. But, until the time when the Sacraments are exchanged, until they are transformed and transposed into perpetual fact, they will be opposed by the enemies of the Church and the rogue atheists who are determined to see Her fail. That is why you must not surrender to them, and why you must continue to pray and hope, awaiting in joyful fulfillment for the Coming of your Redeemer. The skies are not always blue because the Earth needs the showers that quench the thirst of the parched life below. Hence, there will be human suffering as long as there are spiritually-famished souls on the Earth who need the fruits of that Love to transform them into perfect Light.

My children, it is obvious that the Crucifixion of Jesus has already eliminated the stench of evil and indifference from the face of the Earth. But, not everyone on the Earth has accepted that Sacrifice as reparation for the fall of humanity from Paradise. It is not a lacking in compassion by God that makes the world an awful place, it is the blatant

xl

l

lx

refusal of lost souls to wield His power and dignity that   lxx
inhibits the Earth from being the perfect reflection of
Heaven. I ask you to not allow the ensuing days to diminish
your belief in all that you have written and prayed-for. You
are wielding the power you wish to extend over the
blasphemous forces in the world. Human suffering is already
being diminished. Hundreds-of-thousands are already
coming to Salvation in Jesus by your prayers and holy works.
Do you believe the words 'It is finished (?)' Those whom you
believe are being left-behind are already included in the
Divine, benevolent, and healing plan of God. Was the   lxxx
Crucifixion an event that occurred during the mortal time of
humankind? Yes. And, that suffering is still alive because
it is the reparative balm for a tawdry and sordid world of
people who are still running from that same Crucifixion. My
son, you are asking the same questions that tried to frustrate
My Immaculate Heart as I stood beneath the Cross on Good
Friday. I asked God in Heaven—How can this horrible
suffering and tragedy bring the restoration of Redemption for
My adopted children? And, His answer was in the Blood
being poured-out on the ground a few feet in front of My   xc
sorrowful eyes. He calls that 'Love in unbounded Beauty!'
Can you not see, then, that these are truly the End Times?
And, for that, you should be happy! How can My Triumph
be seen by all humankind if My children run about the Earth
saying that it is too dark to see it? That makes no sense either
spiritually or physically. You must remember that the work
that we have done together has already borne fruits upon
which many are already feasting. If God had not dispatched
Me to seek your assistance, how would you have gone on?
My son, your brothers and sisters will come running for the   c
holy confection of conversion once they have first savored the
sweetness of Love inside their hearts, and not before. If you
will continue to pray with Me and all the children of Light,
that day will come. Considering how you feel while looking
at this world, how do you suppose the Savior of the world
feels, He who hung on the Cross and died for the Salvation

of every soul? Do you believe that He is frustrated? The answer is no! He is patient, and that is one of the greatest fruits of His Divine Love. He is waiting for everyone to stumble upon the Truth and accept its overpowering beauty   cx
and perseverance. Many people will profess to follow Jesus in all ways until it comes their time for sacrifice, suffering, sorrow for the suffering of others, and their patience. Please remember that being with Me also means sharing My service as the Lady of Sorrows until God, Himself, says enough! These are the days which are transforming the face of Creation. You are living them now. Frustration and anger toward the Throne of God are the fruits of error and lack of peace. Prayer is the solution. I am assured that you will live only the happiness of the Holy Spirit in all of time to come.   cxx
Please be accepting in all which God provides, wills, and allows. Your Master's decisions are most infallible in every way. At the end of time, you will see this very clearly. You will slap your forehead with your palm and say 'Oh, I get it!' Thank you for praying with Me today. You call with 'Hail Mary' and I have come! This is your holy blessing to help you continue through the ages. + I will speak to you again very soon. I will always love you. Goodnight!"

Our Lady specifically asked me to articulate a heart rending story that was recently recited by one of our parish priests in a liturgical homily. Our pastor had read an account of a small child who was terribly sick and not going to survive unless she received a bone marrow transplant from a matching donor. The child's sibling, himself a small boy, was found to be the suitable candidate. It was explained to the tyke how he could assist in restoring the health of his sister; and from his keen attention to the serious conversations of the adults, he comprehended the dire gravity of the situation. So, he consented to undergo the surgery. However, when he awoke following the procedure, everyone realized that he had not understood as clearly as they had earlier believed when he asked the attending physician, *"Am I going to die now?"* A thunderous requital of sacrificial charity then collided with the earth and the consciences of everyone there. Here was an innocent child who truly thought that, by his consent, he was being asked to exchange his life for his sister's; and yet, he still said yes! Fiat never rang more loudly than this! Oh, for us to be as heroic as that little boy was that day! Our Holy Mother wants every person who opposes the Roman Catholic Church to be just like this little giant among men. Too many people mistakenly believe that they are being asked to relinquish their very lives, when God is simply asking them to help Him heal Creation. Our Lady says that each person who surrenders to Catholicism will awaken again to a Kingdom so divinely beautiful that the heavens will weep that the world has finally prepared itself for the Glorious Coming of the Son of Man. Our Christian obedience means that Paradise can unite with humankind without the need for the fires of justice, without the prerequisite of purifying infliction, and certainly without the recognition that anyone ever opposed the unity instituted by Christ at His Last Supper in the Upper Room. All of those who despise the Original Apostolic Church must realize that they will live again with the same glowing countenance that will undoubtedly surround that young bone marrow donor for the remainder of his days. The family of man must be made whole again; and we need those who reject us because they are the separated ones who will make us complete. This grand vision does not exist outside the Catholic Church, and neither does the salvific aura of spiritual Redemption!

But, let us understand this correctly, for far too many naysayers have hijacked its meaning to accuse the Mother Church of an elitism of which She is clearly not guilty. The logic of the Holy Spirit demands that unity be manifested as oneness, an integrity of wholeness that is reflected within its indivisibility. There is no division inside the circumference of peace, nor are there fractures in anything that is unified, and neither is the mind of Christ divided. By taking on perfect human flesh, Jesus Christ repaired the breach between God and man, creating a oneness between ourselves and the Most Blessed Trinity that had not existed since the Edenic fall of Adam and Eve. Our Blessed Lord secured the promise of our deliverance into this beatified state of grace, even when we were still in sin and knew not His Truth at all. His magnanimous Mercy is our forbearance against God's righteous judgment in mortal time until we become cleansed in the Blood of His Perfection, begetting our justification in His death and rising from the Tomb. Now that the Trinitarian unity has been revealed in Him, there exists a sublime Citadel of sacramental renewal for the inhabitants of the Earth. Those who receive the miraculous cleansing of their souls through the Grace of the Sacrament of Reconciliation and proceed to the Thanksgiving Altar for the reception of the Bread of Life are given the infinite measure of Sanctifying Life, and are transformed by the power of God into the fully-mature Mystical Body of our Savior, capable of submitting themselves before Heaven's Throne to offer worthy sacrifices and praise in Jesus' Name for the redeeming of the world. By holy acts, prayers, intentions, motivations and desires, we propagate His Mercy and absolution to succeeding generations who still fail to recognize Jesus as the Sacred Host. Just as each member of the Catholic faithful has been a beneficiary of the Divine Mercy of Christ, even prior to our immersion in the Sacraments of renewal, those who seem to be outside the Catholic Church in the darkness of spiritual obscurity and disunity are also beneficiaries of the benisons of the Holy Messiah by virtue—the truly heroic virtue—of the sacrificial lives of the faithful followers of Catholicism. Our detractors; yea, even our most ruthless enemies, reside within the universal circumference of the Salvation offered by the Roman Catholic Church through the sacrificial victimhood of its faithful parishioners who compassionately ensoul their adversaries within the premonition of their Christian forgiveness, never losing hope that the world will one day manifest the oneness that Jesus always prayed to overwhelm His Creation. We imitate Christ by maintaining our love for those yet far from the perfect composition of His Mystical Unity, carrying the burdens of secular countercultures which are walking in total darkness, and presenting them worthy for merciful deliverance at the altar during the Holy Sacrifice of the Mass. And, when the Savior of Man peers throughout Creation from His Altar in Heaven, penetrating the souls of His thoughtful children kneeling before Him at our Eucharistic altars throughout the course of the ages, He recognizes the panoramic macroscope of Redemption within us. Everyone we hold in our hearts, God sees as being within the boundaries of Salvation, just as when Our Lord held the ages in His Sacred Heart while hanging on the Cross. *This is the fundamental basis and understanding at the heart of religious ecumenicism.* We love and preserve the opportunity for all fronts and factions of humanity to physically and spiritually coalesce at the Sacred Altar through our open heartedness in imitation of our crucified Lord; because two thousand years ago, He saved a world that did not yet know or accept Him. And, it is His Mystical Body—the Roman Catholic Church—which now carries that Tradition of the salvific Cross in its life and form. We are that sacrificial Mystical flesh, the receptacle for Divine Life, and its transmission through the ages! It is Jesus Christ alive, still experiencing the Crucifixion in His Body, yet maintaining and propagating the Mysteries of Redemption through the collective hearts of His faithful flock which has become His own, witnessing until the end of time to the Universal Unity emanating from the Most Blessed Sacrament. We are living the manifestation of the Miracle of Redemption parceled-out over time in increments through the daily celebration of the Holy Mass. Everyone must realize that the Crucifixion of Jesus Christ is the single event in mortal history that obliterated human sin and the exilic boundaries of time in the same regenerative sweep. One might ask where is the "eternal" when gazing upon the Lamb on Golgotha? I say to you, He *is* the Eternal! His Being and Most Sacred Heart created the fissure in time that united us to the timeless, rending the opaque veil between man and God, and hemming a seam to repair the breach! Everything about the Son of Man while hanging in grief and pain on the Cross was spanning Heaven and Earth, the past and the future, Salvation and condemnation, from its inception to its final consummation! His Body mystically radiated through time and Creation, appearing on every Catholic Altar of history, jubilantly consuming and assimilating into the oneness of God any humanity who would humbly approach the Cross and eat His Flesh and drink His Blood. Likewise, He became one with all who would be the diabolical fodder for His Crucifixion throughout the ages, embracing their decadent humanity and holding the door of Redemption wide open so the wicked might eventually convert and pass over its salvific threshold. Jesus lived human history from the purview of our own souls as He united His Being with the historical spectra of humanity upon the Cross. He experienced our lives 2,000 years ago in the infinity of Calvary by remaining united with our souls to this very moment, undergoing everything we heap upon Him now, whether it be humble prayerfulness and spiritual perfection or putrid egoism and the oppression of our sins. Therefore, when you see the suffering of the innocents, benevolent people undergoing misfortunes, or tragedies yet untold, know that you are witnessing the Crucifixion of Jesus Christ dismantling the boundaries of time, flushing its beauty into the future ages of men. It is Christ suffering the torments of His people. Remember that whatever you do to your brothers and sisters, you also do to Christ, Himself, both now and on the Holy Cross two millennia ago. And, whatever humanity experiences in its multitude of corporeal and spiritual dimensions, Jesus is united with the soul, enduring it also from the Hilltop of Creation. Any person wishing to know the deepest thoughts and visions which gave Our Lord euphoric consolation in His Sacred Heart while He graced the torturing mountain of our Salvation should look closely at the Roman Catholic Church, Her legacy, Her resilience, Her grand design, and Her invincibility. The Catholic Church is Jesus Christ whereby Mount Calvary is made present—in Her people, Her bearing, Her history, Her Liturgies, Her Sacraments, Her hierarchy; and yes, Her future of Resurrection and the dispensation of Immortality.

Sunday, May 9, 2004 Mother's Day   *2:04 p.m.*
St. Pachomius [AD c292-348]
      "This, now, My children is the time during which I   n(130)
ask you to be attentive to My words because I am offering
you the holiness and Wisdom of Almighty God. We pray
again by continuing to seek in Him the granting of

everything on Earth that will make humanity pure. This is Mother's Day—a time when millions who have birthed little children are honored for their faithfulness to the duty of bearing new life into the world. Would the Mother of God not be remiss if I did not magnify My Son's call for the protection of the sanctity of all life on this day? I come to you x *in happiness because My children are honoring Me not only today, but during the entire month of May. This is a unique opportunity for My Church to realize the gift of human Salvation and for the Grace that makes you whole again in the sight of Jesus. When Christians speak of remaking the face of the Earth, the call for the transformation of the human heart is the essence of doing it. I commend you to prayer today and always because this is how Creation is changed. Prayer is the means to achieve the spiritual goals that you have outlaid in your parishes and homes. The true* xx *meaning of loving God is to pray to Him for assistance both now and at the hour of your death. I intercede for you because I am your Immaculate Mother. Thank you for staying at My side for so long, because it is only through your faith that I can succeed. My little ones, it must be apparent to you by now that I am nurturing you to spiritual maturity that you may wilfully call yourselves to duty and service for Jesus. I shall never leave you or allow you to stray from beneath the protection of My Sacred Mantle. However, you must know by now that your spiritual maturation means that* xxx *you take upon yourselves the choices, decisions, and actions that will mend the divisions between nations and peoples. It must become necessary for you to do these things of your own accord and under the Wisdom, guidance, and leadership of the Holy Spirit. My duty is to rear you in Love, and yours is to reflect the Fruits of Love in the most profound ways while you live your mortal lives. How happy I have become to see so many who are, indeed, taking the reigns of Christian responsibility and servitude so that the wounds caused by human sin can by healed by your acts of* xl *contrition, reconciliation, and unity.*

My Special and Chosen ones, it is obvious by now that I come to speak to you with words for the entire body of humanity, but I wish mainly to address My sentiments into the depths of your hearts to display My undying Love for you. So many years you have prayed with Me for the cultivation of your brothers and sisters, and so many millions are becoming the beneficiaries of your dedication to Me. You must also know by now that many things culminate in victory for you, and that it is only a matter of time before you   *l*
see them come to fruition. If there is one more word added to the series of faith, hope, love and charity, it would be the invaluable purpose of patience. I have told you on multiple occasions that humanity is undergoing a vast, wide, far-reaching, and varying reconditioning of the heart that ofttimes takes years to proceed. And, it is during those same years that your Love for God is growing, that your understanding of the purpose of human life is becoming more clear. And, it is during these same years that you understand that every day of your lives is another step toward the   *lx*
Christian perfection to which Jesus has called you. Always believe you will achieve it! Never concede to the relativists who insist that there is no such thing as moral Truth! Fight against the enemies of the Cross who do not accept that the Crucifixion of One Man has mitigated the sins of an entire humanity. Rise-up against the many in your midst who believe that 'compromise' is a better subsistence for the mortal world than Divine Revelation, for there is no compromising the fact of Love that Jesus has laid-out before the world in the Holy Gospel. There is no ambiguity in His   *lxx*
Beatitudes. There is no room for liberal interpretations of the very conservative exhortations which proclaim that the Gate into Heaven is a Narrow one! I arrive with great joy today because I know that My Church stands on the Rock of Truth that cannot be amended by time or the musings of mortal men. When I tell you that Jesus has given you the power and authority to speak on His behalf from the pulpits of the Roman Catholic Church of Christianity, please know that

this is bound in Heaven as it is bound upon the Earth. Do not seek pride for the sake of pride, but be extremely proud of your Roman Catholic heritage. Hold fast to the traditions that have made Saints of the millions who have served so dutifully in centuries past! Never surrender your knowledge that Roman Catholicism is the Church that Jesus Christ intended His Church on Earth to be—and no other! Why? Because He wishes you to partake of the Holy Eucharist and the Holy Sacrifice of the Mass simultaneously. And, this can be done only in His Church, only in the Roman Catholic Church, under the guidance of the successor to Saint Peter, himself.

My Special and Chosen ones, I have decided to tell you these things today because you are about to begin working on a project that will seem altogether too ecumenical for you... And, My Special one, can you now see the commencing of great things that have come to be in the past thirteen years because you have given of your human will to Me? I ask you to continue to do so because you will continue in the line of Marian Saints who are praying for your successful journey through life with your brother in the Church. Indeed, these are happy times because time, itself, is a passing element that you are utilizing to its greatest potential. You love and are in Love. You see well because your sacred vision is clear. This is why all ultimate victory belongs to you, and it is also the essence behind My proclamation to you that Jesus will someday rewrite the history of the world. It is a very beautiful day where you live in your homeland of Illinois! I wish for you to go outside soon and enjoy it, and that means My message for you today is nearly through... The ecumenical work you are about to prepare will predispose thousands more to the Grace and beauty of the Roman Catholic Church by implication... You must be elated at this time by the continuation of your union in the Holy Spirit as you write additional pages in 'To Crispen Courage.' It is a great and holy work of Christian Love and admonition. The mortal world so needs that

lxxx

xc

c

cx

approach...during the present age. Do you remember the
story that Fr. H told you today about the little boy who
donated his bone marrow? Please put that story in your next
book and attribute it as being My request. Let Me assure you
that you are attending Holy Mass at a very sanctified parish   cxx
that is under the care an endearing priest. The story of the
little boy is one that is reflective of My Jesus! However, My
Jesus did die! Thank you for all the hours you are spending
writing about the way the world ought to be... Do you
remember what your brother told you that he wrote in his
brief farewell in his 1976 annual book? The crux of the
matter is that, even at age 22, he was imploring humanity to
set-out to deal with the sheer crisis of human nature. The
acts about which you speak are among those that make-up
that collective crisis. Ultimately, the entire body of error is   cxxx
the product of human sin. If all the world would come to
Jesus, they would rise and sin no more. Thank you for
praying so piously with Me today... Thank you for traveling
to the Saint Augustine Cemetery last Friday... I was there
looking down upon you! And, just as I did that day, I now
give you My holy blessing of perpetual Love. + I love you.
Goodnight!"

The fundamental synopsis of the Roman Catholic Church is none
other than the ultimate Tradition of Ecclesial Unity, effected by the
penitentially transfiguring Sacrament that eradicates any impediment to our
risen perfection and the Bread of Life which impregnates our beings with the
Omnipotent Love of God, Himself. We live in a world where heroes are often
fabricated by desperation, and the mundaneness of life is artificially hyped to
satiate our starvation for some ulterior new meaning. Through a mystical
awareness, the human heart senses the undeniable hints of stellar greatness that
dance at the shimmering heights of our greatest potential. We pine to be
embraced by those larger-than-life possibilities, and united with a reality that
transcends generational definitions and identifies for all future time that we
were one in unity with the ecstasies which cannot be divined from the latter
descriptions of men or engineered by the ghost writers of lost romantic tales.
There is something wholly different between a dark horse competitor who was
never supposed to win seen straining for a finish line in an unexpected triumph

and a darling congenital champion striding into the arena launching a brilliance by which the definition of victory will be henceforth prescribed. One can be claimed a mere fluke in the course of world evolution, the latter a spectacle whose appearance was deigned to give rise to the meaning of "conqueror" in every epoch and era, a predestination whose time before the cynical scope of mortals had come, a providence willed into being with heart and grace that was triumphant from its initial conception. Even in the midst of so many who refuse to acknowledge and respect two millennia of Divine Tradition which honors and proclaims the sole Christ of the human race and the Church He founded with the shedding of His Blood, there are mimicking thespians who hypocritically revere secular traditions without apology, from the coifed green fairways of Augusta to the fanfare of our presidential inaugurations, from the asphalt ovals where our sports gentlemen start their engines, to the Grecian mountains where an olympian torch is set aflame. Yet, they refuse to genuflect before the majesty of a supernatural institution that will last eons beyond the paled extinction of their memories. Apologists for our human legacies are scrupulous in aggrandizing and propagating the greater moments of our ancestors, placing before us in perennial installments the achievements of nondescript mortals who participated, generated or secured many an auspicious instant of being loosed from the chains fabricated by the cowardly mediocrity of fainted-hearted men. Romantics march onto ancient battlefields to reenact liberating conflicts amidst smokescreens of exploding muskets; masted ships sail gracefully into harbors beneath hailstorms of confetti and streamers as on their maiden voyages in days of yore; the skies above our commencements are cluttered with mortarboards and cadet caps every May; and trumpeted color guards in period regalia call our horses to the gate at the running of our thoroughbreds. But, it is God alone who gives men the capacity for these encroachments upon His Crown, the days on which we parade them forward, and the memories we possess to highlight our successes before the swiftly exhausting ages. The human heart can sense that each overwhelming deed that has stricken awe upon the psyche of the masses echoes notes of philharmonic chords reverberating through the sanctified dreams of men, our penchant for unfettered freedom, and the flourishing of our sovereign identity and spiritual omnipotence as the repatriated children of Heaven. Our souls clearly perceive that our Almighty Father is the architect of every destiny within His earthly people, down to the last faint heartbeat of a medical school cadaver lain cold onto a coroner's slab. God is the orchestrator of the polyphonic aspirations of His finely hewn Creation, the ethereal Choreographer of these exilic ceremonies, the Mystical Landscape over which our best opportunities are ordained, the Spirit which bears the fire in the braziers of our triumphs, the Sacred Heart where our strength prevails until the finish, the Wind that billows the canopies of our ambitions for eternal renewal, and the ultimate Author of the epitaphs which will be recorded for the nostalgic perusers of our most cherished literary anthologies, the autobiographies of our friends, and our self-composed valedictory songs.

Our Lord spoke in parables during His travels upon the Earth, using the aesthetics of the nature He created, the natural reactions of the all-too predicable men He loved to embrace, and the benevolent characteristics and inclinations of the many creatures He conceived to populate the skies, the lands, and the seas; thereafter and henceforth pining to reveal the unseen power of His providential Love as the motivating factor behind organic life and all inanimate things. He was queried by His apostles as to why they were the privileged recipients of the deeper meanings behind His parables, while the masses were allowed only to glean their inescapable Wisdom through much soul searching, prayer and revelatory suffering. Even until now, Jesus works in this same manner, touching the hearts of imminent saints as well as the most hardened of sinners, describing the spiritual attributes of an unseen Kingdom that He wishes to flourish unimpededly across the cultures of this planet. There have been examples replete to strike the deepest chords of our humanity and resonate with the highest inclinations of our spiritual senses, transforming the vision of the impossible into the recognizable reach of our too-often failing steps. Coretta Scott King, the widow of Rev. Martin Luther King Jr., made an insightfully prophetic remark about what she witnessed on August 28, 1963 in Washington D.C., the day her husband spoke so eloquently about life—not only to America at large, but to the eternal ages—and about the responsibilities of decent men, the preservation of human dignity, and the intrinsic unity that must come to full manifestation within the consortium of the world. Upon hearing the final words of the speech of this great civil rights hero that day, after articulating his spiring dreams so much mirroring the crucified Son of God, the entire crowd of tens-of-thousands that was fanned-out before him and around the grand reflecting pool at the foot of the Lincoln Memorial burst into a deafening ovation, recording their accolades, adulation and concurrence upon the pages of historians in reflection of the Truth that had just bloomed from the soul of this minister of God. And, standing in that afterglow at his side, his beloved wife Coretta remarked that, for a brief moment, it felt like the Kingdom of God had descended to the Earth. Yes indeed, my dear sister, righteousness did flow down like a mighty stream. It marked the perfection of Heaven before all Americans from the lips of your martyred spouse, eclipsing our world on that heralded day in the late summer of '63. And, the King of Creation has brought this same immensity within our purview on many other occasions with as equally vivid distinction and clarity, but in ways that still render His clearest Revelation veiled as a parable to those who refuse to listen to its highest calling.

Sunday, October 14, 2001 (excerpt)   *12:58 p.m.*

"I wish for you to call on the great parishioners   k(287)
whom you have known for the last decades, especially those
who have died, for they can see more clearly now the impact
of their faith upon the living allegiance of your own. Indeed,
if the Nobel Prize was to be awarded to anyone on this day
in history in 1964, it should have been given to the great
man (Martin Luther King, Jr) upon whom it was bestowed.
He has been a living child of God ever since his death,
knowing that his call to righteousness was a just one to share.
If only more people upon the Earth would follow his peaceful   x
demonstrations of the Truth of Jesus, there would be more
debate and less warring. These are the times when you can
look both backward with the advantage of lessons learned
and forward with hope that you shall never repeat your
mistakes again. With Jesus as your guide, you will know that
you can never err, that Love is the plane upon which you
will always travel, and that Truth is the eloquence by which
you will forever speak, even to the moment of your passing
into death. I have the fond vantage point of having seen the
first words that millions of people have said to Jesus, once   xx
they have seen His Holy Face. Each and every one whose
soul was taken to Heaven stated that they could not have
known how beautiful He was or how horrible His Wounds,
but they knew He was with them all along in their darkest
hours and most intense suffering. This is how they
recognized Him, as He bore these awful things in advance of
their own. Woe to those who have lived their lives and have
had no grief visited upon them by their greedy calculation,
extravagant surroundings, and selfish motivations. I say,
pity those who are about to see that they have lived in no   xxx
way the likeness of Jesus upon the Earth, because their
eternal future shall be very grim. Were it not for the ullage
which is being sufficed from those who lay in infirmaries or
at home while awaiting the surrendering of their flesh, any
others who are indifferent toward the Holy Gospel of
Christianity would perish in a flash."

It was ten years after Dr. King's extraordinary speech that another flash of heavenly brilliance illuminated our country by way of an aesthetic parable to immortalize the triumph of God's creatures. Through a wholly different venue, tens-of-millions of people worldwide watched a victory that was not fostered in any way by the involvement, credit or conceit of the self-serving human will. It was a mystical reflection of nature at its best, inspirited and alive for a brief, shining instant, and a transient occurrence of natural perfection derived from beyond the boundaries of our wildest imaginings. Every spring, the eyes of our competitive spirits focus upon the age-old trilogy of equestrian races that are a source of secular awe. The Kentucky Derby, the Preakness, and the Belmont Stakes are hailed as the proverbial Triple Crown of sporting events, wherein the greatest thoroughbreds in the world gather in succession at these three contests with their owners, trainers and jockeys prepared to challenge one another and the historical legends who have previously laid-down fabled records of stately excellence, expanding the meaning of what our countrymen have always believed winning to be. In 1973, a horse named Secretariat had come-of-age amidst the finest traditions of Kentucky's racing heritage, and his owners entered him into competition, hoping he would produce an exalted moment to be fondly remembered for decades to come. And, Secretariat more than answered the call, not only for those who cared for this gallant specimen, but also for the heart, soul and conscience of all Americans who wanted to believe there was more to life in 1973 than Watergate conspirators and foreign oil cartels. Who could have known that a single horse would capture our national attention and allow our beau ideals to bubble to the surface of our lives in union with our greatest hopes and dreams. After Secretariat's convincing victory in the Kentucky Derby and another prize-winning performance in the Preakness, media experts everywhere trumpeted the possibility of his final achievement, that he was poised to become the first horse in a quarter century to reach the pinnacle of refined accomplishment in these equestrian events—winning all three races in succession and gaining that coveted distinction of being a treble victor among the foals. Millions of people throughout the United States and around the globe, including seasoned racing veterans, Hollywood celebrities, government dignitaries, and nameless common folk who had never even seen a horse race before set their eyes upon New York's Belmont Park on June 9, 1973 at the behest of animal sports enthusiasts, hoping to see if this chestnut steed could actually sweep the races of the Triple Crown, a feat that had eluded so many great horses during the two dozen years prior in almost providential form. Reminiscent of Fatima, Portugal and the 1917 Marian Miracle of the Sun, a crowd of over 70,000 people jammed into the raceway park on that beautiful weekend in early summer; press pool reporters, college students, movie stars, ordinary Joes, mothers and fathers walking children by the hand and hefted onto their shoulders, along with the throngs from across America who watched by television, some too young to even know what a Triple Crown winner was. Even myself, an eleven year old boy, who knew nothing of such games, but who had witnessed the previous two races by random chance while surfing TV channels, was drawn to our family set that Saturday at the urging of my own curiosity and the show-preempting national coverage. There was a seeming unity among everyone who watched; millions exhilarated in expectation, hoping to see a slice of history, pining to see a champion succeed, nervous that it may not come, praying to see something many had never witnessed or may never see again. The pageantry, elegance and fanfare of the event were outlaid in their fullest tradition. To everyone to whom I am writing now, imagine the compaction of emotions pent-up in the shared hopes of the national multitudes, one mammoth essence of potential jubilation still locked behind the verdict of events in time. This sea of humanity was simply hoping to at least witness a win by a nose, as if wishing for anything more would have been beyond any spectator's dream. And, it was in this mystical state that America poised itself as these majestic steeds broke five wide from the starting gate beneath a silent blue sky and beaming sun. Secretariat scrambled into the first turn along the rail with his strongest competitor flanking him stride-for-stride. Huffing nose-to-nose, entering the backstretch they flew, and then...suddenly... it happened. The Providence of God expanded the bounds of the created universe and gave the entire world a gift that was a premonition of His own Kingly Dominion. This preeminent horse in whom our Heavenly Father infused the power of life absolutely exploded with the speed of a mythical Pegasus being called by a Grecian god into the eternal halls of legends. He stormed past the three-quarter mile marker faster than any horse had ever run the Belmont Stakes and accelerated completely into his own domain, exceeding the entire field of competitors like a four-legged rocket blazing toward the horizon, running faster and faster with each expiring second. Three lengths to the lead,...5 lengths, ...8 lengths! Never before had the dyke of human euphoria sprung a gusher of satisfaction with such prophetic foresight—first a tiny trickle giving way to a fuller stream, then a raging torrent, followed by entire tapestries of ecstasy crumbling before the eyes of this trembling melting pot of humanity. The race was barely half run when the crescendo of victory was unleashed like a titanic tidal wave. The realization came upon everyone there like the deigning of a miracle, healing all who yearned so wantingly for the greatness of the moment to be fulfilled. People were crying and wailing in bewilderment, falling to their knees in sudden amazement, no longer able to stand upright because of their heights of raw elation. It was as though the crowd was seeing the Face of the very God who made this creature run.

Expectation and anticipation embraced the brilliance of the heart in a perfect sequence to the soundtrack of thundering hooves upon the soil. Incredulous veterans of the racing industry started cursing the jockey from their skybox windows, claiming he was blowing the race and that Secretariat was running too fast to ever withstand a finish. Neither their souls nor the seasoned logic of their experience could capture the dimensions of the grandeur they were seeing in timeless leagues above their expectations. Ten lengths turned into 14, and into the third turn they went with nearly a half-mile to go. The trackside commentator was shouting above the hysterical pandemonium of the crowd into his screeching microphone, *"He is moving like a tremendous machine! Secretariat is in a position where he's impossible to catch!"* Coming out of the clubhouse turn and with an entire home stretch spread before him, Secretariat charged forward with a look of utter defiance on his face like a runaway locomotive, all alone in time and space, a sprinter dominating a marathon, an apparition of nearly unthinkable proportions permeating the seams of the surreal, surpassing the capacities of his nature, widening the scope of his lead and his overwhelming victory with every stride, redefining the meaning of "beast of burden," and ripping the gate of triumph completely off its hinges. He accelerated and came streaking down the long stretch heading for home, passing before an awestruck crowd standing in wonderment, pounding their breasts in hysterical astonishment—extending the separation of humiliation between himself and his opponents to...16 lengths...20 lengths ...23 lengths ...26 lengths ...30 lengths, to the deafening roar of a crowd shrieking at being blessed to witness something so profound. And, as Secretariat made his final thrust toward the finish line, the shoes on his hooves pile-driving the track, this little eleven-year-old boy was jumping all around our living room, nearly mind-boggled by what I was seeing, although I had never seen a Triple Crown race before or knew what it really meant. I simply realized with my childlike heart that, for this amazing moment, I was witnessing something to remember for the rest of my life. Secretariat defined winning for me on a scale that would sustain me until February 22, 1991, when I was given a premonition of the Triumph of the Immaculate Heart of Mary. He crossed over the finish line, shattering the world record by over two seconds going away, completing the race 31 lengths ahead of his nearest competitor, a feat that had never been seen in the history of horse racing, unequaled to this day. Jack Whitaker of CBS-TV Sports, who was calling the race to the nation, later reflected upon witnessing this marvel of the animal world by saying, *"Everyone was speechless. And, then when it set in, people were crying. I actually saw people crying, it was such an overwhelming event."* Another veteran of the New York Racing Association, Pat Lynch, stated some years later, *"It was like the Lord was holding the reigns. Secretariat was one of His creatures, and He maybe whispered to him—go!—and that horse really went."* And, with a calm, contemplative sigh and a reverent reminiscence in his voice, he acclaimed, *"It was really an almost supernatural experience. It really was."* Heywood Hale Brown, another CBS commentator, perhaps said it most succinctly as he tried to describe what this race and like events really mean, *"At that moment, they were more than life allows."* And, speaking to the legendary golfer, Jack Nicklaus who questioned Brown about his personal experience that day, he said, *"Jack, don't you understand, all of your life in your game you have been striving for perfection; at the end of the Belmont, you saw it!"* The parable was made complete some years later when, upon the death of this great thoroughbred, veterinarians discovered during the autopsy that Secretariat was born with a genetic abnormality, possessing a heart that was over two and one-half times larger than any normal horse. It was not an anatomical birth defect, but a legend-making advantage of sound physiology, impressed by the Creator within his being before birth, assuring him to be born into something greater from his conception. So, there it is, the heart wrapped in a parable of one of God's majestic creatures. Indeed, it is by the heart that we shall all claim victory! And, isn't it fitting that we should remember with each new springtime the stellar performance Secretariat unleashed which, for a brief moment in time, united millions of people inside a vision that seemed to be beyond us all? There is not a secular-minded person around who would refuse to recognize the appropriateness of such remembrances from the annals of humanity's modern history.

Sunday, June 13, 2004 (excerpt)   *3:55 p.m.*
St. Anthony of Padua [1195-1231]
Doctor of the Church, Hammer of The Heretics
   "My little ones, on this Feast of Corpus Christi, I call   n(165)
you to hunger for the righteousness of God. Be near Him in
all things, pray for His Divine Mercy, seek His Salvation,
please the purposes of His Will, regain the dignity your
forefathers forfeited, purify the intentions of your hearts,
enrich the lives of your enemies, seek the conversion of the
lost, emulate the piety of the Saints, embolden the tepid to be
strong, emblazon your future across the horizons, garner the
faith to succeed, admonish the faithless in your midst; and
above all things, Love Jesus, as He is your Savior and King.   *x*
I tell you again today, as I have given the world warning for
centuries, that they who hold fast to their belief in the Most
Blessed Sacrament and receive Holy Communion with

penitential contrition shall be granted Eternal Life in Heaven. My children, your Redemption is this clear and simple. If you can muster the courage to fight for the Truth of Jesus' Holy Presence in the Bread of Life from the Altar, your Salvation in Heaven is assured. Your Mother realizes that there are many transgressions which have yet to be mitigated. There are treacherous life-plans that need to be altered. There are captives in need of release. Yes, there are countless other sins which need to be ended. But, I tell you over and again that all goodness that will purify Creation to the best of all things is found in the Sacred Body and Blood of My Crucified Son. Imagine the strength of belief of the Church throughout the ages, that She has offered the gifts of Bread and Wine to Her priests. Of anything else you can ponder in your mortal lives, think about this Consecration of humanity to the richness of Salvation by God's chosen priests who are humanity. The victory of peace over war is found in the Holy Eucharist, the healing of the sick is located there, the conquering of the darkness by God's Holy Light is manifested in the Most Blessed Sacrament. My children—My Church—your dedication and devotion to Jesus in the Most Holy Sacrament of the Altar is this important in your lives.

  Today, we also pray for those who are leading their brothers and sisters away from the Traditions of the Church. Pray intensely for those who are desecrating the Holy Relics of the Catholic Church in the name of modernization. Pray for the souls of sinners who are perverting the Truth of the sacred Banns of Marriage in the interest of diversity. Be compassionate toward the ignorant and enraged against those who are perpetrating outright heresy and error for financial gain. These are strange and frightful times for good Christians everywhere, but all who come to Me shall be granted shelter during the imminent storms. Bring to Me your most finely fashioned dreams and I will make them all come true. Give unto Jesus your most impossible hopes and He will grant you your hearts' desires. I promise you today above all the other promises I have made—I am speaking on

xx

xxx

xl

l

behalf of your God! I carry the commission to make clear to the world the infinitude of His Glory. I bear to you the Good News of His Holy Will. No humanity anywhere else in or outside of Creation could be more blessed than that which resides on the face of the Earth. I assure you of your good fortune in Jesus, and I tell you with all the sureness of His Resurrection that your Divine Life for which you have long-prayed and suffered gladly is nigh at hand.

My Special son, I realize that you seek in your brothers and sisters the holiness that has engulfed you. They have yet to know and hear from the Mother of God. Feel compassion for them because of this, and know the high status of your own good fortune to have been granted such a gift. I call upon your very soul to speak to your heart, and reciprocally your heart to your soul, that all things are occurring according to God's Plan—as difficult as this may be to comprehend. Your prayers and sacrifices, the intensity of your Christianity pouring-forth into the world, and the miracles that your own miraculous life is manifesting are indeed opening the sleeping eyes of the rest of the world. You often seem to wonder how your Mother can come to you with such great hope and happiness. I sense in your heart the impressions that I could wield My awesome power more widely and prominently. I only ask you to believe for a time that I truly am—I truly am in ways that you have yet to understand. Bear with Me in the same labor that I bore your Salvation into the material world 2,004 years ago. You will soon see the fruits of your labors in rather obvious ways, with overtones that will expand the elements of time and space. You will sense that sacred unity for which you have always pined between the living and the dead. You will begin to have thoughts of the sweetness of your brothers and sisters instead of the oppression by which they are controlling the Earth. And, your perspective will turn to your own sure realization that the End Times have come. Your vision and your tenor will be of reflection, compassion, encouragement, willingness to sustain and be sustained; and that simple,

lx

lxx

lxxx

beautiful, confident, and precious sense of accomplishment will be yours. You have seen this in My predictions which have come true. You have received these things by your own making—by toiling and not counting the cost, and by believing in our work together when only few others would accept. Thank you, My precious little one. Thank you and your brother to whom you have given the greatest of yourself for many years.

xc

I have offered you words about Jesus in the Holy Eucharist because He has been the receiver of your supplications for the entirety of your years. Ever since you were a tiny child in Saint Augustine Church in your little village home, you heard the Sanctuary bells peal to tell you that a Divine miracle was about to occur. This was the Consecration that has preceded your own consecration to My Immaculate Heart. This is Jesus' having physically given you to Me. And, I accept you, I want you, I cherish you, I pray for you, and I will someday see your dutiful and obedient little soul in Paradise with all the Angels and Saints forever to come. You will bring your Baptismal Gown back to the very Holy Spirit who once handed it to you, fully intact and utterly unstained. This is a promise that I make not only to you, but to the God who created Me as well. I have given you the bounty of My Immaculate Heart here today because this is what we do. I offer My Grace to you in a way that the nation of America shall never be worthy to receive... The pageantry of the last week in the death of Ronald Reagan was about the inevitability of death. I am offering you a celebration of Eternal Life in Jesus that has been prefigured since the Dawn of the Ages. I wish for you to not ponder the figurative images of black caissons and mourning widows. I wish for you not to dwell on riderless horses with inverted shoes. No—I wish for you to draw your hearts into that great and noble triumph of humanity itself being borne on the withers of God's own Secretariat carrying His people back to His awaiting arms—so far ahead of the claw-footed world that neither wind nor lightning could ever

c

cx

cxx

hold you in arrears. This, My son, is what you are doing for God here on the Earth, and this is why you will ultimately stand inside the circle of victory with champions' flags waving overhead and a quilt of fresh carnations blanketing your soul... I offer you now My holy blessing for today. + I will speak to you again next week. Thank you for your prayers. I love you. Goodnight!"   cxxx

     If reasonable people can acquiesce and concur to the rightness of propagating memorable moments such as the strides of a famed horse, then are we not even more bound and fully obliged to acknowledge the indubitable Redemptive Remembrance that has already itself proven to be more than simply a mortally constrained contest in time? Should we not parade before every ensuing age that indelibly Holy Sacrifice, composed of the will and the Sacred Heart that engulfs and surpasses the incarcerating parameters of our ticking timepieces, the Salvific Crucifixion which overwhelms our present experiences and provides an irreproachable redefinition to every future that will process from beyond the eastern horizon, the Perpetual Dawn that is already showing its undying presence in the galactic Morning Star, the Splendid Victory which can never be eclipsed, the Eternal Sun that has ignited and enlightened every torch of wisdom, and the Royal Scepter which renders our trotting steeds to be little more than prodigies of the foreboding Truth which declares that Paradise is on the verge of unleashing the last great bastion of human sanctity from behind the Gates of Eternity? If horse races on a spring day or eloquent oratories on the plazas of grand republics are occasions for the elevation and expansion of the human heart, why can't humanity recognize the uncontested Summit of Devotion to which all men throughout every age have been simultaneously transported at the sacred words of Consecration during the Holy Sacrifice of the Mass? If we are awestruck by the self-denial and deprivation sustained and overcome by tenacious people who are driven to conquer the inclement regions of the towering Tibetan Chomolungma, then why are we not breathless in awe at each of the Catholic Saints who endured far more than a summer mountain climb to experience and maintain the spiritual perfection that feeds our sanctified aspirations for immortal deliverance into Paradise forever to come? We can travel to major cities and enter any number of skyscrapers where we are faced with a decision before boarding the elevators. Do we remember that, in the tallest buildings, not every elevator goes to the highest floors? While some take their passengers from the first floor through the tenth floor, others service only higher levels like the fifth to the fifteenth or the tenth through the fortieth. Few of the cars travel from the ground floors and mezzanines to the highest penthouses and observation decks in continuous ascent. If these towering buildings could be viewed as metaphors for the knowledge of God, how high do we wish to go, and which elevator should we choose? What if we take an elevator based simply upon the sensation it gives us that we are rising? If we are in the one that services only the lower floors, will we ever see Creation from the highest point, no matter how long we remain standing inside? Are we preferential to our position, fearful that the view we may otherwise experience will be less palatable to our comfort? The world is filled with such vain logic that has been concocted to fulfill the justifications of faithless men whose only goal is self-enrichment. And, they are the lesser upon whom so many curious people have naively attached their worldly perspectives for dreamy advancement. Far too many men have their intellects buttressed with perceptions that could not be disentangled from the sinful nature of secular gravity in another two millennia. It is these shallow religious arguments that must be replaced by a contrite submission to the vision of the Supreme Witness to the True Faith, the Most Holy Mother of Jesus Christ.   There are events and circumstances providentially scattered throughout our lives that provide degrees and gradations of ascent to the human heart, and which move humanity to a clearer perspective of ordained existence, while each of them raises us to a more proficient awareness of our responsibilities and our all-too-often obscured potential. However, none of these earthbound encumbrances or illusionary distractions is the spiritual elevator which will lift humanity enmasse beyond the incidentals of the future to the highest revelations; for they are but the faltering venues that provide only the measure of ascension allowed by the finite dimensions of their sinful authors and makers, bounded by time and the memories of men. They are the imposters who only mimic the Truth, all the while distracting unwary people from their noblest capacities. Even Einstein's relativistic theories are modern parables about Christianity and the condition of our collective faith. This great scientist noticed that when people entered an elevator where they could not observe the world outside its spatial confines, none of them could distinguish between the sensation of the car actually rising or whether the force of gravity pulling their bodies toward the floor had been increased so as to connote a feeling of ascension. The empirical sensation is identical in both cases, the floor pushing up more firmly on someone's feet. This is the deception within many sects of Christianity that are at odds with the Roman Catholic Church. And, since their congregants cannot yet see beyond the veil of their passing, they feel what they believe to be their ascension in grace, while it is actually the gravity of their obstinance against Jesus, laboring beneath the weight of His Cross to save them. You see, some of them are not on an elevator at all; but they fail to realize it because they are too busy protesting a Roman Catholicism they have not even had the decency to peruse. They are utterly petrified of the powerful magnificence of the Hierarchical Church that Jesus Christ founded because they have been taught for generations to fear and despise its call for penitential self-sacrifice, not realizing that it is simply Our Lord's summons to give more generously of themselves to Love.

If they would only lend their prudence to the Holy Roman Catholic Church and the piety and self-denial She extols, they would understand that the Original Apostolic Church is the Elevator par excellence. It alone is the Carriage of Divinity whose death-defying reaches extend beyond the clouded veil into Heaven itself, providing the ecstatic fulfillment which composes the spectacular envisionment we gain at the towering summit of Jesus' Sacred Heart, that place where mankind touches the celestial domain and communes with his Omnipotent Benefactor. The Holy Mass reverberates the primeval spirit of Creation through a collection of unified hearts, transported in time into the blissful reaches of Paradise through a beatific plume that is opened to the heavens by the Sacrifice of the God-Man, matched to the allegiance of His apostolic servants who have given their lives in faith to sustain a holy priesthood until the cessation of the ages. The recollection of my childhood harks my memory back to a time when I stood on my toes atop an extended kneeler with my nose poking into the air, barely able to see over the back of the pews blocking my view of the Sacred Altar in our small village church. I remember being surrounded by a sea of worshipers, straining my ears with great attentiveness, waiting for those consecrating words from our parish priest and the ringing of the altar bells, signaling to my little heart that *The Miracle* of the Transubstantiation had just taken place. Indeed, every Sunday without exception, I was taken by my parents to Holy Mass to witness the greatest moment in Creation over and again, each time standing in anxious anticipation atop that kneeler, waiting for the instant when our robed Father would raise the round piece of unleavened Bread above the Altar with his hands extended to God in supplication, the Host I was never allowed touch. And, upon hearing the words, *"This is My Body..."* just before the tinkling announcement of the miracle which has forever transcended nature, I knew through my childlike faith that Jesus Christ had come to be with us and hear our prayers, even though I could not see Him. Thus, two millennia of Tradition saw its continuation unimpeded, resilient, marching through the ages, lifting us in dignity and endowing us with the surreal power to outlast the pall of death itself, experiencing the Majestic unbowed, advancing leagues beyond the cynicism of faithless mortals, processing by the Light before which bygone kings have knelt, breaching the ordinary and bringing this epoch of humanity back from the precipice of mental mayhem, focusing our vision upon the paradisial summit, folding us in the silver clouds of Grace and depositing our untarnished souls in the yonder pleats of the raiment of Glory. Can a heart stir so silently with a passion so deafening that an entire world would move into this new Springtime? Can there arise a concussion of Divinity so powerful or could an angelic resonance of harmony be so perfect that it would shatter the obduracy encasing the hallowed potential of the human race to reveal the truest Love wishing to flourish between Heaven and its united people from the day an innocent Man was crucified and rose again?

Sunday, May 11, 2003 Mother's Day   *3:03 p.m.*

"The Mother of all humanity has come to speak to m(131) you today because I wish to bring My Holy Love into broken hearts who have never known the true meaning of Divine affection before. Yes, this is a day that has been set-aside for the admiration of human mothers, but I am calling even these to take refuge beneath the protection of My Mantle and in the sweetness of My Immaculate Heart. My children, I wish to tell you on this special occasion what it means to be the Matriarch of Creation. My role as Queen of Heaven and Earth is one of particular strength and compassion, much like   x the bearers of children on the Earth. But, I own the title of Mother of God, and there is no other. It gives Me great honor for My children to remember Me, therefore, on this day as well. I have seen through the vision of Wisdom and the benefit of the blessings of Eternity that your human hearts are still aching. And, this need not be true. Temptation, sin, impatience, and greed are the cause of such torment. When you enlist the Holy Spirit to be your guide through mortal life, you will see that only your relationship with God is what matters the most. When mothers and fathers love God   xx with the fidelity of the Angels, He will ensure that your children follow alongside you. Being a mother means tending to the needs of her children, but being the Mother of God gives Me the capacity and authority to shape the spiritual goodness of their souls. A mother in the world provides food, clothing, and filial affection. This Mother of God gives the Bread of Life, Eternal guidance, ecclesiastical Wisdom, and compassion for the heart. I am known for all

time and beyond the everlasting ages as the Benevolent Consoler because I accept and embrace the people of the   xxx
Earth, even in their weaknesses. I understand what causes the agony in your lives without your having to explicate it to anyone else. You need not even utter audible groanings with your voices for Me to know that you are in pain. Do you not remember the Sacred Reproaches upon which you meditate during the Season of Lent? Such are also the pleadings of the innocent human heart! The benign nature of little children lives inside everyone, begs to come out, and cowers in the darkness of the brutal world. It is to this intrinsic simplicity that I have come, offering the Peace of God where there is   xl
sorrow and regret. My children, I am the only mother in Creation who can do these things.

    I thank all of My faithful children for acknowledging My Grace during the month of May, and for all of time. I am grateful for the many prayerful ceremonies where a statue of Me receives a crown of flowers. Each 'Hail Mary' of the Most Holy Rosary is a reciprocal kiss on My cheek by the humanity whom God has deigned to call His children. We share a unique and spectacular relationship that transcends the history of the world, which cuts through the darkness of   l
the lost mortal ages, and that pays no mind to matters of the flesh. Together, we form a spiritual bond of Divine Love that cannot be put asunder or affected in any malevolent way by forces of the world. We share goodness, peace, joy, sanctity, purity, and Light through the Resurrection of Jesus from the Sepulcher; and we understand the motivations of God by the power of the Holy Paraclete. Why have I come seeking you with such great intensity? Because you are My babes who are yet calling-out from your nests in the world, craning your necks to see where your Mother may be. I am   lx
here, My little children! Your Mother is at your side, and I will never leave you to suffer harm anymore! I am the same Blessed Virgin Mary who bore your Salvation in My Womb, now holding the Lamb of God who takes away the sins of the world in My Arms as the Thrice-blessed King of all Creation.

His Will is to be done in your time! His little eyes are glowing in acknowledgment that it is coming true! Do not be sorrowful that the unification of the world seems not to be at hand because, in the end, it has already been achieved. Imagine the sorrow I have had for the wait! I watched sadly   lxx *as My Son was Crucified on the Earth. My Immaculate Heart was pierced with a sorrow that has passed beyond the veil. Why? Because too many who are living sinful lives are still crucifying Him! And, I cry compassionately for unborn children in their mothers' wombs whose lives will be ended much too soon. I weep for victims of war and crimes of the heart. I sorrow because there are too few who will turn to Jesus for the eradication of pestilence, disease, famine, plight, and nakedness. Yes, all of these things cause the Mother of God great pain.*   lxxx

      And, if this is not enough, I am sorrowful because even those who have faith in My Son will not wield its power to admonish and rebuke the enemies of the Cross. They cower in the back pews of their parishes and watch as though they are casual spectators while the Holy Sacrifice of the Mass is offered. I ask My little children to participate more fully in the cultivation of humanity in the way of the First Apostles and Saints! Be the activists for the conversion of the world to the Cross, and counteract all the clamoring of the millions who are seeking to abandon the alone, dying,   xc *unkempt, disheveled, and misled. Become the new Saints Francis, Augustine, Matthew, Mark, Luke, John, Juan Diego, Pio, and all the Saints! Pray from your hearts that your next-door neighbors will abandon their lives of drunken licentiousness and turn their lives over to upholding the Gospel of Christianity. Call upon them to embrace the spiritual goodness that has brought many wretched sinners to the contrition that saved their souls! Ask them to espouse the Holy Virtues and the Sacred Beatitudes that Jesus proffered the world in the Sermon on the Mount. Then, when you turn*   c *to your Heavenly Mother and ask how you can better please Me, bear these fruits in your hands as you raise them in faith.*

If you seek more graces for your friends and enemies too, let us meet at the intersection of Heaven and Earth on Mount Calvary, upon the Sacred Altars of the Roman Catholic Church! Come there and tell Jesus that you have brought your gifts of contrition and reconciliation in exchange for His benisons upon you! Be the blessers of other lives, of terrified human hearts, of dying men, of broken families, and of timid little children. Become the health of the sick and consolers of the grieving by making this age of humankind better than any that has ever lived before! And, yet, too many come to Me and say '...but Dear Mother, how do we do these things?' And, My response to the millions who are waging war instead of seeking peace is to ...become every good thing that you are not now allowing to live! I have great patience for the humanity that is Mine, and I will wait through all Eternity if this is what God has planned for you.

cx

On this Mother's Day, the greatest burden that I bear is the lukewarm faith of Christians everywhere. If only My children would adopt the same patience that has become the forte of the Savior of the world, they would try harder to ameliorate the ills of their peoples because they would know that there is sufficient time to succeed. Never believe that it is a contradiction to also know that the Son of Man might return before dawn tomorrow! And, what will He discover you doing? What will the Master of the House find when He enters the door? He is seeking your Love, My children, in exponentially viable quantities! He is seeking the Love in your hearts to be flooding the Earth as in the days of Noah! My Son is a good swimmer! Make the Earth to be the vast ocean of miraculous human affection in which He would like to plunge and take you all under His arms to the safe shores of Paradisial jubilation! When you make the cause of your days the pursuit of this Love, you will lose your desire for the mortal. You will drop the materials in your hands. Your eyes will begin to see the Glory of the Coming of the Lord! Hallelujah! You will learn what it feels like to be Saints before you ever die! When you raise-up the Cross of the Son

cxx

cxxx

of God and His Glorious Resurrection too, all Creation will   cxl
come running to stand beside you as you elevate the very
purpose of your having been given the gift of human life. I
am hopeful and joyous at the same time that I hold the
sorrow in My Heart for those who have not yet tried because
I know, above and beyond the pondering of any modern
prophet, that everything I have ever sought in My children
of the Earth will come true! I have seen it, and I ask you to
believe that I have.

    My Special son, it gives Me great pleasure to speak to
you with high hopes because, as you know, you and your   cl
brother are already two of the most successful of My children.
There are still many things yet to do, notwithstanding those
who behave as though they are your enemies; for many of
them are not, they are only feeding their own indignant
pride.   You had a very good conversation with your
relatives; you are continuing to be the spiritual mentor for
tens-of-thousands in this modern day; and, by your courage
and perseverance, you are becoming the conqueror for Jesus
whom you have always prayed to be... My son, you have
said on any number of occasions that you and your brother   clx
are living in a world where there seems to be nobody else.
Never be resigned to the unfortunate fate to which so many
have subjected themselves in blind errancy! God is always
with you, Jesus is your best friend, and the fellowship of the
Holy Spirit will be with you always, even past the cleft
between your mortal nature and Eternal Life. I have also
told you that self-compassion is one of the greatest gifts you
can give of yourself to the God who lives in your heart...
Thank you for your prayers today... This is My holy blessing
for you and your brother now. + Please continue to be happy   clxx
that you are doing God's Will. I Love you. Goodnight!"

Why has the evangelization of the Truth emitting from the Roman Catholic Church seemed so frayed, squelched and inadequate at times? It is because of the horrible burden under which She and Her children labor that is being inflicted by contrarians who are so offensive to the unity we desire, those who refuse to defer to greater Wisdom, those who would only bend, scandalize and humiliate the Sacred Hierarchical Church of Jesus Christ into oblivion, and then, upon accomplishing its Crucifixion, cheer aloud with a rancorous sense of personal gratification. And, too, because of those who would hold-out in disobedience to Her tenets until they see the flashing white eyes of Jesus Christ. The Creed of the Roman Catholic Church's existence is one of compassion and mercy, bearing with fortitude the deliverance that has been heaped upon the shoulders and fragility of Her people. The Protestant Revolution of the 1500s and the succeeding skirmishes of rogue theologies have done more than draw huge numbers away from the universal power of oneness that has been the hallmark of Christianity since it was first fashioned by the Holy Spirit on Pentecost, AD 33. It has ominously set forth a counter-vision that will never possess the taming parameters to circumscribe the sultry egoism of men who claim illegitimate dominion over the destinies of huge segments of God's children. In that inauspicious past, they blindly transferred the Gospel of Christ from the foundation of loving sacrifice and submission, i.e., the Divine character of Heaven's unity, onto the terminal platform of the unbounded reign of human preference in all matters, mortal and Divine. A portion of humanity intentionally separated from the whole of Holy Christendom and protested without a whit of conscience, "I'll decide!" effectively dooming generations of men to the failed consequences of the most arrogant and assertive among them. Their neo-theologies no longer unveiled successive beauties of Christ's humble submission. Instead, they inaugurated an intellectual foray meant solely to obscure the irreproachable genius of the Holy Spirit who had labored fifteen hundred years through the lives of His most faithful followers, building a castle where men could live in peace as one in heart and purpose amidst the travails that would undoubtedly be greeted upon them throughout every generation. It was no longer the Third Person of the Most Holy Trinity peacefully and prudently advancing the implementation of His Sacred Beatitudes through the annals of time; rather, it became the warfare of innumerable contortions of whimsical human interpretation, splintering humanity into intellectual adversity at the expense of Christian solidarity. Rational batteries arose like arsenals against the mystical, the same intelligence that still divides our allegiances, as tepid theologians strain the gnats from our perfection with cookie-cutter fear-mongering. Consider the almost unimaginable unity before the religious hostilities of the 16th century. What could have been the deepest thoughts of Martin Luther and his renegade contemporaries once he saw the bastion of

Christianity in which he passionately believed fragmenting before his eyes into clustered aberrations that he surely knew must be opposed as being beyond the pall of His Savior? What can we appropriately say of his sordid legacy after 33,000 different denominations have arisen, all claiming to possess the truth of Christianity, and most of whom are at odds with the teachings of the others? Simply scan the Yellow Pages of your local telephone book for the Christian churches in your demographic area? There, you will find a microcosm of our splintered nature, the shards of our shame regarding Christian cohesiveness throughout the United States. The most unfortunate consequence in all of this is the violation of the unity that materializes from the recognition of the Ultimate Truth to which every man, woman and child would gladly submit if it was to be clearly seen! Theological obscurity, haughty agendas, and wilful pride have brought 500 years of division and devastation to fruition, and it is time for that to change. And, change it will at the mighty hands of the Most Blessed Virgin of Nazareth! Those who set forth the fractured course of Christianity almost five centuries ago did not have the prophetic foresight that Christ imbued within His Apostles when the hierarchy of the Catholic Church concretized and came forth to shepherd humankind to the threshold of Eternity. They, instead, left their multitudes unprovided for, forcing them to forage their spirituality all alone, advancing the unheard-of concept that no absolute Divine authority existed among the people, leaving everyone in their ranks to search for their own personal truth. They detached themselves from the authentic Repository of revelatory history, that stately Ark and Guardian of Sanctification and Redemption. And, the overriding casualty of this spiritual train wreck is the very Truth that Jesus Christ spoke and still passionately speaks about, His intention for all humankind to be united at the Altar of Sacrifice to receive His Sacramental Flesh and Blood in the Most Holy Eucharist. The prevailing worldview of a growing multitude is that there exists no Universal Truth to which all men must give their willing assent. Therefore, their new-age sense of righteousness demands that anything envisioned by the human intellect must be respected as possessing an equal emanation of the Truth. Although none of these people would subscribe to such logic in any other area of life, they believe that if the Truth cannot be known, then their own personal truth is as tenably valid as anyone else's. As a result, we have homosexuality forcing its illegitimacy upon our youth, the killing of children in the wombs of their mothers being protected as an inalienable "human right," the sanctity of the family being devastated by rampant divorce rates, and sexuality used as leisurely entertainment. There is even a supposedly Christian congregation with pew-crushing attendance rolls and robust television ratings where a pastor preaches with strains of twisted Scripture, teaching his deceived flock word-for-word from the Bible that Christ, our Lord, has made him filthy rich because he is in good favor with Heaven instead of admitting that he has extorted millions of dollars from impressionable people for his own material gain. Those tithes should be given to the poor, and this so-called "minister" should repent before a Roman Catholic priest, the latter having already sacrificially divested himself of every physical possession on Earth so this prevaricating preacher can be spared from the fires of Gehenna the instant his soul departs his flesh. This "impastor" is headed for the flaming Abyss, and is leading his applauding, Lexus-driving congregation with him, while he is still ironically heralded at ecumenical meetings and accorded seats of prominence as a disciple of Jesus Christ by marauders who have plundered the meaning of religious ecumenism. People who are destabilizing civilization, obscuring the redemptive Truth, and sowing disunity are going to see Divine Judgment from God's own Hand. And, as Forrest Gump would say, *"...that's all I have to say about that!"*

Sunday, June 30, 2002 (excerpt)   11:18 a.m.
"The courage that you muster to fight against the   l(181)
enemies of Christianity is a gift of the Holy Spirit from the
Throne of God. Therein, your every sacrifice is blessed as a
portion of the suffering of Jesus on the Cross because your
souls have become one in union with perfection like Him.
And, if you wish to continue to be like Him, you must worry
not what your adversaries can do to your reputations or the
health and safety of your physical bodies. I am not asking
you to walk headlong into intentional danger, but fear not
when such moments arise that you are threatened by the   x
scalded dogs of evil who surround you now. It is true that
the Catholic Church is both pure and being purified, and
you are a force for good in this transformation. Is the Church
to be crucified as the Son of God was nailed to the Cross? Let
Me assure you that He, too, is suffering the agony of the
ongoing sins of an errant humanity because His Love for
humankind did not cease when He was raised from the dead.
My children, the future of Catholicism is not like a piece of
driftwood wandering about the oceans' crests. My Church is
stationed high and away from the corruption that will fall   xx
every other mortal institution on the Earth. Therefore,
remain very close to the Sacraments, and trust in the Church

Hierarchy because Jesus is guiding them with all the power of God, Himself. You will be accosted for defending your faith, even though your detractors will know that you are in agreement with them about the sins of some of your brothers and sisters. If anyone would wish to castigate the Catholic Church in its entirety as a result of the weakness of a few, such critics are under the influence of Satan. Anyone who is an enemy of the Roman Catholic Church when Jesus calls the world to completion will be cast into Hell. It is just as simple as this.

      xxx

I wish not to speak brashly or abruptly about those who have yet to be converted to the Holy Eucharist, but I belong to the irreproachable Light of Heaven. I cannot be despised by those whose souls will eventually reside in Paradise. As it has been said before, sinners who bear hatred against the Mother of God belong to the Antichrist. Please deliver this message to the world-entire for Me, knowing in advance that the level of danger in which you might be entering will be elevated... Simply place it in your other writings on the schedule you have already planned. My children, your God is filled to the brim with contempt for those who are assailing the Holy Roman Catholic Church... The angels decline to hover over those who harbor hatred against the Most Blessed Sacrament. The Living Wrath of Jesus awaits those who scoff at the Sacrament of Confession. I tell you these things not as doomsday prophesies, but as promises that My Son will cleanse this world of all heresy before His final mission is through. It is only through His Divine Mercy and the prayers of the Catholic faithful that those who belong to other religions and denominations are allowed admittance into Heaven at all. Hospitals and nursing homes are filled to near capacity because God has requested such holy souls to join Jesus on the Cross to defeat the enemies of the descendants of Saint Peter. My children, these are the facts, they are not portions of flowery orations or dimly-lit predictions.

      xl

      l

Should not the Mother of God reserve the right to admonish humanity about its position against My Church? lx *Do I not have the authority to speak with such Truth in rebuking those who refuse to believe in all Seven of the Sacraments? Let Me assure you—I am beautiful and Heaven is beyond description. But, those who declare themselves to be in diametrical opposition to the teachings of the Roman Catholic Church are ugly, unsightly, living outside the state of grace, and in a gravely sinful condition. This is how serious it is for anyone from any walk of life to defame the beauty of the Church, whether it be the media, public leaders, private journalists, other religions, or an anonymous* lxx *man standing on a curb alongside a darkened street. Now, I must tell you that I have spoken these things from the depths of the Love in My Immaculate Heart for those who are guilty. I pray deeply for their conversion, understanding, humility, and prayers; but most of all, I seek a change of heart in them, that they may come to the Altar of Sacrifice to receive the Eucharistic Species of My Son. I ask them to come not out of fear, but because they believe! Indeed, I seek their Sacramental Confession based not only upon My admonition, but because they realize that their souls are* lxxx *otherwise separated from God by their unconfessed sins! There are many wakes to come for the dying who will have gone past the chasm of mortality without laying their lives bare before a Roman Catholic priest. Woe be unto them! Please pray for them now! This is the seriousness by which Jesus is approaching these latter times, and I am the Mother whom He has dispatched to speak on His behalf. I have said to humanity before that it is better for you to hear this from Me at this point in time than for Jesus to bring the backlash of your own obstinance to bear against you on the last day of* xc *the world.*

My Special son, I assure you that I wish not to frighten you in My words today or cause you to lose any hope for the conversion of your fellow men. There are statements in this message that absolutely were required to be made.

When you relate them to your brothers and sisters in a couple of years, I ask that you are sure to be clear to also say that neither you, nor I, are judging the worth of their souls. It is imperative that you assure anyone who inquires that 'The Divine Mercy of Jesus' is the reason that all non-Catholics are saved and allowed to enter into Heaven. In the end, the entire of humanity will know that it has been the Catholic Church, her priests, parishioners, and every semblance of prayer, servitude, and suffering that will have brought the Mystical Body of Christ to the Altar to be wedded with the Sacrificed Son of God. It must be a good feeling inside for you to know that you are on the inside of Grace, looking outwardly at the multiple millions who are about to come running to you as your friends and for leadership in joining you at the center of the Truth.

c

cx

You wrote a very good book in 'White Collar Witch Hunt...' For now, He (the God of your fathers) is happy to know that you have begun yet another book to be published early next year. Can you not see that you will have so many someday that your work, and Mine, cannot be cast-off and ignored? This is why your patience is required now, more than during any other time in your life. You will win sooner rather than later in accordance with how patient you are willing to become... I ask that you never surrender your hope that all the world is better for the acceptance you garnered to your God in February 1991... I give you My holy blessing for today. + I will speak to you again very soon. I Love you. Good day!"

cxx

The Roman Catholic Church has stood in bold contrast to the illicit phenomena that have reared present before righteousness and Truth during the past 2,000 years. We are of one faith, one teaching, and one fold under the generational stead of Saint Peter, assisted by the Angels, led by the Saints, protected by the Martyrs, and claimed by the Queen who bore our sacrificial King to birth, notwithstanding the individual egos within Her flock who wish to assert their wilful contradictions while stating their duplicitous allegiance to Her tenets. Imagine standing on the open field at Kitty Hawk, North Carolina in December of 1903 beside Orville and Wilbur Wright as they prepared for the first powered-flight of their newly-conceived invention they called a "flying machine." What would have been our reaction if God would have inverted history and a Boeing 747 Jumbo jetliner from our modern day was suddenly seen lumbering into view across the sky and, with full-flaps extended and jet engines roaring a high-pitched whine, touching-down on the dusty tarmac and taxiing alongside the wood and wire contraption of these primitive aviators? You see, a large part of humanity is still standing on that arcane field today, listening to men who claim to be right, irreverent rebels who are fielding their prescriptive views for religious piety that are as unreliable as that first aeronautical deathtrap. Ignobly and arrogantly they refuse to acknowledge the gargantuan beatific airship sitting before their eyes in full view of their highest aspirations, that grand transporter with blue mantled stripe whose hull gleams in the sun, looking like the presidential Air Force One inscribed nose-to-tail with the name—Roman Catholic Church—the same Ship of Deliverance that landed in a manger in Bethlehem two thousand years ago which has been resting quietly and peacefully ever since, awaiting its nuptials with the sky. Foolish human beings somehow believe that the Hierarchical Apostolic Church is some strange, obsolete, inanimate behemoth from a rare foreign archeological dig, incapable of satisfying their insatiable desires or sustaining their post-modern ambitions. But, what will they think when Jesus Christ draws the boarding steps away, speeds the engines for take-off, carries His Church to the end of the Earth's rolling fields, and pilots our Deliverance into the Eternal Dawn? I tell you, there are many poor souls who will experience that day and stand horrified that their spiritual deliverance has just escaped their grasp. Until then, our Matriarchal conductor has asked me to shout with urgent persistence, "All aboard!"

Sunday, February 27, 2000 (excerpt)   *3:43 p.m.*

*"My dear children, you are seeing many false attempts   j(058)
by man to unite himself with God. Unless a soul is led by the
Holy Spirit, it will not find everlasting Life or true meaning
in mortality on the Earth. You, My little ones, have been one
in the Holy Spirit for many years, especially the most recent
eleven. You know that I own the reason for the only success
that you can achieve, and He is the Child of Bethlehem who
also owns you. Can you see how the human mind has taken
many ponderers down many stagnant and errant paths? The
Holy Spirit of Jesus will guide and teach you always. His   x
Light is the Wisdom by which you walk. Take comfort in*

knowing that you are one with Him and traveling the road to everlasting Salvation. In that knowledge, nothing can discourage you.

Existentialism can be described as a dungeon. One is quite correct in describing such darkness and captivity. Only Jesus is the Light, and only Jesus can save your soul. The so-called peace that others feel who follow existentialism is not the peace of the living Spirit, but the stillness in the wake of their dead souls. That is why there are no choices in Christianity. There is no alternative to perfect Love and seamless obedience to the Truth of the Holy Gospel. If a man decides to choose, he must choose God, wherein any further choices are rendered obsolete. By choosing God, the decisions are already made which affect the purity, dignity, and destiny of the soul. The decision is already made to bow in deference to the King of all Creation and to relinquish your will and sovereignty to Him. There is no autonomy in this righteous state because the human soul cannot claim Salvation without Him. Hence, you are one in God through Jesus, and this is both your freedom and reward. No one should wish to exist anywhere separate from Him. Do you see how such philosophies as existentialism come to be? People will not accept the Cross of Mount Calvary or the Trinity of God. No wonder they are blind! Jesus saw their blindness during His Agony in the Garden that you are praying right now. His wish of 'Come to Me and see, and be seen' was being ignored by the barrage of self-interest by those who fell asleep! I ask what else He could have done before that Maundy Thursday to prove His role as The Christ! His miracles, prayers, and teachings seemed much too frail that fateful evening. And, I have told you that modern-day life is an image of the Passion of this noble Man! The world is again that garden on that sedentary night. But, the Son of Man has risen! This time, those who sleep are being awakened by the horrific Truth that they cannot fail this Master again! The twenty-first century has opened to be the night in the garden where no eye can fall asleep! This

xx

xxx

xl

time, millions are awakening and crawling prostrate to the Altar to say 'I am here to serve You, I will not rest until my soul sleeps in Thee!' This is why there is great hope in the modern-day world. I am pleased to announce that rather than sweating droplets of Blood, the Savior of the world is shedding tears of joy that so many are following Him. Rather than looking into the sky and saying 'Let this cup pass Me by,' He is now saying 'Let Me drown in this chalice of Love from My people!' Oh, how prophetic was that night that has brought this living day! How you will remember on March 8ᵗʰ (Ash Wednesday) as you recall your destiny before Him. You may be marked with ashes, but your spirit will soar anew with the joy that all you have come to be is made perfect in His Grace. You will remember that human suffering is not inevitable because the God of Israel will take it away. All you need to do is ask the Messiah, My living Jesus and Manna of the Altar, and human suffering will be no more. My children, the world suffers not at the hands of Love, but because humanity will not take the Hand of Love. This is a collective manifestation composed of individuals who suffer alone. But, their collective agony is the Light of the Cross still glowing in the darkness of the world, and will continue until the last lost soul can see his way Home. I ask you to continue to pray for those whose lives have been given to join the power of the Cross. Indeed, they have not lost their dignity. They have found it there! They are claiming it for those who still refuse to know! They rest in grief over the pits through which many would fall into the fiery abyss, laying in wait for souls who could not find God without them. Remember that each time you see a soul on his deathbed, he is blocking a place in Creation through which other souls might fall into perdition. These saints are proud inside to fill this role. Just ask any one of them, and they will tell you. They are too noble to complain, too loving to say no, and often unaware as to the reasons why. Jesus has spoken to their spirits and asked them to join Him in the Redemption of man. In their own holy subconsciousness, they say in reply 'Our Lord, to whom else could we turn?'

l

lx

lxx

lxxx

My Special son, that is the essence of what I have come to tell you today. I am very happy about your plans. Whatever you give to God in His Name, He will use for the conversion of souls. I know that your heart keeps asking when? Perhaps the answer will come when you prove that you accept the timing of His Will. The ark is not fully loaded yet. Allow Him to proceed without living in anxiety. Waiting in joyful hope is a fruit of your patience. Thank you for your prayers. This is My holy blessing for you. + I will speak to you again very soon! Please remember to pray for those who have nothing to eat! I love you. Goodnight!"

xc

Section Five
His Blood's Red Glare,
Bombs Bursting in Air

In your time, the innocence will fall away
In your time, the mission bells will toll
All along the corridors and river beds
There'll be signs, in your time

Towering waves will crash across your southern capes
Massive storms will reach your eastern shores
Fields of green will tumble through your summer days
By design, in your time

Feel the wind and set yourself the bolder course
Keep your heart as open as a shrine
You'll sail the perfect line

And, after all the dead ends and the lessons learned
After all the stars have turned to stone
There'll be peace across the great unbroken void
All benign, in your time
You'll be fine, in your time

In Your Time
by Bob Seger

So, we must collectively redress the world we have so awkwardly and painfully wrought, the lands appointed by God to be wrapped in wonderment and reverential awe, but instead lie justifiably prostrate beneath calamitous regret and bewilderment with the storied pages of human existence flipping at a frenzied clip from beneath our oppressive thumbs. Our days are traversing the epic of human existence from the scrawlings at the dawn of man to the etchings of our final hour, and decreasing in number to that ineffable clash between Heaven and Earth which every race and legend of peoples know to be approaching in subtle, but ever more glaring, increments of diplomatic and evangelic failure. Inasmuch as we have declined to surrender into permanent oneness in anything heretofore, let us be united at least in conceding that the many centuries of humankind absent of our collective obedience to the Holy Gospel of Jesus Christ have yet to manifest a systemic goodness, either in the social strata of our civilizations or within any rendition of cohesive civility having been legislated, inflicted or devolved upon the ages. Beside these waters should we ponder—perplexed, even if only for a brief moment, at the crashing of history's waves, wondering about the reasons why it has taken two millennia for our human hearts to sufficiently mature through the burning examples flamed within our cyclical rotisserie of sinful disengagement from Divine Mercy and Eternal Love. Our provocative ruminations call us like a mystical muse, pleading that we reflect more deeply upon the reasons why our vision is so obscured from the spectacular Essence in the Providential Wisdom of the Slain Messiah of Creation which thrives evermore brilliantly with each of our passing defeats. Let us cast our mystified gaze with heartfelt courage upon the ingenious beauty residing within the hallowed sanctum of our breathtaking marrow. It is there that the consecrated presence of God exists in communion with our interior joys, but lies besieged behind the defenses we have erected to deflect the poison injected into our lives by those external forces emitting only the darkness of volatile aggression and self-fulfillment. We need not be left to stumble over the footprints of their final desperation or the quickened sultriness of their cynicism that is imprinted upon our spiritual character. Hopeless pragmatism is their lifeless credo, which is nothing more than a dead weight that they ultimately glance to us through their repeated failures to invoke the supernatural faith to combat their rejection of the Lamb of God. It is only through the escalating advocacy of the Holy Spirit that we may embrace humility once again and recognize the poverty that has become our passionless conviction, our personal insufficiency in defining the ultimate goals of our human existence without the guiding hand of Divine Light, the indifference by which we have obscured repeated attempts by the heavens to clarify our holiest vision, and the stifling paranoia fronted to those courageous few giants who have spate upon the material world and lifted their hearts in bold faith to the sanctified elevations where the jewel of our perfection resides. Humankind need not fear the legitimate obligations which accompany the revelation of our Christian identity, for these sacrificial benisons must be thrust with heartfelt devotion upon our wilful dispositions until our egos shall cease their selfish recoiling from the beatific romanticism of the highest realms. No longer can we merely hint at the dignified composure of our blessed potential for fear of offending the decadent slanderers of decency, they who are the illegitimate progeny of partisans too selfish to shoulder the redemptive works of self-denial and noble charity required for the advancement of the human race to places that only the most unbridled of dreamers have dared to climb. We must rise to this timeless occasion like warriors whose hero has finally come to lead us Home. Our Lady is the grand guard of the King who cannot be struck down by anything or anyone. All the despicable forces of Hell aligned in one marshaled advance are but the fluttering of a tiny mosquito which She can quickly disarm with the blink of Her beautiful eyes. She has already made troubadours of brutes, squires of scoundrels, and princes of beasts; and Her commission of world sanctification is not yet complete.

Sunday, February 13, 2005 (excerpt)   3:04 p.m.
Saint Catherine Dei Ricci, Stigmatist [1522-1590]

"*My little ones, when you ponder the illnesses of*   o(044)
humanity on physical terms, consider also the spiritual agony
that is overwhelming the Church. It is true that you fight the
enemies of relativism and secular humanism. There are
oceans of heretical thought around you that are attempting
to dilute the Truth for which you stand. I assure you that
you have the strength to swim against the tide. You are
given the power to walk atop the crests of egregious error
that are facing humanity, and you will survive the fight with
valorous courage. I ask you not to wade too deeply into the   x
abysmal debate that is taking so much time away from others
who could be accomplishing God's work. There are certain
messengers who have been chosen to engage the enemies of
the virtues of the Cross and to admonish sinful humanity for
its errors of commission and omission. I call upon these seers
and chosen ones to continue speaking the Truth with
Heaven's acclamation as your guide. I am the Mother of
God. I give you assurance that My intercession throughout
the ages has been a way station of strength and guidance for
many before you. Call upon Me during these perilous times.   xx
Be not afraid to repeat 'Mother, I need your help.' Jesus has
given Me the commission to comfort and console His Church
during these present hours of trial and persecution. He has
allowed Me great latitude in telling you the impending
events of the future that will correct the course of a misguided
humanity. My children, I take My role in the conversion and
redemption of humankind very seriously. Why? Because I
wish to see each of you at My feet someday in the beauty of
Heaven. Give Me your hearts and minds, and make every
action one with the Divine Will of God. If you become like   xxx
Jesus in every way, you will succeed.

My Special and Chosen ones, I assure you of My
continuing participation in your lives as the future continues
to unfold. The miracles of My coming here would be wasted,
it would seem, if you had not decided to live in compliance

*with My wishes. But, you have obeyed, and have consented
to be My workers in the vineyard of the Earth to make all
Creation a better place. How can two words 'thank you' be
sufficient to express My gratitude? The coming 'morrow and
all the rest of your days are an expression of God's happiness*   xl
*with you. We do not concede to the deadpan slowness of the
element of time because we realize that every ensuing
moment is critical in the remaking of the future of man.
Every thought you entertain toward that goal is another
blessing for the Earth. Whenever you sit down and write-out
your faith and love for God's people with pen and page, you
are praying for the re-arrival of the Son of Man. It may not
be clear to you now what I am saying to you, but someday
soon, one day in the very near future, you will realize what
a blessing you have been."*   l

When considering the multitudinous definitions and prescriptions
divined from America's microcosm of dimensions, our cultured democratic
experiment is a land where each of our countrymen understands the meaning
of one nation, indivisibly united, marching nobly toward a future that seems to
be somewhat unknown, but never found insufficiently pliable to give-way to
our aspirations as if we were kings and queens, royally processing the aisle of
the great cathedral of time, itself. And, it is to this identity that the Queen of
Heaven has come calling, bearing the supple intention of eliciting a full-
throated response from humankind that corresponds precisely to the biblical
prescriptions of Divine Love that were engraved into Creation through the
Mystical artistry of Her Crucified Son—for nothing else can save us. Everyone
should realize that there is no inherent legitimacy in our freedom to choose,
just as there is no navigational value in the needle of a compass without the
colossal polar attraction engineered by God into this celestial sphere. The
entire worthiness of our everlasting being is manifested through the power that
draws our hearts toward Jesus' Divine Legacy and Redemptive Salvation.
Those who refuse to tender their souls according to the sacrificial precepts of
Christ's Love offer little benevolence or spiritual evolvement to the future of
mankind. They lack forward momentum toward our unifying destination in the
crux of human perfection at the foot of the Sacred Altars of the Roman
Catholic Church. There may be alternative pathways to God, as some might
hypothetically boast, but know true that every authentic spiritual boulevard
proceeds in deference, allegiance and submission before the Most Blessed

Sacrament of Roman Catholicism before it reaches the Deity-Father on High. Notwithstanding the undeniable implications of this irrevocable reality, no one is omitted from the opportunity to accept the Eucharistic Body and Blood of Jesus because the supernatural emplacement whereby all humanity converges came into being at the shattering of the boundaries of time. There are millions of mortals who accept Jesus Christ for the very first time only upon seeing Him Face-to-face. Every created soul from centuries past has knelt before the Risen Christ in submission after departing this world; every yogi, Apollonian, Dionysian, Aryan, secular humanist, every person of Judeo ancestry, every king and queen; and all the soldiers and samurai, politicians and pressmen, shaman and medicine men, witch doctors and voodooists, Roman legions and ancient Druids, Nazis and Fascists, agnostics and atheists; down to the last man, woman, and child, they have knelt, each and all gazing upon the coalescing affection of the Crucified Christ who still lives! And most, for the first time in their lives, realized the unconquerable Truth that they were simultaneously looking upon the Eucharistic Host that has resided fully-apparent in the Tabernacles and Monstrances of Roman Catholic churches for nearly two millennia, passionately hoping to have embraced them with the Universal Truth of His Merciful Love—the only Redeeming Principal in the universe. What an awesome awakening this has been for generations of people who have rebuffed the gift of the Holy Eucharist! Imagine rising to the unsurpassed vision of the Bread of Life and the emblazoned revelation of Almighty God unprepared! The Most Blessed Virgin of biblical history has descended into our mortal realms during these present hours preceding the grand opening of Eternity for the purpose of preparing us to meet the Truth of Her Son, the Rock of Ages. She wields God's Love like a glistening saber, honed to such perfection that the fortunate targets of Her intercession often do not realize they have been struck with Her Divinity until they shun Her, and the pangs of their depravation rise to such intensity that they scramble back to Her embrace for relief. The Queen of Divine Truth processes through Creation, paying no deference to the protesters who peddle misconceptions about the Most Blessed Sacrament which Her Son instituted at the Last Supper before His Passion and Death. Neither is She slightly concerned that anyone might be offended by Her declarations that there is only one Bread of Life from One Sacred Altar! This irrevocable Truth reveals in itself that the whole of humanity is spiritually ill-equipped to withstand the searing revelation that our deliverance to Final Judgment portends.

The most prolific movement of this age is given definition and clarity only in our reorientation toward the Holy Cross and the Messiah who was slain there. This revelation must rise pre-mortem to inform our intentions and supplant our unbridled, self-serving nature, even surpassing our patriotic fervor by light-years on end. The Holy Mother wishes to ask us why we join as a proud nation on the fourth day of July every year and gather beneath the nighttime skies with our faces upturned? Do we look to the heavens simply to see a more entraining use of our gun-powder and pyrotechnic abilities? Are we no more than momentarily "aesthetic," while awing below our annual sky-faring artistry by which ornate explosions of colors are choreographed? Or, are we celebrating a gift from Almighty God which He ascribed to the visions of our European ancestors, they who wanted more than the ability to choose for choosing's sake? Our forebears embodied a diverse montage of deeply-seated yearnings that were collectively inflamed and drawn toward beauties inspired by the Holy Spirit at the center of their souls. They pined for God to grant them the freedom to pursue their hope-filled dreams of perfection that laid impeded and dormant beneath the tyranny being subjected upon their spirits. They envisioned greater possibilities for humanity than the secular drivel of maniacal despots and selfish misers who were profiting by the enslavement of their talents and toils. The Supreme Architect of Creation dispensed His power to our ancestors to compose their future in response to His call to reach for His Omnipotent Breast, bestowing an almost sacred inheritance upon a random segment of growing humanity, chosen to play-out their dreams and aspirations in concordance with His creative heartbeat, and in ways uniquely profound and reverberating in unison with the sublime ecology of classic Christian doctrine. History has witnessed a grace beyond measure in seeing the United States of America having been endowed by its Creator to climb to its infant feet, clothed in the vast potential to reach the most mesmerizing plateaus of human civilization. But, our generation, with its proliferating post-modern horror, is the ultimate forfeiture of that sacred birthright; for as a nation, we have more than compromised the Gospels and agrapha of God's pious genius. Indeed, we have rejected Him outright and with such rogue impunity that our fully-extended stride into the dark Abyss seems nothing more than another of our complacently-negotiated maneuvers to avoid righteously engaging the Roman Catholic Truth that authentic Wisdom demands. There is no virtue in defending a way of life when that existence is based in flagrant denial of purity, peace, and love; immersed instead within the putrid stench of personal greed and haughty materialism. True freedom is on its deathbed these days, heaving its last mortal rattle, because the Breath of Life has been exhausted from the lungs of our righteousness by those who care only whether their compressions of liberty will resuscitate their own egoistic prosperity. America will be tossed into the crematoria of disemboweled history if our steps continued to be motivated by prudish complacency and financial gain. Our Lady summed it up rather succinctly when She told me that every member of our republic must change their statements of "I want!" and "I need!" to the more passionate declarations of "I will!" and "I do!" Our real enemy is not the tenant down the hall, the neighbor across the street, or foreigners beyond the seas. The greatness of tomorrow rests within the numbers who will throw away their gold-encrusted goblets and sparkling diamond pendants, drop to their knees in contrition, take a Rosary in their newly-calloused hands, and search the lost reaches of their hearts for the hidden pathways revealed to them through their newfound trust in the Immaculate Virgin of Nazareth, the Beatific Lady who processes with heroine perfection through the chambers of their forgotten holiness. The love of country must proceed from our devotion to the highest ideals we can possibly muster through the witness of our sacrifices and the blood dripping from our veins. We must envision ourselves as that cornucopia of plenteous piety from which the world can voluntarily consume the regeneration of life and the spiring beatitude of the inspirited human heart. Hereafter, our desires must conform into communal alignment with the genial wisdom of those generations who sorrowfully lamented in their long-standing soliloquies the happier destiny that escaped them simply because their spiritual disciplines were purchased by hollow whims, rotting their conviction from within, leaving their humanity shorn of vision, thereafter unable to summon the strength to avoid reaping their own cultivated calamities. We must walk through their dark valleys of regret with them and learn from their vacuous desolation. We must pity their weeping over bygone morning battlefields, lain in state and covered by the requiem haze of the blood-letting contentiousness they brought to bear upon the feuding families of humankind. Look upon the Cross of Mount Calvary! The God of Abraham has never left His Creation unattended. The right answer has always been preserved! Humanity has never been allowed to drift very far away, or be too appalled by the torments of the world, or fall too deeply into an uncharted oblivion that is without provision for the deliverance of its victims, because the Holy Spirit has always mercifully implanted steadfast pillars of saintly Light into the bedrock of our historical fabric and pile-driven them into the foundations of our existence, just below the burial crypts of our dead human consciences. This is why the Torch of Christ is being so finely touched to the rekindling of our hearts, which are rapt in eternal joy by the Queen of Paradise to save us from the ruins.

Friday, July 4, 1997

"Good evening, My little children. You are My g(185) *pretty hearts that flicker and glow perpetually in a world of darkness. Your love is not derived from flash powder, nor is its resonance but a bang ringing through the air. No, My children, your service is of a higher making. Your light*

never fades, and the sound of your love for God is ever upon your lips. Your Mother is the Patron Saint of your country. Hence, this is the Land of Motherhood. For that reason, I again plead for your prayers to end abortion. I indeed wish your country a happy anniversary of its founding. And, I ask you to recall the reason for this foundation, that you may honor God freely. My Special son, these are the years during which I have addressed you upon this occasion—1991, 1992, 1993, 1994, 1995, 1996 and 1997. These cumulative years represent your true freedom, not the country in which your heart resides or its government. How many years is it? With the Grace of God and your prayers, we will continue. We will continue to redress the grievances of broken hearts, to fight evil and indifference with prayer and holiness. We will strive to usher the Kingdom of God into a world which is at its peak of rejection of that Advent. We shall not desist. We will continue to hope in the fruits of our prayers. No other nation in the world is so developed as the United States of America; and yet, no other which knows God so well is rejecting Him so willfully. I assure you that I am advocating and interceding on your behalf. Today is a time of reflection for your country. But, not enough of its citizens are in unison with the God whose Grace you beseech. When Jesus returns to the world, it will not be a far-off event announced by wise men. It will be the fatal realization of all mortal men and women. There will be no time for theology or reflection. As Jesus reclaims His Kingdom, only the voice of 'yes' by the human soul will be important. This 'yes' must be as swift as the 'Fiat' which first began the downfall of evil at the Annunciation. Those who proclaim and live in accordance with the Apostles Creed have already pledged this 'Fiat.' I am your Mother and teacher, and Mother of your Teacher. You will never go astray by heeding My call. You will always know your lessons by praying to understand. I have spoken with you for many years. But, from where I come, I have only begun and am already finished. Your patience and effort make these simultaneously possible in the passing

x

xx

xxx

xl

world of time. I love you dearly. I have always loved you dearly. It is not possible for you to comprehend at this time where you are in My plan. But, you are on course and in union with the march of Creation toward the victory of My Immaculate Heart. You know Me, however. In your love, you know Me best. There are many changes and constant motion in the world. Your bodies are growing older in an exile subjected to pass. But, your heart will never grow old. Your heart does not age. Indeed, it perpetually feeds your wisdom to anticipate God and fully accept His Will. Through glory and pain, alike, you know Him. I assure you that God will end this seeming repetitive pulse on Glory, in Glory. I am your Sign of the Ages. I am the reason why Creation has come to this. I am the reason that victory was born into the world. From within My Womb and out of My Bosom blossomed the Flower whose beauty won the Heart of God. His Name is Jesus. The Christ of God is the Son which He so loves, and yet still sacrificed for those who would not love. By the sin of lost humanity, God was brought into humanity to prove His own power. God knew from the beginning that sin would never prevail. And, to whom does Glory belong? That same Son sacrificed so that Glory could be won again, perpetually forever. At the sin of Adam, God cried. He set a mirror before Adam so that Adam could see himself, the one he truly worshiped when he sinned. God said 'if it is your will which you honor, it is but your face you will see.' And then, God did what He does best. He forgave. He came to Earth to redeem. He became the image in the mirror that Adam would see when trying to find himself. At the Love of God, Adam cried. But, these were no tears of sorrow. They were tears of joy and thanksgiving. God mended humanity by healing His own broken Heart. He healed His own broken Heart through the courage of one Sacred Heart. God said 'I love you' thrice and breathed Life into a Trinity of means through which He would prove it. And, you live amidst that Most Blessed Trinity to this day. Therefore, you need not be 'Adam sinful,' but 'Adam

l

lx

lxx

redeemed.' You need not heed the call of evil who fell the   lxxx
first children, but rather obey the desires of God who washes
you clean in Mercy. God is your Teacher who spells Mercy
thus—Crucifixion. As you accept the Sacrifice of Jesus, Mercy
is concurrently yours. You are given the fruit by taking the
seed inside. My little children, this is the story of true
independence. This is the reason for the lighted sky and
lifted faces. This day will pass, and through God's will,
another will follow. But, Jesus is the true tomorrow of your
hearts. When you receive the Holy Eucharist, you are
assuring your soul of its own early light of dawn. There will   xc
be no prevailing darkness. There will be no sorrow or plight
come the new Morning. As a very young child, the first thing
you learn to recognize is the face of your mother before you.
And, you come to know the face of your father. These are the
faces you will know when God sets your soul free from
mortality to come to Eternity. You will know My Face and
the Face of God, just as Adam saw Jesus' Crucifixion in the
mirror before him. You will be miraculously and beatifically
present at the place of your judgment. You will then know
that there is no mirror. You will actually be at the door of   c
your new Home, greeted by all those with whom you will
reside..."

What reprehensible malfeasances have we committed, allowed and
festered upon our hallowed mainland? As if beyond all moral imagining,
leaders who have taken oaths to preserve, protect and defend the people of our
union from enemies, foreign and domestic, have embraced the grotesque
notion that pregnant mothers of America somehow have the right to rip their
children from their wombs as a mere economic convenience, creating killing
fields and weighted stations of carnage unmatched in modern history. Do we
have enemies within the borders of our country that are bringing us to ruin?
I tell you through the prophetic voice of the Holy Spirit of Jesus Christ that
future generations, should there be any, will all but condemn the unrepentant
who are responsible for the legalizing, upholding, procuring and propagation
of abortion. This industry, its proponents, and the leaders of this country who
refuse to stop it are nothing less than willing accomplices to premeditated
murder, the conspiring reflection of the Nazi genocide that mortally assaulted

the eastern hemisphere during the mid-20th century. Mine is not inflammatory social rhetoric, grandiloquence, or hyper-religious zealotry; it is a revelatory declaration of the highest domain, ushered in Truth directly from the Throne of God. This is why Our Lady pleads with the guilty ones to come into Her embrace where She will encourage them to repent and accompany them to Her Son's merciful absolution, exonerating them from culpability, and restoring their sinless perfection that was stolen from them by the Evil One, himself. Then, they will engage the good fight through the virtue of their own reborn souls. Once our societies are finally liberated from this hellish inhumanity against the dignity of our most defenseless citizens, we will be escorted in conscience by God's avenging angels to face the legacies of our lands and the others who followed our nightmarish example; and we will be given a renewed vision, just as the German people were enlightened when their conquerors paraded them through the concentration camps to witness the murderous assault of their indifference against the sanctity of human life. In the not too distant future, civilization will renounce our generation with the same disdain and incredulity with which ours now looks upon the ethnocentrism of Hitler's Third Reich, wondering how our society could have been so lost as to kill babies in the wombs of their mothers. It is absolutely astounding how such an insidious darkness can blanket the human perception almost unawares, sometimes feigning even the most benevolent intentions. How easy it seems to obscure the lie with feminist worldviews and twisted contortions of the facts, leaving us susceptible to the barbaric missteps of previous generations, although in creatively different forms. The citizens of the approaching age of awareness will see us clearly for who and what we are. How is it possible that people in our country have become so encased in such blindness? Allow me to give you a view of God's impartiality. Consider how the Angels gaze with crystalline clarity and unabashed rebuke upon the duplicitous legacy of certain Jewish leaders who portray nothing but hypocritical indifference as they urge modern societies to remember the extermination of their religious brethren, while casually omitting the *other* five million innocent people who suffered the same terminal fate during Adolf Hitler's Holocaust of World War II. Average citizens the world over do not even know that there were nearly *eleven million* victims of the Holocaust. Common people do not realize that six million Polish people were killed by the Nazi regime—only three million of which were of Jewish ancestry. And, who were the rest? Let us remember that Poland's population was 98% Roman Catholic. Our children are not taught that one in every three Catholic priests in Poland was slaughtered alongside the Jewish members of their homeland. Why? Was the anguish and fear of these forgotten Martyrs any less intense in their final agonies? Were they not also children of God, a chosen race, who were entitled to their dignity from the moment of conception in their mothers' wombs? And, even more egregiously, does there not exist a colossal hypocrisy, a deficiency in fairness, and a lacking of good judgment when these same Semitic leaders close their eyes to the contemporary holocaust of unborn children with as much impunity and culpability as the German citizenry ignored the plight of their flock during the Second World War? Please do not assume that I am in any way slighting the suffering of any human being or group of people. My desire is to neutralize the convenient soundbites and misconceptions of shallow historical views. There have already been far too many accusations leveled between people that foment interpersonal mistrust, lack of peace, and the destruction of unity nowadays. I give this example only to show how easy it is for darkness to stealthily enshroud even those dedicated to the most righteous agendas. Nobility and piousness are the progeny of the consistent conviction of the Mother of the Messiah who speaks to the past, present, and future with seamless validity. The Queen of Heaven cannot be intimidated by the posturing of human beings to speak anything other than the Truth. Her articulations of Wisdom are reliable and spiritually fertile with the possibility of reconciliation and the advancement of a newfound peace. No person or group is beyond admonishment or rebuke when refusing to engage the battle for the preservation of human life, in our age or in any other, against those who are willfully destroying it, no matter what their justification or religious affiliation, remembering that in the most perilous and gruesome circumstances, prayer often becomes the only weapon at our disposal for the preservation of our own species. But, since the sacrifice of human life is not required for deliverance of the unborn, the individuals and organizations who are crying "never again" must become the greatest defenders of prenatal children that human civilization has ever seen, lest the horrific plight of previous generations shall never achieve the resounding harmonics of spiritual divinity before the Face of God. Abortion is the same hideous madness, the identical deadly nature, veiled by the same inane ideologies, packaged in the recurrent lies of liberation, perpetrated by the same soulless evil, and destined for the selfsame eternal judgment. The legalized infanticide of unborn children over the past three decades, some 46 million in number, is a gross and flagrant horror of unprecedented proportions. The Supreme Pontiff is right! Genocide and Infanticide are two horns of the same apocalyptic beast! In our post-modern age, only the methods of extermination differ, albeit they are more clinical, clandestine and tend toward cognitive desensitization. Partial Birth Abortion is where a fully-developed child is completely birthed from a mother's womb except for the head, whereupon the baby's skull is pierced and brains extracted in a pain-scalding moment of death. This procedure should send spine-tingling chills to the bone marrow of every pious Jew, Christian, Mormon, Buddhist, Hindu, Islamist, atheist, agnostic, capitalist, materialist, wiccan, judge, senator, representative, president, and on and on; but especially to the heart and soul of the Jewish people because they justifiably affirm that no one knows suffering more deeply than themselves. And, since I concur with this personal claim, I call them one and all to lead us in eradicating the scourge of abortion from the face of the Earth! Shame the abortionists, the politicians and the Supreme Court justices with your suffering, my friends! Fight the nobler fight! Shake yourselves from the enamoring chimera of a war from ages past that is slipping beyond the memories of men, but honorably engage the same evil in the present tense! Show the world that your martyred loved ones have not died in vain! I beg you to convince the precious Anne Frank who now rests in the bosom of the Almighty Father that you also believe in the beauty residing within every soul given the breath of life. Hear her words: *"I still believe, in spite of everything, that people are still truly good at heart... I simply can't build up my hopes on a foundation consisting of confusion, misery and death. I see the world gradually being turned into a wilderness; I hear the ever approaching thunder which will destroy us too; I can feel the sufferings of millions; and yet, if I look up into the heavens, I think that it will all come right, that this cruelty will end, and that peace and tranquility will return again ... I must uphold my ideals, for perhaps the time will come when I shall be able to carry them out."* Anyone who refuses to forcefully condemn the demonstrable evil that currently spreads its fury of insanity upon our dignity as children of God is lost amidst their own self-serving and damnable agendas. They have doused the light within their own souls with this wickedness. All moral authority is lost the instant someone callously refuses to speak to the equivalent evil that manifestly and disgracefully lurks in time before our immediate purview, the same death of the soul that denigrates and destroys human life, no matter what the generation of man. Our medical communities have followed the legacy of Dr. Josef Mengele by finding a way to accomplish the diabolical killing of life in the womb, believing that the flesh somehow veils their satanic actions from the view of our consciences, and likewise from the all-seeing Judgment of Jesus Christ, who is planning a blitzkrieg of His own against these predatory fiends. As in the Holocaust, human abortion is an insidious, collective darkness that no one seems to have the power to stop, very few the conviction to impede, even less the moral vision to speak against, and almost none the courage to lay down reputations, lives, limbs and fortunes to end with any sense of urgency or immediacy. The atrocity of abortion is not wrapped in a hot war that is destroying cities and redrawing borders; its victims are not our shop-keepers and bankers; its screams are not blood-curdling; and its consequences have remained covertly subtle through the silent complicity of the national media. America's culture of death has found an acceptable juxtaposition to our cultural identity without having to be too aggressive to our psyche or showing a face of social domination or national ideology. Why? Because the only appreciable opposition to it is comprised of a few pebbles of hapless rhetoric from our pulpits, while editorial boards who are excised of any noble character brainwash the public with devilish, journalistic advocacy for those who wish to kill! When these diabolical death clinics surrender the fetal remains from their homicidal bloodbaths to private mortuaries for cremation as a method of disposal—as they presently do—is it not a harrowing parallel to the Nazi crematoria of World War II? Consider the question! Are not pro-abortion marketeers, its sympathizers, and the American media lost in the same hellish darkness and psychological inversion that fueled the propaganda of Hitler's regime? Are not the doctors who perform such inhumane barbarities simply the next incarnation of evil in the flesh? Our modern medical profession is the providential generation of a centuries-old institution that has its roots based in the dogma articulated by Hippocrates and his peers who lived in ancient Greece 400 years before the Birth of Christ. He composed and professed the following oath whose truth has survived into our contemporary age because of its devotion to dignity, a profession of integrity that doctors and medical practitioners have upheld for over two millennia, but whose lofty tenets have been forsaken by vast numbers of spiritual vagrants who illegitimately claim the sacred title of "physician" in our modern day

Hippocratic Oath

I swear by Apollo the physician, by Æsculapius, Hygeia, and Panacea, and I take to witness all the gods, all the goddesses, to keep according to my ability and my judgement, the following Oath.

*"To consider dear to me as my parents him who taught me this art; to live in common with him and if necessary to share my goods with him; to look upon his children as my own brothers, to teach them this art if they so desire without fee or written promise; to impart to my sons and the sons of the master who taught me and the disciples who have enrolled themselves and have agreed to the rules of the profession, but to these alone the precepts and the instruction. I will prescribe regimens for the good of my patients according to my ability and my judgement and never do harm to anyone. **To please no one will I prescribe a deadly drug nor give advice which may cause his death. Nor will I give a woman a pessary to procure abortion**. But I will preserve the purity of my life and my art. I will not cut for stone, even for patients in whom the disease is manifest; I will leave this operation to be performed by practitioners, specialists in this art. In every house where I come, I will enter only for the good of my patients, keeping myself far from all intentional ill-doing and all seduction, and especially from the pleasures of love with women or with men, be they free or slaves. All that may come to my knowledge*

in the exercise of my profession or in daily commerce with men, which ought not to be spread abroad, I will keep secret and will never reveal. If I keep this oath faithfully, may I enjoy my life and practice my art, respected by all men and in all times; but if I swerve from it or violate it, may the reverse be my lot."

In 1993, Robert Orr, MD and Norman Pang, MD surveyed 157 deans of allopathic and osteopathic schools of medicine in Canada and the United States about the use of the Hippocratic Oath. They found the following:

1. 98% of schools administered some form of the Oath

2. Only 1 school used the original Hippocratic Oath

3. 100% of current Oaths pledged a commitment to patients

4. Only 43% vowed to be accountable for their actions

5. 86% failed to include a prohibition against euthanasia

6. 89% failed to invoke a deity

7. 92% failed to prohibit abortion

8. 97% failed to prohibit sexual contact with patients

Are not these reported statistics truly enlightening? Can it not be seen that the original Hippocratic Oath which had served us for centuries is now unacceptable to our modern medical establishment? We can see what they did not like by considering what they removed: To be held responsible for their actions; to protect those who are suffering agonies, especially during their transition from this life into the arms of God; to lay their vocation before the Great Physician as a witness to their actions; to be held accountable for the birth of all children; and last but not least, to be held responsible for sins of the flesh perpetrated against their own patients. In 1993, none of these moral precepts was apparently worthy of being mentioned as a sufficient ideal upon which to pattern the continuation of the sacred vocations they received from far more noble men and women than themselves. Representatives in their ranks gutted the elevated grandeur of Hippocrate's oath in exchange for a culture of sanctioned licentiousness, godlessness and death to which many of their colleagues have declared allegiance as its sacrilegious henchmen. We have descended a long way from an honorable man promising God and the ages that he and his fellows would do no harm to human life to, now, doctoral deans at prestigious universities requiring students to become proficient in the satanic procedures of stripping unborn children from the wombs of their patients, lest they never see the initials "MD" behind their names.   This is the pure, diabolical work of Satan, himself.   Who is going to stand-up against these Godless practitioners who are destroying human life?   I will do it, while also standing at the side of the Immaculate Queen of the Universe who towers to infinite heights of authority above me! Hear this voice, America—then answer Her! *How is it that men could know that abortion was evil in 400 BC, and we knew it in AD 33, but you no longer believe it in AD 2005?*

Sunday, March 14, 2004 (excerpt)   *3:58 p.m.*
St. Leobinus, French Bishop [6th C.]
    "As your journey through Lent continues for 2004, I   n(074)
ask you to remember that your strength is your faith, and the signs for the long road ahead reside in your Love for Jesus. As you emulate that great devotion for the purification of humanity that My Son has for His created people, ponder anew how He felt while the world awaited His great Passion and absolving Sacrifice. You have often considered the Feast of Christmas as the happiest time of the year, but I wish for you to also pray deeply about the imminent Easter Triduum that you shall celebrate in a few weeks' time. Your Lord sees   x
every trial and tribulation that you face during your walk of mortality upon the Earth. Indeed, He has been there before you. He knows of the darkest hours of your grief and loneliness, and how you are tempted by the forces of evil to leave the pathways of righteousness. Remember Jesus' responses when He was tempted in the desert. Man does not live by bread alone. Hold deeply in your heart the certitude by which Jesus remembered the reason why He was born as Man. Hold inside your thoughts all the ways that My Jesus stayed with you, even until Death. And, ponder the many   xx
ways that He recalled that the Holy Spirit was within Him while He completed the course for you. He said to Creation in the desert that God could not be tempted to forsake the people He came to save. Yes, please always acknowledge this commendation of Love that He continues to bestow upon

you as you live-out the days of Lent 2004. It is wholly true that you must become like Jesus in order to accompany Him back to the Light of Paradise. Let no mortal man ever try to persuade you to believe that you are incapable of perfect Love. I have told you on a number of occasions that you will xxx *be ostracized for embracing the Truth of Christianity by your fellow sinners. You will be cast-away as dreamers and zealots. Your faith will be looked upon as the making of fanatics. However, My children, please stay the course with Me in assuring your detractors that you belong to the same Christ who is the meaning of life and the making of your seamless perfection from this life into the next. I have given you the benisons of a grateful God because you have not yielded to the forces of doubt that accompany so many along your journey through Lent and through human existence* xl *entire.*

When you pray for the cultivation of the world during this Holy and Sacrificial Season, I ask you to remember to ask Jesus to rescue those who are being punished for their faith. Ask Him to deliver the downtrodden back to the sweetness of their dignity again. It is not too late for you to ask God to end abortion with swiftness and jurisprudence. I know that you often wonder how it can be true that so many unborn children have died in a land which purportedly so values a single life. Americans somehow l *believe that unborn children are expendable commodities that can be destroyed at the will of its doctors and the faithless mothers who bear these tiny ones in their wombs. And, yet, others are known as criminals if they inadvertently take the life of a child in the womb whose mother 'intends' to bring it to birth. How can the former be called a practitioner of the medical profession and the latter a murderer? The Truth and Light about the sanctity of human life is that an unborn child is a living human being from the very moment God places a soul inside a mother. There is no* lx *room for debate in the matter of protecting the sanctity of unborn human life. This Season of Lent is an appropriate time for all My children to ask God to end the scourge of abortion once and for all.   Christians everywhere should band together in a united front against the enemies of unborn human life. You should marshal your forces to protect the innocents who ask with silent anticipation for the opportunity to be delivered to birth. This, My dear ones, is My special request for you today.*

And, to My Special and Chosen ones, I realize that you also understand the value of the sacrifices you make during Lent and for the whole of the Liturgical Year. You recognize the cleansing power of the Rite of Reconciliation and the peace you feel inside because you are so good. Thank you in all ways for living the holiness that I have so invoked you to embrace. And, My Special one, I wish to tell you something that your brother said to Me and the Angels as his bedtime prayer last night and upon awakening again this morning... I tell you this now so you would know that this is a serious dedication that he is offering to you with the intercession of Me. He said in his prayer that he has seen generations of awesome people come and go before him. He has seen the summits of the mountains ranges at the U.S. continental divide. He has seen the whitecaps of the Atlantic Ocean from thousands of feet in the air. He has seen the ancient cities of places like Dubrovnic in all its elegance, and all the cultures which have come together there. He has been to the summit of miracles at Medjugorje and also here. He has seen healings and conversions with his own eyes to rival no other age. And, he says that he has even seen the face of the Mother of his God. However, in all of these things, My Special one—of all the miracles that anyone could hope to see in a span of 50 years, the most profound and heart-touching is the way that you love him. This eclipses anything and everything that he has ever seen, heard, or experienced. Jesus' legacy is alive and well in this 21st century world in you, and Creation is all the more blessed because God has given you life. And, you are sharing that life with your brother in a way that has miraculous overtones that not even

lxx

lxxx

xc

*I could impress upon his soul.   This is his gratitude, My   c
Special one.   He shall always say 'yes' to Me and to your
Savior not only of his own accord in Love, but because of the
example that you have placed before him.   When you get to
Heaven someday soon, you will also see with great clarity the
gratefulness that Jesus has for you.   Jesus can rewrite history
and reverse the effects of time.   He can amend the course of
human existence even after the annals of history are through.
I wish for you to remember this all the days of your life.
Why? Because Jesus will amend the course of human events
based upon the lives of people like you.   By simply living the   cx
way you do, with all the hoping and reaching-out to the
poor, and praying with such dedication everyday, you will
see upon your entrance into Paradise that many of the things
you are concerned about now will have not even occurred.*

*My Special one, you can see that I am speaking to
you of miracles again.   Yes, I am referring to the miraculous
manipulation of the times of Creation by the God who
fashioned it.   My Son can do anything He pleases with His
Eternity and with His people.   I ask for you to remember
during the times when you are disappointed that history will   cxx
be rewritten by the holy things you say and do.   It will take
all the power of the Saints among whose number you will
join in many cases, but I assure you that goodness and purity
will prevail.   Women who have fallen to the temptations of
lust will become virgins once again.   Priests who themselves
became victims of the forces of Satan will see that they were
chaste all along.   No one will have ever starved to death,
they will have simply fasted for too long.   I am speaking to
you on this day in March 2004 about that remaking of the
world—that breaking of a New Dawn that you say should   cxxx
have already come, the one that was meant to be.   I come
today, My Special son, to give you hope anew that your life
in dedication to Jesus is of vital importance to the Son of your
God Most High.   Never despair, always be steadfast in hope,
and know that Jesus is always near.   And, where there is
Jesus, there is the Holy Spirit, and the Mother of them both!*

Thank you for believing the miracle that is still unfolding before you now. Thank you so kindly for believing in Me, for understanding that God has given His humanity to Me as My children. Be confident in what you believe to the depths   cxl *of your heart... I have completed the message that I came to offer you today. I am sure you can see how happy I am with you and your brother... Remember that no greater miracle has your brother ever seen than the way you love him. I offer you both My holy blessing for today. + I will speak to you again next week. Thank you for your prayers. I Love you... Goodnight!"*

For those who are looking for answers or wonder how the collective disorientation of our peoples arose, it was not a matter of the occurrence of a single event or the culmination of a few. In a very profound way, evil was given latitude with a most palatable face through the converging of certain circumstances, ideologies, and technologies that came to the fore during the historical errancy of the twentieth century. The United States recanted her loyalty to the Saints' biblical imprimatur, ignoring the Holy Gospel's call for strict moral values, virtuous standards and higher honor, choosing instead the allurement of materials over the hallowedness of the imperishable, and conceding to the stimulation of the flesh, while shirking their duties as Christians and shrinking from spiritual nobility. America violated her oath of pursuing heroic sacrifice in millions of dynamic increments of human valor, witness and interaction, exacerbated by the swift machinations of the mass production of goods and the immediate canvassing power of communication. Nature, with its recurrent themes of renewal and steadfast consistency, had always been the purifying decree of hope that bore the soothing influence of Christ's Divine discipline upon the erratic nature of passionately impetuous men. Our pathways of life were accompanied by the consoling metronome of God's pulse of new life, nurtured by the repetitive cadence of His paternal care, and protected from desperate hopelessness with the prophetic knowledge that another sun would always rise unscathed by the clouds of former days. Yet, this stabilizing beauty was drowned-out by the din of a 24/7/365 modernism that danced to a sensual drummer and scattered our interior devotions without apology or restraint into the whimsical chaos of carnal temporality. An entire generation was sheared from its underpinnings and lured out of the kingdom of the honorable heart. Once the constant struggle to maintain our basic needs was overcome, the pursuits of preference became self-indulgent and epicurean as masses of people focused on their personal pleasures, and were drawn to the stimulating drunkenness provided by a glut of slothful venues that arbitrarily reproduced without abatement throughout the capitalistic landscape. Both sensual and extreme experiences have replaced the universal procession of our ecstatic union with God with a fizzling firecracker whose amusement lasts no longer than a flashing instant. In this context, I am not articulating anything of wholesale revelation to anyone, neither am I saying that life cannot have its pleasurable pursuits and enjoyments. But, when something as sacred as the bearing of our children becomes suppressed under tyrannical assault by anyone or anything, it is long passed due time to reevaluate what disproportional mindlessness has found sway over the consciences of our citizens. It is fully apparent to any honest person that in this cultural menagerie of descending decadence, women by the millions have been hoodwinked by a baseless agenda of self-possessed lies into rejecting the greatest manifestation of their feminine dignity that Creation will ever know, the sacred vocation of their motherhood. They have been brainwashed into believing that the destruction of their babies will settle the supposed infringements upon the freedom to live according to a false definition of life that is peddled by other members of their same sex. Feminine anarchists who embrace the hissing serpent of early Eden have dishonestly concocted a patriarchal caricature that is a shimmering deception, a rotten fruit offered by the father of lies, himself. And, with carnal satisfaction in one hand, a false image of oppression in the other, and wearing sheep wool to disguise themselves as freedom fighters, these malignant women have connived their naive sisters into believing that the Wisdom of Jesus Christ, through His Hierarchical Church, is the perpetrator of their unhappiness. This ploy is the ultimate bait-and-switch routine! Therefore, the battle against the dignity of men in the hierarchy of Divine Love has commenced throughout every locale across the national domain, especially within the sacred bosom of the family, leaving a swath of emotional and cultural carnage that has been recorded in every civil court in this land, bar none! We need look no farther than the posturing in the Garden of Eden at the beginning of time to see what is happening. The cognizant manipulation was never articulated so clearly than in a composition by the writer Sabine Barnhart, who grew-up in post-war Germany, and who witnessed the strident composure and strict values of the women who rebuilt her homeland after horrific desolation was inflicted there during the Second World War. In her poignant and often heart-rending style, she composed a polemic masterpiece to contrast the sound character of her grandmother's generation with the wanting example being set-forth by the modern American women she came to know after immigrating to the United States in the early 1980s. I believe Ms. Barnhart's courageous and honest words are like the sun emerging to burn-away the storm. Here is an excerpt of her feminine wisdom.

The legacy of the post-war woman, whose story is captured in the Bible and pre-modern time of Western Civilization, is a testimony to her endurance and stability. They have witnessed for centuries that she is capable of rebuilding her family and community side by side with her husband and making man her ally. Her role as a helper was not yet redefined by the secular interference of society. The modern woman has gradually chosen to transgress against her own nature by removing herself from that role. Her cries are not tears of sorrow, but of unhappiness and dissatisfaction. Her lamenting is not grieving the dead and stillborn, but the burden of raising her illegitimate children alone or rejecting them from her womb. Her impatience is not her eagerness to await her husband's return from imprisonment, but to keep him imprisoned through her legal battles. She chases after favors from her adulterous relationship with her false husband, an institutionalized state.

Modern woman's quest to manipulate her society with her crippled perception about her "hardship" has influenced most Western nations. It is seen in the legalization of her false image as a minority and victim. The feminist spirit impregnates her land with selfishness, complacency, apathy and dependency; leading men into bondage. Her world consists of worshiping the idol of her own image. She seeks absolution from her sins through secular counseling, bringing her to a false sense of contentment and security.

The emancipated woman has lost her ability to empathize, to sense the sorrows of her own people that she partially created by rejecting her own role. Thoughtlessly, she drifts into the vices that make her dependent on objects and useless causes, bringing her only temporary feelings of happiness. The man who once cherished her is never good enough to take his rightful place by her side. She holds him responsible for her unhappy state, and boycotts her marriage vows. She emasculates his very essence by enslaving him to be her master. Modern woman has turned into Potifar's wife, imprisoning an innocent man before he could prove his innocence.

She births heartless children who find no comfort at her cold breast. Her milk is a bitter poison. I am from that generation of women who had bought into the lie that a woman can be like a man. Many women of my generation are divorced women, who found themselves more confused after their failed marriages. Their shattered lives looking like a war zone, these women can't figure out where their issues stem from and repeat their follies all over again, continually blaming men for their failures. I heard their stories many times when I counseled them through their pains in my ministry to the divorced. It became obvious that the legal status of woman has gone beyond good intentions, and is rather destroying the very thing she seeks.

The images and message of a post-war woman of the past can teach modern woman that she too can come out of her war zone, if she makes man her ally. Today's woman is given more assistance to complete her tasks than in any other time in history. She no longer has to deal with the high loss of infant deaths or diseases. She has the ability to learn and build upon her knowledge so that she can start new ventures for herself and her family. Most of these inventions came from man, her partner. Recreational time has increased for her, and yet she cannot find peace with herself. Rather than continually distancing herself from her man by making herself the victim, she can close it through a reasonable approach by knowing her role. She has the natural abilities to be a nurturer, mother, and lover. The woman who shows loyalty and support to her man will be the more satisfied woman. She possesses an aura of sweetness that does not diminish her capacity to think and reason.

Women and widows of my grandparents' generation were still married to their real husband in a physical and spiritual sense. For the most part of their lives, they were able to trust that they would be provided for by their spouse through sickness and in health. In their faith, they were married to their spiritual Husband who sustained them through their widowed and single years. The way their rural life was organized, it caught their sorrows and plights in a nurturing network in which they could draw on their own resources. They excelled through their trials and hardship and had enough left-over to pass on an inheritance to their children. Their examples and lives should not be discarded and forgotten. German women and women everywhere can see that it was the spirit of the post-war woman that gave purpose to their men to rebuild.

The legacy of women in war torn countries are readily observed by their behavior. Women who bedded the institutionalized society committed adultery because they took that role away from their men and husbands. A woman who relied on society for her emotional well-being committed a spiritual adultery. Their offspring will most likely reject the role of the real Father, both in a physical and spiritual sense. Women are, and always will be, the keeper of the hearth, watching over the fire to keep it burning. Her warmth and gentleness will keep her man in the folds of her family, if she submits to the loyalty of her Husband.

It is in her relationship with her man that the heart and mind of both genders meet and unite as one flesh. Women who reject the role of her man will find her environment declining into a merciless wasteland of poverty and immorality. It's up to woman to choose how she wants to act in her current circumstances, so that she can regain her honorable status again. And that will be the day when man will praise her with his lips again and call her "blessed."

The Heavenly Mother of Paradise appeared to me again one recent day. I had been contemplating the situation I often encounter concerning the adversarial position that American women often take against men, more specifically, wives against their husbands. You see, I have been blessed by the Providence of God with a wholly unique perspective. My eyes have gazed upon the perfect Woman whom no other female will ever surpass, but whom God expects each to emulate. All the dreams I ever had of such Beauty, the ones that have bounded elusively through my heart, are now discernibly and mystically real to me. Barring any excuses, I understand the potential and possibility that is easily within reach of every mortal woman who has the humility to summon the Immaculate Heart of Mary to the core of her being, and to defer to Her every grace without any pejorative objections. I realize there are people who would never lay down their life for me, but I also know of the Magnificat of the lowly Handmaiden in Saint Luke's Gospel who *has* already said "yes" in complete submission to God so my soul may be raised into Heaven someday. She is the Mother of Jesus Christ, who responded to the Archangel Gabriel, *Fiat Lux! Let there be Light!* And, I live inside the comfort of Her Immaculate Heart, where Her unfailing Love staves-off every force that might ravage my vulnerabilities, confronting my enemies like a shield, accepting the piercing of arrows and the slashing of blades so I can remain composed enough to wield the righteous sword and fight as Her warrior-son on my own intrepid feet. I understand what it means to have valor beckoned from the shadows of my uncertainty by unrivaled feminine Grace, having my attention rapt in the sparkling glint that twinkles from Her thankful eyes. My innate being rests in Her hypnotics of ecstasy, my arms raised in filial surrender; and Her response has been to don my spiritual frame with the angelic armor worn by heroic Saints from ages past, tailoring it to fulfill my best potential, encouraging me to wear it with an honorable gratitude spread-eagle over the legacies of my faithful predecessors. She won my allegiance with a single tear, a droplet of hope the size of Creation's seas. She petitioned me with the regal bearing of Her Queenship to gaze at the depths of the love She offers, and to accept with confidence the liberation of the Holy Spirit residing within my trembling heart, allowing Jesus to explode outwardly like a nuclear blast of divinity into the souls of God's lost progeny. This power pulsates at the core of every man waiting to rise at the triumphant reveille that Courage reports, summoning us to capture our most passionate dreams. The purpose and longevity that is mysteriously bred within our spiritual beings transfigures us into the sacrificial "has," while magnifying the embodied opportunity for happiness-forever-after to be presented to the nations. Notwithstanding any preordination since my birth or the supernatural grace of the Roman Catholic Sacraments, for over 14 years now, my heart has been divinely nurtured and sublimely caressed in its remotest realms by a soothing gentleness and plenteous forgiveness that is as gargantuan as a mountain range whose foothills are a sprinkling of Everests. This image of noble domination thrives within the unexplored folds of our emasculated hearts, but rarely meets its manifestation, only in flashing moments, which are stolen as soon as they appear, replaced by the societal sentence we are unjustly asked to bear for the redemption of the delicate creature who was brought-forth to complete us. Every man's heart pines to experience that undefinable tenderness that gives him rejuvenating love and places his mettlesome feet on a course of conviction in lockstep with the historic imprints of saintly giants. This is the gift that women were created to be for the souls of men! The wind beneath their wings, indeed! And, what will a man do from those lofty heights? He will lift the elegant beauty of a woman upon his shoulders and foist her to the pinnacle of Creation so that every living thing can venerate the breathtaking princess she has become. It is reciprocally real and alive in the Immaculate Woman that Jesus is lifting-up before Creation.

Anyway, as I knelt to quietly pray before our Heavenly Queen that day, pondering these images, I lamented how sorrowful it was that God has created a female gender endowed with an almost endless capacity to touch the beatific reaches of men's souls, with the power to embolden them to heroic stature with the vision of Heaven, but who too often abuse that inspirited potential by intentionally inflicting selfish violence without conscience upon the most sacred vestiges of another human soul. A man can endure physical exhaustion, punishment and pain all day long, but the lance thrust through his private heart is the most profane of domestic abuses. After I was finished outlaying what I see, the Perfect Woman of Heaven responded, *"There has never been a man who has stripped a child from his womb."* She then asked me to record my petition, along with Her poignant response. And, with that task completed, we move forward into greater solidarity.

Sunday, February 27, 2005   *3:01 p.m.*
"Today, I would like to speak to you about the condition   o(058)
of the Church in America. I wish to convey to you the deep
Love that Jesus has for the priests and religious who are
trying to fight against such a reckless culture. It must be
made clear to Americans everywhere that those who are
accused of being violators were victims before they were
claimed to have victimized others. All are victims of the
same evil that has been an enemy of human Salvation since
the beginning of time. I stand by My priests. I believe in the

powers of contrition and absolution. I call upon the citizens   x
of the United States, especially those with prosecutorial
powers and members of the media to stop feeding on the
weaknesses of their mortal brethren like sharks and vultures.
No one is immune to the temptations of sin. How can it be
true that secular institutions claim the moral high ground
when it is their own lacking in righteousness that has
exacerbated the problem? They have created a monster over
the past forty years, and now are complaining that there is a
monster on the loose. Therefore, do not be disconcerted at the
purification that is ongoing both inside the Church and   xx
outside. However, collective America should not single-out
a particular person as an 'example' of evil in your midst.
You will be very surprised come the end of time to see where
evil is really lurking around you now. It is not in the
convents and rectories. It does not exist the first place you
might imagine. No, My children, the greatest evil is found
where human beings refuse to stand beside other people in
their weakness, but instead, stand-out in arrogant pride and
point fingers as if to say they, themselves, are free from sin.
Does humanity not recall the reluctance of the people in the   xxx
Sacred Scriptures to stone the woman who was accused of
adultery? Let Me tell you now—all of modern secular
America is guilty of adultery! Humanists and relativists of
all stripes are groping the innocence of holy people
everywhere by lying to them for capital gain, backslapping
their patrons in the name of fortune and fame. They cannot
be betrothed to their religious faith and to the material
world, too!"

Concurrent to the aforementioned secular happenings, the inoculation
of the moral conscience of society against the disciplining guidance of the
Roman Catholic Church was achieved by rogue revisionists, opportunists, and
demagogues who wilfully hijacked the somewhat nebulous pastoral decrees of
the Second Vatican Council, which was convened during the early 1960s by
Pope John XXIII. These thieves of the Truth climbed aboard the stallions of
divinity that were given birth by the Cardinal Princes of the Church, and rode
away holding the golden reins of Catholicism that they lacked the authority

from God to grasp. Thereafter, the patriarchal deposit of moral reasoning choreographed by the Mother Church for our modern day and Her voice of righteousness were silenced, leaving the flock to a rapacious pack of wolves for their greatest immoral field day. Our deluded western civilization was sold the fallacy that the Catholic Church had somehow "changed," purportedly bringing Her to Her contemporary senses, begetting the moment when masses of alleged faith-filled people exhaled a sigh of temporal relief and ducked from under their yoke of charitable self-sacrifice and obedience to revealed religious dogma, taking with them the very manifestation of their faith in the Gospel of Jesus Christ. The Holy Church was stripped of its transcendent garments and prepared for the Cross clad in a nihilistic image of self-fulfillment for the sole purpose of assuaging the fears of those who would protest against Her from behind the veil of their pride. "I'll decide" became the mantra of the American church; and the preferences of disordered consciences scattered the traditional rose petals of our unity to the adulterous affair we began to engage with our physical senses. Whimsical predilections and willful absurdity were forced to the surface of our pious identity by people who had no foundation or stability in the genius of contemplative holiness and sacrificial human love. Historical revisionists mysteriously gained an illicit respect and social notoriety that their resumes could never have procured for them among the venerable theologians and historians of previous generations. The living examples of the holiest Saints of Christendom were scrapped as being medieval aberrations. Those who were most disenchanted with their spiritual lives were allowed to engineer a new, hollow religious regime, a revamped counter-culture that disparaged and submerged the celestial brilliance of ancient reflective liturgies and timeless Traditions, the spoils of our Faith which had been protected and transmitted to our modern times by the blood of Martyrs and the generosity of the greatest witnesses to Jesus Christ who ever lived. The Christian world was turned upside-down by these renegade revisionists who flip-flopped against the ecclesial Truth, leaving the Apostolic Church to be falsely accused and convicted of irrelevance in absentia by the minions of the western world unless She conceded to their popular, bohemian demands. Roman Catholicism and its Sacred Traditions which have outlasted the centuries and entire civilizations came under sudden diabolical attack from every conceivable direction, flanked by the mass-media's New Age culture, each front boasting ranks who falsely claimed to be the latest victims of its oppressive religious rigidity. And, too, as in most every secular forum, women again launched their vertical offensive against the all-male priesthood that they have been hoodwinked by feminist America to despise. Ironically, there has never been an institution or group of believers in the entire history of Creation who has sacrificed as generously, proclaimed as emphatically, preached as fearlessly, shed blood as copiously, documented as meticulously, elevated as nobly, or defended as heroically the dignity of women before the presence of God as the Roman Catholic Church. It is simply that this current contingent of post-modern women denounces God's definition of pristine feminine beauty that is exhibited by and comes to perfection and fruition in the Most Blessed Virgin Mary. Their claims of subjugation will be silenced upon seeing the True Victim of the Cross whom the Church has been urging them and the rest of humanity to focus upon for the past 2,000 years.

Throughout this evolutionary tide, few theologians in the past half-century have been visionary enough to predict or recognize the colossal impact that instantaneous communication to the masses would bring, reminiscent of the splitting of Christian unity caused by early Protestantism through the use of printing press technology in 16th century Germany. Influence and precedent were established in the western mind, going unchecked and untempered by Wisdom realized through the solitude of prayer. The population of the United States felt relieved from the strictures of self-denial at the same moment the sexual revolution was peaking, tantalizing libidos in search of moral casualties. Divisions arose like wild beasts between people who quickly understood what was happening and those who were hellbent on leaping from their windows of opportunity to recreate both the Church and the secular void into their own God-forsaking image, free from the subservience and obedience they owed to their Eternal Father through His Magisterial Hierarchy here on Earth. Priests were coerced through a surging militance to symbolically abdicate their sacred roles as spiritual fathers and model moral guardians. They were stripped of respect and, consequently, lost their pastoral authority to admonish and rebuke their people. Shepherds were looked upon as old, backward, ignorant and spiritually on par with common laymen in the pews, their life-long learning, sacrifice and commitment demeaned to the level of some strange, anonymous worldlings. The miraculous and mystical aspects of Christianity were re-framed as being an unbalanced utopianism, absent pragmatic reality. And, perhaps the greatest tragedy of them all, faith-filled apologetics died as if wiped-out by a plague. The renting force of modernism was brought upon the world stage and allowed to incise the social fabric of our secular and religious communities and the families that would have borne the next generation of holy priests and nuns, plummeting the number of vocations to levels of near extinction. After all, what young male acolyte would be drawn to the priesthood when its entire patriarchal foundation had been tossed into the gutter, while the whole material world was now to be gained without a pang of guilt, and sexual pleasure t'boot? The power to persuade, mold, mesmerize, divide, provoke, desensitize and destroy was given unbridled venue within the souls of sinners who no longer had the spiritual discipline or moral capacity to fight it; and not one Apostle of

Jesus Christ was allowed to strike a wolf, even if it was howling at the midnight hour of our holiness. All manners of worldliness began to be justified, as long as they could be construed as the magnification of our merited gifts or a flushing example of the "Spirit of the Council." And, from this insolent mindset, a newly synthesized predator of darkness began to prowl unchecked, preying upon, coopting and devouring nearly every mass-communication and entertainment medium in sight. The broth of Hell finally came to a boil. One such example comes to mind from 1981, when I was sitting with a friend in his living room, watching for the first time the Music Television phenomenon, more commonly known as MTV. Although I was familiar with its format of broadcasting continually-televised music videos through discussions I had with my prep-school and college friends, I had never seen it personally because it was only available through paid cable television, to which our family never subscribed. To this day, I vividly remember my thoughts while reclining on that sofa. I recognized the appalling visual impact, engrossing nature, and illicit messages that were being subtly transmitted to everyone who watched, especially the latchkey children who were being raised at its novel breast. I anticipated the depths of depravity to which this medium would eventually descend because, even at that time, the public resolve to check societal immorality was inhaling its last few breaths. Speaking to my friend that day as he relaxed in a nearby recliner, I said, "MTV is going to destroy this generation of children someday." Be reminded that this was two decades ago when the entertainment industry was still puritan by contemporary standards; the rest is recorded as present malcontent in the psychological and emotional defiance of today's rebellious youngsters, adolescent teenagers, and impressionable twenty-somethings. The wary Christian ministers of the 1950s now seem somewhat prophetic, the ones who are repeatedly mocked as moral prudes in present-day depictions by the same amusement companies who are reeking havoc on our spirituality to this day. There once was a time when courageous, responsible men stepped directly into the fray, warning legions of innocent children and their lax parents about the slippery slope that inexorably leads to moral and societal perdition. Yet, they wailed like a playpen of spoiled toddlers for the self-indulgent right to tear down the righteous customs of modesty, purity, and temperance so as to ingratiate themselves with the licentious fads appearing under the guise of popular music without a twinge of reproaching conscience. Even then, the Holy Spirit was admonishing them and us that our lives were being seized, grilled and quartered for serving to the nightmare of outrageous entertainment and pagan impurity in these present days. Am I demonizing those who have been given the talents of musical composition and theatrical performance? Not in the least. I am only making clear in the realms of this agonizing uncertainty that those who have placed their God-given abilities to the service of Satan by inciting the sensual savage within us and provoking the immoral beast, not to mention profiting through an abject agenda of assailing the sanctity and patrimony of the Catholic Church at every diabolical turn, are headed for the fires of Eternal Damnation! We live in a generation of fifing marauders and malefic hate-mongers basking at the pinnacles of nearly every secular venue who are being allowed to hide behind some hedonist judicial interpretations of their constitutional rights. Hear me out, my sorely misguided friends! You may have convinced your haughty bench-sitters wearing long black robes that purveying wide-scale societal perversity is your inalienable right, but be awakened and reminded that the heavens have granted no such forbearance to your wild animosity against the Commandments of God! These perfect laws exist, and they are immutably inscribed in the Firmament with the Blood of the King who owns your lives. And, His righteous commands will leave you no option but to be indicted as reprobates and evil co-conspirators before His High Throne someday. Beware, for the hour of accountability draws nigh!

Sunday, July 4, 2004   *2:34 p.m.*
St. Elizabeth of Portugal [1271-1336]

"*Of all the greatness possessed by the Lord, the greatest*   n(186)
is Love! My children, I have come today to speak to you
about this Holy Love which is the bastion of purity,
goodness, and peace that your souls are silently seeking. I
have not come today to speak about patriotism or secular
freedom because the greatest chains of bondage known to
humankind have come from the hatred that is espoused by
governments around the temporal world. In and of itself,
individualism is not freedom. If quoted out of context, Truth
is not freedom. And, if used for sinful purposes, emotions and   x
affections that bind men's hearts together are also neither the
producers nor result of freedom. I wish to speak to you about
Love today because it is the core of the freedom that the
world can neither give nor ever take away. What of this
Divine Love? Why should you accept it? Why should you
emulate it? Why should you embrace and extol it? The
answers to these questions require your openness to accept
your helplessness before Jesus as contrite sinners whose only
means to Everlasting Life is in Him. Your personal and
social consciences are founded in the One Truth that is God   xx

in Him. I wish for you to ponder these things because the annals of history prove that you are helpless to discover the true meaning of freedom on your own. You cannot reach perfection of your own accord. You cannot survive either physically or spiritually without the intercession of Heaven. Those who choose to deny this are already dead. So, while you see and hear the fireworks displays around America today, remember that you are only a self-serving society of selfish rogues whose materialism will be the reason you shall never own the Grace from God you proclaim to possess. If you do not turn your hearts and minds to the spirituality that you require to see the world the way it is, and indeed how it should be, you will never be granted that Perpetual Light of Divine Salvation. The colors red, white, and blue have nothing to do with the perfection of the human race. They are a collective symbol of imperialism and idolatry. They are the three vices which keep you imprisoned in a nation without conscience. They are the three swords with which you are lancing your own dignity. But, what will your peoples say when told that the Mother of God is displeased with the insolence, audacity, and selfishness of the country over which She reigns as Patroness Saint? Can 287 million people understand that what lies within your borders, save the Roman Catholic dioceses, has nothing to do with faith, trust, hope, prayer, and deliverance? And, what about those who refute what the Catholic Church teaches? Ask them precisely what it is they are protesting against!

I realize that it seems to be such a contradiction that I tell you that I am displeased with the conduct of the people of the United States, and yet I come to you as a happy Matriarch of God's Creation. I am happy because I already know the outcome of the world. I have seen the Victory of the Cross which has come to fruition within the Triumph of My Immaculate Heart. How could anyone be sad when they know that this moment is at hand? I am asking you to look at the Earth with a new perspective, to realize that it is your temporary home, and see for yourselves that your impending

xxx

xl

l

deaths are your release from the bondage of human mortality once and for all—only inside the Crucifixion of My Beloved Son! I have ofttimes told you that Jesus' Sacred Heart is filled with Mercy, and His Judgment is one of understanding. He knows the temptations that lure you in other directions, and He also knows the ones who are trying to take you onto another path. He has already amassed a stockpile of millstones and created a cauldronous fire for those who reject Him at the last. My purpose here today, as always, is to assure you that there is hope for the millions who yet do not understand the power of the Cross. In that Cross, you will discover the ultimate fashioning of true freedom in the way that God wishes you to be free. Knowing this to be factually true beyond the capacity of any of His creatures to refute, I come to you with joy and in the expectation that, in your good capacity to reason, you will accept the Crucifixion as expiation for your sins. If you will only give yourselves time in peaceful pondering to comprehend what I am saying, you will know why there is time, and why you are in it. I have told you this long ago on many occasions, during a special series of messages in the opening months of 1991.

My little Special and Chosen ones, I understand that you are also happy along with Me because you realize that everything I am telling you is true. You have learned nothing new in My message to you today. However, I wish to reinforce My Love for you by asking you to take some of My words to the outerworld societies that will not listen to other modern Christians. You give of yourselves to Jesus because you know and accept everything He has given to you—Grace atop of Grace that are juxtaposed to your other efforts—and gifts that you offer in accordance with the obedience of your own personal will. You shall be granted sainthood for this! I tell you with the fervent Love in My Immaculate Heart that the future belongs to you, that you have already conquered the element of time and your enemies, too. And, if only you will find in yourselves that your timely discussions about the perils and evils of the world

are not an undue focus on the negative, you will become
happier as you live-out your daily lives. It is alright to see
what is happening, but please do not become distraught that
they are not changing quickly enough that you somehow
internalize your own spiritual fatigue. I wish for you to be
wise in the way you view the horrible aspect of the material   c
world. See what is happening, discuss possible solutions,
pray for them to come, and be happy that God has given you
such recourse in Him. This is one of the venues to freedom
about which I am speaking—not in a secular sense, but in
terms that will strengthen your trusting relationship with
Jesus and with God. You are wise little children. You have
stood by Jesus through countless agonizing moments. You
have never once surrendered your faith. These things cannot
be said about very many people! You shall be sainted for
this! My children, in all of these things, you should be happy   cx
along with Me. Why? Because My happiness is not full
unless you are happy with Me. If the Mother of God can see
the countless ways that My Son's Sacrifice is being ignored
and desecrated and still come to you with a smile on My
Face, surely you can muster the joy to know that anyone who
is guilty of these things is being conquered by the obedient
gift of your lives... I will continue to speak to you if you will
allow it... Thank you again for your prayers, this has been
a very good day. I offer you My holy blessing now. + I will
speak to you again next week. I love you. Goodnight!"   cxx

Creation can bend one to marveling when our conscious awareness
steps back from its pandering engagement with our physical senses; and being
freed from the bondage imposed by fleeting demands, begins to survey the
mysterious dynamics of life with the higher sentience of a contemplative heart.
There is an ethereal liberty respected by the universe which allows our mystical
souls to permeate substance and transcend the seeming incarceration of every
exilic boundary. We swim in an inherent reign of freedom which pales the
caricature that nations have attempted to manifest in their secular-humanistic
governance. These boundless realms compose an imperishable domain which
lies beyond the reaches of our wilful manipulation, an orbit of sanctity that can
never decay into the fiery strictures of the human psyche, where all holocausts

are born. Earth-bound reality is terminally marked for people without faith as being only those commodities they can physically manipulate through their consolidation of peripheral power. They are guided only by the application of their individualistic parcels of practicalities that their experiences and biases anemically provide. It is the minute attributes of these pragmatic options that cause the vast majority of human beings to be enslaved within the confines of avoidable sin and its fallout, which is never condoned by our Almighty God, He who presides over the infinitude we refuse to see with our spiritual eyes. Every heart can touch the boundless generation of unending Light that the heavens emanate; and we do so in numerous moments of exhilaration and grief alike, but most often in our liturgical prayers and religious devotions which prove our highest intelligence and most resilient allegiance. Then, it seems, the dailiness of our ostensible captivity hails derisive repetition upon our belief once again, and we fall from hope that life must be something more, and that our good intentions are actually securing this new reality. Overcome by acute fatigue, we unknowingly succumb without malice aforethought to the wiles of mortal oppression, one veiled strike at a time, until its weighted impartiality drives sorrow and despair into the softest lamella of our heart like a searing brand; itself a grace that inspires us with its painful annoyance to flee to the starlights of our contemplations again in search of the partner whom we once adored, the Christ, who patiently awaits us to enjoin Him in the next steps of our waltz to His choreographed Divinity. O' the elegance by which He floats above the celestial balconies of our souls, stepping with the flowing rhythm of Divine Love across the historical expanse of the loggia of time as if it were the most inconspicuous crack in the main dance-floor of Creation. How difficult it seems to be amidst so much lethal distraction to entice the children of men to become mesmerized more by the infinite beauties a heart can envision than the dying fantasies our weary eyes are shown. We live within a diminished world of aggressive factions that are at war with our hearts and the delicate beauty contained therein. The composition and completion of our inner-most being begins its manifestation at the conception of our souls; and wholly sorrowful are they who are deprived of recognizing their essential blessedness as children of God upon being vested in the flesh. Much too often, we are disoriented from the beginning, trained in captivity at the outset, and subdued in potential before life has ever begun to flourish, a tragic bevy of tiny doves slapped from the sky on their maiden flight. This is why the acceptance of the Kingdom of Heaven must be embraced as if we were little children. We must sense a sacramental rebirth of opportunity that provides the revelatory re-engineering of our intellects to the prophetic levels of galactic spiritual genius. Then, and only then, will we be able to participate in life through an eclipse of divinity and an overshadowing brilliance that sparkles at the horizon of the paradisial borderlands like a diamond on a sleeve. Our lives must emanate the royal dominion and regal power of the Most Holy Trinity by coming into harmonious union with the immortal dignity that we assumed and never relinquished the moment our Divine Creator fired His first thought of us in the kiln of His Infinite Truth. We were not cast as an amulet of frailty in this limitless sea of emblazoned Light; there were no flaws in His architectural design when He fashioned our frames in His Love; stain did not know us at the outset, nor was there a premonition of being hopelessly crushed to an oblivion of shame and defeat without the Grace needed to survive. Mankind assumed this blemish upon entering the world, a disfigurement that the Blood from a Sacred Chalice has summarily wiped away. Here, know now that it was for the spiring pinnacles at the never-ending reaches of conceptual and regenerative Love that we were drawn from the depths of God's highest desires and raised from the dust to stand clothed in our inherited nobility once again. The human heart was created to be nothing less than a lightning rod for our Lord's insatiable enchantment and the holy receptacle of His invincible power for universes yet unseen. He has smelted the definition of humanity to perfect temper in the furnace of His Omnipotence, using all the assorted ingredients of sanctification that man would allow. The Lord of all Creation has placed His trust in the lion-hearted passion of His honest human family, knowing that we would match His Love with our own. History has shown that devotion has withstood suffering, conviction has outlasted desperation, resurrection has conquered degeneration, courage has vanquished fear, victory has survived defeat, faithfulness has consumed godlessness, deliverance has banished horror, love has obliterated hatred, and life has transcended death. Hail we must!—this sacrificial crucible of soiled terra firma upon which we reside. This sacred domain, mastered by the Deific Son, circumscribes the life-giving spectrum of salvific Love, making it the purpose of both our sacrifice and our reward, the agony and the ecstasy paraded before time and Eternity, past the purview of civilizations, stars and planets, afore the vision and gratitude of yet unseen races of living creatures who have been told our arrival is near, all of us returning heroes of the celestial motherland who were sent abroad to the blood-drenched Earth to wrest re-creation from the jowls of destruction and high-noon daylight from the midnight of eternal death, gracefully striding in our return to Paradise, into the Celestial Cathedral among the Living, wearing crimson war-wounds as our crowns. We shall live there in peace as bold conquerors from an immortal battlefield where the chains of time, themselves, fell to the floor of Creation in submission and defeat, worn-out ages which now humbly record with ecstatic wonderment a legacy of tenderness tempered and tested to unknown limits, spectacular highlights of Grace elicited from an almost unimaginable agony and depravation, prophetic visions of Mystical destiny which no time-bound mortal could ever grasp, rising from God's hope like a fire-branded phoenix, transfigured and purified to the tenor of a simple dove as we entrain our hearts in the communion reality for all the hallowed heavens to see. This is the Savior race, the Mystical Body of Jesus Christ, at its shining moment of homecoming, all because the Lamb of God forged His Sacred Heart in this temporal arena of unimaginable suffering and sorrowful Deicide, inflicted by the very same creatures His Father deigned to save. The Messiah of the Cross gave humankind the ring, the circle of Everlasting Life between the Persons of the Most Blessed Trinity, when He clothed Himself in the raiment of this terrible war—the flesh of a Child in a Manger—and ushered us through His crucified example to the Paradisial Summit we possess from the Alpha of our Creator's vision.

Sunday, August 6, 2000   *4:15 p.m.*
Feast of the Transfiguration

    "Now, dear children, I approach you again with hope   *j(219)*
and anticipation because your lives are their fulfillment and your prayers bring holy constancy, the peace of genuine Love, and the light of Divine Grace into the darkness where lost souls are squandering their valuable time in mortality. This is indeed a day of the celebration of the transfiguration of man because, in Jesus, you are sent to be Wisdom to the peoples. Every day is the remembrance of an earth-moving event in history, whether it be the awful blast of an atomic weapon or the passing of a Holy Pontiff into the Light of   *x*
Paradise. Yes, Pope Paul VI is twenty-two years the happier today to see the fruits of his life on Earth to have so nobly advanced the Church of Faith in the revelation of God. Dear children, please know that I continue to bask in the knowledge that little Jesus is as anticipatory as you. He provides many signal graces and holy blessings so that every day of your lives is connected to the previous multitude by the continuing awareness of your Salvation. Please always remember that the Son of Man requires the enlistment of your faith to recognize these things. That is why you can know   *xx*
that the rainbow of last week was a reflection of your previous message. It is why you understand that each Hail Mary and Our Father and Glory Be you pray sets the wheels

into motion that carry the poor souls in Purgatory into the happiness of Heaven, simultaneously compounding the number of Saints who intercede for you at the Throne of God. We have made the world a place of many gifts because we love in the same Holy Spirit who dwells with Me in Glory and in your hearts. Can you not see this interwoven majesty of supernatural unity? Can you not see how the days xxx *truly belong to Christ the King? That is why these special moments of messages are an intrinsic and unique part of the unfolding of the Plan of God for the Redemption of the human race. Jesus intended for these days to come from the Miracle of the Cross. These messages began there, and will culminate upon your arrival at the right hand of the Father who ordains them. Your Creator loves justice and right! It is He who collects the days into one immortal basket of plenty. He makes them to be connected by the universal intentions of the Church Triumphant, reflected by the* xl *petitions of His faithful in the world. Why else would your Bishop first see your brother's letter of request for a vocation on the Feast of the Saint of Vocations, Saint John Vianney? What is perpetually occurring just beyond your immediate comprehension is an orchestrated plan of cultivation, conversion, and deliverance. You are in attendance at the great dance of human history that has been unfolding in many ballrooms since the beginning of the ages. You march in step to the same song of victory as the Apostles who first saw the Risen Christ. The tone, cadence, and melody of* l *Love have not changed since Thomas uttered the words of piety and admission 'My Lord and My God!'*

Dear children, the world is a replication of Thomas, and all in it will soon raise their voices in the song of unity, 'It is true! There is no doubt!' The celebration has been brought from that first Easter, all the way to sunrise this morning and beyond. This is the truth above all things, over the passing fashionable products of capitalism, beyond the obstinance of those who are too encapsulated by kharmas, high and away from a cerebral meditation which transcends lx *the psyche, and overpoweringly destructive to any political locomotion that may pass through the city in the name of enhancing the lives and fortunes of the rich! Do not believe their false claims that they are pro-life when their chosen representative single-handedly refuses to stop the execution of scores of sinners whom he declines to forgive in the name of state-sponsored justice. Do not believe their lies! It is all for fame, money, power, and egoism to the exclusion of aid to the poor and pity upon those whose parents never taught them any better or left them with a pittance of opportunity during their formative years. These are among the reasons that I tell you that politics is as dark as Free Masonry. Neither of them will lead you to see the cold, hard facts of human misery or the mitigation of a horde of sins. Only the graces of the Roman Catholic Church will deliver all who call themselves human; only the Sacraments of repentance, reparation, and renewal can bring humanity to Light. The Tabernacles contain the Candidate who has already won the Victory, and it is He who has been elected King by the unanimous and popular vote of the singular God of all Creation. There is no democracy in that because there is no dissension! There is no question to put before the people because God has already selected the Master who reigns over all in the world. It is Jesus! It is Love! Now, the referendum is whether the societies of the world will accept their own fate and follow Him to Salvation. My children of the Earth, your own souls are on the ballot! It is you who must be the elect! I wish for your fortunes to be great indeed, but a wealth of knowledge and power deigned by Jesus for those who love Him! That is why you know that My words are not just hypothetical images of what might have been if the world were more perfect, but accurate descriptions of the entire universe as it will soon come to be! I do not rely on your dreams to make you happy, but upon the factual existence of Divine Grace which has awakened you from mortal sleep! So, feel the skies shake with the ballroom dances which those before you are enjoying! Someday, you will again think that it is thunder, but it will finally be your soul piercing the veil into everlasting Life! The flashes you*

lxx

lxxx

xc

see will not be lightning, but the countless camera bulbs   c
being held in the hands of the Saints as they encapsulate your
passage into their midst! And, the many thousands of moist
droplets will no longer be the rains, but the happy tears of
your Heavenly Father whose Heart is so touched that you
have finally arrived back Home again. When you feel this
gladness land softly upon your cheeks, know that they have
just fallen from His. It is My high honor to watch this Glory
unfold each time another soul sails gleefully back to Paradise
upon the tears of which you spoke in your Diary, those of the
faithful on Earth whose suffering made the image of the   cx
Cross perfect for every last sinner to see.

       My dear Special one, it is part of that fulfillment that
calls Me to this place every day and every week, to ratify
your lives in My Son, to thank you for your holiness, and to
pray with you so no one will be left behind when Jesus
reclaims every last inch of the Kingdom He owns. I hope
that you continue to be happy that I have loved you so, and
that nothing can take My Immaculate Grace away from you.
No amount of time can carry you away because, quite the
contrary, you are traveling closer to Salvation every day.   cxx
Always remember that Christianity means that time is on
your side; it is not your enemy because it stands for your
passage into Eternal Life. Those who grieve growing older
do not truly envision the victory at the end. You have an
exception to many of the circumstances—those who hold the
dignity of Jesus Christ in their hearts. There is no grief or
hopelessness in the heart of My dear MJ! Look at the majesty
that is residing there! The Truth, the light, the piety, and the
faith! Before the mortal world has ended, I promise that your
Diary will have drawn millions to be like her, and I promise   cxxx
that you will have seen many of your enemies at your door.
This is My blessing for you now. + Thank you both in an
everlasting peace for your faithfulness, service, and prayers.
I will speak to you again very soon. I love you. Goodnight!"

America! America! Has the hollow sensation of materialism and flesh totally expunged our desire for the soul-enrapturing caresses of our Heavenly Father? Are we going to die in the wreck of this world and descend into the dismal pit without so much as a fight? Have we completely relinquished our intention to be found worthy and beautiful at the impending Return of our Messianic Deliverer? I beg you to declare that this is not so! Fix your guileless eyes across your rolling lands, and look at the unmitigated greed and perversion that have become your guiding lot. Incline your ears to the canyons of your wanton revelry, and listen to the eerie silence where thundering reproaches once echoed from your walls, rebukes that arose from the convictions of passionate men in holier times, whose cowardly progeny are now too afraid to mount the Holy Cross and stare-down with righteous defiance the arrogance of prideful antagonists at the risk of an onslaught of retaliatory strikes. How ironic it seems that so many have been enticed to prove their independence from Divine authority and simple common sense by fanatically searching-out the abysmal edge of the great plateau of Deliverance. What madness causes individuals to push the envelope of Jesus' merciful patience to the depths of the Crucifixion? Is the answer found in their manifest hatred of the Catholic Church who implores their egos to take-up their crosses, bear their yokes, and don their ruffs in humble love? Multitudes of people are being deceived, hoodwinked and driven to dive headlong into outright diabolic works that will condemn them to the fires of Hell, just for the satisfaction of saying, "No one can tell me how to live or what to believe!" Our democratic ship of state is listing toward its own demise in the rebellious cesspool of sin wrought through the abuse of the modest principles by which this nation was founded! Millions are hurling themselves into the decimation of their eternal legacy; and the curtain is poised to descend on this age, and the lights of divinity will rise in the earthly hereafter, revealing their despicable works according to the Truth laid alongside the cornerstone of Creation.

Does it seem like I am hopelessly lamenting this situation, or that I am worrisome or despondent about offering my part while holding on until the conclusion of the world's final act? Please, never for an instant entertain such a notion of my surrender! My instructions are to courageously respond, *"No, I am not your judge; but I am to tell you how you will soon be judged! And, I have yet to truly suffer for the good of this cause!"* The Truth is far more sobering than we first thought. My task is to take anyone who will listen to the desolate foundations from where the Triumph of Our Lady will rise like a skyrocketing tower of Light that cannot be felled! There is a baseline of modern reality existing beneath the libertine smoke of this age; and from that dias in the bowels of our intentions, a voice is being raised, communicating to these last auspicious moments of human existence the unequivocal fact that the

Matriarch of all, who will spare no man's pride, is providentially preparing to wipe-clean the slate of humanity with the sacred adroitness of the Universal Mother whom She so nobly is. I am announcing the eternal dismantling of what we visually see, and declaring in the Name of Jesus Christ that the ne'er-do-wells and evildoers who have desecrated this planet will be certified as the most fortunate opportunists if they run now for their lives to the confessionals of the Roman Catholic Church and lay bare their souls in repentance before an ordained priest in the line of Melchizedek to gain sanctuary from the coming Purification. They should rush without reticence and absent of fear into shelter beneath the Catholic garment of sacramental perfection, because they are about to be backlashed by the baneful record of their lives as their selfishness is revealed beneath the spotlight of the radiant Beauty of the Queen of Heaven and Earth. The ecstatic vision of Her Immaculate Heart will crush them! Oh, they may not be killed outright, but will wish the mortal part of their being was already dead and buried beyond Her penetrating gaze. Their sins will chill their blood and cleave to them like millstones as their eyes fall upon the depth, power, beauty and gentleness of Her spectacular purity and breathtaking Love. The panacea of Her maternal embrace will be so overwhelming that they will endure a literal cauterization of their souls as they wish for death in the flames of the cleansing fire they will not be able to escape. There, their existence will stand in abeyance as She meticulously and mysteriously sanctifies their essence, clean of the filth they deployed to stain the Creation that Her Son hung on a Cross to purify. Know beyond any shadow of doubt that those who lay in the burn-units and rehabilitation wards of hospitals are their mystical deliverers; they are their parable, they are Christ for them! Call to mind the medicinal baths in which these pitiable patients are scrubbed. Envision the pain searing their charred limbs as they are peeled of their dead skin to make way for the new. These innocent ones are enduring the punishment for other sinners so the latter can be forgiven and admitted to Paradise at the instant of conversion. Nevermore wonder why the blameless are suffering such unjust atrocities of misfortune and pain. No longer be stupefied that a benevolent and loving God would allow these precious people to endure such indignity and disgrace. It is for obstinate sinners who lead lives of hellions! They should witness the love that both God and His people have for them!—and recognize the hope their proxy-sufferers maintain for the possibility of miraculous conversion! Be alert in faith, as well, for the fateful day is quickly approaching where this sacrificial mercy, this liberating exoneration, will reach its culmination and these sacrificial victims for Christ will be called to perpetual Redemption. Our victimhood in union with our Beloved Lord will be complete, and the world's lost sinners will be left to suffer their own torments with no saintly composure or strength to sustain them. Justice will descend like a monsoon of incandescent fire that they will never outrun in all their steps of Eternity. Mountains and hills cover us, indeed! No longer will the faithful children of God have to endure the hellish consequences of other people's high crimes and misdemeanors. The adversaries of human Salvation wilfully entice the world to the hilt of unimaginable impurity, indecency and sin, pulverizing society with a hailstorm of immorality that pocks the benevolent landscape with craters and canyons of iniquity. They slander, impugn and brow-beat decent people who speak-out as courageously robed stewards of this vineyard, and shipwreck the lives of thousands upon millions for financial and statutory gain. The floor of Creation will literally collapse beneath their feet someday, and the chasm of eternal perdition will open-wide to engulf them in its endless flames; and plummet they will to the place they prepared for themselves, wearing their tee-shirts that arrogantly proclaimed they had "no fear." Fire and brimstone cannot begin to describe their bleak future if they do not repent. Yes, they should "fear this" description of their destiny. For them, wisdom begins in fear of the Lord. And, for us, the children of God and partakers of the Most Blessed Sacrament, we are fearless in the Truth. Heaven is ours, and we shall soon tread this Earth again like kings! Consider how Christians surround the ancient Roman Colosseum as our Supreme Pontiff carries the standard of our Savior's Crucifixion in triumphant procession on Good Friday. No one from that ancient pagan empire would have believed the prophecy if it had been told, but the Mystical Body of Christ now marks time to our victorious destiny, and has surpassed and abolished the murderous fate of a hideous circus which leveled ruthless ignorance and inhumanity upon our martyred brothers and sisters in centuries past. The faithful progeny of those Martyrs now own the storied lands of their captors, along with the pomp and circumstance that garnished their pride, while possessing more elevated visions and presiding with newer rites of Grace amidst the ruins of their fallen empire. This is our sign of hope, O' people of the American nation! The children of Christianity are destined to be lords of this homeland again, governing according to an almost forgotten Grace and unending Love. Our late Holy Father, Pope John Paul the Great, said on January 29, 2005 to an audience of judges and lawyers of the Church's central appellate court, *"One must resist fear of the truth, which at times might stem from fear of wounding persons. The truth, which is Christ Himself, frees us from all forms of compromise with prejudiced lies."*

Sunday, July 20, 2003 (excerpt)   2:09 p.m.
"One Giant Leap for Mankind"

    "Please remember Me when deep in your prayers,   m(201)
little children, for I will amplify them with My exemplary
Grace before the Almighty Father. My intentions are benign,
My purposes are always benevolent, My Immaculate Heart
is sincere, and My power to effect the change you are seeking
on Earth is unprecedented in the Sacred Heart of Jesus. I call
upon you so that you will reciprocally call upon Me to be
your holy guide in living-out your days. How I truly wish
for you to be happy! I have told other messengers throughout
the ages that I cannot make you happy here on the Earth   x
compared to the rejoicing you will do in Heaven. However,
compared to the dismal lives many people have led before,
I can assure you that your blissful faith will open the
doorway for your anticipation of the Eternal Salvation of
your soul. My children, God has granted Me the gift of being
your benefactor so that you will be fully prepared to accept
this Salvation. What is it that I give to you? I bring you
Wisdom in the form of undying Love. I offer you the
compassion of a Perpetual Mother. I console your hearts
when you are in pain. And, with the Light of the Love of   xx
Jesus, I make your pathway clear to the Holy Cross. You
surely must remember that I stood beneath that same Cross
on Good Friday when My Loving Son was Crucified. What
does His Sacrifice tell you? That you are saved by the power
of His Blood! And, that you know that human life is never
wholly shed of sorrow, but such sorrow need not give you
cause to surrender the fight for righteousness. You are more
than conquerors in Him who has Redeemed you! Your
dignity has been regained in the indignity of the Passion of
My Slain Son. I am the Mother of all of this supernatural   xxx
Grace, and My call is for you to be strengthened in your
sorrows. Never give-up or give-in to the sadness of the world,
because the happiness and joy of Life Eternal has vanquished
it for the good of your future. There is hope in these things,
there is new life, Resurrection, and the knowledge that you

are free to choose the holy pathway of mortal life. This is the goodness to which you are called. My children, if this were not true, I would have told you very plainly heretofore.

I am calling upon My humanity to come to its feet for the change that is needed all around the world. You are but little children, and you have done many mighty things in technology, medicine, communication, and travel. You have taken that very small step for (a) man, but have you chosen as a collective people to make that giant leap for mankind? Have you decided for God as a unified species? Do you acknowledge Jesus Christ as the Savior of humanity from every hamlet, borough, city, suburb, and summit? Are you yet so divided that you cannot see past your own indignance? Time is a very short passing for you to endure. You see the ages which are affected by the elements and edifices. Your hearts are buffeted by rejection and sorrow. To what do you attribute these things? Is the world so blind that its inhabitants assume that human suffering is inevitable? If so, then you must open your eyes to the Truth which has been borne to Creation in countless miracles throughout the history of all histories. I give you My solemn Word, My Son—your Savior; and your reaction and response must be one of peace and hope; for if you do not, your future is indeed hopeless! Every venue by which you can see the fruitful beginnings you have been seeking for centuries is available to you now in the Salvation you have gained in the Cross of My Son. You must crucify your own will so that it can be raised again in unity with God through the Resurrection of Jesus from the Tomb. This is what it means to be holy people. When you see tragedies and losses occurring around you at a seemingly more regular pace, do not place their attribution at the doorstep of your Loving God! Humanity is to blame for every teardrop that has ever been shed! When you turn inside to ask yourselves why, you will see your absence of holiness there, completely banished from your spirits in favor of the grief that you have asked the Almighty Father for instead. Call upon the Angels to give you comfort!

xl

l

lx

lxx

Ask the Holy Spirit to guide you through the darkness! Become filled with allegiance to the Crucified Son of God, and anything that burdens you will be lifted from your shoulders, cleared from your pathway, and erased from your recollection.

I have also told My people that if you pray with the intensity of the Saints, you will not realize your passing from this life into the next. I have asked you to be united as one humanity under the Holy Cross in the likeness of no other age. And, if you continue to decline to do these things, you will make no giant leaps in any direction that has anything to do with Divine Love! All of your accomplishments in the past are only metaphors for your own vanity and the way for you to say 'We are proud!' Your Almighty God is asking you to answer the question, ...proud of what? Please tell Me that you have not spent the past 2,000 years pining to seek other worlds when you have yet to perfect the unity of the very one on which you stand! Please tell Me that it is not true! Please assure the millions of Holy Saints who reside in Heaven that your purpose in being the leader of the nations is not to become better at making war, fabricating pretenses to conquer your foreign neighbors, cheating the very friends upon whom you have relied so many times before out of their very next meal, and self-aggrandizing your capacity to wave a red, white, and blue flag and say 'I'm free!' My people, tell the Mother of your Omnipotent God that your intentions are more benevolent that this! I pray you, tell Me that it is not true! What about the giant leap of faith that My Son has asked you to make headlong in knowing that His Life, Death, and Resurrection is God's gift to you in absolute Love? This is the priceless act that He is seeking in you now. Give your souls to Him as though you were diving into a deep ocean from atop a towering cliff! This is the giant leap! This is where your courage lies! The stern admonishments that your Immaculate Mother might give you now are nothing compared to the division of the sheep and the goats which will occur come the end of time. I am kind and

lxxx

xc

c

gentle, and God is fair and mild. And, Jesus is very much   cx
filled with Divine Mercy for those who can read the signs
that are ongoing on the Earth today. Indeed, the many who
understand the Truth of the Holy Gospel and reject it
anyway are in grave trouble! We must pray for them! We
must pray for them! Someday, the sizzling sound you will
hear will be the agony of their souls in the blazing flames of
Hell! We must pray for them!

Therefore, when you see suffering, loss, tragedy, and
sorrow in your midst today, remember that it is the egregious
arrogance of a lost humanity that is making it so. And, the   cxx
obvious question of millions in your midst '...when will all of
this end(?)' is entirely dependent upon when the sinners
decide to relinquish what they are doing and turn their lives
over to Jesus. It could happen by the end of today if only
everyone would believe. Or, it could occur tomorrow if Jesus
decided to provide a large enough miracle. Is this any way
to urge a people to embrace their faith? Is fear the only way
to guide the lost into the righteousness of the Light? These
are such questions to which humanity, itself, must respond.
I will tell you something that may give many of My children   cxxx
great hope, others apprehension, and millions a signal of a
long-earned sense of relief..."

Our Lady then showed me a poignant vision and told me of
certain future events that will accomplish the final purging of evil
from the world. They were utterly horrific in nature, but filled
with the triumphant majesty of Almighty God. This prophecy
must remain confidential for now because humanity does not yet
possess the spiritual temperament to embrace the truth of such
things while Divine Mercy still reigns for every living soul!

"...Please read the Book of Revelation! The righteous shall
have their fill! I promise that this is what will happen if the
millions who have rejected the Cross of their Salvation do
not bend in contrition before it, amend their lives, and never
return to such baneful ways again. And, for those who know
the Mother of God as the Gentle Maiden who reigns as the

*Queen of Peace over Heaven and Earth, I assure you that
there will be irrevocable peace on Earth once this righteous*   cxl
*purging has been done. I give you My solemn promise that
all of these things are true. Lucky will be the villains who
will die between now and then of their own accord!*

   *My Special son, it has not been My purpose to
frighten you today. The historical nonsense that happened
on this day 34 years ago has nothing to do with human
Salvation. I am calling for a '...giant leap' that involves the
surrendering of the will to God, of sacrifices from the wealthy
on behalf of the poor, and the deposing of popularly-elected
democratic leaders in countries whose agenda are to only*   cl
*profit for themselves. You have been told that the world is
upside down, and Jesus is about to invert it to the pleasure of
every Martyr who ever died trying to prove it in their day.
Thank you for allowing Me to speak to you with such
profound seriousness today... Thank you for doing your part
in a very holy way. You have been a very easy little boy for
Me to guide. And, your brother has been one as well... Yes,
it is true. Some of the things I told you today were also told
to Saint Joan of Arc... This is now My holy blessing for you.
+ I Love you. Goodnight!"*   clx

    It seems somewhat difficult for a growing segment of our society to
accept the possibility that the generation of their thoughts and the bases for
their personal convictions may not be as well grounded in realism as they
originally perceived them to be. In fact, vast numbers of secular groups refuse
to recognize how negatively their view of existence is influenced by a state of
discernment that is wholly compromised by flimsy, prejudicial biases. Let's
face it, millions have been indoctrinated in nothing more than mundane
worldly perspectives since birth, rendering them devoid of any functional
understanding of the substantive meaning of human life here on Earth. They
are immersed in an alien vernacular of acquired vagueness, ignoring the
historical significance of Jesus' Life, Death, and Resurrection, His ongoing
involvement in the material world, and the contemporary miraculous signs He
dispenses to jump-start their faith. The examples that confirm this deficit in
religious ideology are much too numerous to ignore. While there are ample
numbers of people who don't even realize the spiritual aura evolving in and

around them, there are multitudes more who do, but sadly have already given-up on participating in the perfection of civilization because the sacrifices are simply too heavy to bear. Moreover, most of them could care even less what this means as long as their immediate vicinity remains relatively peaceful. It is easy to distinguish the constraining bonds of these bland, agnostic and atheistic perceptions when faced with life's unexpected tragedies. Their inability to see beyond the immediate consequences of our mortal condition leaves these people replete with vain, vacuous excuses to explain away the oftentimes unpredictable misfortunes that occur—saying that the afflicted ones were in the wrong place at a most inopportune time, or they did not work dutifully enough to outpace their hardships, or they were born weaker than the rest of us, or suffered a hideous malformation of genetics, or they are experiencing their predestined lot in life, or they deserve what they have made of themselves, or that fate simply dealt them a poor benefit from the luck of the draw, and on and on, ad infinitum. How this banal nonsense takes on such forms is quite a mystery, all of its renditions no more than varying ways of saying, *I haven't the foggiest notion why such a fate has befallen them, but thank my lucky stars or God, if there is one, that it was not me!* The minuscule breadth of secular cognition is further cordoned within a world that reveres only the measurable "equal and opposite reaction" of physical dynamics. The mindset of being sequestered inside a cocoon defined by the blindness of sin, and being separated from the vast reaches of a more productive existence is neutralized through an impenetrable faith in the Omnipotent Person of Our Lord, Jesus Christ. Materialistic actuaries allow themselves to become nothing more than organic dominos, stood on end by the forces by which they are mesmerzied, surrendering to an ill-scripted prophecy that functions toward sequential conclusions that have no greater possibility than lying end-to-end on a tabletop with dollar signs numerically matching within their closest proximity. Wouldn't it be better to entertain the prospect that our Divine Creator embodies a definitive, redemptive purpose within every moment and action, permeating the multiplicatus and conjunctive manifestations of His active or passive Will? Is it dysfunctional to believe that the temporal parameters of the material world are committing the ultimate act of fraud against our perception? And, are our "absolutes" truly as strict and clearly cogent as we conclude them to be? An enlightening example may be our recognition of which direction is right or left. When making this decision, we are faced with a precise choice, whereby most people know which way to look when asked to point in either direction. But, since God finds Himself facing both forward and backward, up and down, north, east, south, and west, and inward and outward through Eternity, all at the same time, which direction is His right of center? You see, there are no opposing or conflicting choices for God because right or left is any direction

He wants them to be. His Divine Will unilaterally articulates and extrapolates our bearings at any given moment, and defines the direction of our return to His presence. And, because Sacred Scripture tells us that there truly exists a "right hand of the Father," how do we determine this orientation? By looking where Jesus Christ is physically standing—at the right hand of the Father upon the altars of the Roman Catholic Church. God revealed to humanity the direction He was looking when He sent His Only Begotten Son to the Earth. Mortal reasoning has now been relieved of its diminutive stature and empowered with the ability to contemplate Heaven, unfettered by the parameters by which our logic is usually constrained. And, it is from this elevated plateau that we search for the answers to our questions about the providential angst, plight, torment, agony and reparative suffering of our fellow brothers and sisters.

The Most Blessed Trinity is the Creator-Thrice who simultaneously enshrines within His Deific Glory the infinite realities He has deigned to conceive. This does not imply only a number we cannot seem to count. It is a vibrantly flourishing, regenerative definition where the sanctity of God is incalculable, perpetual, and inclusive of all the dreams, aspirations, hopes, sentiments, and yearnings of every person who has been given the breath of life. The collage of possibilities that we envision in the Light of the Holy Spirit exists in its *fait accomplis* within Him, meaning that all things we consider as our hopes and dreams already exist as concurrent realities, living in complete synchronization with the unity of God's Divine Will; and at the same time, distinctly and separately, much like the Holy Trinity, itself. But, what are we witnessing from our secular cultures instead? We are habitually conscripted into materialistic societies that are blind to the prescriptions of Everlasting Life and ingratiating themselves in pleasures of the flesh as if there is no tomorrow. The refusal of human creatures to generate any sanctifying hope has come with the dispensation of our free will and the abandonment of faith in the unseen. Humanity has become blinded to the vision of seeing itself anywhere inside the realms of universal redemption. We are declining the overt invocation of Divine Light without a whit of desire to surrender our unifying expectations into God's Omnipotent Providence, a supernatural action that would entwine us within the fabric of His enlightening revelation. Everyone should concern themselves with the possibility that people can be excluded from the "all" of Paradisial Creation by refusing to tender their lives as miraculous participants in God's Redemptive Plan. Yet, He still maintains His presence within our souls as the "Beatific-All-in-all" throughout the broad parameters of time by annihilating with the Divine Mercy of the Lamb of God every vestige of sin that has tainted Creation thus far. There is a transfiguration occurring at this very moment through the salvific work and sacrificial witness of the Mystical

Body of Christ through His Roman Catholic Church.   Imperfection is becoming extinct as we speak, being rescinded through the power blazing from the Holy Sacrifice of the Mass into the hearts of the faithful who suffer humbly, while effecting a restorative grace for those whose faith is too puny to realize how their lives are being consummated by the Divine. Everyone must acknowledge and imitate the redeeming nature of God, as Love, to understand the mystery of human suffering and the far-flung realities of His Kingdom which are prophetically revealed through our Christian faith. And, where does this transcending annunciation take place? Within the mystical prowess vested in the human soul when we desire to seek-out the meaning of existence and search for the reasons why Creation has been so animated by the spark of new life, i.e., when we set upon the voyage to discover the mysteries of our being here, hoping to find the purpose of our days with as much excitement as when the first sails were hoisted in search of a new world, when our egoism is sacrificed on the altar of our consciences for the freedom to partake in holier things, when our distractions are finally laid to rest so we may survey our indwelling motivations, when our self-sufficiency is broken by conceding to our need for affection and affirmation, and when we arrive at the simple conclusion that Love is the mightiest power in all the universes that have ever been created. Only then will we recognize the multi-dimensional coexistence of all possibilities emanating from the Divine reaction of God's creative Will. I believe there are many people who simply resign themselves to dead fate in the midst of their calamities because they know of no other means to change their lot. But, those who rise to the call of Our Lady delve into the miraculous knowledge imprinted into the world by Jesus Christ. And, with the exhibition of heavenly virtue, the cross-section of our understanding of life grows like a panoramic scene of expanding dimensions, transcending ever after the anemic boundaries of sensual experience and the fantasies that our minds may conjure. We come to new life in the triumphant clarity of our redemption, while those who decline Mary's offer often revert to possessionism and self-ingratiating actualization in vain attempts to nullify the difficulties of life. Such faint-hearted individuals have nowhere else to turn for self-identity or substantive meaning because they are lost in the wiles of their own conation. And, they must be found before death implores them to retreat! This is surely why something so spectacular as Mary's intercession to my brother and me has occurred. The floodgate in the ocean of Heaven has been removed, and humanity is witnessing God's Glory, previously draining upon the Earth in sprinkles, now erupting into absolute torrents. A final deluge has commenced, and the prophetic Ark is loading. It is now as it was in the days of Noah. So, awaken and be counted two by two, millions upon millions. Let the nations and cultures of the modern world come arm-in-arm to the boarding plank. Be not afraid to set aside your carnal attire, for it is only passing away! We will begin again in the Light of perfection, where the old order will be transfigured into the priority of the new. There is a sacred Cross within each of us, and our obedience to its calling is the deliverance of ourselves and all who will soon see the unshaded lamp-stand of our souls from the other side of time.

Palm Sunday, March 20, 2005   *1:46 p.m.*

"This special day is made even more holy by your   o(079)
dedicated prayerfulness on behalf of God's people who are chosen to suffer in exultation of the Cross. On this Sunday, as you honor the King of kings who was welcomed into Jerusalem only to be slain for the sins of the world, place your own sorrows in Him. Know that your enemies are despising Jesus when they speak ill of you, and be glad to partake of the Passion of the Son of Man. You shall inherit His just Resurrection! My children, you have many reasons to thrust your spirit of thanksgiving onto the world stage.   x *Christianity is much the better for your embracing it, and Catholicism remains contemporary as you extol the Traditions of the Church. I have asked you on more than one occasion to decry the movements to modernize the Roman Catholic Church. Remember the Saints who fought to keep holy the great relics that have been handed-down to humanity from Saint Simon Peter to Pope John Paul II. Trust with all your being that Jesus is pleased by your faithfulness, because maintaining your allegiance to the Traditions of the Church connect you not only with the First*   xx *Apostles, but with everything the Faith Church will discover come the end of time. You can no doubt sense this circle of continuity in which you are living, the chain of loyalty in which your lives are links, from the Birth of Jesus in Bethlehem to everything you can imagine to facilitate His Kingdom before His Glorious Second Coming. I have asked My children to be not only God's people, but God's holy people. Comprehend the spiritual continuum manifested by the faith you hold so dearly in your Crucified Lord with that same Christianity reflected by your predecessors in faith.*   xxx
Each time a priest offers the Holy Sacrifice of the Mass, he

codifies the union of the ages with God's Christological Truth. You are one with every other person who is rescued by Jesus from the perils of death. And, by virtue of the consistency of the Sacraments and the Grace of the Holy Spirit, all time is one in Him. The millions of anonymous Saints who have died heretofore reside with you now in the resilient power of the sanctity of God. They are your counterparts in the Mystical Salvation of humankind, and I ask you to call upon them for Wisdom and guidance. Should you desist in sparing some sense of hopefulness for the sorrowing among you, please recapture your spiritual strength and rise above the darkness that keeps you from seeing the jubilation of the Holy Spirit clearly.

xl

Today, I have come to thank you for the faithful service you are giving to My Son. I ask you to realize the blessings you have been accorded by Him in the works of peace and justice you are so lavishly bestowing upon this broken world. For all the corruption and the effects of human sinfulness that you see everyday, I ask you to place your sights upon the bright imaginings that keep your hopes aloft. It may be true that you cannot return to some places here in this life that once brought you broader reflection and consolation. However, I assure you that harboring fruitful fondness for life's perspectives in your hearts will ensure that you will live those great moments again—even if after you have completed your journey of mortal life. You are bound for Heaven, and happiness cannot escape you there. No elation is beyond your grasp. No hope is left unfulfilled. You should remember that life on the Earth is a preparatory process whereby you are amended and changed, and your souls are bolstered by the awesome commission of Jesus Christ to manifest perfection in you. There will be many great discoveries before the Earth is through that will convince even the hardest of heart that God loves them. There are revelations yet to be unveiled and miraculous signs from beyond the skies and past the tortured silence of the heavens that will perpetuate unparalleled belief in millions of lost

l

lx

souls everywhere. I ask for an enhancement of your patience while these things come to pass, knowing that many of them may occur after you have come to Heaven. Knowing that the world is now being purified and cultivated should always give you hope. The delight of your faith, itself, is allowing the Will of the Almighty Father to be done in His own time. Pray to always be in union with Him as the generations come to a close. God will provide the signs and wonders to assure your Christian eagerness that you are on the right path.   lxx

And, what of these signs? What is it about the world that lay in wait, hoping for discovery, rediscovery and resurrection? Does it include the thousands of shipmates at the bottom of the seas, burdened by the unwary darkness their lost captains could have never fathomed? And, will you be visited by strange and unheralded vestiges or extraterrestrial beings as signs from Heaven that the Son of Man is near? I tell you today that such are not necessarily the signatures of the Final Ages, but they comprise the cosmic paraphernalia of a transfigured universe poised for the grand closing of the chasm between humanity and the Creator of the Universe. Indeed, what of these signs? Will you decipher cryptic messages or discover hidden sequences in manuscripts and ancient artifacts? Your Lord would have warned you in advance of the testaments of His Truth even so! You need not search the chambers of the world to discern the culmination of time. You only need Jesus Christ! Every sign, every message God ever gave the world about the transformation of humankind from 'lost individuals' to 'found people' is clearly revealed in the Nativity, Life, Passion, Crucifixion and Resurrection of Jesus of Nazareth. He would have you translating cryptic messages as a matter of course if He thought it to be significant in the greater Providence of the Plan of God. But, Jesus is God's message, and the messenger, too! He is the full accord you seek between this world and the next. He is the genius whom God has dispatched to teach and inherit the Earth; and by   lxxx

xc

c

His Holy Sacrifice, He has made the world complete. Jesus has brought the dominion of God to bear over all the lands sprawled across the latitudes by His Father before the ancient days began. He represents Heaven, both in Wisdom and premonition, to everything that was lost when Adam and Eve were first cast down from the Garden of Eden. And, His invitation is for humanity to begin anew in the justification that has been wrought by reason of His Divine Love; that this same humankind, now healed, shall be perpetuated before God's unapproachable Light. I assure you of this—My Jesus will succeed at the last. He will make of the world what He chooses, and He will lethally destroy and craftily repair Creation according to His vision of the perfectness of life. Being in unity with Jesus means understanding one's place in the universe before the backdrop and purposes of Heaven. And, if any man wishes to be brilliant in the ways of great novelers and expeditionists, he should come by simple understanding to defer to the Son of Man in all things true. He should embrace the beautiful with profundity and obedience, and with a stellar heart filled with the prescience of the majesties of God; for it is in these things that you will discern His willingness to ratify your peace and good wishes on platforms of silver and gold.

Therefore, My message to you today, My little ones, is a sublime dictation of happiness and Truth. I call upon your deftness of spirit and knowledge of Love to be always and everywhere aware of the slow transpiring of human conversion that your work is benefitting. Be fond of Me, and love Me dearly. I am a benevolent Mother and charismatic Queen who calls upon you to espouse that Christian romance which softens the hearts of the stoic and tenders the lost to the absolution of Jesus so wilfully given to the forgiveness of men. I ask you to pray fervently for the conversion of the world as you begin to celebrate the Easter Triduum. My children, as you can see, I have come today to assure you that Jesus is with you through your trials and tribulations, and in your suffering. I bid you a very good day on this Palm Sunday.

cx

cxx

cxxx

cxl

Why? Because this is the Feast of Palms, the palms laid beneath the pathway of the King of Creation. You realize with great imagining after the passing of centuries that these palms would lead the path of the suffering of My Son. Please accept the text of this message that is given to you heretofore as My intentions for you and the world.

Now, I wish to continue speaking to you in a consoling tone. There is, indeed, a dark pall that comes over the human spirit at times. It is one of helplessness and fear, one of questioning and lack of understanding. Sometimes the human soul feels so out of control of its future. I assure you that Jesus and I are closest to you during these times. You are My lovely and living children, and you are faithful to My call... Can you see how even the most simple hearts among you can be attacked by evil, and in a way that feels uncontrollably dark? It is true that you have fought such a fight before. You see, when someone is in such a state, their sense of perspective is factually destroyed. Their ability to conceive happy thoughts is impaired. And, even when they muster a sign of happiness, they see it only as a self-imposed ruse to cover the truth. There are millions of people the world-over who are suffering this now. And, they include not only the poor and abandoned, but many who have simple and productive lives. You see that the 14-year-old prodigy could not conquer the darkness that overcame him, and he took his own life... I offer you now My holy blessing for today. + I will speak to you again at the great High Feast of Easter! The Paschal Mystery will be complete! I love you. Goodnight!"

cl

clx

clxx

It is commonly known that the individual facets of any mechanical device must function with symmetrical perfection, or it will inevitably destroy itself. Consider the multitude of moving parts composing an automobile engine operating in synchronicity so the purring motor of a Cadillac Coup de Ville is barely audible beneath its polished hood. Or, think about the precision reflected in the compendium of mathematical knowledge required to even design such an engine. The behemoth amount of calculations, summations, ratios, values, measurements, quantities, and quotients must be accurate to the degree of absolute, with the rules governing their manipulation being a rigorous requirement for the determination of their products and remainders. Consider our natural environment, how we build our houses, layout our streets, promulgate our laws, defend ourselves against foreign enemies, and reside within the patriotic whole. In all of these examples, we search for the optimum utopia of perfection as we know it to be, with harmony among the participants as our primary barometer of success. There is an almost innate respect for the organization and achievement of our intentions in any mortal endeavor. Our hearts beat with admiration at anyone who has pushed the circumference of possibility to wider realms—*except in the domain of sacrificial Christian love!* President John F. Kennedy rallied the spirit of our American nation on May 25, 1961 to implant a human footprint on the surface of the moon, the glowing globe in our nighttime sky. But, could you imagine the knee jerk reaction if our current president attempted to inspire us to manifest spiritual perfection with all our might and resources before the next decade expires? Why did so many Americans take delight in the possibility of the first choice, yet twice as many now shriek at the prospect of accomplishing the second? Saint Paul did not hesitate to admonish those of ancient Greece about the folly of their ludicrous beliefs in multiple gods and their sensual worship of animals and birds. He was a man who knew the desires of the supposedly unknowable God, a child of revelation and a contradicting mystery to the image makers, fad purveyors, and cultural procurators of that age. The Holy Spirit commissioned him with a Divine mandate and thrust him into a cauldron of darkness whose citizenry knew no better. He walked with the true Light that could not be out-witted, out-reasoned, extinguished, impugned, disconcerted, or overcome. And, that singular Truth still lives in the hearts of the Catholic faithful, thriving in the midst of this spiritually arcane 21st century. Imagine how this servant of God, a man truly ahead of his time, would be chided today by those with beliefs contrary to the Wisdom of the Triune God of Israel. Nay, look at how the secular millions responded to Pope John Paul II with mockery and utter disdain, and how religious liberals everywhere are already turning a deaf ear to his successor, Pope Benedict XVI. Can you imagine a businessman living a posh life in a downtown Chicago neighborhood deciding to climb the world's highest mountain, then spitting at the instructions of a Tibetan Sherpa saying, "I don't need your help. I'll do it my way(?)" Is this not what a person striving for spiritual perfection is doing if he rejects the Wisdom of the Catholic Saints and the teachings of the Roman Catholic Church, an institution which has stood tall in moral rectitude for nearly 2,000 years, notwithstanding how many contemporary reprobates have tried to sully Her legacy through their outright lies, half-truths, and cheap characterizations? The Saints understood the clarity of charismatic reality better than any of the great physicists of the world have comprehended the tangible forces of nature. But, those who refuse to defer to the redeeming genius of the greatest human beings who ever lived, while wishing God would step aside and make room for their ingratiating betise, feel compelled to deride and obscure our faith in the Messiah's existence, slander His Apostolic Church, and whitewash two millennia of Christian Truth into a pluralistic sector of spineless platitude in order to make their case against the magnanimity of organized religion.

Most fittingly in the sight of God, the Roman Catholic Church is 2,000 years out and has had everything shy of the kitchen sink thrown at Her—well, perhaps that, too; but She still stands as an illuminating array of sacramental holiness, pleading with welcoming arms for humanity entire to enter into Her redeeming embrace. Who could possibly refuse? And, why? What part of Roman Catholicity is so despised? I can tell you—It is the submission required of the faithful flock that is so starkly repulsive to the pride of men! Remember, however, that we cannot sacrifice ourselves for others unless we offer our complete autonomy to the authority of Jesus Christ, which He embodied within the Magisterium of His Church. Bible-believing Christians claim to be bound to God through the written tenets of Sacred Scripture. But, too many of them have loosed the bindings of their allegiance by granting themselves the leeway to interpret the Holy Word as they see fit. By doing so, they are essentially subjected only to themselves by maintaining the right to re-frame the meaning of the Holy Bible and modify their understanding of the New Testament according to what is most beneficial to them at any given moment in time. In other words, they claim the agency to regulate their personal relationship with God through mutated ruminations lacking in the Wisdom of the Holy Spirit; and in that, there is no authentic, complete, or sacrificial obedience to His authority. They never quite make it through the Garden of Gethsemane and onward to their perfection in the Holy Cross as individual followers of Christ. This is why there are over 30,000 different Protestant interpretations of Sacred Scripture. There is no plenary Deposit of Truth to which Protestants submit. They never deny themselves the unilateral power to "decide." And, unfortunately, the authentic reflection of Christ's sacrificial witness is lost somewhere in the mix. The Roman Catholic view is much different and more globally universal than theirs. Every member of the Catholic faith is called to recognize that they are not the head. Our submission and obedience has the potential of rising to the perfect image and likeness of Christ because we have surrendered our desires to see the world in our own likeness, leaving us bowed in humble deference to the ofttimes mysterious ways of God. His Will does not have to be palatable to us because, when we engage Him in trust, Love is magnified within us; and in that is our true joy. Jesus is glorified in our submission to His Will, which has been deposited within His

Faith Church on Earth; and henceforth, the world sees our Lord personified in His people. With this Wisdom, it can never be an offense against the peace and order of society to call out of the darkness those who are wandering near its perilous traps. Lucid sense seems to be relative for most. For those who are disoriented, things possess a logical coherency only as long as the circumstances are conducive to exercising their passions and sentiments. Freedom becomes their most valuable asset. If they can imagine, desire and attain it, then they conclude that it must be within the realms of permissible conduct. The justifications they make to determine interior consonance is with the sensual impressions they have allowed to be imprinted upon their psyche. We, as human beings, begin making mental impressions of things that "feel" good from the primal moments of our mortal existence. They are infused upon our psychological and physiological identities in the mysterious functions of our brains and nervous systems. The animal instinct of our constitution is a self-fulfilling mechanism which thrives on things that ingratiate our senses, causing us to be constricted by undue pleasures of the flesh. God's Divine Love, on the other hand, initiates the expansive, outward mobility of our existence into unbounded realms of spiritualism that vigilantly provide for our authentic happiness. When love is denied admittance to the heart, and the wounds of that deprivation become more acute, especially if the soul does not know to search for the compassion of God, it turns inward and gravitates in leaps and bounds toward the lower tiered, animalistic, and carnal satisfactions it has imagined or experienced in the past. It is as though we frolicked as children in an open meadow with the taste of true freedom flowing through our rapture, when a storm came upon us and chased us into a nearby cave. With the memory of the hail of discomfort, we grew to accept the confinement of the cavern as a safer domain for our existence. Worldly passions and enticements are only "feel good," supermax prisons that prohibit us from returning to the Omnipotent freedom in the meadow of supernatural Love which flows from the mountains of Paradise. This is why the Blessed Mother asks us to reevaluate our momentum and to discard our fears of momentary spikes of spiritual unease. Thus, we are asked to cast away any feelings of rebellion against the Roman Catholic Church. The Virgin Mary asks us to instead make our leaps and bounds toward the center of our hearts without looking back over our shoulders toward the sensations that have dimmed the awareness of our liberating dignity and spiritual unity. Now is the time to return to the Infinite Love at the Altar of Sacrifice, for therein rests the destination for our intimate communion with the celestial heavens. Nothing in the world can draw us away from God once we receive His Eucharistic Body and Blood, and experience His true Love emanating from within our deepest beings. Our sanctified identity returns like a blazing fire, and we awaken as if having been doused in the face by a trough of cold water. The darkness is then seen for what it really is, and is overcome by the Light, freeing us from the ill-winds that forced us to believe the fallacy that the highest mountains could never be climbed, that once-sparkling cities would never shine like pearls on their hilltops again, and that republics as secularly ingrained as the United States of America could never be immersed within the genius of the Holy Spirit of Jesus Christ.

Sunday, July 4, 1999 (excerpt)   *5:21 p.m.*

"To you, who are the children of My Immaculate   i(185)
Heart, I bid peace and comfort on this day which celebrates the country in which you live. Your God has planned a great future for you! An awe-inspiring cultivation is near at hand! My children, the soul of America is not a barren one, but it is sorely lacking in conscience. There are too many hearts that are asleep in the senseless trap of materialism. They will awaken from their slumber to the call of this Morning Star who is about to shake them into complete union with the Holy Spirit. I am She who is from God, your   x
Patroness who has come calling for servants and spiritual companions to usher-in the age of piousness. Who else will act if My children fail to act? What other body of humanity will walk forward to reach-out for the torch? If you will continue to be patient with Me, you will see the last one-fourth of this year as greater than all of your July 4ths wrapped into one."

This was personally fulfilled for me when the first seven years of my diary *"Morning Star Over America"* was published.

"It is an opportune time for Christians in America and around the world. The collective anticipation of your people is towing in the direction that bodes well for the revelation   xx
of My intercession. It is wholly true, the roads of human life cannot elevate mankind from them of their own accord. I bear the plan that many will follow. This has been true for the past two millennia. I cannot tell you in too strong terms that My children will know Me. And, My faithful children

are many, in the millions and the multitudes. And, what of your life outside of Jesus? There is none! There is no life separate from the Word of God. All of the speeches in the world cannot capture His eloquent Grace! I wish you could already see the end of time and the effect that your work will xxx *soon have. Every day, you move closer to the realization of the hopes that cannot die. It is your dear Lord and Savior who keeps them alive. This is the new rise of freedom that cannot come from the hand of mortal man. This is the re-opening of the promises that have been handed-down through the ages since that all-defining moment on Mount Calvary, the Legacy which has been feeding humanity the nourishment of spiritual vindication for your true survival. I cannot tell you today the exact hour that Jesus will return to take your souls to Paradise, but I can tell you with* xl *confidence that it is a time that will soon come-to-pass. Let no one tell you otherwise; the Son of Man is alive, and He is as hungry for your Redemption as you are famished to be saved. You must recall the Holy Gospel passages that speak of the Second Coming of Jesus. God has spoken to the prophets, and their prophecy is soon to be fulfilled. My children, I am that Lady with the Crown of Twelve Stars, not the twelve tribes of Israel! This Mother is your source of Wisdom, as I have been for centuries past. You who wait for Me like the dawn will not be disappointed, for I bear in My* l *arms the reason for your joy!—Yes, the Giver of Everlasting Life! I hold the Christ-Child, the Anointed One, who beckons Me to show Him the children I have claimed for His Father. He wishes to be united with the brothers and sisters that God promised He would be granted on the day of His Passion! You are those children! You are the descendants, the last of those who wait to see the Eternal Light of Glory! I bid you the peace and gladness which lives in the Divinity of the Holy Spirit, the same Love who has brought Me to speak to you today..."* lx

The contrast has been struck. The tenor of our political discourse and the composition of our remedial values display a haunting digression from the virtue any truly great nation should espouse. Witness the words of the Queen of Heaven. Are they not foreign to the mainstream thoughts of our society? The miracle of this country has been turned on its head. There once was a time when immigrants were drawn to this land because it provided fertile opportunity for life unencumbered by tyranny. America possessed a solidified base of respect for goodness, if not in the overall conduct of its diverse populations, then at least in the inscribed resolve of her founding documents. There was an age when American leaders subscribed to honor, respect, virtue and devotion, a time when men and women of conscience defended the universal truths which they humbly acknowledged to be self-evident. Moral prudence was implied from the first sentence of our national charter to the last. Heroism in defense of the highest orders of common decency was a natural commodity that could not be sold, bartered or bought. The halls of our democracy were filled with men whose nobility could not be diluted or compromised. Honor and Truth were defended at the expense of the estate. Today, however, our public leaders worship the capitalist empire, instead. I dare ask, why did radical fundamentalists crash jetliners into the World Trade Center towers instead of our spiring cathedrals and churches? And, while the winds howled with militarism and retaliation in the aftermath of that ill-fated day, the Queen of Heaven offered what should have been our only response to the world. A contrast, indeed!

Sunday, September 16, 2001   *3:56 p.m.*

"My dearly beloved little children, I ask you to   k(259)
remember at this time in your nation's history that the
conversion of humanity often comes at great cost, and is not
so much in what God wills to happen, but rather in what He
allows so that all races of people will realize how far they
truly are away from the perfect transformation toward
perfection which is discovered in the depths of the Holy
Cross. All suffering, agony, desperation, and realization are
profoundly placed in perspective from the purview of Mount
Calvary. Therefore, it is only through the Love of the   x
Almighty Father that you are placed inside the Being of
Jesus, and He in you; and the Kingdom of Heaven is glorified
not by your error, but in the Truth that you are all being
slowly taken there on the wings of those who have been

chosen to be His instruments of peace and destruction, alike. I am the Patron Saint of this great American nation, and I have seen the essence of suffering and horror from the highest pinnacle of human existence. It is you who are participating in it now, for it is you who are loved; and it is your Creator on High who has placed you in His favor, even to the point xx *that you are worthy to be among those who are given an allotted portion to agonize for those who will only turn their backs and run.*

If you wonder whether it is God who has wrought these terrible things upon your country, do not be tempted to blame Him for the error of sinful man. It is He who mitigates all that is yet ill in the mortal world, through His own mysterious ways. While there are so many ironies that surround the meaning of human existence upon the Earth, and so many other paradoxes that seem to take your hearts to xxx *despair, please remember that nothing in the material world is worthy of transfer across the chasm of the ages into the incorporeal universe and onward to the celestial heights. Why has Jesus ordained such a pathway where your steps are so intrepid and dark to the tone? Because it is He who has tread there before you; it is His Sacred Heart who is now providing you Light; and it is His liberty which is setting you free, not the flames and smouldering rubble that seem so poignant to your sight, not the rushing scenes and blaring sirens, and not the watery eyes of the New Colossus who* xl *stands so prettily in the harbor, helpless to do anything more than she has been capable of doing since her arm was first raised there so many generations ago.*

Therefore, I tell My children and My country to rise again, to be lifted past the angst which is pulling your hearts aside, to remember those who have fought to their deaths for the righteousness which has set you free, and to call upon the Sacred Mysteries of the Trinity of God for consolation, renewal, resolve, and strength. This is not the time for war, there is no time for war between men when only their l *political sovereignty is at stake. The true battle that matters before God was begun twenty centuries ago when He asked you to be not unlike His only begotten Son, He who has been Crucified to take away the sins and the effects of the transgressions that you are seeing to this modern day, He who is still your Shield and Help in time of trouble. My children, the events of this past week did not begin in the hours, weeks, months, or years before they occurred; they began the moment that the Son of Man asked you to be perfect as He is perfect and proclaimed that anything short of that Divine perfection would result in certain devastation and annihilation. You are seeing history repeat itself inside a mortal parameter where good men continue to be silent about the Christian Gospel, and then call for the use of weapons of mass destruction in the wake of the awful effects of their own indifference.*

There are no comprehensible words that can truly mend the hearts of My children who have been so afflicted by the loss of those they love, only to know that they are now in the presence of the Creator of the universe, and to move ever so swiftly toward the Sacraments which will again make them whole. There is nothing in human grief that is of a lateral accord, other than to share it with your brothers and sisters, because such grief is always of the vertical elevation that belongs to the Heavens. Hereafter, your nation will forever be closer to the Paradise which engulfs the entire globe and clothes you in its Grace. Millions of people will hear My words of this day only long after I have given them, and another war has been commenced, only beyond the terrible explosions of new conflagrations and the counting of increasing tolls of casualties who will be numbered as being among the dead. I again tell you that there is no war short of dying for the Son of God that is worth the waging; for anything less than this is only vengeance, or the lion who will chase the flea who has bitten him and left a swelling mark on his flesh. There is only a false nature in the unity which springs from patriotism because constitutions and waving banners cannot take you to the pinnacles of holiness;

lx

lxx

lxxx

they are only distractions along the way to divert you from the true Will of God to remake the face of the Earth into the   xc *authentic likeness of the Holy Gospel through the Messiah who has redeemed you. Once the terrible years before you have passed into expiration, you will see that My words here today are the true orations which should have been lifted, along with the proper Requiem Masses which are already being offered in reflection of the commendation of the dead into the Holy Arms of God. Please seek your solace there, in your awareness that their battles are through, that their souls are now facing the Light, that they now number in the thousands among those who are praying for you from the*   c *other side of life.*

    List not those offenses that you will count among many for which you will seek justice, for Justice is a gift which only God can dispense, and you are a part of the Peace from which Justice is grown. Be the seeds of hope from which forgiveness may blossom; turn your other cheek and be the noble ones who must now have a newer sense of purpose in the Passion of Jesus Christ; and go not backward in revenge, but only forward to the meaningful reunion that all humankind will find in the Glory and compassion of His   cx *Sacred Heart someday. Thereupon, I pray for your consolation during these times of distress; I seek you to bask only in the happiness that you are all worthy in sharing the power of the Cross; and I call upon you to remember the meekness and determination of the Lamb of God Who has taken away the sins of the world by bowing in Grace before His persecutors and reminding them that, outside of time, they have already been defeated. This is not the moment for a shameless search delving into the portals of time-honored hatred or a reason to reclaim the limelight before the nations*   cxx *of the world. The American society, the sublime purposes of democracy, and your national pride have not been shamed by the events of this week, but only glorified and taken closer to the Throne of God. Let not your hearts be troubled by thoughts of retribution, lest you become equally as dark as*

the wretches who have brought you to tears. This is the age of the Resurrection of Jesus from the Grave, and it means for you to turn to Him instead of your arsenals of war. This is a testing moment when your hearts are shaking, rather than the underground where the detonation of other bombs would   cxxx
otherwise make the Earth to tremble by mistake. Wear your wounds of battle proudly for God, and know that He is your Peace. Come to Me, instead, all who are torn apart by the throes of human life, and I will truly take you to the Doorway of Heaven where the Prince of Peace will give you every sensation of Love for which you have yearned since you were only little children swinging on the playgrounds of your fathers' homes. Let this be your remembrance of this awful time! Call not upon your response to the hatred which has befallen you, for it has already been defeated by the   cxl
Messiah on the Cross. Go forward in the confidence that Jesus is the Providence of God who has chosen you, too, as His worthy Nation of many races to be united in Him once again.

     My dear Special son, I hope that you will transfer these words of consolation to your suffering people someday. They will be consoled both retroactively and in absentia for, by then, they will all accept that I began speaking to you on February 22, 1991. Please know that all of your thoughts about the terrible destruction in America being a portion of   cl
the conversion of humankind are true. God does not wish for death and horror to befall His people, but you can also see how many are only now coming to know Him from the first. I will cease speaking to you now in reverence for those who have passed into Jesus through My intercession. This is My holy blessing for you now, to be passed along to every soul who is alive in your country today. + Thank you for saying these prayers today! I will speak to you again very soon. This has been a very good week! I Love you. Goodnight!"

There are people who still possess the high hope that America can become a sterling example of common brotherhood and a catalyst for peace and good will around the globe; not a new world order per se, but a more sanctified whole, a union of piousness consecrated in Divine Love beneath the Cross of Jesus Christ. Numerous are the Christians who remain in vigilant awareness of the voice of the Holy Spirit within them, laboring in a silent martyrdom for a change of heart among the callous dregs of societies and civilizations. But, these holy people are not the individuals who believe that women have the right to kill the babies in their wombs before their births, or thereafter by strapping on bombs to murder complete strangers they perceive to be their enemies. They are not the materialistic empire builders or the flesh inebriated minions on night club stages. Neither are they wolfish judges and juries who believe that the execution of convicts who violate our public laws is justice as God ordains, nor are they the executive leaders who sympathize with invading and occupying other republics in order to spread our vacuous example of capitalist democracy. I harken to our earliest American immigrants. Have the hopes of our countrymen again become enslaved beneath the tyranny of colonial imperialism? The facts would render it no longer questionable that carnal and material captivity have befallen the true independence of the people of the United States, and have thrust us into a cyclical mindlessness of celebrity worship, egoism, and faddishness. It is evident that self-satisfying multitudes have succumbed without a fight to their own imbibing gullibility, becoming spiritual vagrants who have sold their last red cent of moral responsibility to the devil, standing verifiably hustled out of the value of their sanctified toils, and swindled of the noble attire their honorable forebears wove to deck the respectability of their temperance. Yet, the Queen of Heaven relentlessly calls each of us from the vaults of Heaven, petitioning us to ponder whether there survives even a morsel of character that has not been hocked by the lies of worldliness.

Sunday, February 13, 2005 (excerpt)   *3:04 p.m.*

"My little ones, while so many in your midst look   o(044)
skyward to discern what type of thunders the heavens choose
to roll, you turn instead to the Seat of Wisdom for eternal
knowledge. I invite you to continue to share the glories of
Paradise from your position in mortal time through My
intercession, until the moment when you shall join all the
Saints in that lasting benison of unending Light. I come to
you with great joy and hope today in the realization that My

people on Earth are bringing great cultivation to the world. You are changing the face of the Earth by embracing the Truth of God's Kingdom. Therefore, you are making this a special season of Lent for 2005. Please remember to include all the needy in your daily prayers, especially while you recite the Sacred Mysteries of the Most Holy Rosary. And, pray for Pope John Paul II as well. Yes, he does lead the Church with the vision of perfect Love in his heart. There will be no greater pope to live in your age, My children. Please heed his call to holiness, and defer to him in all ways. Protect his legacy to the death, and follow his teachings as you would the Word of God, Himself. The Holy Father is making his valedictory speeches as these waning days of his life continue to pass. When you think of peace and justice, remember that Pope John Paul II has been a prince among you for the elevation of the poorest of the poor. His call for peace is written everywhere, and only the just among you have chosen to respond. I ask you to stand-up for him when you hear the heretics of the world attempt to impugn his good name. All of this is the espousal of your own testament of righteousness on behalf of Jesus Christ. My Jesus mandates a Creation filled with purity and the decency about which He has spoken for centuries on end. He calls for your service without recompense, for humility despite the unsightly face of your enemies, and compassion even for those who persecute you. You are the children of this final age of time who are growing the sacred vestiges of the Saints for your own successors to pursue. When you recall the magnanimity of the sacrifices that the early Christians made, ponder how easy it is for you to live-out your convictions today. Here, especially in America, you enjoy the freedom of speech and expression. May the words of your mouths and the meditations of your hearts be acceptable in the sight of Almighty God."

x

xx

xxx

xl

Will our nation of paralyzed courage voluntarily suffer the hallowed marrow of our longevity to absolute extinction for false promises that will never sustain the nourishment of either our temporal contentment or our everlasting happiness? Are we a people who still possess a stabilizing sobriety of thought and action that cannot be swept away by nationalized rhetoric of civic superiority, or the mind-numbing timbre of the drums of battle, or the sycophantic premonitions of elected politicians predicting the demise of our "way of life" that have been irresponsibly launched into the winds of our public worldview? Are we going to be sieged into compliance with the unholy agendas of irrational war-mongers who attained office through a judicial coup d'etat, instead of the bonafide will of the people? Arousing the nationalistic passions of the civilian masses of any country without the most pristine of intentions has always proved to be one of the most irresponsible actions ever perpetrated by political leaders throughout history. Robert F. Kennedy once stated that the voice of the mob is madness. Horror appears from continent to island cove, and from the orbits above the Earth to the bunkers beneath the deserts when people blindly relinquish their thoughtful, reasoned composure to the unbridled passions of patriotism that are often whipped-up by radical ideologues with clandestine agendas whose scopes and breadths they could never convince a well-informed public to embrace. This is the sum total behind the worldwide leadership that has marked the opening of this new millennium. There is not a man alive who can rightly claim to be guided by the Spirit of Jesus Christ who acts in utter defiance against the sanctified guidance of the Supreme Pontiff in Rome prior to the outset of any military conquests. It is now an unarguable fact on the historical record that George W. Bush, his closest advisers, and the sparse number of world allies they cajoled into prosecuting the war against Iraq defied with outright impunity the wisdom of (the late) Holy Father, Pope John Paul II, a spiritual mountain of a man who once stared evil squarely in the eyes while experiencing the gruesome horrors and consequences of a monstrous, neo-pagan nationalism when his Polish homeland was ravaged by the lathered frenzy of a German military machine rumbling across Europe in direct contravention to any sound moral compass. George W. Bush, a supposedly pro-life president, native son of the West, a secular prince of a former democratic king, a man whom late-night comedians once said made Dan Quayle look like Britain's Winston Churchill, and who had done little more than grace the VIP suites at baseball games and preside as governor of Texas over the most inmate executions of any state in the history of the nation, could not summon the courage to withstand the inevitable retribution that would have been leveled against him by the secular media and the revenge-hungry electorate of America had he not figuratively spit in the face of one of the holiest and most visionary human beings to ever set foot on this planet, the Vicar of Christ, whom he publicly abandoned in the lineage of Pontius Pilate for fear of risking his political future. And, it was not him alone, but thousands of Catholics and other professed Christians, nay I say millions, had their obedience to their Savior pilfered by rogue priests, pastors, ministers, theologians and other disobedient demagogues who stood on their inflated egos and brash temperaments to debate the Holy Father's celestial Wisdom, arrogantly rebuffing his sanctified guidance when he authoritatively spoke for the Body of Christ against the evils, travails, and perils of illicit war, rejecting mercy to extract an eye before an eye was ever taken. Our Lady told me that this philosophy of life only renders both sides blind. It is intriguing how people, both worldly and religious alike, recognize the power in patriotic, secular unity for the advancement of war, but refuse to be awestruck by the unifying power of Sacred Scripture and Divine Catholic Tradition which have been sewn together into an impeccable fabric of perfection flowing-down from the Sacred Altar like a wedding train bridging the chasm of time. How many people believe their own wisdom and cerebral instability to be of greater depth and composure when making such profound decisions for the cohesion, course and outcome of the collective human race? Now hear this!—No one can even remotely remain in union with the Will of the Savior of the world or in communion with Divine Love while living in contradiction to the teachings of the Supreme Pontiff of the Roman Catholic Church; and America is going to learn this grief-stricken lesson as the tragedies of our country's diplomatic decisions continue to unfold, bringing the dark abyss of sorrow and loss to thousands of living rooms and door stoops, multiplying the moments of silence for the fallen, and increasing our collective wisdom through suffering instead of patience aforethought. Peace comes by being a peaceful, religious and merciful people. This is "our way of life" that has been stolen from us, not by terrorists, but by a marred sense of patriotism foisted upon us by leaders who can nevermore claim the title of peacemakers before the Throne of God. We must pray with passionate hearts that they may one day repent and be allowed to regain their title of children of Light because, in these time-bound moments, they have made themselves agents of the Antichrist.

Sunday, September 23, 2001   *1:47 p.m.*
"Every child of God who resides on the face of the   *k(266)*
Earth should consider it a grave dereliction of his spiritual
duties to fail to remember the repose of the souls of the
faithfully departed when attending the Holy Sacrifice of the
Mass. When you are numbering your blessings, you should
always count among them the Truth that your Savior listens

to your petitions for the betterment of the station of all people everywhere, inclusive of the living and the dead. Yes, this is the universal consideration which makes humanity whole, beyond and past the mortality that always falls at the feet of your Divine Creator for His greater Judgment. I have come again to this home, where two of My very pretty children live, to bless and guide you, to teach, to pray with you, and to seek your participation in the enlightenment of all the world about the power of the Holy Spirit. If ever a home was blessed, My children, it is this one! Please remember that this is not a reward for your past contributions toward the conversion of the world, but God's recognition that His Son will always be welcome here.

I wish for you to listen very carefully as I speak to you today, even more clearly than you may have in the past, because I know that the past weeks and ensuing months will try to be a great distraction from the work that we have set-out to do. If you are pulled into the ongoing discussions about the merits and demerits of international conflicts and political rhetoric, you will not fully understand Jesus' desires for you to remain at peace. Indeed, if the entire world had been admonished to this Wisdom long ago, there would be no such temporal discourse occurring in America today. Every soul on the face of the Earth should be concerned about the terrible words of the leader of the free world on September 20, 2001 as he and others were clamoring for a new global war to begin. This is no more than selfish vengeance at its best and the type of approach which will lead other nations into a global panic and world-wide anxiety. I have called more recently for all peoples of every race to return to prayer for consolation and not to arms for revenge. Sadly, however, My call is being ignored, and many millions are about to suffer the consequences as a result. Does the fate of the material world have to be this way? Of course not! The Almighty Father is a very merciful God of good will, and this is the response that He expects from those who profess to know Him. There is no such phenomenon as avenging an

x

xx

xxx

xl

evil if those who seek it also employ the practices of outright evil themselves. This kind of duplicitous action will lead only to greater destablization for those who are innocent of any wrongdoing. My prayerful request is that everyone will turn to Jesus in contrition and peace so that intercontinental conflict can be avoided by all means.

You have entered a changing season now, where there will be that new autumn reminiscence about which you have often written and proclaimed. My call is for you to remember that you must be an innocent society of peaceful hearts. When there are losses that try to take you to despair, your response should always be of prayerful contemplation, always! All of this talk about readying armies for conflict and drawing battlelines has little to do with international accord, and nothing to do with justice! Therefore, My call is for more offerings of sacrificial Love in the face of personal loss, for actions of reconciliation over those of retribution, and for the entire world to gather under the Cross to see what true Dominion really is. There is no pain that My Jesus has not known! Call upon Him during times of disappointment and personal agony, and He shall make both of them take leave of your individual lives! Is it possible that the Mother of God could admonish every soul on the face of the globe for not seeking the reversal of the call to arms that the United States is now enlisting of its forces? My response is that those who are preparing for war are entering a grave condition of sin. Listen well to those who are asking for penance and forgiveness, those who have for so long been praying for peace, whose advice is now and already being thrown aside. I ask the peoples of the world to consider the plight and future of the innocent millions who have nothing to do with governmental struggles or international policies which affect only those who decide where the wealth of the world will reside. Think of those whose plight will only be worsened when the destructive reign of unleashed armaments beings to unfold.

l

lx

lxx

I have built a mighty army of souls who are the true   lxxx
children of God, those whose destiny is to live for the
everlasting ages in Heaven with the King of all Creation.
My army has amassed a force of goodness that no evil can
affect or destroy, no matter what is deployed against it. No
one who belongs in My army can visit or encamp the horror
and terror that the faithless will see as the years continue to
pass, because My legions of children have already been led to
Victory in the Sacred Heart of My Son. I say to you today, if
you wish to amass an invincible lot of souls who can destroy
any evil in its path, take-up your Holy Rosary and get in   xc
line! There are many good souls who are working quite long
and hard to help those who are afflicted these days, from
infirmary to triage; and I must tell you that there are Saints
in great numbers who are making the charge for peace where
there are only the echoes of war. They know what suffering
is like; they understand the hollow calls for bloodshed and
violence anew! When you make peace instead of stooping to
the ignorant bias of battle and knife, you move even closer to
the nobility and humility that Jesus has asked of you.
Therefore, find your peace in Him; enlist His command to be   c
your guide, heed the lessons of the New Covenant Gospel,
remember the sacrifices of the Saints, be faithful to the
miracles of the Sacraments, place your futures along the lines
of Grace, imitate the temperance of the Christ of all blessings,
and take every concern in your lives to God in prayer. I tell
you today, by the time you have done these things, there will
be no momentary or present requirements for war, and no
desire to prosecute a campaign of conflict against your
neighbors. When you remember how great is the God of
Abraham, you will remember the call to Peace that His Son   cx
has placed before you in His Sermon on the Mount. When
you stand high atop the mountain of absolution someday, He
will ask you if you served His people by taking them to the
foyer of pardon, rather than to the docks in defeat.

If only I could turn the attention of every soul alive
to the Mystical experience of perfect Love, that you might

stand and pray at the foot of the Cross until you fall to your knees in final understanding, you will tear-down the walls of your own skyscrapers and burn your stocks and bonds in the furnaces of your worst enemies to keep their spirits warm. cxx *Once the nations of the world realize that compromise is no substitute for absolute Love, even though it may temporarily resolve a boiling conflict, then you will know who God is. It is more important to eliminate the desire for hatred than it is to refrain from exercising it from the start. Hatred is evil; revenge is the work of Satan, and any nation that practices either of them for their own individual advancement has no place in the Kingdom of Paradise. There are chastisements that are in place to change the hearts of humankind, but I must tell you that the destruction which you have seen to* cxxx *date around the globe pales by comparison to those chastisements, should God decide to dispense them to His unwary people. The things you suffer now are no more than a mild breeze compared to the cyclone that Jesus is about to bring upon those who continue to cast His holiness aside. Please remember that My Motherhood is one of Love and compassion for all of My children, and this is the reason that I am telling you these things.*

Those who oppose the Sacred Mysteries of the Holy Roman Catholic Church are an impediment to human cxl *Salvation! Let there be no mistake; theirs is a bleak future if they do not enlist the faith required to understand what God wants from those who will live in Paradise with Him! A rejection of the Truth of the Holy Eucharist portends a horrible future for those who attempt to desecrate its purity! If you continue to ponder the reasons for the inexplicable violence in America today, it is because those who live across this blessed land are refusing to bow before the Most Holy Eucharist! My call for prayer, fasting, penance, confession, and conversion is being ignored by a nation of people who* cl *are being blinded by three colors of a banner with stars and stripes they are wrapping around their eyes. The victory you seek is not found therein! It is found inside your hearts! It is not the false unity of a government of people, it is the Truth and destiny in the Son of God! This is where you should place your sights, because it is upon your hearts that He has placed His own. I promise you with the authenticity of the Divine Nature of your Redemption, itself, that those who travel any other pathway than this which has been laid-out by Jesus are quite the errant ones; and such error will*   clx *continue to yield untold suffering and injustice inside the borders of your continent and the world at large. I plead with you to understand and comply with all that I have told you here today, for there is no one who lives today in America who has seen the true Glory of the Coming of the Lord!*

    My Special son, I hope that you understand the need for Me to address the issues that I have today because there is great disharmony and fear ongoing in your land right now. Your brothers and sisters are weeping from grief and crying-   clxx *out for revenge. The former is redressed by their faith and understanding, the latter must be expunged from occurring at all. I thank you mightily for taking time to pray with Me again today, that you have such foresight to know that only Jesus can bring the restoration and consolation that is so missing around you now. I ask you to remember that you and your brother are larger souls than to be shaken from your mission for Me, even if the battles arrive within inches of your front door... This is My blessing for you now. + Thank you for your prayers! You are My little ambassadors! I Love*   clxxx *you. Goodnight!"*

We protract offensive warfare because our faith in the Prince of Peace never seems to take the leap of courage from the futile squalls of vengeance into the heroic realms of peaceful coexistence, depriving us of the sinews that would otherwise allow us to invoke the better angels of our nature, as Abraham Lincoln once said. Our basic instincts for exacting revenge and retaliation would have us believe that the order of the universe somehow demands an equal and opposite reaction to every unpleasant circumstance or interpersonal conflict we encounter, or becomes thrust upon us. Wild beasts do as much. In many quarters of America, our countrymen have become utterly ruthless when adjudicating the societal and global consequences of our fragile nature. We routinely dispose of human beings created in the image and likeness of God with outright impunity, casting their lives into the throes of unimaginable desperation and hopelessness, whether it be through our penal systems or capitalist oppression. People who are exploited and poverty-stricken will be the first to enter Paradise, and multitudes of repentant death row inmates will be welcomed into Heaven long before the right-wing, judicial partisans and prosecutors who disposed of them into long-forgotten obscurity in the dustbins of the world's dungeons and prisons. Jesus Christ teaches that the miracle of restoration and unity for any nation of peoples is found on the farther side of the chasm where forgiveness, forbearance, and exoneration shimmer with the highest honor. Yet, we seem to inevitably stand amongst our carefully crafted weaponry, targeting where they must be strewn to their most destructive effects, because our fallen nature is repulsed when asked to mount the Holy Cross and bear the inflictions of our mutually-shared brokenness. Imagine what damage the Son of God could have done to this world while wielding the full power of the Omnipotent Deity if He would have responded to the mocking call of his executioners by stepping down from the Cross and dispensing His absolute vengeance. The withered fig tree in the Gospels is our parable. No one but His Virgin Mother would have survived the purging if He had wanted to eradicate sin from the Earth in that solemn instant. I learned this lesson of indelible peace one time from a young man named Jeff Buhl, an underclassman I knew from my years at Ashland High School in Illinois. His family was not wealthy, and I'm unsure whether he was even close to being the best academic performer in his class. If he was, no one would have known it by looking at him. But, he was one of the most friendly, kind-hearted people anyone could ever meet. He had a self-deprecating sense of humor, someone who could laugh at himself in a flash for something foolish he may have done. To be honest, I wish I would have taken the time to get to know him better, because soon after high school, God called him home to Heaven; and I know why. His life here had been completed by bringing the image of Jesus to perfection in a brilliant moment that has now become a timeless lesson for humanity through a charitable gift of his benevolent heart. I was standing outside the main portico of our high school building one day in the spring of my senior year with some friends, where we were congregating after lunch before being called back to class. The weather was beautiful then, and several dozen of my classmates and I kidded amongst ourselves, trying to keep the horseplay to a minimum, when another young man became upset with Jeff for personal reasons. It was over nothing really significant, but this angry kid unexpectedly struck Jeff flush in the face with his doubled-up fist. The unrestrained brutality of the act made my soul bristle with anticipation to be the next one to throw a punch in retaliation against this bully's senseless physical-aggression. But, before I could even flinch, Jeff shrugged-off the offense and turned his compassionate face toward his assailant saying, "You're my friend, I'm not going to fight you," whereupon the angry classmate struck him point-blank in the jaw with his fisted-hand again. And, without a hint of anger, revenge or aggression in his voice, my angelic friend turned a gentle gaze toward his attacker once more and said with resolute calmness and placid determination, "I'm not going to fight you." Then, almost unimaginably, he was struck in the face a third time, and delivered the same merciful response again. Their altercation ended without another word. The aggressor could perpetrate no more violence because Jeff's peacefulness and composure rendered his physical abuse to be absolutely useless; and he walked-away, disarmed and humiliated, while the rest of us returned to class not really believing the spiritual humility we had just been privileged to see. And, to this day, my soul cherishes Jeff's magnificent example in my heart because it touched me with such beatific light; and my eyes well with tears when I recall it today. My heart holds the highest-tiered admiration in honor of Jeff Buhl because I know my vision that day fell upon one of the greatest human heroes who ever lived. He extolled self-possessed grace to the fullest! I was face-to-face with the finely hewn, impenetrable power of a human heart filled with genuine good will, supported like a fortress with Divine love. We all witnessed perfection in Jeff during those spring days of 1980, and God took him unto Himself soon after that, because what more could this prodigy of Love have done to magnify Jesus Christ with any more sanctified brilliance? Therefore, America, what say we don the courage of my late friend, and set a new course toward the spiritual perfection he achieved?

Sunday, December 15, 2002   *2:22 p.m.*

"Indeed, I have sought the intercessional Providence   l(349)
of the Love of God on your behalf because, knowing Him
well, it is clear that there are many blessings still residing in
Heaven that He will dispense to you upon your prayerful
invocations. When I come to you to pray, My children, it is
always in thanksgiving because you are more holy than the
time before, your petitions are focused more upon the plight
of the suffering, and the conversion which is worthy of all
humankind stands with much greater clarity. You are
walking gently upon the ground because you know that   x
charity begins in your meekness—not in some cowardly

way—but in the peaceful intellect that is the Wisdom of the Holy Spirit. I speak to you today during the mid-season of Advent to remind you that your anticipation of the Return of Jesus in Glory to take your souls to Heaven must become the enveloping reason why you bask in the Light of His Birth. There are too many who continue to wonder why the West is so entangled in the materialism that has brought such destruction upon your country. Other nations around the world who espouse Christianity look at the United States of America with shame and horror to know how you have perverted the true meaning of Christmas. At a time when Jesus is asking His disciples to embrace the Spirit and abandon the flesh, Americans everywhere are diving more deeply into corporeal matters, an inexplicable infatuation with material possessions, and a brash reluctance to receive the Sacrament of Reconciliation. Whatever happened to the grand nation whose forefathers would build their freedom upon? Where now is the trust and honesty that were integral parts of the development of a country of peace and justice? You can see now, My little ones, why they are eluding you! Please do not allow anyone else's desire for material things to distract you from the Nativity of the Prince of Peace. Be on guard against those who would offer you tangible goods in exchange for your fond favor toward them during the Solemnity of Christmas. I am asking for your understanding that the Birth of My Son is meant to take your hearts and souls closer to humility, self-denial, chastity, and to the Sacred Beatitudes which will eventually transform your land into the real city on a hill that will draw the lost into the piety of the followers of God.

    It is not enough, it would seem, that the horrible events that befall America are cast aside as the hatred and misunderstanding of another human race; but to vengefully use massive forces against them in retribution even makes your country more ugly in the eyes of the Heavenly Father. Let Me assure you on the date which is only ten days away from the celebration of Christmas, if the people of the United States enter their cathedrals, churches, and sanctuaries asking

xx

xxx

xl

for the peaceful blessing of Jesus Christ on the occasion of the   *l*
recognition of His Nativity and thereafter set-out to prosecute
another war of military aggression against your perceived
enemies, the retaliation that will be brought against you from
them will be unprecedented in the history of all humankind!
It is not My intention to frighten you with these words
because they will reach the ears of those for whom they are
intended long-past sufficient time to alter the course of
modern events. But, know for the record of history that I
have given them, so that when God justifies His vengeance
against America on any number of future occasions, you will
all know why. My Jesus is angered and sorrowful by the way   *lx*
the people of the United States have turned their backs on
the unborn, the poor, and the homeless. What nation on
Earth would expend billions of dollars in capital wealth to
utilize armaments to slaughter tens of thousands of innocent
children overseas in the name of political revenge instead of
using those monies to keep your own little children from
freezing to death in their homes, on the streets, and hidden in
abandoned cars and cardboard boxes in alleyways and
basements beneath bars and brothels? If the leaders of the
United States of America wish to see true justice, then all   *lxx*
they need to do is wait for the Son of Man to return and see
their actions tossed with justifiable Wrath into the fires of
Gehenna. What He shall do with their souls is a matter for
His Divine Mercy and the Final Judgment to come.

It is one of the aspects of the world that makes Me a
Sorrowful Mother to be required to tell you these things.
Imagine how the Hosts of Heaven are looking upon you!
What must they be saying about a nation that has
proclaimed the Most Blessed Virgin Mary to be its Patroness
Saint, and then live in a way that defies almost everything   *lxxx*
that Her Crucified Son gave His Life for? I will tell you at
a later date because, like the faithful of the Church, I am
praying with you that certain circumstances will be
eliminated and mitigated before I am forced to place such a
reprehensible text into discernable words. I do not wish to
tell you that there are millions of Americans whose souls are

on the pathway to perdition, as true as it would seem to be!
I wish I could make it clear to you that all souls are blessed,
and that they are equally praising God in the way that He
has prescribed in the Sacred Scriptures. It would give Me   xc
great elation to describe the United States as the perfect
union of freedom and prosperity, but I cannot! These things
are obvious to those who know Jesus well, but seem to be a
source of great irritation—even a distraction—to the people
whose choices are made only by what they can gain. We
pray for these people because they are the ones who are now
the farthest from Grace. They are the reason why innocent
victims are suffering here and around the globe. I tell you
again—My Son is not going to allow this callous disregard for
His Crucifixion and Resurrection to continue for very much   c
longer.

Our Lady then made mystical allusions to terrible occurrences that
God would allow to come upon us if we did not convert our
hearts.

...and then the entire platform of selfishness upon which the
Western capitalist system is built will come crumbling to the
Earth. Please understand Me without any confusion about
what I am going to tell you now...in the scope of the Eternal
Vision of the Justice of God, it will be a good day! For
Christianity! For the retrieval of goodness, piety, and
prayerfulness in a nation that has chosen to abandon all
three! Who would come forth to say that the Mother of God
would never speak of such horrific destruction only ten days   cx
prior to Christmas? Let that man approach His Holy Mother
and justify the silence of the people of Light in a nation
where such is lauded by members of the media, corporate
executives, and lazy clergy everywhere! Let a man who has
an ounce of righteousness in his bones approach the
Immaculate Virgin Mary and say that God does not have the
right to sanctify all 50 states in the matter of an instant on a
bright sunshiny afternoon, and then let the poorest of the
poor around the globe pump their fists in the air that the

great devourer in the West has finally been slain! I dare   cxx
say—let any holy man approach Me and say that the United
States of America does not deserve to be castigated...for
having killed millions upon millions of its own unborn
children in their mothers' wombs outright, with malice
aforethought and ruthless indifference. If the American
people so fear the terrorism of other sinners, they have not
seen chastisement on a massive scale until the God of their
fathers repays them for embracing the evils of Satanic works
with seeming joy and jubilation... When the Holy Fires and
Silver Sword of Justice return to the modern world at the
Sacred Hands of Jesus Christ to end the element of time,   cxxx
sinners of all stripes who will then see the Truth with perfect
clarity will bow at His Holy Feet and beseech Him '...slay
me first! Please, slay me first!' They will look back upon the
peaceful Nativity of Jesus through a much different set of eyes
then! And, they will have nothing of material wealth to
protect them from the devastation which will become their
daily mantra for the rest of the ages!

My children, I have given you no new revelations
today than that which you have already anticipated because
you can clearly see the condition of the world. The   cxl
possessions of other men are immaterial as far as the spiritual
Truth is concerned. They are like millstones around their
necks, balls and chains that will keep them from running
into God's Kingdom as though they had the fleeting swiftness
of the Angels. I beg you during the latter portion of this
Advent Season to never relent in your pursuit of Justice on
behalf of the Cross. I ask you to gain strength in the
knowledge that you are living in the age of the Resurrected
Christ! Be humble when you know it is fitting, be bold when
circumstances warrant, and slay the opposition to your   cl
holiness as though you had silver bayonets in your hands.
You are the members of My Army of Souls for Jesus. You are
the warriors who search for peace by rooting-out those who
live in such hypocrisy against the New Covenant Gospel.
You are activists in the culture of Life! And, I assure you
that what you shall bind on the Earth in the Name of Jesus

for the advancement of Divine Human Love shall also be bound by God in Paradise. These are the sacred promises by which you have lived before, the very faith that you have taken to heart in many times past; and it is the precise perfection in which you will also deliver your spirits over to God upon the happy occasion of your deaths so He will receive you in Jesus' Arms for deliverance to your mansions of beauty with and alongside the Angels and Saints. So, why is Christmas such a holy time, one of peace, a period of reflection of the silence in which Jesus Christ was born? Because the Baby who came into the world like a Lamb will terminate the evil in it soon like a roaring Lion!

clx

My Special son, thank you for praying with Me today and receiving these words on behalf of a suffering humanity—those whose lives are left in ruins by the many around them who are taking more than their share. You have been told by the likes of Saint Thomas the Patriot that you should pay your own way, make the world a better place than when you first discovered it, and pray like the dickens that Jesus Christ will take your soul to Heaven when you finally die. These wishes are rather appropriate as the world moves to its conclusion. I wish for you to gain strength in what I have told you, to not care whether anyone approaches you with any hints that you are a dignitary in their midst, and that you can sense with better perception that everything that causes a tint of darkness to form around your heart is being slowly but surely destroyed by the work you are doing for Me here... I wish for you to always remember that the world would be poorer in Spirit and hope if not for your having given your life to Jesus... This is your holy blessing from your Mother now. + I will speak to you again very soon! I Love you! Goodnight!"

clxx

clxxx

cxc

Could it possibly be true that the United States of America has finally provoked the heavens into showing utter disdain for us by requiring the most benevolent creature who has ever set foot on this planet to issue such flaming rebukes from Her Queenly Throne in the vaults of the High Kingdom? The irrefutable answer is "Yes!" Human arrogance has reached its zenith, and it now has the misfortune of being crushed beneath Her Immaculate Heel without so much as a buffer-zone or respite of retrieval. So many of the faithful flock have contemplated for decades the meaning in the prophecies of the Triumph of the Immaculate Heart of Mary, and by what intonation that occurrence will be brought to fruition. The words I have delivered from the Matriarch of the Universe are revelatory in answering and clarifying these questions. Our worldly existence was never meant to be an immoral free-for-all of spiritual contradiction by which we oppose, slander, demean and mock the Perfect Life manifested by God in His Son, Jesus Christ. Those who refuse to accept Him by emulating His virtuous and sanctified personification will be separated as indignant goats from among the sheep and chaff from the fruitful grain, discarded thereafter to blazing destruction in the horrific fires of Eternal Damnation. The Lord of Creation will thunder, *"Away from me! Enter into Hell, the place prepared for you! For when I was hungry, you gave me no food. When I was thirsty, you gave me no drink. When I was a stranger, you gave me no welcome. When I was naked, you did not clothe me. When I was ill and in prison, you did not comfort me. I declare to you now, whenever you did not do it for the least, you did not do it for Me!"* And, how is one befallen by this infernal destiny outside of time? Beyond any doubt, by becoming immersed in the rancid abomination of the dreaded culture of death in the United States of America. Think about it! Spiritual condemnation is a decisive, universal consequence that is only avoided by our repentance and renewed allegiance to the Crucified Messiah whom the Creator of the Universe dispatched to save us from this same Divine Judgment. Jesus Christ is "Sacrifice" personified! He is Love Incarnate! Human sin reeks of the anti-Sacrifice because it is anti-Love! Our obedience to heavenly virtue is the yoke of nobility. Only a babbling fool would declare that if someone rejects Holy Wisdom, Hell will not swallow him! But, is this not the mantra of people who wish to convince humanity that God is so merciful that He would never condemn the wicked? They simply wish to invoke a license to sin without conscience, while demanding they not be required to endure a redeeming syllable breathed upon their dead souls. The only question that remains is where we go from here. I say, for my part and to those who will listen, let us return to the daylight! Prayer, contemplation, meditation, conversion, sanctification, service, and sacrifice are the mainsails of our spiritual vessel! Let us depart from this abyss and set our course for the crest of divinity, out of the dismal reaches of militarism, away from the dim shunt of our dubious future, toward the restoration of purity and light. Let us rise to greet the everlasting dawn! Awaken, my friends! In the Name of Jesus Christ, the Messiah and King, I say, rise! Christians unite! Protest no more! Have the courage to repair the breach of your 16th century predecessors by your humble sacrifices to God! Heaven is calling to its prodigal sons and daughters, "Return!" Live and extol the convincing witness of our Resurrected Messiah—"that they may be one!" Announce the presence of His Immaculate Queen, and gather in peace at the site of His Holy Sacrifice, beneath the Cross, in communion at the Sacred altars of the Roman Catholic Church!

Sunday, December 29, 2002   *2:22 p.m.*
Octave of Christmas, Feast of the Holy Family
     "My little children, I wish to speak only for a few   l(363)
moments—only for time-sufficient to tell you that My Love for you is as wholly and Holy profound today as it was when we began our intense work for Jesus many years ago. Therefore, I come to you in an appreciative tone to offer you the thanksgiving of the Lord, to assure you that neither time nor circumstance can divide or separate you from Him now. You have been the warriors for a Kingdom of Holiness that is only now growing wider because of your dedication. This will be My final message of 2002, but I assure you there will   x
be as many as the Almighty Father will allow into the future. What can be said of 2002? It would never be improper to tell you that the world is more shapely in Divine Love by your works and prayers. I assure you that your piety and service have borne the fruit of consolation for tens of thousands of agonizing souls, the food of compassion for innocent priests around the world, and the first step for millions more on their pathway back to Grace. You live in a nation that is yet celebrating the Octave of Christmas, but is speaking of war—military aggression against foreign lands   xx
such as Afghanistan, Iraq, and North Korea, and this only days past the celebration of Christmas. How ironic it is that your country celebrates the anniversary of the Prince of Peace by coveting warfare as a means of international diplomacy, so much so that your government is now wishing to reshape the steel from the fallen World Trade Center

Towers into a brand new warship named the USS New York. All the talk about world peace from the United States is a hollow lie. You only wish to conquer the enemies of your own consumerism, materialism, your assumed right to strip your unborn children of the gift of life, and to placate those who refuse to stand-up to your obstinance against the Commandments of God. This, My children, is the legacy of America for 2002, but your work here for the King of Love, My Jesus, has been the mitigation of many ills. I have been praying with you while you have written your memoirs about your obedience to Me, about the righteousness that needs to come to your land if it is ever to be the likeness of Paradise.

xxx

My commendation transcends your physical works on behalf of God to include the meditations of your hearts and the words of your mouths which have been the instruction of sinners in the ways of Wisdom. I beg you with a Motherly pleading to not give-up the fight now. I am with you for all and everything that is of God. I hold you dear to My Immaculate Heart for all the reasons you have been Baptized into the Catholic faith. Indeed, I will be with you through the end of time and upon your entrance into Heaven to live with Me and all the Saints, cast brilliantly inside and within the Divine Domain of the Holy Trinity. Providence has you doing these things with Me because you are creatures of a Love so omnipotent that you cannot escape the breadth of God's grasp. You belong to Him and He to you in this Love, so that by waking to every new dawn with your mission for Him in your hearts and spread across the expanse of your thoughts, your lives are the living legend of the conversion of the entirety of humankind. Let there be no mistake—the Holy Spirit has done this in you, and I have been your advocate before Jesus to keep your Love aright. There is no weakening in the resolve of the blessed—although there may be dark moments sometimes—your goals and objectives are clearly to the enlightenment of Creation to its Eternal Redemption in the Blood of the Cross. All of this will live

xl

l

lx

well beyond your own mortal days, past the closure of the ages, and into the infinity which is the power of God. You share it now within the parameters of time because you are the contemporary Saints who are expressing the Will of God to the modern mortal world. I tell you again that there are things you cannot comprehend about the actions of other men, but the Sacred Mysteries of the meaning of human life lxx *have all become clear to you now. Thank you for rendering your writings about the Kingdom I have tried to describe to you only in words, for your profound expressions have become the way in which untold millions of people are returning to God.*

    My Special son, I thank you, I thank you, I thank you. I know not what else to say. My Love for you and your brother has no boundaries, and all the adjectives in your language still leave Me speechless as to describe how you are blessed. There are still so many things to do, so many more lxxx *words and sentences to connect in the process of bringing the knowledge of God to your fellow men. It is all in you now, and it will come out if only you will disregard the seemingly everlasting dailiness of human life. There is only one more mountain that you need to climb, and it is the very sorrow that keeps you from understanding what I am telling you with greater revelation. There is peace in the world, but humanity will not search for it. There also is healing, consolation, international cooperation, and Divine courage. You and your brother are helping My many other messengers* xc *around the globe to make clear the good faith of Jesus to deliver His people to the New Jerusalem with their absolved souls intact. We seek for this to occur earlier rather than later, and with their contrition rather than their arrogance. But, you can see wherein lies the fight when things are not this way. You have already won, and you will win. Jesus has already returned, but not yet. Therefore, go into 2003 with the realization that you have lifted your feet onto the next higher step toward the transformation of the Earth into the likeness of Heaven. I shall never remove My protective* c

Mantle from above your souls or your very lives because you belong to Me. You are My living possessions. You, indeed, are My children. And, I am your Immaculate Mother whose Love knows no end; My determination has nothing in Creation to block My success, and the dreams you hold for the future world will all come true in the Triumph of My Immaculate Heart. I do not tell you these things to give you false hope or to somehow get you through the darkness of night without really telling you the Truth. My messages to you for nearly twelve years have been candid and open. I cx *have reprimanded both you and your brother when the occasions were ripe, and I have given you praise over all other things. And, this is the reason I have come to you briefly today, to give you the prime assurance that your God is pleased with you. Thank you, again, for responding to My call. I know you are happy to be in Love with Him... You are the champion caretaker of the greatest nobility. This is now your holy blessing. + I will speak to you again very soon! Thank you! Please remember to pray for the unborn, for the end of poverty and disease, and for all the other* cxx *petitions we both hold so close to My Son. I Love you! Goodnight!"*

There are those who would wait for a time-bomb to detonate beneath their living room recliners before taking anyone's word that the ticking they hear is a harbinger of their imminent doom. Well, the hands on the clock of the explosive Love of the King of Creation have just clicked to their vertical pose, and the counter is flush with zeros across its luminous display. Each message from the Immaculate Heart of Heaven's Queen is an ominous stroke of Eternity which has commenced the tolling sequence of the high-noon reckoning of mankind with God. Therefore, I shall proceed with hope and confidence in the Blessed Assumption of Mary to renew this evangelic message in an attempt to jostle untold sinners into reconsidering the majestic nature of our familial bonds within the Catholic Faith-Church on Earth, hoping for a collective realization that each and every soul around the globe is called to be an active participant in human Redemption at the Altar of Sacrifice through a consortium of charity and self-denial for the sake of loving humankind enmasse. Peace comes only through the strength of God, and prayer invokes the wielding of His power.

Sunday, March 23, 2003   *2:18 p.m.*

"With all the Grace from Heaven by which Creation   m(082)
has been blessed, I have come to pray with you for world
peace. These are the difficult hours about which men of
peace have told you since the first shot was fired in the war
of human sinfulness so many ages ago. My children, when
we pray for the reaffirmation of the hearts of the lost to be
regained by Glory again, let us not forget to include those
who claim to be united in the Sacred Heart of Jesus who are
only murmuring His Holy Name while they seek materialism
and disgrace for themselves. It is a very dangerous world   x
where there lives a lot of free people whose culture does not
allow them to see the reasons for defense of the enemies they
despise. Such is the misunderstanding that accompanies a
globe so large, with so many regions, and with so many
values and assumptions about the role of God in the
reclamation of man. Today, you can readily see the ongoing
conflagration about which I spoke on September 16, 2001.
Why has this come to be? Because of the vengeful nature of
humanity. It has come because too many will not exhaust all
avenues of peaceful unity. And, now, too many thousands of   xx
innocent people are paying a terrible price. The ongoing war
that the United States and its allies are prosecuting in the
Middle East is an outright mortal sin. It is the collective
efforts of a republic which has given its wiser side to the
skullduggery of Hell. While I am the Patroness of America,
I am weeping mournful tears of sorrow because My people
will not heed My call for peace and unification. My little
ones, please keep this message in a place of safe keeping
because, soon, the United States will pay deeply and dearly
for this onslaught of naked military aggression. How can the   xxx
leaders of the West be so adamant about eradicating the
oppression of other societies when its own people are
enchained in the horrific effects of material wealth, lust,
arrogance, and lack of spirituality? How dare anyone
proclaim that God has shed His Grace on Thee! You will see
more accurately that He will dispense His Holy Wrath upon*

your lands instead! I do not bring messages of doomsday
cults or the rubbish of the darker age. I am speaking about
the Truth of the present-day world in which the haughty
isolationists who inhabit the United States of America are   xl
fighting only for the right to spread its capitalism to the rest
of the continents...

People will say '...How can the humble and meek
Mother of Jesus Christ issue such a stern condemnation of the
freest nation on the Earth?' My response to them is that I
have seen the very God whose Wrath is justly waiting in the
wings. I have heard the mourning of the pious little children
of Light all over the world who look to the West in sorrow.
I hear the groaning of Creation under the burden that the
United States of America has placed upon it by the   l
horrendous weight of it sins against the dignity of life!
Americans kill helpless unborn children in their mothers'
wombs and call it the right of free choice. They allow the
poor to die of starvation in their own streets and in ghettos
around the globe and call it self-imposed poverty. They
inject poison into the veins of poor lost sinners and call it
secular justice. My children, I have been dispatched by the
God of your fathers to tell you without equivocation that He
calls all of these the actions of a country that is wholly under
the influence of Satan. All the speeches about freedom and   lx
international dignity are the product of a hollow rhetoric
that is dying into the dust. Indeed, tell those who might
proclaim that the Mother of their God would not be filled
with such disdain for America that they have never been
more wrong in their lives! I will weep! I will cry tears of
sadness when God allows His Holy Justice to rain absolute
horror onto the land of the free and home of the brave. You
are the land of the obstinate and the lifeless! You espouse the
culture of death so that you can nourish only your own life!
Yes, I will weep because too many generations have passed   lxx
without any response to My apparitions. I am telling you
that the future will be filled with deep agony for Americans
everywhere, and it will be a necessary function of the

cultivation of the West that so many will suffer. Am I telling you this so as to prophesy a new kind of chastisement? Please pray with Me, and God will give you the answer.

My Special one, you have seen with your own eyes the destruction and lack of concern for innocent human life that is ongoing in the war in Iraq. This entire conflict is based upon political and financial motivations! We pray together that more and more will come to understand this as the weeks ahead continue to unfold... Thank you for saying your prayers together with Me today... This is My blessing for you both now. + I will speak to you again next week! I Love you... Goodnight!"   *lxxx*

Since such Divine warning has been invoked, know that it originates in the righteous Truth which resonates from the Sacred Heart of Christ the King, and finds its compassionate culmination in Divine Mercy, where penitent people have always surrendered to the magnificent articulation of Love, and found perpetual absolution. Our final Judgment will be sealed with the spikes of our own arrogance if we fail to read the signs of the times and convert our hearts to Jesus. No greater premonition of the unveiled Truth could have been granted than the vision given humanity upon the passing of Pope John Paul II and the majesty of the succession to the Pontifical Throne the world witnessed at the Vatican in Rome.

Sunday, April 24, 2005   *2:58 p.m.*
Dedicated to the Papacy of Pope Benedict XVI
    "Now, My little children, you are living in the year of   *o(114)*
Pope Benedict XVI, and your journey toward Heaven is much closer than when it first began. I am the bringer of Great News in that you have continued to be chosen to enlighten your brothers and sisters about the supremacy of God and the provisions He has made for your exculpation and deliverance to the mansions of Paradise. As you ponder how the future months and years will unfold, I ask you to pray for the intercession of the predecessors to My holy Pope Benedict XVI. Indeed, call upon the strength and Wisdom   *x*
that took Saint Peter to martyrdom in the name of human

absolution. Today has been dedicated to the installation of Pope Benedict XVI, and represents the opening of Eternity even wider for the conversion of lost souls to the Grace of Almighty God. Jesus has planned for His Church to live into its present hour since the beginning, and it would be too rhetorical to assert that the Papacy of Benedict XVI will be more brief than that of John Paul the Great. As you have moved past the age of 40, both of you have been allowed to see the many transformations of the modern era that will lead to the culmination of all the ages. You have seen histories of terrible wars and the burdens that have been placed on innocent lives. You have fought against the evil forces that have besieged your ancestors and tried to take from them that very peace for which your hearts still yearn. Throngs of agnostics have assaulted your characters, and evildoers of all stripes are yet attempting to bring ruination to your good names. Even in the wake of these things, I ask you to bear forward in the acknowledgment that your victory in Jesus has already been won. There is great hope in the world today, little ones, because the Shepherd that Jesus has chosen to lead His flock is a tried and true Roman Catholic Christian who will not change his stripes according to the direction of the wind. My Pope Benedict XVI comes from a lineage of courageous fighters, and his honorable service to the Faith Church on Earth will be so admired that he will be long hailed as one of the greatest Pontiffs to ever reign at the Holy See. Therefore, this is a very good day for Heaven and Earth.

I ask of My children today that you pray for My new Pope. Ask Jesus to keep his spirits always aloft and give him the Light of Justice as his guide. Pray that no one would ever attempt to take him from this world until his service to God is through, and that Jesus will uphold his dignity as in the greatest servants in the days of old. Please tell humanity, My children, that Pope Benedict XVI has the kind and gentle heart that is most reflective of Jesus than anyone who has ever been elevated to the Papacy. He loves....O' how this

xx

xxx

xl

Pope loves Jesus' people. He understands the oppression that befalls those who live in places where human freedom is oftentimes ignored. He has held fast to the Faith, he has been a pillar in a wavering world, he has fought the good fight against the liberal forces wishing to dilute the Traditions of the Church, he has suffered greatly over the inequities between peoples and nations, he has given his life to the spreading of the Holy Gospel, he has prayed like none before him for the conversion of the lost, he has been unselfish in giving to the poor, he has been the most reflective about God's creatures since the great Saint Francis of Assisi, and now, at long last, he has become the Vicar of Christ on the Earth! He is more than your Holy Father now, he is the very imitation of the Son of Man incarnate in the world. And, how I love this Pope! How My Immaculate Heart pines that My people will embrace this Holy Father with the admiration of the Angels! He is My Pope! He is My gift to you! He is your intercessor to the Hosts of Heaven by his very invocation. His blessing will grant you the Plenary Indulgence that can shake the worst evil from the depths of any man! I ask that you give him your hearts, your souls, your spirits, and your dedication. Love My Pope like you love Jesus, Himself, because he will lead you during his brief Papacy to the foyer of the Promised Land of everything you have ever wanted from the Throne of God.

    My Special and Chosen ones, you have witnessed on April 19, 2005 that majesty, mystery, and mysticism of the Roman Catholic Church in the election of the 264th successor to Saint Peter. And, he has presided over an installment Mass in the past few hours that moved the heavens to tears of joy. His homiletics are utterly profound pronouncements of Eternal Truth that issue from the lips of God. When you think of every impassioned admiration that you held for Pope John Paul the Great, prepare to treble that fondness, love, and devotion for Pope Benedict XVI. He is the future of your faith in the Church, your vision of human Salvation for all the world, and your source of ecclesial guidance for his

l

lx

lxx

lxxx

tenure in Rome. Watch carefully how he is received as he travels the world. Pray for the protestors who might heckle at the utterance of his name, because they are under the influence of evil legions. I know that both of you are true to your trust in Jesus and the infallibility of the Holy See. It will not be difficult for you to continue in your seamless service to My Sacrificed Son under the guidance of your new Pope. Your work for Me is yet incomplete. You have many more prayers to recite, miraculous messages to record, and contemplations to write. You have countless other lives to touch, hearts to soften, eyes to open, and souls to convert. This is the mission to which God has assigned you, the one you have chosen to accept, and the reason you will someday rest in My Arms in Heaven with Jesus and all the Saints. I hope you understand the importance of your continuing to decipher the difference between what the world defines as good and what your hearts tell you to be Fruits of Goodness. You see clearly because you have been accorded the vision to see Heaven clearly. Let not your hearts be troubled by the calling of the flesh or the seduction by your friends to lend to other pursuits. Your goal is the reaching of Heaven and helping your brothers and sisters understand the reason for their seeking that goal as well.

xc

c

I will ask you to tell Me what it felt like to see, hear, and witness the events in Rome this week when the new Pope made his appearance. I wish for you to try to capture your feelings in words based upon the heartfelt victory that you have just described because, in a small way, that is the same elation humanity will feel upon the Return of Jesus in Glory. Do you remember that His Return will be announced like a surprise gift by the Holy Spirit just prior to His breaking through the clouds? 'I announce great joy to the world! Habemus Papam!' And, with these words, your souls have again been granted the Protection of My Immaculate Heart from a Pope who is deeply devoted to Me and who has venerated Me as His Mother since he was first able to utter audible words. Send the word forth, My children, that this

cx

cxx

is My Pope! You have, indeed, witnessed this week the beginning of one of the greatest pontificates in the history of the whole of Roman Catholicism. Be grateful to the Lord for bestowing this great gift upon humanity! As this humble servant labors in the vineyard of God, humanity will indeed walk more gracefully to that Glorious Resurrection that Jesus has given to you all. My children, I end My message today with the same joy in which I came. I commend you to the service of Pope Benedict XVI and the Divine Mercy of Jesus. I remain your Protectress and Benefactress. Please continue to emit the jubilation that is befitting of your obedience to Me... My Special son, you know that I tell you things that are awesome to hear, but what you have seen from Rome this week is awesome to behold!.. I give you now My holy blessing in the Name of the Father, the Son and the Holy Spirit. + Be of great joy! Habemus Papam! I love you. Goodnight!"

cxxx

In the grievous aftermath of the passing of the Supreme Pontiff, Pope John Paul the Great, the Cardinals of the Roman Catholic Church sequestered themselves in Conclave in the Sistine Chapel at the Vatican in Rome. While only in their second day of voting, the world was not anticipating the election of our next Pope so early in the balloting. However, in a surprise gift of the Holy Spirit, the ceremonial white smoke billowed from the stack above the Sistine Chapel just before 11:00 a.m. CDT United States' time on Tuesday, April 19, 2005. In unison with the churches in Rome and others throughout the world, the bells of Saint Peter's Basilica pealed the joyous announcement of the conclusion of the sacred gathering and the election of the Successor to the Chair of Saint Peter. I was sitting at my office desk, intermittently checking the online media throughout the morning for news of the Cardinals' progress, when I received a telephone call from a former colleague who had retired several years earlier. He excitedly said, "William, we have a Pope!" I quickly thanked him, grabbed my jacket and immediately ran along with the rest of the believing world to watch this revelatory celebration on television. As I was driving home, I could not help envisioning the millions of people across every culture of the globe fleeing from their physical stations in time, as was I, to poise themselves to receive an Apostolic Blessing from Christ's newly elected Vicar. With people rushing-in from the streets, commoners abandoning their temporality, children called-in from their play, assembly lines skeletonized, and the eyes of the secular mass-media refocused, our attention was ripped from our ordinary pursuits to gaze upon the history of Roman Catholic Christianity playing-out the salvific procession of renewal before our consciousness in all its Divine splendor. So much seemed at stake during this Papal transition. In years past, there have arisen sinister forces both inside and outside the Church which have diminished the regal bearing of Her stature in the eyes of Earth's people. The Sacred Traditions of Roman Catholicism have been under assault by modern opportunists over the decades since the Second Vatican Council of the 1960s. Too many people had hoped with great expectation that this would be their next chance to liberalize the focus of the Church hierarchy, thereby furthering their errant, mundane, rogue, and sacrilegious agendas of sexual licentiousness and willful epicurianism. Many fallen-away Catholics rejoiced upon hearing the news of the death of the great Vicar, John Paul II, and now saw their chance to wrest control of the Church from its more conservative Fathers. The larger, more obedient mass of Catholic Christianity pined for the continuation and protection of 2,000 years of Sacred Apostolic Tradition and Orthodoxy, handed down through the ages of the Church's Magisterium by Her faithful priests. I had been praying passionately in union with the Church that God would allow this exceptional succession of virtuous benison to be transmitted to the ensuing generation of the Church Militant. I was somewhat nervous, along with many others, that this would be a treacherous turning point in the life of the Catholic Church, and Christianity as a whole, in this moribundly secular age.

I arrived home and seated myself in front of the television set with my brother, watching the coverage from the heart of Italy. Just as I had imagined, the people of the Eternal City were pouring into the streets in throngs, scurrying to the piazza at Saint Peter's Square to join the tens-of-thousands who had been vigiling there since the beginning of the Conclave. I felt a strange spiritual transcendence while observing the events unfold, as if we were watching a miracle happening from beyond the parameters of our mortal existence. My senses were heightened and expanded to realize that humanity was participating in a hallowed moment of history that will be fondly remembered until the final moments of the Earth. There was an extraordinary connection with the deposit of the past, and a prophetic relationship with the completion of the future. It is as though humankind was stepping out of the darkness into a corridor of timeless divinity that exists from one end of Creation to the other, just beyond our casual awareness. Unbeknownst to many people, humanity was being flushed into the beaming Light of Jesus Christ. The omnipotent Providence of God had placed the world front-row, center seat alongside the Holy Gospel of the first century. The Keys to the Kingdom of Paradise were about to be transferred to a new Papal Rock before our very eyes with all the majesty and tradition contained in the Bosom of Christian fidelity! Only days earlier, on April 2, 2005, nations and peoples from every continent, culture, and way of life had witnessed the solemn passing of one of the greatest servants to ever dignify the Roman Catholic Papacy in the person of Pope John Paul II. And, for 17 days thereafter, a feeling of death seemed to subdue the Church, especially after we placed the remains of this magnificent Polish Pontiff in a tomb in the Sacred Grottoes beneath Saint Peter's Basilica. The Supreme Representative of God on Earth had again laid down his life in defense of the unalterable Truth, witnessing to the potential and perfection of the human species through the Divine Love and Mercy of Jesus Christ and the holiness He asks us to sustain. If the Magisterium of the Holy Church the Messiah founded 2,000 years ago is the visible essence of Jesus Christ as the head of His Mystical Body, the world certainly engaged the Sacred Triduum of the Passion, Death, and Resurrection of the Lord during the events of April 2005.

With such pondering of spiritual thanksgiving, I was taking-in the mystical phenomenon unfolding before the purview of the temporal world. We later learned that some two billion people were rapt in attention that day, watching the curtained doorway above the ornate facade of the Seat of Christianity to learn the identity of the 265th Roman Catholic Pontiff. As we waited, a stirring began, the rubrical curtains parted, the pane-glass portal opened, and out stepped Cardinal-Deacon Jorge Medina Estevez of Chile onto the loggia amid the flushing roar of the people who rose in anticipation of his ecclesial declaration. And, with a trademark composure that only Cardinal Estevez could effect, he proclaimed in Latin, *"Annuntio vobis gaudium magnum; Habemus Papam!*—I announce to you news of great joy! We have a Pope!"* And, I kept thinking how giddy the Archangel Gabriel must have felt when the Cardinal-Deacon told us the news of great favor, knowing the former had heralded the same blessing to the Blessed Virgin Mary twenty centuries earlier. Anyway, at the pronouncement of these words, the soul of the world rested in anxious anticipation for the sign that the Church would be unyielding against its secular foes who wished to open the gates of Hell. It was almost as if time had stopped while we were poised in expectation; and then the name rang forth through the strains of a dead language which was transfigured to give life once again, *"Eminentissimum ac reverendissimum dominum, dominum, Josephum."* Cardinal Estevez had just told us that the new Pope's baptismal name was Joseph. Then, after a pause that seemed to last forever, he said, *"Sanctae Romanae Ecclesiae Cardinalem RATZINGER!"* A detonation of triumph erupted from the faithful flock of Catholics and people from other faiths crowded in the square; and even the voices of the religious-media commentators cracked with emotion, as they were unable to contain their joy. My brother and I were catapulted with the masses of faithful people into tearful jubilation as we simultaneously screamed, "Yes!" This is the Pope we had been praying for the Cardinals to elect. I tell you now, hope still lives! God's newest Secretariat, a faithful son of Germany who was born to be something greater, had just thundered out of the misty haze of our faith, bearing humanity atop his humble shoulders with a bountiful heart that has been straining for the finish line of Paradise since the moment of his baptism. Pope John Paul the Great had just passed the torch of ecclesial divinity to Joseph Cardinal Ratzinger from his mansion in Heaven, and the Roman Catholic Papacy was given new life. Indeed, it was a premonition of God's Church being raised from its sepulcher upon the return of Jesus Christ in Glory!

We remained fixed to the television coverage, watching the Basilica balcony being hastily prepared for the initial appearance of Pope Benedict XVI. My soul was transported into ecstatic wonderment by what I was witnessing with my very own eyes. Truly, the Holy Gospel was being preached to the world. Matthew 13:16-20 super-emblazoned with mystical relief across the conscience of humankind. As the world awaited the first appearance of the newly elected Pope, the greatest collective unity in history was simultaneously experiencing a mystical vision of the anticipation immediately preceding the Return of Jesus Christ in Glory. Like our Savior, everyone knew that our beloved Holy Father was alive, chosen and present, and would presently appear before our eyes. The air bore the sensation of the moments before the dawn, awaiting the miracle of Easter, the Messiah rising from the dead, the stone rolling away from the Tomb, life conquering death, and the continuity of everlasting Salvation given the renewal of the breath of life. If the death of John Paul the Great seemed like Good Friday, the election of Pope Benedict XVI felt like Our Lord's Paschal Resurrection—unstoppable, invincible, the Rock of Saint Peter, the Faith of the First reigning until the Last! God declared to humanity on April 19, 2005, *"The world is still Mine!"* Roman Catholicism lives even still! Soon, the Vicar of Christ walked from behind the balcony doorway, into the full view of the throngs of his faithful children. In one enlightening instant, the Apostolic Church of Roman Catholicism seemed to rise like a Phoenix from the ashes of the Earth, breaking past the wilderness, appearing from out of the fog of our times, and taking-on the presence of a mighty aircraft carrier turning her flight deck into the wind for the positioned launch of her storied dogmatic squadrons with an heroic giant of traditional engagement manning the tower. My heart was in utter ecstasy, overwhelmed by feelings of triumph. It was almost as if an exorcism was taking place as I envisioned the haughty enemies of Roman Catholicism reeling with futile exasperation before an overwhelming power and dominion they could never hope to conquer. My soul acclaimed with reverential pride, "I am a Roman

Catholic! This is my Holy Father! I am a child of Eternal Destiny; and I believe, I submit, and I obey!" The mystical cord which binds the history of humanity to the Cross of Jesus Christ has again been tossed into the future and over the wall of time. God's family has been united once again with the Good Shepherd who will reach with his impenetrable faith beyond our veil of tears and petition for us the benisons of our Eternal Deliverance. It is as though Jesus Christ said, *"The Succession of the Truth now marches onward! Death has no power over My Church, for it has been banished once again by the faith and allegiance of a Princely College of Cardinals who acceded to the voice of My Spirit, surrendering themselves as the instruments of God for the Salvation of the world!"* Yea, She is whole and everlasting beyond monarchies, congresses, kingdoms and civilizations before our eyes, withstanding derision from diabolical legions, elevating dignity from the beginning of the ages with the knowledge that She will preside over the final internment of man at their apocalyptic close. On April 19, 2005, the world once more witnessed the humiliation and benevolent annihilation of the adversaries of God's Christianity upon the election of Pope Benedict XVI. Satan was further crushed in defeat! The fatal strike convoked with the historic repetition of an authentic Successor of Saint Peter, who has arisen to the custodial providence of Christianity with a vibrant and living faith at the ready, and who has taken the earthly reigns of Christendom, accepting the Keys which unlock loving unity and paradisial deliverance for us all. What a grand day was recorded in history that Tuesday, and one I shall remember as long as I live. Indeed, please hear me now!—*This Pontifical Election, as a single, unveiled event, has eclipsed the miraculous intercession of the Immaculate Virgin Mary in my life.* It was as soul-shaking as any supernatural event a human being might see in a thousand lifetimes. It has been a vivid, providential sign that has illuminated the whole of Creation for a brilliant, shining moment, and whose effervescent afterglow will remain forever haloed above our souls!

CONCLUSION

The Blessed Virgin Mary spoke in Her September 16, 2001 message about a "...perfect transformation toward perfection" of the mortal human species. For all we have been told about our sinful nature, and everything we are asked to cast aside by the teachings of Christ and the Wisdom of the Holy Spirit, would it be presumptuous to suggest that the perfection about which Our Lady is speaking has more to do with honing our spiritual skills in ushering the Kingdom of God unto the Earth with our hearts than with simple pious platitudes and grandiose physical gestures? This is not to say that the work of our hands is unimportant while we serve to manifest goodness and moral order in our not-so-great societies. When I ponder the ways that Our Lady has tried with an almost incomprehensible passion to draw us toward an interior discipline never before seen in the history of man, I cannot help but arrive at the conclusion that some people among us are already there. I see it in the broken bodies of the famished, the elderly and infirm, and in little children's eyes, and in summer sunsets and rainbows. I often wonder if the perfection that the Holy Mother is talking about has more to do with common decency than some rare, metaphysical heroics that only few people in the world have ever achieved. I think Divine Love is this simple; and I believe that this is the perfection to which Our Lady is referring. When Tim Parsons-Heather spoke almost too generously about my personal desire for the spiritual conversion of humanity in his *Foreword* of this book, he recognized that we are indeed a fractured people who are in need of the cohesion that can only be procured from the perfect peace of God. And, not just any god, but the God of Abraham, the God of our Fathers, the Almighty God who begot Jesus Christ from His Own Preeminent Will, and sent Him to live among us as a seeable and knowable example of what human perfection is. We are told that Jesus is perfect, bearing a perfection that was once concealed in living human flesh. He looked so much like everyone else that He was chided, ridiculed, mocked, and even slain as being a heretic from any other walk of life. Jesus was like us in every way except sin. Hence, if we renounce sin and promise God that we shall hereafter do everything in our power to become the likeness of Jesus, will this not also make us perfect in His image? This, too, is my impression of Our Lady's words in Her September 16, 2001 message. As She has told us many times before, if we were incapable of achieving this manifest piety that God deposits in the epicenter of our lives, She would not be here speaking to us now with such hopeful overtones.

This book, *To Crispen Courage*, is filled from cover to cover with expositions, designs, parables, spiritual paradigms, warnings, prophecies, blessings and teachings from the Mother of Jesus Christ. She once asked me to consider what it was like for Her on Good Friday upon the Deposition of Jesus' Body from the Cross as He was laid in Her lap. And, when I think about it, a strange mixture of sublimity and terror crawls up my spine. How torn were Her feelings to realize that Her innocent Son had just been executed to redeem a world who hated Him outright? Yet, She knew that His horrible death would fulfill Her promise to God through the Archangel Gabriel and the Sacred Scriptures, too. Out of Christ's mortality comes the absolution of our souls; and out of Mary's grief comes the harmony of our hearts. The world is codified in the perfect splendor of human agony in the lives of Jesus and Mary; and our poor attempts to equate our suffering with theirs sometimes seems too little. But, they care about it deeply. I think about Our Lady's messages as I have recorded them here with humble submission, anticipating a great future for the culmination of the Earth, and with pity for anyone who refuses to believe that everything She has told my brother and me will eventually come to pass. I feel a deep, interior sorrow for people with ostentatious egos who lean only on themselves in times of trouble. The human psyche cannot muster the strength they will ultimately need. Human arrogance has long been seen as one huge, ungrateful abomination by God because we rarely, if ever, give Him credit for our successes; and we always blame Him for our failures. We should never mind the alignment of the stars, or how the dice will roll across the crap tables in Las Vegas next week, or what our chances are of winning our state's lottery anytime soon. There is no sure bet for success in life because our premonitions do not lead us into the world, but outward and beyond it. That is the way God planned it, and it is the reason we should continue to pursue that internal presence of the heart where His divinity lives. Awesome wonder does not refer to how fast an F18 can fly, or who gets to sit at the controls during the next launch of the Space Shuttle Endeavor. Indeed, did we not learn from both Challenger and Columbia that futility resides in a curiosity that seeks not to explore the spiritual realms of our yonder galaxies, too? Our goals and objectives should always strive to be greater than the simple mission of satisfying human curiosities or collecting gamuts of artifacts and superfluous information to bequeath to our children in the name of science and industry, or attempt to rectify past wrongdoings through revisionist historical accounts and secular nostalgia. The inroads we have made in Christian awareness will forever outlive the legends we make of ourselves in the eyes of our children, our grandchildren, and their ensuing generations of friends and peers.

And, this certainly does not infer that our self-immolations must consist of bloody sacrifices that in no way serve to eliminate the egregiousness of our transgressions, because the Sorrowful Crucifixion of Jesus has already accomplished that. Whatever we suffer along the lines of personal agony is complementary to the Sacrifice of Jesus on the Cross, for He calls us to take up our crosses, no matter what they may be, and follow Him with deific courage into the material world. If God deigns us to accept a particular form of suffering, it is not just some meaningless palliative to show the world that suffering is an end in itself. We unite with Our Lord in further alleviating the effects of the sins of humanity in reflection of the Passion of Jesus; and in some cases, we have no alternative than to comply with the inescapability of death. In most cases, however, through God's compassionate Wisdom, He gives us doctors, healers, and lenitive compounds to help ease our pain and sometimes stop the deep physical and emotional burdens by which we are oppressed. The involuntary responses of our bodies reveal the expanse of His Will in the invisible battle between good and evil that often rages-on under medical microscopes, in research laboratories, and in cultured petri dishes around the globe. We learn at last that we are culpable for the wrongdoings we commit during our passage through mortal time, and God calls upon many innocent sufferers to bear the cost on our behalf in the likeness of Christ. We are not innocent, it would seem, until proven guilty of our original sinfulness unless we receive the Sacrament of Baptism. After that, we are expected to enter a constitutive pact with our fellow man, especially our sworn enemies and even those who live half-a-world away, so that human sin can be avoided in all its gruesome forms. If we listen to the lessons of the Mother of God, we will know not to simply repress our grievances with other people while continuing to harbor a perpetual hatred for them, citing separate but equal international treaties as a contractual subterfuge. Indeed, we are asked to expunge our thoughts of disdain altogether in favor of a new world order by which the many cultures, creeds, the two genders, and all other attributes of human diversity are pooled together in the Sacred Chalice of the Blood of Christ for reconciliation with the God of all thought, action, form, freedom and expression. This is the real evidence that we as a united people have accepted our commonness beneath the guiding hand of one God. Our Lady told the Medjugorje seers to not question the Will of God in such matters of human coalescence, but to do it out of faith and obedience. She said, *"My Heart is burning with love for you. For you, it is enough to be converted. To ask questions is unimportant. Be converted; hurry to proclaim it! Tell everyone that it is My wish, and that I do not cease repeating it. Be converted! Be converted! It is not difficult for Me to suffer for you. I beg you, be converted!"* Hence, we see that even the Mother of our Lord is still asked by God to pour-out Her Love in sacrificial ways so our hearts will be given to Him. Our Immaculate Mother continued, *"I will pray to My Son to spare you the punishment. Be converted without delay. You do not know the Plans of God; you will not be able to know them. You will not know what God will send, not what He will do. I ask you only to be converted. That is what I wish. Be converted! Be ready for everything; be converted!"* (April 25, 1983).

For all the mental contortions we put ourselves through in an attempt to make some logical sense of why God allows certain things to happen in the world, as though we are destined to be left in the darkness by fate and temporal blindness, Our Lady is clearly telling us that to know the reason for Her Son's decisions is not as important as ensuring our compliance through means that amend His Will in more merciful ways. This is how we can determine our destiny in Eternity from our helplessness here on Earth. And, this is the crux of the messages from the Virgin Mary to my brother and me. Her persistence in telling us that we live haplessly in a world of constant change, often for the worse, appears to be God's schemata for warning us about the perils of remaining ingrained in the embattled futility of the physical world. We are lions who refuse to roar, doves who will not fly, champions who are too afraid to fight, travelers who are too slothful to move, visionaries who decline to see, and image-makers whose spiritual innovations are becoming lost in the dust. We need to remember that the Blessed Mother stands to gain nothing of Her own by coming to speak to the world. She was conceived without sin in Her mother's womb. She never committed a single transgression against God in Her entire life. She is the Queen of every facet of supernal Creation that God ever made, and Her reign with the King of Glory will never end. So, why is She so concerned about our conversion to the Cross? Because She accepted us as Her children on the day Jesus was Crucified—He asked Her to do it just before He died. And, what Mother with as tremendous love as the Immaculate Virgin Mary would not travel to the remotest places in the universe to bring Her children home?

There is an extremely divergent clash of cultures that exists between the world humanity has manifested and the one our Holy Mother sees with Her eyes. All we need to do is look around at our glut of irresponsibility, and toward our collective recidivism into mortal sin, to the social degradation that has overtaken our cities' streets, alleys and neighborhoods, and the almost inconceivable profanity that spews from the mouths of adolescent children. I have addressed in this book the need for God's little girls to become the image of His Mother once again. Here in our own country, newspapers and magazines often publish articles about the so-called "liberation" of American women, and the kind of men with whom they choose to share their lives. It is not unusual to see teenage females with images of spikes and devils tattooed across their backs, or multi-colored rings of barbed-wire inked beneath the epidermis of their arms. And, some of them look for male companionship with young men whose eyebrows are pierced with silver rings and crossbones. However, the old argument that we should just turn our heads until they reach adulthood is not going to wash anymore. We all know about the inequities between nations and peoples around the globe; and we should work dutifully to rectify them. However, do we not also owe our children in the western hemisphere the capacity to recognize right from wrong in interpersonal, social, cultural and economic matters? After all, greedy American consumerism is the root of the problem facing many other countries because we are too reluctant to share our goods and services with them. So, when the Blessed Virgin Mary says "be converted," I am convinced that She means to be caring, selfless, helpful, charitable, prayerful, peaceful and pure. There is no doubt that She is especially calling Americans to live-out the promises we have made—not only to our own citizens, but to operationalize the factual decree that all men are created equal, no matter in what nation they reside. Our young people should remove the bongs from their bookshelves and replace them with bibles and statues of the Saints; and they should trade-in the blunts and one-hitters in their pockets for iconic medals and Rosary rings. And, not only that, it should be something they are willing to do because they know it to be a ratification of their spiritual conscience, not some act of political correctness or a temporary reversal of course to make them eligible for a secular accolade. We can change our appearance on the outside and fool our fellow Americans into believing that we have begun anew. But, we will never deceive the Son of Man into accepting our new identity unless we commit to it from the inside out. Beyond any doubt, this is the conversion about which the Mother of God is speaking. She is laying-out an awfully progressive agenda in Her messages around the world these days, calling for radical change in our conceptual perception of personal achievement and social success. We cannot pretend to deny the indictments Her Son is leveling against us now, nor can we claim ignorance about the Messianic Law; not now, not after almost 2,000 years of Christian evangelization, countless people martyred in the downtown square in front of thousands of heckling cowards and infidels, the occurrence of images and apparitions the likes of no previous age, unprecedented attacks against the traditions and piety of the Church, rebukes and counter-charges by institutional prosecutors and money-grubbing lawyers, and other factions from all walks of life who believe that God has just dumped us here because He does not love us anymore, or that He doesn't exist at all. No matter how we fashion our opposition to Mary's call to Christian Truth, we cannot escape it at the last. We can never say "no" to a Kingdom of sanctity and peace that wishes only to supplant this burdensome beast we call the Earth with a new sphere of Divine Love, and to wipe-out our transgressions, vindicate our culpability, eradicate our suffering, bear our sorrows, and renew our creative spirits in complete wholesomeness, even when we grow too old and much too gray to care anymore what happens to us or our loved-ones for whom we have worked all our lives to elevate to a more dignified poise of stately being.

If we ponder the meaning of the words "pristine," "elegant," and "regal," do we not conjure images of higher places with gold and platinum appointments; or thoughts of charismatic mysticism, regeneration, jubilation, unending light, and the pinnacle of life's fulfillment? If our hearts struggle to discover the definition of "ecstasy," isn't it true that we are thinking about something we never really expect to achieve? The Holy Mother wants us to search for these imaginings because She knows we stand to inherit a better fortune than we ever thought human existence could be. Our feelings are much too suppressed by the negative blueprints of our youth; and undue pressure is implanted upon us to succeed in ways that will never contribute to the fulfillment of our faith. I have seen a great deal of suffering in my life. My friends have agonized over internal tensions they could never overcome because they were too spiritually weak to fend for themselves. I have met impressionable young people who have been maligned, molested, neglected, exploited, assailed and abused. And, the one thing they all have in common is the persistent question of "why" God would allow such torment to come to them. We may never know the answer in our day and time, but we can be assured that the toils of human life are an effect of the far-reaching chasm we have created between ourselves and perfect human love. Unsuspecting people of all stripes have been shorn of their innocence because those in their midst took them for granted. Indeed, we have all been despised at one time or another simply because of the fallacious ways the world perceives us to be. I have written on many occasions that living inside us all is a greatness that is yet unknown to the exterior world; and this is why we think we live in a reclusive shell like termites inside a fallen tree. Quite the contrary, we are spiritual giants whose growth has been stifled only because humanity has rejected the true heroism living inside our hearts. Drunkards and drug addicts lie on street corners, in alleyways, along dark boulevards, and beneath railroad trestles not because they want to be there, but because life forces them to conceal their greatest potential behind the disdain from others who have cast them aside. Some wives drive their husbands into bars and brothels because they want to be left untouched once their children are born; and then they callously say that they married crack-heads, criminals, sluggards and despots. Just because individuals grow-up to be who they are does not imply that their childlike need for nurturing love ever goes away. It would be easy for most of us to become embittered by the everyday drudgery of the temporal word; and many people do, and their loved-ones and friends bear the brunt of the bruises. Many preachers and public orators have said throughout the years that our children are urgently desperate and bitter, and that they were not born that way. The environment in which we have asked them to live has bred this despondence. We are often the source of the interior scars that form on the hearts of other people; and those tattoos and piercings about which I speak are some of the visible effects. In the final analysis, the words of Wisdom from the Mother of Jesus Christ represent the last great bastion of hope for the dregs we have made of many helpless men. She has come delivering messages and speeches of calmness, devotion, emollience, healing and assurance. If it is true that our lives are but a speck on the head of a pin or a grain of sand on the beach, then what do we have to lose by allowing the Patroness of Creation to lift us up to Her Son, to bind us to the Hem of His Garment, and allow Him to take us like wounded lambs to our spiritual restoration once again, to the triage of the Most Blessed Trinity, where we will be united not only with one another outside of time, but with that same God who is pining to hold us with the longing of a father seeing his only begotten son limping back from the battlefields of war.

There is a strange opinion held by some people nowadays which says that God is somehow going to cannibalize this world in order to create a new one that will last beyond a thousand ages. The fact is, the Earth as He knows it will be just fine, and Jesus Christ will sustain the beauty of Nature precisely the way we see it in its most evocative forms. We, the people, laden to the globe by the laws of physics and the exile we were consigned to serve away from Heaven are the ones who must ultimately change. Wherein the Bible says that the old world is passing away, it means that everything in existence that has nothing to do with the perfection of Paradise will expire upon the Second Coming of Jesus Christ. We must shed our corporeal skin to make room for the new spiritual fermentation we shall hand-over to God upon the closing of the ages. And, in this, there are no obsolete particles that can be redacted in the construction of the new. This brings us to the critical mass to which Our Lady is leading us now—prayer from the heart, personal penitence, a genuine subscription to willing self-denial, openness to the vast cynosures of God's intercessory Grace, and to parol the fact that we are ultimately responsible for our own spiritual demise. And, in more practical terms, we are expected to be on guard to recognize the demonic effects the American mass-media are having on human morality and against organized religion today, and the turmoil and degradation that leftist elements are perpetrating against the popular piety and common decency of well-intentioned people everywhere. Countless civilizations before us have suffered the wailing of their spirits in search of Eternal Truth, hoping against hope for some material evidence of God's signature on the wall, or in something greater than their ordinary faith. Indeed, the supernatural intercession of the Blessed Virgin Mary is the manifest satisfaction of their metaphysical hunger; and we must believe in Her power, for if we decline, then there is no cure for that. We no longer need to starve from the absence of Heaven in our daily lives because Our Lady is brokering the peace between God and humankind in ways never before seen at the invocation of the Holy Spirit. Everything we strive to achieve, the inexplicable dimensions of human life, the unknown galleys of the bellowing future, and the proverbial brinkmanship that has long festered the rift between Jesus Christ,

Our Redeemer, and ourselves as the heirs of His Redemption all make sense in the context of Our Lady's most recent messages. Even the providence of human suffering, torment and bondage, when seen through the perspective of the Holy Cross, begin to take-on a clearer meaning, greater than the facts and connotations we assign to them through the bibliographical discernment of our theological works. We must eventually realize that miracles from Heaven are crucial in the broadening of the freedom we are seeking, and in the signs and wonders for which we pine during the hardships of everyday life. I have often said that thoughts of our impending doom force upon us much more than a mild dose of apprehension because, when we die, we are going to a place we have never been before, to stay forever. But, in the grand scheme of things, would we wish to be remanded to this world of strife and inequality for an infinity of years? It is more than just wondering whether the grass is greener on the other side of life. From what we have gleaned from the Church in centuries past, we will someday walk down glistening streets of gold, wearing crimson velvet vestments around our souls, and never once look back at the exasperating plunge we took to escape the prison of our flesh. Paradise is the solvency we gain by a forward-thinking faith; and our hopes are thus well-founded. So, let us heed the call of the Immaculate Woman whom we know to be our Queen of Peace and Mother of Perpetual Help. For all the strains of unity we have ever sung as men, let these be the refrains that finally bring us to stand as one melody of love, humankind united as the Mystical Body of Christ. There is a great deal of work yet to be done in the conversion of this world— eliminating the neglect that still suffers our children in the streets, dismantling our offensive military arsenals, exchanging extemporaneous lies for the permanency of Truth, and proclaiming before the world that we accept the Resurrection to which our Lord has promised to raise our souls someday. The adage may be truer now than in times past, that, "...if old cemeteries could talk, we might wonder what they would have to say." Let us speak for those bygone ages now, showing up as one people on the welcome mat of Salvation that the Son of Man laid at the doorstep of the Earth twenty centuries ago, and offering our Holy Mother the infinite bouquet of the entire deposit of the human race, telling God that we are justifiably His to take. We embark upon and conclude this sacred journey in the midst of the stars, the Angels, and the Saints during our celebration of the Holy Sacrifice of the Mass in the Roman Catholic Church. When the gifts of bread and wine become the Body, Blood, Soul and Divinity of Jesus Christ—that Divine Annihilation about which I speak—we partake of the everlasting Fiat by which the last vestige of our former selves is supplanted by the new.

Notations

CPSIA information can be obtained at www.ICGtesting.com
Printed in the USA
BVOW06s2317060816

458168BV00004B/32/P